The Political Lives of Saints

The Political Lives
of Saints

Christian-Muslim Mediation in Egypt

Angie Heo

UNIVERSITY OF CALIFORNIA PRESS

University of California Press, one of the most
distinguished university presses in the United States,
enriches lives around the world by advancing scholarship
in the humanities, social sciences, and natural sciences. Its
activities are supported by the UC Press Foundation and
by philanthropic contributions from individuals and
institutions. For more information, visit www.ucpress.edu.

University of California Press
Oakland, California

Library of Congress Cataloging-in-Publication Data

Names: Heo, Angie, author.
Title: The political lives of saints : Christian-Muslim
    mediation in Egypt / Angie Heo.
Description: Oakland, California : University of California
    Press, [2018] | Includes bibliographical references and
    index. |
Identifiers: LCCN 2018019550 (print) | LCCN 2018023056
    (ebook) | ISBN 9780520970120 | ISBN 9780520297975
    (cloth : alk. paper) | ISBN 9780520297982 (pbk. : alk.
    paper)
Subjects: LCSH: Islam—Relations—Christianity. |
    Christianity and other religions—Islam. | Coptic
    Christian saints—Egypt. | Coptic Church—Egypt. |
    Islam and politics—Egypt. | Copts—Egypt—Politics
    and government. | Christianity—Egypt.
Classification: LCC BP172 (ebook) | LCC BP172 .H46 2018
    (print) | DDC 281/.720962—dc23
LC record available at https://lccn.loc.gov/2018019550

Manufactured in the United States of America

25 24 23 22 21 20 19 18
10 9 8 7 6 5 4 3 2 1

For my parents

Contents

Illustrations

Note on Translation and Transliteration

All translations of my interviews and my chapters' epigraphs are mine. When I draw on original Arabic texts in the body chapters, the translations are mine. The mistakes are also all mine.

Throughout this book, I use the standard system for Arabic transliteration followed by the *International Journal of Middle East Studies* (IJMES), with some modifications. I use diacritical marks for transliterated terms that do not appear in the English-language dictionary. I also use the Arabic form of the plural for terms that are not in the English-language dictionary (e.g., *mawālid*, not *mawlid*s).

I do not use diacritical marks on proper names (e.g., of person, place, organization, etc.) or book titles. I do not italicize proper names and Arabic terms that appear in the English-language dictionary. All other Arabic terms and phrases are italicized (or set in reverse italics if the surrounding text is italicized). Applying these rules sometimes leads to curious differences in transliteration. For example, *ʿadhrāʾ al-tagallī* ("Virgin of the Transfiguration") designates a local term of visual iconography, whereas al-ʿAdhraʾ al-Mughitha ("Virgin of Relief") is the proper name of a church.

In the Egyptian colloquial dialect, the "j" sound is pronounced as a hard "g." I retain the "j" when referring to a standard Arabic term (*al-jasad al-muḥannaṭ*). I apply the hard "g" when quoting the speech of my interviewees (e.g., *al-turāb min gizmithu*) and when referring to

Egyptian names of persons or places (e.g., Gabal al-Tayr), or special terms particular to the Egyptian context (e.g., *Aqbāṭ al-mahgar*).

For the names of places, I also follow the English-language spelling in cases in which there is a clearly established spelling (e.g., Cairo for al-Qahira). In cases in which there is no clearly established English-language spelling, I follow the IJMES system. I also omit "al-" for the names of places (e.g., al-ʿAur), unless it is part of a phrase (e.g., Gabal al-Tayr). When a proper name appears in a longer Arabic phrase, I follow the IJMES system even if there is a different established English-language spelling (e.g., Maspero but Madhbaha Masbiru).

For the names of persons, I follow the English-language spelling in cases in which there is a clearly established spelling (e.g., Isaac Fanous or St. Bishoi). In instances in which a person has published in English, I honor his or her own preferred spelling (e.g., Magued Tawfik or Bishop Moussa).

Acknowledgments

This book was made possible by the boundless generosity of friends who have become my family in Egypt over the last two decades. Bumping into Nivin Fikri during a procession in Mallawi was one the best accidents that ever happened to me. Wherever I'm heading, the Fikri family in Imbaba has somehow never failed to find someone there, and just in time. Nivin, Faiza, Vivian, Mina, Irini, Ilham, and Milad have thoroughly infused my life with tenderness and laughter. Bishop Murqus and the students of the Clerical College in Shubra al-Khayma threw open a network of churches and monasteries to me, and entertained all my questions with great patience. I am especially grateful to Juzif in Qiba', as well as 'Abd al-Masih and Mari in 'Ayn Shams. Outside the Coptic Church, I am privileged to know Samy Gerges and Magdy Samaan, who each availed their experience and charisma. For a home away from home, I count myself most fortunate to rely on Fadia Habashi and Nashat Salama, and Anne O'Neill and Nashat Megalaa, in all circumstances. Words are not enough.

The intellectual growth of this book rests on many conversations with the most inspiring of teachers and interlocutors. It started as a dissertation in the Department of Anthropology at Berkeley, under the expert supervision of Bill Hanks, who introduced me to semiotics and the anthropology of Christianity. Charles Hirschkind and Saba Mahmood pushed me to consider secularism, Islam, and Egypt in ways that would always and only make my work better. I grapple now with Saba's profound impact on my life in her sudden absence. Stefania Pandolfo and Alexei Yurchak prompted me to think about aesthetics and technology in exciting directions. Daniel Boyarin imparted his insights on a range of topics from the literary life of late antiquity to what it is like to have a Coptic priest as your neighbor.

Before Berkeley, my desire to become an anthropologist had initially taken root during my undergraduate years at Harvard, where I found timely encouragement from Jennifer Cole, Engseng Ho, Lorand Matory, and Marcelo Suárez-Orozco. At Luther Seminary in Minneapolis, where I spent a most productive gap year, I am indebted to Lois Malcolm and Mark Swanson for their support.

My first job after Berkeley in the Department of Anthropology at Barnard College is where my book really began to take shape and when I experienced the Arab uprisings from abroad. Nadia Abu el-Haj, Fadi Bardawil, Cassie Fennell, Paul Kockelman, Brian Larkin, Brinkley Messick, and Ozge Serin kindly read and commented on drafts in perpetual motion. They join my other colleagues Elizabeth Castelli, Severin Fowles, Alex Hartnett, Nicole Peterson, Beth Povinelli, Lesley Sharp, Audra Simpson, and Paige West in having lent me support and pleasure throughout my first stint in Manhattan.

In the following years, I held postdoctoral positions at Emory University and the Max Planck Institute for the Study of Religious and Ethnic Diversity. At Emory, I discovered lifelong anchors in my friendships with Deepika Bahri and Natalia Aki Cecire. At the MPI, Peter van der Veer extended years of funding and faith in my ambitions for which I am grateful. I will never forget Nate Roberts and Rupa Viswanath, who were the ones to first put Göttingen on the map for me, along with my most winsome memories of Ajay Gandhi, Weishan Huang, Jin-Heon Jung, Sam Lengen, Rumin Luo, Tam Ngo, and Sarover Zaidi. Jie Kang and Ming Tang gifted me with wisdom and perspective beyond their years, and Roschanack Shaery's inextinguishable verve spurred me on.

I am honored to call the University of Chicago my home, where I find creative energy and discerning interventions from all corners of campus. At the Divinity School, I owe a debt of gratitude to my colleagues who continue to overturn my assumptions and hold me accountable to my best self. Among them, Alireza Doostdar and Sarah Fredericks stand out as my treasured comrades ever since my arrival. Beyond the Divinity School, I quickly came to appreciate my writing group as a rare haven of confidence and fearless criticism, without which this book would never have surfaced. I wish to acknowledge members of my writing group who saw my work and personality through thick and thin: Alireza Doostdar, Sarah Fredericks, Andy Graan, Elina Hartikainen, Ghenwa Hayek, Darryl Li, and Kareem Rabie. Hussein Agrama and Orit Bashkin have always succeeded in sending warmth and wit my way. Co-teaching with Orit has been most rewarding for many reasons, and I thank her and our undergraduate students from Jews and Christians in the Middle East for their feedback on select chapters. I have also found Ph.D. students to be one of Chicago's most prized assets. Among them are Rachel Carbonara, Aaron Hollander, Andrew Kunze, and Elsa Marty, whose rigorous comments on my entire manuscript have enriched my writing and thought beyond it.

For several years, I moved from institution to institution, slowly figuring out that my most permanent residence lies in the conversation partners I have built over the years. The inestimable impact of two research collectives on this book's development deserves special recognition. In 2007–8, my dissertation's earliest versions were forged in dialogue with members of The Vision Thing, a group convened by Bill Christian and Gábor Klaniczay with funding from the National Endowment for the Humanities. I thank the following scholars whose work on divine visionary experience has nourished me: Francesca Braida, Deirdre de la Cruz, Knut Graw, Ágnes Hesz, Jacqueline Jung, Mayte Green-Mercado, Amira Mittermaier, Vlad Naumescu, Ana Ofak, Katrina Olds, Lehel Peti, Janine Rivière, Valérie Robin, Monique Scheer, Jalane Schmidt, Anthony Shenoda, and Xenia von Tippelskirch. In 2012–14, I developed the most recent drafts of my manuscript in discussion with members of the Sensory Spirituality group, headed by our PI Sonja Luehrmann and funded by the Social Science Research Council's New Directions in the Study of Prayer initiative. I have been fortunate to gain comparative perspective on Orthodoxy outside the Middle East from Daria Dubovka, Jeffers Engelhardt, Jeanne Kormina, Vlad Naumescu, and Simion Pop.

A number of minds have engaged this book's drafts at various stages, and all have displayed some formidable quotient of brilliance, experience, and industry. I am indebted to the following readers who have given me invaluable feedback on various sections and chapters: Deepika Bahri, Andreas Bandak, On Barak, Andy Blanton, Simeon Chavel, Maria José de Abreu, David Frankfurter, Mischa Gabowitsch, Sarah Green, Vivian Ibrahim, Alice Kim, Rebecca Kirkpatrick, Alan Mikhail, Jun Gyu Min, Sylvia Nam, Sally Promey, Nate Roberts, Randall Strahan, Monique Scheer, Samuli Schielke, Jeff Stackert, Nelly van Doorn-Harder, Isaac Weiner, and Joshua Yoder. I find it impossible to express fully my gratitude to the following individuals who have combed through my entire monograph (and remarkably for some, twice): Michael Allan, Febe Armanios, Carlo Caduff, Natalia Aki Cecire, Steve Davis, Matthew Engelke, Kathy Foley, Ajay Gandhi, Sankaran Krishna, Brian Larkin, Vincent Lloyd, Margaret Mitchell, Valentina Napolitano, Anne O'Neill, Kabir Tambar, and Jeremy Walton. Sending me pages upon pages of detailed comments on each chapter, Febe, Natalia, and Kathy have especially set the bar high for what scholarly engagement is, and I will always remember what generosity and excellence look like through them.

At University of California Press, I cannot ask for a better editor than Eric Schmidt, who has overseen this book's publication with skill and grace. Archna Patel and Maeve Cornell-Taylor helped me navigate all the necessary steps throughout the whole process. I thank the four anonymous reviewers for California, whose comments significantly improved my manuscript's frame and arguments. The writing of my book benefited from Andrew Frisardi's and Anitra Grisales's light yet meticulous copyediting, which saved me from nothing short of embarrassment. Allison Brown provided expert assistance with Arabic transliteration through patient rounds of back-and-forth. Bill Nelson remains my go-to cartographer, and I thank him for his maps for this book. Dale Mertes came to the rescue in the last months with his skills in graphic design. Without Phil Grant, this book would suffer from the absence of an index.

My friends and family are the ones who backed my strange drive for this ethnography and its long career in the making. Grace, Henry, Joe, and Liz knew me before I knew my passion for fieldwork and writing, and they crucially remind me. Memories of Chris Chan and Nathan Foley-Mendelssohn remain alive to move and sustain me. Alice, Carlo, Cassie, Dee, Ro, Syl, and Zé have given me deeply meaningful adventures of friendship that I believe everyone should be so lucky to experience. My sister Susie's expressions of love and care arrived when I needed them most. Finally, my parents have steadily endured and marveled alongside me from start to finish, so much so that I am challenged to view myself as this book's single author. It is to them that I dedicate this book.

My fieldwork research was funded by the National Science Foundation, the Social Science Research Council, Barnard College, and the Divinity School at the University of Chicago. My writing was enabled by the Fox Center for Humanistic Inquiry at Emory University, the Max Planck Institute for the Study of Religious and Ethnic Diversity, and the Seoul Institute. My final steps to publication were supported by the Center for

International Social Science Research at the University of Chicago. I am grateful to Magued Tawfik for permission to reprint video stills from *Al-Shahida Marina* (1993) and Father ʿAbd al-Masih al-Basit of Musturud for permission to reproduce images from *Zuhurat al-ʿAdhraʾ fi Misr* (2010). I also thank Jordi Camí Caldés, Marc Dosch, Phil Jackson, Father Bula Saʿd, and Dana Smillie for use of their photographs.

Introduction

The "Virgin of the Apparition" (*'adhrā' al-ẓuhūr*)[1] is a touchstone figure in the Coptic Orthodox imagination today. This image of the Virgin, her arms outstretched and robed in blue and white, looks very much like the French Catholic Mary of the Miraculous Medal.[2]

Yet, any tourist in Egypt, from Aswan to Alexandria, is far more likely to encounter this icon of the Virgin than the classic Byzantine icon of the Eastern Orthodox Theotokos (*wālidat Allāh*). While claimed as Egypt's own, the Virgin of the Apparition also evokes a lost ecumenical history in holy saints throughout the Mediterranean Basin. From the ancient shrines of wonderworkers to the medieval lore of relic thefts, saints have served as common currency for Jews, Christians, and Muslims in Egypt, extending their relations with religious affines elsewhere.[3] In the modern era of anticolonial nationalism, the Virgin Mary in

---

1. Copts also refer to this image as the "Virgin of the Transfiguration" (*'adhrā' al-tagallī* or *'adhrā' al-tajallī*). For more on how this image serves as a site of Christian-Muslim interaction, see chapters 3 and 5, "Territorial Presence" and "Public Order."

2. The image of the "Miraculous Mary" or "Mary of the Miraculous Medal" is based on the Virgin's appearance to Saint Catherine Labouré in Rue du Bac, Paris, in 1830.

3. As an ethnographic study based on fieldwork, this book focuses on Christian-Muslim relations to the unfortunate exclusion of Jews. As of 1948, there were seventy-five thousand to eighty thousand Jews living in Egypt, and twenty thousand of them were indigenous Arabs or "Karaite" Jews. Currently, there are less than fifty Jews living in Egypt. For more on the Egyptian-Jewish diaspora after 1948, see Beinin 1998. For more on how this common context gave rise to the Arab nationalization of Copts, see chapter 2, "Redemption at the Edge."

particular has possessed unique potential to unify Egypt's citizenry across boundaries of faith, and after the foreign rulers and missionaries had already left their marks.

The Virgin of the Apparition refers to the Virgin Mary's culminating appearance at a church in Zaytun, a neighborhood in northeast Cairo. Arguably the most significant event in modern Coptic history, the Zaytun apparitions began in May 1968, on the heels of the 1967 Arab-Israeli War and at the height of military territorialism under President Gamal Abdel Nasser (1956–70). Seen as bursts of bluish-white light against the dark midnight sky, the Virgin of the Apparition was soon elevated into the consummate image of Egypt's blessed status as Holy Land. Crowds of Christians and Muslims gathered in Zaytun, consecrating the Virgin's status as the holy saint of Christian-Muslim unity. Indeed, Copts often emphasize that Zaytun's first eyewitness was a "Muslim" mechanic and that Nasser donated state property so that Copts could build a larger church building in the Virgin's honor. Infused with nationalist value, the Church of the Virgin in Zaytun is the second largest church in Egypt, following the Patriarchate of St. Mark, the seat of the Coptic Orthodox Pope and the symbolic center of Christianity in Egypt.

In May 2014, I visited the Church of the Virgin in Zaytun. The overall mood in Egypt at that moment was one of overwhelming fatigue, and for many Egyptians, anger and disappointment. Since the revolutionary uprisings that had toppled President Hosni Mubarak's thirty years in power (1981–2011), the country had endured instability and chaotic transitions in political leadership. During the previous summer of July 2013, General Abdel Fattah al-Sisi's bloody ouster of President Mohamed Morsi and the Muslim Brotherhood from power put a brutal end to more than two years of protests and demonstrations.[4]

Since 2001, I had been visiting the Church of the Virgin in Zaytun at least once a year. That spring was the first time I spotted an army tank parked outside its main gates and a Coptic police general on guard asking for my passport. Composing 6 to 10 percent of Egypt's population,[5]

4. Sisi oversaw the Raba'a Mosque Massacre that resulted in the deaths of over one thousand Muslim Brotherhood sympathizers (July 2013). The massacre has been described by leading international human rights groups as "one of the world's largest killings of demonstrators in a single day in history." See "Egypt: Rab'a Killings Likely Crimes against Humanity," Human Rights Watch, August 12, 2014, www.hrw.org/news/2014/08/12 /egypt-raba-killings-likely-crimes-against-humanity (accessed May 6, 2018).

5. The percentage of Coptic Christians in Egypt is a wildly contested figure. According to the Egyptian state census, Copts make up 5–6 percent of the national population, a significantly lower figure than the Coptic Orthodox Church's estimates of 15–20 percent.

Coptic Christians are widely regarded to be the Arab Middle East's largest "religious minority." After Sisi's coup, Copts confronted a steady surge of church torchings in Upper Egypt and the Delta over a period of two weeks in August 2013. In Zaytun, the church's amplified security addressed the fears and anxieties of those Copts who expressed that a repressive police state was more important to them than the unwieldy ideals of liberal democracy.

On the face of it, the Church of the Virgin in Zaytun had transformed from a national site of Christian-Muslim unity into a sectarian fortress of Christian identity. Compared to 1968, when it had attracted mixed crowds of Christians and Muslims, in 2014, it functioned as an imposing security checkpoint for sifting "Christian" insiders from "Muslim" outsiders. The Virgin of the Apparition, an integral element of the church's history, was also entangled in these transformations. Having once provided the image of nationhood beyond religious difference, it now represented the demand for bolstered minoritarian protection under the new Sisi regime.

On closer examination, however, the Church of the Virgin in Zaytun also hinted at more enduring legacies of postcolonial nation-building that had engendered Egypt's current landscape of sectarian differences in the first place. For Copts, the key institution in question is the Coptic Church, and more specifically, the pope-president pacts that have governed Christian-Muslim affairs since Egypt's full independence from Britain in 1952. The reason for my visit in May 2014 was to see the new museum for Pope Shenouda III that had opened earlier that month in the church's back courtyard. The late Shenouda, perhaps the most influential leader in modern Coptic history, reigned for over forty years (1971–2012), outlasting the Mubarak regime. Toward the end of his life, Shenouda's main claim to fame was mismanaging conversion scandals, bringing him into disrepute in the Muslim world from North Africa to Southeast Asia. His most important legacy, however, was the fulfillment of his ambition: "to integrate the Copts—every single one of them—into the church" (Hasan 2003:130). The new museum promoted the memory of Shenouda's

---

Scholarly literature generally agrees on somewhere between 6–10 percent. Of this 6–10 percent fraction, over 90 percent of Copts are Orthodox, with Catholics and Protestants composing the remaining percentage. Although the Protestant churches command disproportionate weight in Coptic affairs with respect to their small numbers, the Coptic Orthodox Church is by far the most influential, centralized organization that represents Coptic Christians in Egypt. Throughout this book, I refer to the Coptic Orthodox Church as the "Coptic Church," or just "the Church."

lasting impact, in his double role as a political broker of intercommunal relations and the spiritual head of Coptic revival and reform.

Powerfully juxtaposed, the images of Pope Shenouda and the Virgin of the Apparition reinforced an alliance between national histories of authoritarianism and religious imaginaries of holy presence in times of war and violence. Whatever ruptures the 2011 revolution and the 2013 coup had wrought, Copts and Christian-Muslim politics in Egypt were beholden to the firmly entrenched forces of their authoritarian making. The Church of the Virgin in Zaytun honors the orchestrated convergence of mass miracles and state militarism, carrying forth cultural continuities from its Arab nationalist past into the postrevolutionary present. Under current threats of sectarian attack, the church further enshrines the legitimacy of Sisi's enlarged security state and its origins in military nationalism.

Meanwhile, the Virgin of the Apparition also communicates other historical origins of memory and imagined belonging toward fashioning the story of Copts and Christian-Muslim relations in Egypt. Having traversed a variety of Christian and Islamic traditions, the Virgin Mary indexes the rich heterogeneity of ritual practices beyond religious identitarianism under the Egyptian nation-state. While collective imaginings of sainthood have been subject to the space and time of modern nationalism, they also offer an inheritance that exceeds the Coptic Church's institutional grip on miracles, in their secret lives and their sectarianizing fates. This book excavates this inheritance to understand how Coptic Christians envision their ties to Muslims and negotiate their fraught place in a new Egypt.

. . .

This book examines holy saints and their imaginaries as sites of Christian-Muslim mediation in post-1952 Egypt. By "Christian-Muslim mediation," I signal two different kinds of mediation: (1) Orthodox Christian traditions of divine intercession that have long brokered ties across various faiths and denominations; and (2) the Coptic Church and its state-authorized role as an arbiter of Christian-Muslim affairs. An ethnographic study, this book journeys to the images and shrines where miracles, martyrs, and mysteries have shaped the lived terms of national unity, majority-minority inequality, and sectarian tension on the ground. At the forefront of its analysis is the Coptic Church and the religious forms of authority that have rendered Copts into a communal unit to be governed and regulated by the Egyptian nation-state and its authoritarian tactics of security and military control. Rather than taking holy saints to be an expression of an underlying Christian essence, which risks relegating Coptic Christian beliefs and practices to a minoritarian ghetto, I insist on analyzing how images of holiness—like the Virgin of the Apparition—organize Christian-Muslim unity and Christian-Muslim difference in Egypt. In the chapters that follow, I claim and demonstrate that saints and their imagined activity have played a key role in both advancing and challenging the marginalization of Copts and Coptic Christianity in contemporary Egypt.

Penned in the political present of the Sisi regime, this book's focus on Egypt's Copts also gains renewed significance in an anxious period of tragic violence. In the wake of the Arab Spring and Mubarak's downfall in 2011, Copts have been increasingly identified as the collateral damage of revolution and regime change. In addition to numerous local conflicts between Christians and Muslims,[6] a string of events since 2011 displayed shocking levels of violence toward Copts, unprecedented in scale and design. Weeks before the Tahrir uprisings, the bombing of an Alexandrian church had left twenty-three dead (January 2011). Under military interim rule, the army's clashes with Coptic demonstrators resulted in twenty-eight deaths, referred to as the Maspero Massacre (October 2011). After the Muslim Brotherhood's forced exit from power, acts of retribution included the torching of over forty churches nationwide (August 2013). In the first years of the Sisi presidency, Copts additionally faced terrorist attacks from ISIS (Islamic State of Iraq and Syria) fighters, with the kidnapping and beheading of twenty migrant laborers in Libya (February 2015), the bombing in the Coptic Patriarchate that resulted in twenty-eight deaths (December 2016), and the bombings in Tanta and Alexandria that resulted in fifty-six total deaths (April 2017). Given this lengthy chronology of bombings, torchings and killings, Coptic Christians have become more vulnerable than ever to facile equations with victimization, persecution, even extinction.

Providing another frame for understanding violence, this book approaches the quieter corners of divine intercession to deprivilege the sensationalizing din of persecution politics and Islamophobia that

---

6. Under military interim rule in 2011, attacks on Coptic churches and property occurred in Sul, Helwan, and Imbaba, Giza, in addition to clashes between Coptic demonstrators and the army in Manshiyyat Nasir, Cairo. Compared to Cairo and Alexandria, local incidents of sectarian violence more frequently occur in Upper Egypt, where estimates place the percentage of Copts as high as one-third of the population. The Egyptian Initiative for Personal Rights, a human rights organization, has documented at least seventy-seven cases of violence against Copts between 2011 and 2016 in the Minya governorate alone. See "Egypt's Cruelty to Christians", *New York Times,* December 22, 2016.

currently overdetermines the global portrait of Copts. My aim in doing so is not to downplay the horrific nature of atrocities that beset Egypt's Copts, nor to diminish sympathy for the threats that they suffer on a regular basis. Rather, I seek to broaden our notion of violence beyond discrete acts of bombing and torching, shifting our sights to the less punctual and more permanent structures of repression, dispossession, and seclusion that have defined Coptic experiences of suspicion, fear, and rage. Anchored in extensive fieldwork that spans a period of tumultuous political upheaval in Egypt, this book offers empirical glimpses into the broader set of conditions that have made Copts a barometer of national unity and a bull's-eye for sectarian violence over the last several decades. By drawing our attention to the political lives of saints, it delves into these conditions from a particular angle, extending ethnographic and historical insights into the relatively durable images and practices that are too often overshadowed by numbing digests of isolated incidents of attack. Viewing sainthood from the vantage point of the margins enables us to approach politically fraught issues of communal authority, territorial conflict, and fears over security with serious attention to the religious worlds that make them possible.

This book is divided into three topoi—"Relics," "Apparitions," "Icons"—of Christian-Muslim mediation. It is a study of the materialities of sainthood, with a strategic focus on how Copts imagine their relations with Muslims and how the Coptic Church legislates and regulates their imaginings. By "materialities," I mean to signal the diffuse set of everyday practices that establish the space and time of commonness by shaping social styles of embodiment and interaction. Relics, apparitions, and icons are all Orthodox media of sainthood, each indicating a particular genre of imagination: relics are fragments that, in relation to a whole, convey ties of belonging and exclusion; apparitions are visions that activate collective and individual modes of perception; and icons are pictures that circulate traces of personhood in the public. These genres of imagination, given their overlap with Islamic histories of saint veneration, forge senses of both communion and friction among Christians and Muslims.

To grasp the politics intrinsic to holy images, this book further traces how relics, apparitions, and icons order relations between Christians and Muslims through hierarchies of national and religious belonging. More precisely, I analyze how Orthodox material aesthetics shape the Coptic Church's management of national unity and Christian-Muslim difference. In the chapters that follow, I draw on three helpful frames for tracking Coptic modulations of the nation-state and nationhood: "community," "territory," "security." Imaginings of sainthood endow the Coptic Church, its popes and senior clergy, with the authority to transform Copts into a centralized community that is legible to the nation-state. They are also what transforms church buildings and shrines into cherished elements of the nation's status as "Holy Land" and into sacred territories that conjure memories of violence and require special police protection. The realm of saints is thus one core domain of instituting national interfaith unity, while also installing infrastructures of segregation and security. In a variety of ways, ritual phenomena such as pilgrimage, martyr commemorations, and public miracles tether religious coexistence to the overarching sign of the nation.

Saints, their holy images and social imaginaries, provide key glimpses into the more general terrain of communal mediation without which Copts cannot even begin locating themselves in the nation. This book's analysis of relics, apparitions, and icons is an account of how Copts uphold their imagined origins and mobilize the religious grounds of their collective agency. It is my desire that this book will allow us to dwell on the more ordinary textures and settings that define minoritarian experiences at the margins while also considering what they hold for redefining future possibilities of belonging and moving toward horizons of hope: In the remainder of this introduction, I provide an abbreviated historical background of Copts and the Coptic Church in contemporary Egypt. I then elaborate on my theoretical approaches to the material aesthetics of sainthood and the national politics of religious difference, charting how these two fields of inquiry together inform my analysis of Christian-Muslim mediation. I close with a brief account of my fieldwork methodology and an overview that spells out my chapters' themes and the larger arc that ties the people and places together in this monograph's story.

COPTS, THE COPTIC CHURCH, THE COPTIC QUESTION

In contemporary Coptic studies,[7] there are two burgeoning trends that seem to suggest a contradiction. The first trend accounts for the modern

7. Contemporary Coptic studies is relatively small within the international field of Coptic studies. Sociologist Sebastian Elsässer (2014) provides an insightful appraisal about the state of Coptic studies (ancient to contemporary), pointing out that Coptology in European and North American universities has historically focused on classical antiquity due to the central location of Greco-Roman Egypt in the origins of Western civilization. As a result, the vast majority of scholarship on Copts and Coptic Christianity has developed in the scholarly disciplines of theology, history, art, and archaeology.

"Coptic renaissance" (*al-nahḍa al-Qibṭiyya*), including the religious activities of revival and reform that parallel the late twentieth-century "Islamic awakening" in Egypt.[8] At times celebratory in tone, this research focuses on the explosive growth of youth education, organized pilgrimages, media channels, iconography, and music—all inextricably linked to the Coptic Church's expanding influence within Egypt and throughout its diasporic communities worldwide. The second trend examines the social and political challenges that have defined Copts as a "religious minority" (*al-ʾaqalliyya al-dīniyya*), directing attention to the systemic repression and marginalization of Coptic Christians in the Egyptian state and society on the basis of their religious identity.[9] If religion is studied according to this line of inquiry, it is frequently through the violation of religious rights across a range of domains (e.g., religious conversion, religious education in public schools, building and repairing places of worship) that questions of discrimination and denials of equality are explored. These two directions of study—both empirically grounded—attest not only to a scholarly division of labor, but also to a core paradox in the contemporary history of Copts: the cultural revival of religion coincided with its political repression. In this book, I aim to analyze these two concurrently lived realities—religious growth and minoritarian regulation—in order to explain not only their coexistence, but also their mutual reinforcement.

To enter into this paradox that continues to define the political present of Copts and Christian-Muslim relations, one must first understand the centrality of the Coptic Church in the making of the Coptic community and the Egyptian state's authoritarian formula for governing Christians and Muslims under the sign of nationhood. Nearly all accounts of contemporary Copts include the Coptic Church's two key popes after the Free Officers' coup of 1952, the two actors who have exerted the most influence on Coptic communal affairs throughout the presidencies of

8. For this literature on the various cultural aspects of modern Coptic Christian revival, see van Doorn-Harder 1995, 2017; Armanios 2002, 2016; Meinardus 2002; Voile 2004; Mayeur-Jaouen 2005; van Doorn-Harder and Guirguis 2011; Ramzy 2014; du Roy 2014. For ethnographies that touch on the Islamic awakening (*al-ṣaḥwa al-Islāmiyya*) in contemporary Egypt, see Starrett 1998; Mahmood 2005; Hirschkind 2006; Mittermaier 2011.

9. For literature on the political sociology and legal aspects of Coptic minority politics in Egypt, see Zeidan 1999; Hasan 2003; Makari 2007; Ibrahim 2010; Scott 2010; Iskander 2012; Tadros 2013; Elsässer 2014; Guirguis 2016; Mahmood 2016. For literature on minority communities in the Middle East more broadly, see Hourani 1947; Pacini 1998; Bengio and Ben-Dor 1999; Masters 2001.

Gamal Abdel Nasser, Anwar Sadat and Hosni Mubarak: Pope Kyrillos VI (1959–71) and Pope Shenouda III (1971–2012). More than spiritual heads who led religious revival and reform on a mass scale, Popes Kyrillos and Shenouda ensured the Coptic Church's dominant political position as the institutional representative of all Copts vis-à-vis their Muslim conationals, while consolidating the communal identity of Copts in a shared religion. To the dismay of Christian and Muslim secularists seeking increased liberalization and an enlarged realm of individual rights unencumbered by religious identity, the pope and his highest-ranking bishops served as the appointed spokespersons for the Copts and the Coptic community. Across a range of settings, from outbreaks of sectarian violence to conversion scandals, the Church stands at the center of managing Christian-Muslim disputes. Only in light of this history of the Coptic Church's collusion with the Egyptian security state is it entirely logical that the Church had prohibited its flock from participating in the revolutionary downfall of Hosni Mubarak in 2011, eventually, in 2013, after cautiously observing the Muslim Brotherhood in power from the sidelines, throwing its support behind Sisi's military regime.

Of course, the Coptic Church was not always so central to intercommunal governance. Since the turn of the twentieth century, the task of defining the place of Copts in Egypt—what became known as "the Coptic Question" (*al-mas'ala al-Qibṭiyya, al-milaff al-Qibṭī*)—was intertwined with the question of Egypt's independence from foreign, colonial rule (Elsässer 2014; cf. el-Amrani 2006). As Ottomanists have shown, it was not the clergy, but the Coptic elites with their impressive portfolios in finance and foreign affairs who had previously served as the main channels of arbitration between the community and the Ottoman Empire.[10] Moreover, during British colonial rule, it was the Coptic secularists who joined the liberal Wafd delegation to the Paris Peace Conference in 1919, when the League of Nations made minorities' protection a core condition for recognizing new nation-states. Eschewing their status as minorities marked by religion, these Coptic leaders upheld the revolutionary slogan: "Religion belongs to God and the Nation belongs to All!" (Bahr 1979; Hanna 1980; Ibrahim 2010). Gifted with an internationalist perspective, Egypt's anticolonial revolutionaries were conscious

10. In her work on Coptic Christianity under Ottoman Empire (2011), historian Febe Armanios has shown that intracommunal politics had been largely defined by the Coptic Church's battle with the Coptic "archons" (*al-arākhina*), the financial and landowning elite who would later comprise the Coptic Communal Council (*al-Majlis al-Milli*) under Ottoman and British rules. See also Seikaly 1970; Guirguis 2008; Swanson 2010.

of the British "divide-and-rule" strategy and further strategized to avoid the intercommunal fate of Hindus and Muslims in India (Carter 1986). Secular-liberal designs of national unity before religious identity emerged with anticolonial aspirations for national independence.

The methodological compulsion to recognize and study Copts in the key of "religion" therefore cannot be taken for granted. Historians of modern Copts agree that the key turning point leading to the Coptic Church's hegemonic status occurred under Gamal Abdel Nasser after the Free Officers' coup of 1952. Tasked with building a nation-state, Nasser ushered in pivotal changes toward remaking state bodies of rule and law, organizing sectarian differences, and incorporating the nonelite into its citizen ranks. Establishing the state's deep ties to parallel orders of religious authority, Nasser effectively transformed the centuries-old institutions of the Coptic Church and al-Azhar,[11] one of the world's most respected and influential centers of Sunni Islamic learning, into state-regulated bodies of control. Consequently, the Coptic community was subjected to an authoritarian formula of rule which has been characterized in scholarship through a range of terms including the "church-state entente" (Tadros 2009), "corporatist-sectarianism" (Elsässer 2011; cf. Bianchi 1989), and the "millet partnership" (Rowe 2007; Sedra 2014). At the risk of overstating my point here, the fact that today's Copts are integrated into their community through religious practices and understand their rights in terms of religion is thus not a natural outcome of primordial attachments to a "tradition" or "worldview." It is, rather, a historical outcome of Egypt's development as a postcolonial nation-state, and more specifically, its political arrangement of managing Christian-Muslim affairs through the Coptic Church—a communal institution centered around religion and religious authority.

Integral to the making of the post-1952 Coptic community, religious revival and reform resulted in the mass popularization and modernization of Coptic Orthodoxy. From the 1960s onward, religion played a critical role in shifting the weight of communal authority from the socioeconomic

11. Established in 973 C.E., al-Azhar has long functioned as Egypt's most important religious institution and negotiated its autonomy under various rulers and empires. When Nasser came to power, he claimed the appointment of al-Azhar's grand shaykh to be his executive prerogative, replacing the previous system of internal election. State authorities also gained control over al-Azhar's finances and secured fatwas legitimating their policies. For more on al-Azhar's relationship with the Egyptian state, see Zeghal 1999; Moustafa 2000.

elite toward the clergy,[12] incorporating the rapidly expanding middle class and waves of rural-to-urban migrants into the Coptic Church's fold. On the scale of sheer numbers, the Coptic renaissance included the exponential increase of church buildings, monasteries, schools, hospitals, and orphanages, along with an entire generation of highly educated Copts seeking to serve the Church as priests, deacons, monks, nuns, teachers, and volunteers.[13] Due to mass industries of technology and transportation, the organization of religious education and pilgrimage activities reached a far broader base of Copts than ever before, resulting in more reported miracles and saintly images in the public. According to the widely respected bishop of youth and education Bishop Moussa, "the Holy Virgin Mary kept appearing to many people since the first century after Christ, but her apparitions [have] noticeably increased in the 20th century" (Bishop Moussa 2010:16). What this mass reform and revival meant on the ground was that ordinary Copts were not so much becoming "more religious," as they were acquiring techniques and skills, new ways of knowing their past and their ties to Egypt, along with new frames of social interaction with others. In short, as the politics of communal authority changed, the nature and contents of "religion" also changed.

This book examines the centralizing and assimilating effects of religion and how they sustained the institutional legacy of the Coptic Church's authority over Copts after 1952. By attending the ways in which the life of religion escapes and exceeds the Coptic Church's control, this book also approaches the breakdown and limits of this authoritarian formula that has defined the modern Egyptian state's governance of Christians and Muslims to date. To be more specific, this ethnography covers the last decade of the Mubarak regime, a critical period of both experimental liberalization and fortified securitization. These shifts, which unfolded broadly throughout Egyptian state and society, placed internal and external strains on the Coptic Church, in ways that hint at connections between religious transformations and political dynamics. In particular, internally, the Church faced a short-lived

12. The Coptic Church's democratization of the laity served to centralize its authority over communal affairs with the Egyptian state's backing. After the 1952 coup, Nasser dissolved the Coptic Communal Council, opening the door for Pope Kyrillos and the Coptic Church to reconstitute it with the church-abiding faithful. As a consequence of this new formula, the power of the secularist privileged elite began to shrink in favor of the church-attending rural masses, who would later become the upwardly mobile, educated middle class in the 1970s and 1980s. For more, see Sedra 1999.

13. For a magisterial overview of the scale of the Coptic Church's growth during the papal reigns of Kyrillos and Shenouda, see Guirguis and van-Doorn Harder 2011.

advance of secularist activism from within the Coptic community, while externally, it saw its position weakened vis-à-vis the state's regulation of Christian-Muslim strife.

On the first count, from the early 2000s, a rising number of Copts challenged the clerical hierarchy's privileged access to the regime, pushing for an enlarged civic space that would bypass the Coptic Church altogether. Concurrent with liberalizing waves in media (Iskander 2012) and political activism nationwide (al-Ghobashy 2011),[14] they established organizations like the Maspero Youth Union and Coptic 38, which advocated for state recognition of individual rights, punishment for sectarian violence and new legal channels for facilitating personal status cases (Tadros 2013; Lukasik 2016).

Many of these Copts, characterized as "secularists" (al-'almāniyyūn) for their political stance against church intervention, hailed from a new generation of youth who were raised, educated, and liberalized from within the Coptic Church itself—as priests, deacons, and lay servants. This sociopolitical demographic is significant because it adds more complexity to a somewhat caricatured binary between the pious laity devoted to religious and spiritual affairs, and the secularist activists driven by human rights and supported by international NGO's. Part of this unique development of pious insiders into critics of repression owes to the Coptic Church's growth, in ways which democratized the laity (el-Khawaga 1997), targeting the working and middle classes and investing in women and youth for the first time in its history. Raised from within churches, this group of Coptic secularists became increasingly troubled by the insular and exclusionary nature of their communal institutions, recognizing the limits of their appeal to Muslim conationals outside the purview of the Church. Rather than abandon their churches altogether, they sought to redefine the orthodox terms of religious authority towards revolutionary action against authoritarian rule.

The internal affront to the Coptic Church's centralized power coincided with the development of significant cracks in the church-state partnership toward the end of the Mubarak regime. Two major conversion

14. Political sociologist Mona el-Ghobashy's insightful analysis of the Tahrir uprisings in 2011 shows the convergence of what she identifies as three distinct currents of protest—labor, professional, and popular. Copts were active in all three currents. The most powerful opposition movements to the Mubarak regime included Kifaya ("Enough"), a coalition of professionals and activists that opposed Mubarak's transfer of power to his son, as well as the April 6 Youth Movement which supported protests for factory workers and labor rights. See "Politics by Other Means", *Boston Review,* November 1, 2011.

scandals and a string of church attacks caused significant breaches in Shenouda's relations with Mubarak and the security state apparatus. In 2004, and again in 2010, the alleged conversion of two Coptic priests' wives,[15] Wafa' Qustantin and Kamilya Shahata, escalated into Christian and Muslim riots nationwide for the souls and rights of these women. Widening the rift between Christians and Muslims, the scandals further polarized the public debate surrounding rights to religious freedom along communal lines. At the request of Shenouda, police forces returned the women into the church's fold and placed them behind monastery walls, catalyzing further rounds of protests against the state's violation of individual rights (Guirguis 2016; Mahmood 2016). In the long run, the scandals resulted in widespread national criticism of the state, and international notoriety for Shenouda and the Coptic Church (for having prevented conversions to Islam) throughout the Muslim world. In the eyes of the Coptic community, these bad marks against the church-state pact were further compounded by a sense that the Coptic Church wielded minimal leverage in its dealings with the police and security forces. At an alarming rate, incidents of sectarian violence, such as the Nag Hammadi shootings and the 'Umraniyya clashes at the end of 2010, seemed to confirm Coptic hunches that state evacuations of police protection at churches under attack were deliberate and strategic. Especially in times of heightened vulnerability, it had become increasingly evident that the Coptic Church was a weak communal arbiter against the state's ability to withdraw security and allow for violence to take its course.

Under President Sisi and Pope Tawadros II (2012–) in the wake of the July coup of 2013, familiar signs of repression took hold in the public imaginary. Like many disbanded human rights organizations, the Maspero Youth Union was seriously enervated if not dissolved, with many of its members jailed and arrested. When over forty churches were destroyed after the military's bloody show of force against the Muslim Brotherhood, Pope Tawadros announced that their burnings were sacrifices for the sake of Egypt. Eerily reminiscent of the 1952

---

15. The Qustantin and Shahata controversies are explosive examples of a general sectarian phenomenon: on one side, Copts suspect that Muslims are kidnapping and subjecting Coptic women to forced conversion; on the other, Muslims allege that the Coptic Church is imprisoning and torturing new converts to Islam. It is widely known that Qustantin and Shahata suffered abusive marriages. Due to the Coptic Church's strict regulations regarding divorce and remarriage, Coptic Orthodox in search of loopholes resort to conversion (to Islam or Protestantism) in order to be allowed a divorce. Up until 1971, the Coptic Church permitted separation, imprisonment and abuse as legitimate reasons for divorce; since Shenouda's papacy, it has limited divorce to adultery.

coup and earlier alliances of nation-building, the rehabilitation of the church-state formula of communal rule was further enshrined among Copts through visual portraits of Tawadros and Sisi, paired with those of President Nasser and Pope Kyrillos. Now after a few years of Sisi in power, ISIS attacks on Coptic Christians and the Egyptian military have only further underscored the difficult fact that the Coptic Church has no choice but to rely on the security state for its future.

The Coptic Church functions therefore as an institution of political mediation, an arbiter between Copts and the Egyptian state, and the principal organization that defines the parameters of the Coptic Question. In effect, the Church is an organ of authoritarian rule, concentrating the politics of communal representation in the hands of the highest-ranking clergy and delimiting religious practices and controversies that cause problems for Christian-Muslim relations. It is the Egyptian state that regulates the Church through a range of disciplinary acts, from denying permits for places of worship to withdrawing security in contexts of sectarian tension. The church-state alliance is far from a reciprocal exchange; it is, rather, a hierarchical relationship that is also deeply marked by repression and marginalization. Under these conditions, religious revival and reform also give rise to new mechanisms of discrimination and disenfranchisement on the basis of Coptic communal recognition as "religious" in nature. To quote one frustrated Coptic secularist, "What will Copts gain with one more church?" Over a quick fifty years, Coptic Christianity has spread widely and assumed new forms and expressions; concurrently, it has also been increasingly subject to public scrutiny and political regulation.

Approaching the religious dynamics and everyday texture of revival and repression is a challenging task. The vast majority of historical and political sociological accounts of Copts are actor-centered, featuring the Coptic community through the decisions and strategies of its leaders, with relatively less focus on ordinary Copts. Much work on religion— that is, religious practices, discourse and ideology—has advanced its functionalist role as the cultural assertion of identity, and in the case of Copts, that of a beleaguered minority struggling with discrimination and sectarian strife. The widespread assumption is that religion merely serves as a cultural instrument for shoring up social and political structures of authoritarianism (e.g., clerical hierarchy) or identity politics (e.g., communal recognition). If it is religion that serves as a medium for defining the Christian-Muslim divide in Egypt, how might we access its activity and effects without reducing it to a mere vehicle of institutional reproduction or minoritarian expression? What does the study of religious mediation offer for an analysis of the imbricated dynamics between revival and repression on the ground? By examining the micropolitics of divine mediation, this book seeks to deepen our grasp of the very practices at stake in the modern making of Copts and Christian-Muslim relations under the Egyptian state.

MEDIA: RELICS, APPARITIONS, ICONS

Egypt's cult of saints indexes long histories of divine mediation, or "holy intercession," extending from its desert monasteries along the Red Sea to the Sinai and toward a larger Mediterranean sprawl of wonderworkers and their shrines. The religious life of Copts, regarded as the "early Christians" who trace their lineage back to St. Mark the Apostle,[16] therefore includes a ritual repertoire of images and sensibilities that have been around far longer than the Coptic Church's revival and the modern Egyptian nation-state. As scholars of North Africa and the Levant have described in rich detail, centuries of commingling among Jews, Christians, and Muslims forged a heterogeneous tapestry of sainthood.[17] Following Peter Brown's somewhat nostalgic characterization, saints' festivals and pilgrimages were occasions for "lowering social boundaries," conveying a "warm breath of hope for a lost solidarity" (Brown 1981:102). Martyrs, miracles, and mysteries therefore are not only signs of an otherworldly cosmology; they also extend clues into a social universe that existed before mass literacy and religious identity, when "the simple people" would go and seek a blessing at the same shrine or ask for miracles of healing from the same holy men and women of the village.[18]

16. A rich and formidable body of Coptic scholarship on ritual, magic, aesthetics, and theology exists in late antiquity and early Byzantine studies. For a helpful beginning in the anglophone literature, see Bagnall 1993; Frankfurter 1993, 1998a; Brakke 1995, 2006; Brakke and Crislip 2015; Davis 2001, 2004, 2008a; Bolman 2002, 2016; Emmel 2004; Schroeder 2007; Mikhail 2017; Torallas Tovar 2017. Other important references include *The Coptic Encyclopedia* (ed. Atiya 1991) and *The Claremont Coptic Encyclopedia* (ed. Gabra), an online digital resource available to the public at: http://ccdl.libraries .claremont.edu/cdm/landingpage/collection/cce (accessed May 28, 2018).

17. For work on sainthood and the commingling of religious communities, see Brown 1971, 1981, 1983; Crapanzano 1973, 1980; Gilsenan 1973; Ghosh 1992; Sanders 1994; Hoffman 1995; Cornell 1998; Taylor 1999; Meri 2002; Cuffel 2005. Aside from the topic of sainthood, there is also significant work on the religious aspects of Jewish, Christian, and Muslim interaction in law, trade and urban life. See Greene 2002; al-Qattan 2007; Campos 2010; Bashkin 2008, 2012; Sharkey 2017.

18. For more on the political and ethical life of this image of "the simple people," see chapters 5 and 6, "Public Order" and "Hidden Faces."

In their essay "The Other Christianity?" (in Hann and Goltz 2010:1–32), anthropologists Chris Hann and Hermann Goltz take issue with stereotypes of Eastern Orthodox traditions as backward, stagnant, and authoritarian by nature. Challenging Protestant-centric approaches to language and ideology,[19] they propose that attending to the material specificities of Orthodoxy can helpfully shift the comparative enterprise of religious studies, showing how Copts, Ethiopians, Armenians, Syriacs, and Greeks share more with particular strands of Islam than they do with Christianity in the West.[20] Given their multiple historical layers of encounter and exchange, the material cultures of sainthood provide an entryway for delving into the heterogeneity of overlapping Christianities and Islams in Egypt: the Coptic Orthodox have common intercessors with Roman and Eastern Catholics, journeyed to the same shrines with Sufi and Shiʿi Muslims, and confronted opposition from Protestant Evangelicals and Salafi Muslims who both oppose the mediation of saints and their representations. In such contexts, the categories of "Christian" and "Muslim" are curiously unstable.

This book centers on three genres of saintly imagination: relics, apparitions, and icons. By studying how they organize everyday social relations between Christians and Muslims, I approach these material images as media of Christian-Muslim relations. By invoking the term "media," I consider these images as communicative vehicles across two related domains.[21] In the theological domain of holy intercession, relics, apparitions, and icons serve as conduits which mediate the heavenly

19. Since the late 1990s, the anthropology of Christianity has steadily emerged as a subfield of anthropology and advanced new approaches to the study of conversion and materiality, among other themes. Although much of the inaugural work focused on Protestant traditions such as Pentecostalism and Calvinism, more recent work has engaged varieties of Catholicism and Eastern Orthodoxy. For more background, see the excellent edited volumes Robbins 2003; Cannell 2006; Robbins and Engelke 2010; Hann and Goltz 2010; Robbins and Haynes 2014; Norget, Napolitano, and Mayblin 2017; Luehrmann 2018. Another helpful resource is the online Anthropology of Christianity Bibliographic Blog or "anthrocybib," founded by Jon Bialecki and James Bielo: www.blogs.hss.ed.ac.uk/anthrocybib (accessed May 28, 2018).

20. For anthropological work on Orthodox interactions with Islam, see Mayeur-Jaouen 2005; Valtchinova 2010; Albera and Couroucli 2012; Bowman 2012; Keriakos 2012; Bandak 2014. For ethnographic work on Orthodox Christianity, see Herzfeld 1982; Stewart 1991, 2012; Dubisch 1995; Kan 1999; Naumescu 2008; Rogers 2009; Zigon 2010; Luehrmann 2011; Kormina 2013; Engelhardt 2014; Martin 2016; Pop 2017; Boylston 2018.

21. In the interdisciplinary study of religion and media, a growing number of scholars have pushed to consider "religion as media," regarding processes of technical and technological mediation to be intrinsic to the concept and practice of "religion." For insightful reviews of this literature, see de Vries 2001; Stolow 2005; Engelke 2010.

and earthly realms, representing otherworldly figures and acting in the world on behalf of holy others. In the political domain of governing religion, these same media also constitute public sites of martyr veneration, collective memories of sectarian violence, and national horizons of intercommunal unity. By conjoining these two domains, I seek to direct attention to the ways in which deep histories of interacting with holy saints create new problems and possibilities for modern Christian-Muslim coexistence.[22] Furthermore, I resist studying these Coptic images as objects of varied interpretation relative to various audiences; in other words, my ethnography is not a comparative analysis of how Christian and Muslim communities attribute different or similar meanings to the particular relic, apparition, or icon in question. Here, I do not mean to suggest that these other methods are "wrong." Rather, they elide important analytic insights about the instabilities of Christian-Muslim difference that are internal to social acts of imagining saints and their mediation of divine authority in the world.

Relics, apparitions, and icons offer rich sites for exploring how Orthodox materialities of mediation shape the ways that Christians and Muslims imagine one another. An ethnography of the present, this book examines traces of Coptic Orthodoxy in its "open dynamic of means and effects" (Pfeiffer 1994:3), in its sustained continuities with the distant ancient past and in its fragmentary remediations under forces of modernization—all of which reveal myriad interfaces with Islam.[23] With this aim in mind, I study images of sainthood as a diffuse complex of practices and styles of mediation. To develop my approach toward media and materiality, this book builds on a body of theoretical literature in anthropology, semiology, and media studies which enables my analysis of the collective dimensions of religious aesthetics and their implications for the politics of Christian-Muslim relations.

22. My approach to relics, apparitions and icons thus departs from the distinguished tradition of studying art and artifacts as carriers of Coptic heritage and civilizational identity within the broader historical canvas of Greco-Roman and Islamic influence. For current surveys of Coptic art historiography, see Du Bourguet 1991; Skalova and Gabra 2001; Immerzeel and van der Vliet 2004; Bagnall 2007; Farag 2013; Gabra 2014.

23. I find inspiration from media theorist K. Ludwig Pfeiffer's emphasis on effects rather than hermeneutic depth: "Communication here is not supposed to connote understanding, coming to terms, mutuality, exchange. It unfolds as an open dynamic of means and effects" (Pfeiffer 1994:3). Intrinsic to any study of Christian-Muslim relations is a theory of communication. By taking a materialist approach to communication, I take the grounds of "commonness" to lie in dynamic contexts of technical and technological effects that exceed any one religious tradition's ritual forms and practices.

My approach to holy images is material, but the materiality of holy images requires some explanation. Rather than approaching relics, apparitions, and icons as distinct categories of discrete objects, I take each to represent a set of techniques and technologies that form a distinct genre of imagining sainthood. Much of this book's study is therefore devoted less to particular images in shrines or on the streets, and more to the whole range of embodied skills and media technologies that characterize an image and demarcate its bounds. For example, my two chapters on relics do not so much engage a select collection of relic parts (e.g., St. Mark's head or St. Marina's hand) as they do a diffuse set of sensibilities (e.g., visualizing death at the location of the body, or touching the edge of a fleshly fragment) and a wide variety of their material supports (e.g., a glass case or a television screen).[24] These techniques and technologies of intercession are constitutive of human capacities to inhabit the world and imagine other worlds. Borrowing from the anthropologist Daniel Miller's formulation of the bodily habitus, "much of what we are exists not through our consciousness or body, but as an exterior environment that habituates and prompts us" (Miller 2005:5).[25] What Miller's approach to materiality emphasizes is the transformative and fluid nature of human perception as it is externally shaped by objects like relics, apparitions and icons. As the media studies pioneer Marshall McLuhan has further specified, there are "sensory ratios" for different media, troubling the idea that there is an exclusive domain of sensation referred to as the "visual" (Mitchell 2005a).[26] In my study, I pay special attention to the visual-tactile aspects of engaging Coptic images of sainthood as these images interface with multiple fields of mediation, from the print and photographic industry to other religious traditions of intercession such as Roman Catholicism and Islam. This

24. Following my approach, there are no essentializing features that distinguish "relics," "apparitions," and "icons" from one another. For example, a martyr's hand exhibited on the television screen is both the representation of a body-part ("relic") and the display of a visual appearance ("apparition"). Conceived to be different zones of imagination, relics, apparitions and icons are characterized by overlapping styles of sensory interaction that reveal their blurry boundaries and challenge the idea that they are distinct categories of art-objects.

25. For other theorizations of habitus as developed by Aristotle, and later by Pierre Bourdieu, see Mahmood 2005 and Hanks 2005.

26. A fruitful range of anthropological work on the sensorium has shed light on the politics of visuality and perception. For a useful beginning, see Howes 1991; Taussig 1993; Seremetakis 1994; Ivy 1995; Morris 2000; Pinney 2003; Hirschkind 2006; Mazzarella 2013; Spyer and Steedly 2013; Classen 2014. For sensory approaches in the field of material religion, see Morgan 2007; Meyer 2009; Promey 2014.

multiplicity speaks to the openness of Orthodox mediation, as it reconfigures practices of visuality and as it is reconfigured by mass modernity across the religious divide.

Moreover, because holy images have specific characteristics, they require careful inquiry into the status of representation. Images of intercession are also the likenesses of saints, raising issues at the heart of anthropological theories of personhood: how is a holy person represented? How does he or she circulate? Imagining saints and their activity in the world is a material practice of interacting with ordinary signs of extraordinary presence in space and time. Relics, apparitions, and icons are all vehicles for disseminating the special qualities of saints, or their virtues, to enhance their social recognition, or their "fame," through the "mobile circulating dimension of the person" (Munn 1992:105).[27] As the philosopher Marie-José Mondzain (2002) suggests, the Orthodox icon, in particular, participates in a vast semiotic operation of incarnation which fulfills the universalizing reach of Christian territorial rule. Beyond Orthodoxy proper, the icon is also a classic representation of holy personhood, a "likeness" that intercedes by virtue of its similarity and semblance to its prototype (Peirce 1955). Inasmuch as Christians and Muslims are both invested in religious significations of holiness, my approach throws doubt on essentializing characterizations of Orthodox Christianity as an "iconophilic" tradition on the one hand, and Islam as an "aniconic" tradition on the other.[28] This book, rather, examines disputes over holy representations by entering into the semiological legislation of any given image, its materiality and its authoritative truths. This task involves accounting for "people's assumptions, either tacit or explicit, that guide how they do or do not perceive or seek out signs in the world and respond to them" (Keane 2014:314).

Ultimately, the circulation of relics, apparitions, and icons activates multiple "social imaginaries," or the ways in which people imagine their

27. Personhood is a classic anthropological topic that explores social systems of value and embodiment, inspiring work on themes including gift exchange, organ transplants, property, and ownership, and the social ontology of art and things. See Appadurai 1986; Strathern 1988; Munn 1992; Gell 1998; Sharp 2000; Myers 2001; Palmié 2006.

28. In recent years, world events including the Taliban's destruction of Bamiyan Buddhas in Afghanistan 2009 and the cartoon controversies in Denmark in 2005–6, and then again in France in 2015, have driven stereotypes of Islam as iconoclastic and aniconic in its essence. As art historian Finnbar Barry Flood has pointed out (2002), these hasty conclusions fail to problematize the vocabulary of iconoclasm in Islam, in the ways that the abundant literature on the Byzantine controversies over the visual representation of images has done.

belonging to a collective whole. As many scholars have shown, these imaginaries are central to modern political formations of mass-mediated participation such as the "nation" and the "public" (Habermas 1989; Anderson 1991; Taylor 2004). Crucially at stake in these imaginaries of belonging and exclusion are social imaginings of "Christian" and "Muslim." Images of sainthood are the constitutive vehicles of imagining the self and its limits: the relic-parts of martyrs mediate the transcendent unity of the Coptic "community," and the iconic "holy fool" mediates the anonymous, fleeting outsider. The reverse is true as well: images of sainthood are also subject to the social epistemologies of the nation-state and its instruments of collective representation, which, for Copts, include the category of "minority." In the case of the Zaytun apparition of 1968, for example, what the collective imaginary of "Christian-Muslim unity" entailed was the enumeration of witnesses and the subsequent drive for "Muslim" testimonies. It is worth pointing out that this imaginary aesthetics of majority-minority difference internal to religious mediation can be found in postcolonial societies elsewhere, at times, with threatening effects. In her work on Hindu monuments and majoritarian recognition in India, for instance, art historian Kajri Jain argues that the commensuration of images with specific communities meant that "an attack on an [image] was construed as an attack on the community" (Jain 2017:19; also Spyer 2008; Larkin 2013). Imaginaries of sainthood lead to uneven registers of religious difference, signaling both national unity and sectarian threat in imagined relation to others. Holy images, therefore, both create collective forms of belonging and are subject to the institutions that manage the politics of collective belonging.

We can see the latter dynamic in the ways that the Coptic Church attempts to regulate the representation and circulation of saints. The regulation of religion's public forms, or the "public expression" of religion, is intrinsic to the politics of religious difference.[29] The cult of saints is public by nature and has enjoyed centuries of crossing boundaries between Christians, Muslims and Jews. Relics, apparitions, and icons

---

29. The public/private distinction and the status of religion in the public sphere are core themes that have defined the interdisciplinary field of secularism studies to date (Casanova 1994; Asad 2003; Calhoun, Juergensmeyer, and van Antwerpen 2011). Anthropologists of religion and media have directed attention to how religious practices reconfigure politics of authority and difference, giving rise to new multiple "publics" (Hirschkind and Larkin 2008; Meyer and Moors 2006; Eisenlohr 2012). Recent work inspired by linguistic anthropology has further studied "publicity" as a communicative effect of making a phenomenon, such as religion, public (Cody 2011; cf. Engelke 2013).

are all public media of holiness, expanding the social recognition of any given saint through the material expression and circulation of miracles that, in theory, know no borders. As such, the cult of saints presents a tricky challenge of public relations on behalf of holy figures. For the Coptic Church, the modernity of revival has moreover led to new, unintended forms and practices in the intercessory imagination that, at moments, exceed the Church's purview and disciplinary powers. From the Egyptian state's standpoint, the religious mixing of Christians and Muslims presents a serious problem of governance and poses a threat to public order and security, topics I will discuss further in the next section. Religious mediations reveal inequalities and cleavages internal to the national public, giving rise to other competing and fractured publics (Hirschkind 2006; cf. Rajagopal 2001; Warner 2002). Insofar as they index the state's management of the religious divide, images of sainthood also expose the ways in which "secularity and publicity are inextricably linked" (Engelke 2013:xxiii). I underscore throughout this book the ways in which the political regulation of Christian-Muslim relations involves extensive transformations of how holy images can act and move. More than a mere matter of keeping miracles inside homes and off the streets, the politics of public sainthood entails interventions in various styles of communication and their social effects.

The material aesthetics of envisioning saints, then, forge social imaginaries and political horizons of belonging and action. Against the impulse to romanticize holy intercession as a timeless, special domain of liberation from communal identity, it is important to recognize that the religious lives of Egyptian Christians and Muslims today are largely carried out in entirely separate and distinct spheres, and by governmental design. At the same time, it is also crucial to understand that the Christian-Muslim divide is not a natural, primordial condition but rather pivots on an imaginary politics of access to the divine which is subject to contemporary transformation. Holy images thus afford one strategic venue for accessing the disparate histories of mediation that underlie Christian acts of imagining "Muslims" and Muslim acts of imagining "Christians."

By placing relics, apparitions, and icons at the center of my analysis, this book sets imaginaries of sainthood on empirically defensible terrain and engages with the material elements of Christian-Muslim difference. By beginning from Orthodoxy's asymmetrical status with respect to Islam, it additionally specifies the broader conditions of marginalization and insulation that have rendered Copts a coherent and distinct community. In doing so, this book exposes what the communication of images reveals at the precarious limits of national unity and minoritarian belonging in Egypt.

MEDIATING CHRISTIAN-MUSLIM RELATIONS

In narratives of modern belonging, it is the hierarchical frame of the "nation" that inscribes the nation-state's authority over religious difference. After an incident of sectarian violence in Egypt, one may safely expect the reinvigoration of stock religious symbols marshaled toward the performance of interfaith coexistence.[30] The telos implicit in these political imaginaries is one of Egyptian national unity, captured by symbolic couplets such as "the cross and the crescent," "the church and the mosque," "the priest and the shaykh," in addition to the Virgin Mary and her beloved status above and beyond confessional lines. Scholars of religion and postcolonialism have convincingly shown how the modern project of instituting nationhood ended up naturalizing categories of recognition once foreign to the fabric of native life: "minority" for explaining the unequal status of Copts and Baha'is in Egypt (Mahmood 2016),[31] "sectarian" for documenting the ascendancy of the Lebanese confessional state (Makdisi 2000; Weiss 2010), and "community" for describing the nature of Hindu-Muslim conflict in India (Pandey 1990; Kaviraj 1997). On a global scale, the secularizing powers of state law and nationalist historicism have resulted in the rise of religious identititarianism and the concomitant reconfiguration of religious worlds. National imaginaries, instead of transcending matters of religion, hinge on the state's most intimate entanglements with religious difference at its multiple orders of mediation.

30. Civic repertoires of Christian-Muslim brotherhood and interfaith harmony are common, especially in moments when the nation's status is under threat. Months after Mubarak's downfall, the interim cabinet established "The Family House" (Bayt al-ʿAʾila), an organization devoted to training priests and shaykhs in interfaith dialogue and developing educational materials to promote shared religious values. Critics of these methods of rehabilitating pluralism have argued that these exercises are overall cosmetic in nature, at worst providing an alibi for the state's inaction after incidents of violence.

31. In *Religious Difference in a Secular Age* (2016), anthropologist Saba Mahmood interrogates the concept of "minority" and "minority rights," analyzing the contradictions internal to secular-liberalism's ideal of religious equality. Due to its potential to invite foreign intervention in Egyptian affairs, the Coptic Church and leading Coptic figures have historically rejected the term "religious minority" (al-Gawhary 1996; Makari 2007; Scott 2010). For studies of minority politics and the limits of secular pluralism elsewhere, see also Tambar 2014 and Fernando 2014.

Accounts of religion's role in the politics of inclusion and marginalization invariably risk smuggling in assumptions about what "religion" is and what it does. To the extent that it reiterates static expressions of belief or ideology, the interfaith industry of "Christian-Muslim relations" reinforces identitarian models of religion and its analytic disassociability from the realpolitik of states and societies. The result is a bewildering methodological impasse that is perhaps nowhere more evident than in the mirrored formulations averring that sectarian conflict has "everything to do with religion" and "nothing to do with religion at all."[32]

This book advances sites of Coptic Orthodox mediation as sites of Christian-Muslim mediation to trace the work that religion performs toward the making of consummate nationhood. Underlining the creative instabilities characteristic of nationhood's making, my ethnography thus focuses on the ways in which imaginaries of holy presence invoke and refurbish horizons of Christian-Muslim unity, and arguably more so under conditions of threat, violence, and repression. As I have suggested so far, the imaginary domain of sainthood, as a realm of richly fragmented pasts and a mosaic of religious pluralism, offers one fruitful perspective into grasping what is gained and lost in holy modulations of unity and difference among Christians and Muslims in Egypt. Here, my approach hinges on the observation that religious and national imaginaries are dynamically interlinked; in short, that nationalism did not so much "supersede" religion as it had derived its cultural forms through its "strong affinity with religious imaginings" (Anderson 1991:12, 10). From a slightly different direction, I am also interested in retaining the scholarly problematic of the "imagination" and entertaining the inadequacies of modern nationalist epistemology. Borrowing from historian Dipesh Chakrabarty's hypothetical scenario, "what if the real, the natural, and the historically accurate did not generate the feeling of devotion or adoration?" (Chakrabarty 2000:149). By tracing continuities between religious and national mediations of belonging, I study how saintly mediations produce imaginaries of Christian-Muslim difference under the hegemonic sign of the nation. By also lingering on their discontinuities, I seek to draw out the ways in which various histories of mediation elide the primacy of the nation, leaving remainders of difference that lie outside the nationalist rubrics of "religious" or "communal" identity.

---

32. For an insightful discussion about methods of approaching connections between religion and conflict, see *American Historical Review*'s forum on "Religious Identities and Violence" (2007).

This book's focus on sites of Coptic Orthodox mediation as sites of Christian-Muslim mediation, moreover, tackles the unwieldy dynamics of sectarian difference internal to the making of national unity. Indeed, the term "Christian-Muslim relations" itself falls short of capturing social and political relations of marginalization and exclusion that inhere within religious semiologies of nationhood. To understand minoritarian belonging to the nation, I pay special attention to the flexible calibration of Orthodox Christian imaginaries from the margins—what may be regarded as the "lived" aspects of the Coptic Question. As I argue it, everyday slippages between national unity and sectarian enmity speak to the limits of the hierarchical frame of the nation-state over religious communities and the promise of nationhood as the solution to otherwise irreconcilable differences.[33] Mediations of Christian-Muslim difference articulate with structures of nationhood and state regulation, further offering clues into the disciplinary remaking of the religion and the ways in which minority worlds mobilize interventions into spheres of imagination. In the remainder of this section, I flesh out three core axes of political belonging—"community," "territory," and "security"—that ground this study on the encounters of sainthood with minoritarian nationhood and state power from below.

To be recognized as part of the nation, Copts rely on images of self-representation that render them into a coherent body politic—a "community"—vis-à-vis the nation-state and Muslim-majority society. As I described in my historical discussion of post-1952 Egypt, the Coptic Church's rise into the centralizing vehicle of communal recognition resulted in the mass incorporation of Copts into the Church institution and the making of Orthodox Christianity within the terms of modern nationhood. Given the Coptic Church's origins in martyrdom, the ritual memory of violence provides the "common traditions" through which a "local community define[s] its own identity and project[s] its image to others" (Pandey 1990:8). When the Coptic community confronts an incident of sectarian attack, Orthodox imaginings of martyrdom and violence mobilize multiple, at times contesting, horizons of communal belonging to the nation. What is the value of a martyr's death? Which clerical and state authorities are accountable to the memory of violence? Linking religious and national registers of mediation, "the cross and the

33. A historical version of my argument asserts that "sectarianism" had not preceded the nation-state as a premodern phenomenon to be solved, but rather co-emerged with modern institutions of colonial and national rule (Makdisi 2000).

crescent"—the classic image of Christian-Muslim unity—is subject to the flexible recalibrations of "the cross" and its semiotics of remembering sacrifice and redemption. By specifying mediations of authoritative origins in holy death, we can examine the making of the "community" into an addressable whole and in imagined relation to Egyptian tropes of brotherhood and national history.

Territorial imaginings of Egypt as "Holy Land" are another key domain in which Orthodox Christianity modulates ties and tensions between Christians and Muslims. Representing a sacred geography of pilgrimage, "the True Egypt" for many faithful Copts is claimed through its ancient images of sainthood availed in places like Muqattam Mountain, desert monasteries, and shrines tucked inside the urban city landscape. The onset of modern Egyptian nationalism placed the material mediation of Christian-Muslim coexistence within a bounded territorial space that generated new conceptions of spatial reality and linked nation-building with epistemic truths (see Abu el-Haj 2001). Collective experiences of dispossession, both national and minoritarian in nature, resulted in different horizons of territorial identification at various points in history. At the height of Arab anticolonial nationalism after the 1967 Arab-Israeli War, for example, Christians and Muslims were allied against the losses of the Holy Lands and the Church of Zaytun was transformed into a holy site of majority-minority unity. Deeply felt territorial losses gave rise to modern epistemologies of holy appearance and Christian-Muslim difference. Not long afterward, identitarian aspirations for more church buildings propelled Orthodox imaginaries of territory in a more sectarianizing direction. The national image of neighborly coexistence ("church and mosque") slipped into the sectarian image of minoritarian marginalization ("church versus mosque"). This slippage exposes the sectarian difference internal to imaginings of national coexistence.

As Coptic churches turned into sites of minority identity, they also increasingly served as sectarian strongholds of national security. Threats of sectarian violence led to enlarged police and military presence at prominent churches, along with hired security guards, ID checks, and/or surveillance machines at many other churches. Religious mediations of Christian-Muslim sainthood incite anxieties about conversion, the potential for disorder, and risks associated with unsanctioned activity across communal lines. Regulating the boundaries between Christians and Muslims for the sake of public order and stability, the Egyptian security state enforces "spatial and social segregation" (Guirguis

2016:57). In this context of institutionalized identitarianism, the state's protection of minority rights must strike a tricky balance between "uphold[ing] the sanctity of religious belief" and "limiting its public expression" (Mahmood 2016:177). On one level, preserving national order via Christian-Muslim harmony is a state priority. Yet the public nature of religion—of appearances, miracles, and virtues—is thoroughly transformed through coercive tactics of Christian-Muslim segregation. Furthermore, the securitization of religious practices generates imaginaries of threat and violence, rejuvenating structures of Christian-Muslim division that are attached to secrecy and fear. These continuities between national security and sectarianism mobilize minoritarian desires for protection against further isolation and vulnerability.

For the Egyptian nation-state, the status of Copts and Christian-Muslim relations has always been a highly politically sensitive issue. Many of the state's authoritarian impulses turn on its capacity to bolster national unity above sectarian strife and guarantee order and protection for its minorities. Analyzing the logics of "community," "territory," and "security," this book examines how religious mediations calibrate relations between Christians and Muslims, ordering hierarchical distinctions between national and religious belonging. To critically interrogate the statist telos of interfaith harmony, it moves past the formulaic dichotomy of "conflict versus coexistence." My analysis rather considers how the national frame of Christian-Muslim unity itself produces new dynamics of marginalization, dispossession, and threat. This ethnography also draws out the fresh traces of holy intercession in everyday contexts that pose practical challenges to the state's regulation of Christian-Muslim difference. Understanding Orthodox mediation therefore helps us navigate the political lives of saints in the ways that it both fulfills and exceeds minoritarian structures of the nation-state.

FIELDWORK AND OVERVIEW

I conducted the bulk of my fieldwork during a period which unexpectedly coincided with the final years of the Mubarak regime. This ethnography, therefore, covers select sites of Christian-Muslim tension leading up to Mubarak's downfall in 2011 and offers limited glimpses into ordinary life under unstable turnovers of rule, from the Supreme Council of the Armed Forces in 2011 to the Muslim Brotherhood in 2012, and finally to Sisi's military state in 2013. Although it springs from a defined period of unprecedented tumult nationwide, this book aims to track the longer, more durable legacies of authoritarian rule that have shaped the institutional imaginaries of violence and vulnerability that Copts continue to face today. As the anthropologist Talal Asad once anticipated in his critical reflections on the Egyptian "ruptured state" in the wake of the Arab Spring, the "danger of an eventual return to authoritarianism is real . . . because of the logic of the fears that issue from the fluid political situation" (Asad 2012:272). Christian-Muslim mediation is one recurrent domain of harnessing such fears. It is a historical by-product, moreover, of religious transformations that preceded a state-centered timeline of revolution and counter-revolution.

This book is grounded in thirty-four months of fieldwork carried out over multiple trips of varying duration during the following years: 2004, 2006–7, 2009–15. It reaches different neighborhoods in greater Cairo including 'Abbasiyya, Muqattam, al-Azhar, Old Cairo (Fustat), Warraq (Imbaba), Shubra, Shubra al-Khayma, Musturud (Qalyubiyya), Heliopolis, and 'Ayn Shams. North of Cairo, it also features sites and people from Alexandria and Maryut, Mansura in the Delta, and Port Said in the Suez region. Southward in Upper Egypt, it reaches Beni Suef and villages in Minya such as Manahra and 'Aur. By providing insights from various regions in Egypt, I seek to avoid a Cairo-dominated account while also recognizing that what I am giving here is far from a geographically even picture of Copts and Christian-Muslim relations.

The chapters move in three parts according to the genre of imagination: relics, apparitions, and icons. Each chapter works through a specific style of holy intercession to consider the politics of saintly imagination. All three parts consist of two paired chapters that are crafted in counterpoint, each chapter providing a slightly different political angle to the same genre of imagination. Throughout the book, I begin with the material aesthetics of sainthood to show how religious transformations constitute social and political relations between Christians and Muslims.

In "Relics" (part 1), I focus on the communal institution of the Coptic Church and its authoritative making into a "national" church. "Remembering Martyrs" (chapter 1) explores ritual practices of visualizing death and resurrection to analyze the internal dynamics of communal self-representation vis-à-vis the Egyptian state. This chapter analyzes the Two Saints' Martyrs, the victims of the 2011 bombing in Alexandria, whose collective memory catalyzed emblematic performances of Christian-Muslim unity calling for Mubarak's resignation. Martyrs' relics incorporate the laity into the body politic of divine sacrifice, transmit signs of papal authority, and set moral limits to the

MAP 1. Major cities and monasteries in contemporary Egypt. Map by Bill Nelson.

clerical hierarchy. At the heart of this chapter is the question of communal transformation and political accountability for violence. In "Redemption at the Edge" (chapter 2), I attend to the external dynamics of the Coptic Church, tracing its tactile expansion through pilgrimage and the sympathetic flow of *baraka,* or "holy blessing," across the Christian-Muslim divide. Highlighting the bordering "edge" of relics, I chart out the material reproducibility of saintly parts in contexts of dispersion and dispossession, as well as mass-mediated rituals of virtual extension among the diaspora. More historical in its orientation, this chapter also studies how the Church's ritual making of Egypt into

"Holy Land" intersected with the anticolonial making of the Egyptian nation-state and its territorial borders. It thus ends with the timely coincidence of two anticolonial returns in the spring of 1968: the Roman Catholic Church's return of St. Mark's relics in the wake of Vatican II, and the Virgin's apparitions in Zaytun after the 1967 Arab-Israeli War. These two imagined returns solidified the hierarchy of Christian-Muslim nationhood over the "ecumenical" ties of Christendom.

"Apparitions" (part 2) considers mixed settings of Christian-Muslim interaction and the fraught implications of overlapping practices between Christians and Muslims. Taking off from the Virgin of Zaytun, "Territorial Presence" (chapter 3) demonstrates that the same national image of Christian-Muslim unity in 1968 transformed into a sectarian image of Christian-Muslim enmity in 2009. This transmutation in the saintly apparition's meaning (but not form) originated in territorial contests over churches and mosques in one of Giza's more industrial neighborhoods. By unpacking the phenomenon of "collective apparitions," this chapter further reveals how modernizing epistemologies of visual objectivity organize differences in "Muslim" versus "Christian" witnessing. The key principle governing this sensible form of Christian-Muslim difference is majority-minority identitarianism. In "Crossovers and Conversions" (chapter 4), I shift attention from collective apparitions to a collection of individual encounters with otherworldly presences such as saints, angels, demons, and jinn, as well as with the figures who mediate them such as exorcists, magicians, and holy men. I make the case that there is enough overlap between Christian and Islamic practices of dreaming and prophecy to yield ambiguities and transgressions. This chapter foregrounds heterodox forms of holy intercession which take place outside of churches and mosques—in shops, homes, villages, and marketplaces that escape the purview of state-sanctioned religious authorities. The chapter also includes a narrative of conversion from Sufism to Christianity which suggests the degree to which Christian and Islamic worlds of messengership, visionary experience, and folk healing can intermingle, crossing over and folding into one another.

In "Icons" (part 3), I engage the public nature of holy personhood by examining how the Coptic Church and Egyptian state regulate the publicity of miracles across the Christian-Muslim divide. Building on the overlap between Christian and Islamic worlds of holy visions and healing, "Public Order" (chapter 5) turns to the case of a Coptic woman whose dream led to controversy between Christians and Muslims along the Suez Canal. This chapter centers on the miracle icon of the Virgin in

Port Said and the efforts of security state officials to manage its public circulation. I argue that the policing of public order led to the polarizing segregration of Christians and Muslims, transforming the material circulation of holy power in the process. The containment of the icon, made into a "communal" image, continues to generate new suspicions, rendering open shrines into outposts of secrecy. In "Hidden Faces" (chapter 6), I trace the effects of insulating Copts into communal enclaves of withdrawal from the larger mixed Christian-Muslim public. My focus is on the cult making of contemporary saints and the mystical imaginaries that yield the collective image of "the simple people." I show that one key outcome of containing and repressing signs of sainthood is an amplified imagination of secrecy and hiding. This covert politics of holy secrecy, moreover, can further serve to ameliorate an authoritarian narrative of communal belonging under the nation-state.

Finally, I close this book with an epilogue centered on the Libya Martyrs, the twenty-one migrant laborers who were beheaded in 2015, and the alarming rise of ISIS across North Africa and the Middle East in 2013–14. Despite its unprecedented nature, I show how the terrorist execution of Copts and its immediate aftermath activated older strands of religious mediation that I have described throughout this book: the communal dynamics of martyr commemoration, Arab nationalism versus Christian Rome as competing referents of political belonging, the outbreak of contests and threats tied to church territory, and the cult making of contemporary martyrs in the Coptic Church. By recounting the Libya Martyrs' various contexts, the epilogue invites reflection on how acts of violence that exceed the Egyptian national frame—through impoverished Coptic migrants and pan-Islamic militant groups—exacerbate old structures of sectarian tension in a new era of postrevolutionary militarization.

As a whole, the book offers an analysis of Christian-Muslim mediation through the political lives of saints in Egypt. By engaging the materialities of holiness, it seeks to enrich our perspectives on millennia-long traditions of instituting authority and their contemporary interventions in spheres of minoritarian repression and authoritarian state rule. It is my hope that this work may also shed light on the more ordinary vistas of belonging, including the roads that have been taken and have yet to be fulfilled. On that note, we turn now to the Copts on New Year's of 2011, the revolutionary opening for the Tahrir uprisings.

PART ONE

Relics

CHAPTER I

Remembering Martyrs

Martyrdom is a love sacrifice burning. . . . Its scent fills the whole universe, attracting all hearts of purity and filling them with jealousy and desire so that they can go along on the heavenly road.

Mothers of the Convent of Amir Tadrus, Harat al-Rum, "An Introduction to Martyrdom," preface to *The Biography of the Great Martyr Prince Tadrus al-Shatbi* (*Sirat al-Shahid al-ʿAzim al-Amir Tadrus al-Shatbi*)

This anonymous hero is very ancient. He is the murmuring voice of societies.

Michel de Certeau, "To the Ordinary Man," preface to *The Practice of Everyday Life*

ALEXANDRIA OF 2011: BETWEEN THE PASSION AND THE RESURRECTION

On January 1, 2011, a car bomb ripped through the Two Saints' Church in the Sidi Bishr neighborhood of Alexandria.[1] The blast left twenty-four dead and over two hundred injured, transforming the New Year's Eve mass into a bloody midnight nightmare. In the following weeks, red-and-black posters of the cross with the crescent covered the Mediterranean promenade and permeated the urban squares of Cairo's neighborhoods. These posters of Christian and Muslim solidarity

1. The Church of St. Mark and Pope Peter in Alexandria is also referred to as the "Two Saints' Church" (Kanisat al-Qiddisin or al-Qiddisin).

FIGURE 1. Contemplating St. Mark's life and death, Tomb of St. Mark the Martyr, Patriarchate Cathedral of St. Mark, ʿAbbasiyya. Photo by author.

publicized sentiments loud and clear: "No to Terrorism, Yes to Egypt! [*Lā li-l-irhāb, na'am li-Miṣr!*]."

For mourning Coptic Christians, however, the target of public reproach was neither terrorism from abroad nor sectarian conflicts at home. Their message of protest was rather directed at the failure of their political and spiritual leaders to protect them. On January 2, the funeral for the twenty-four new Alexandrian martyrs, or the "Two Saints' Martyrs" (Shuhada' al-Qiddisin), was held in St. Menas Monastery where an audience of thousands gathered with indignant rage. Seated in the front rows were the Church's highest-ranking bishops and Egypt's state dignitaries, including Alexandria's Governor 'Adil Labib. Behind these church and state leaders, the mood was stormier. Waving hand-held wooden crosses up and down in their hands, the crowds bellowed inside the cavernous cathedral: "With our souls, with our blood, we will redeem you, O Cross!"[2] One martyr's relative cried out in pain: "Yā Samu'il! [Samuel!]." Others in the crowd demanded recognition from the Coptic Church's top figure Pope Shenouda who was absent at the event: "We want the Pope!"

Cameras for Aghapy TV,[3] the Coptic Church's satellite television channel, broadcast the funeral live for Coptic viewers all over the world. At the center of the broadcast were the wooden coffins carrying the victims' bodies. The television footage alternated between the speakers and the people in the pews. Bishops Yu'annis and Bakhumius presided over the rituals of remembering the martyrs, speaking above the crowd's cries. Bishop Yu'annis invited the audience to reenvision the bodily fragments of martyrdom in Alexandria: "Dearly beloved, the event was terrifying [*rahīb*]. So terrifying that fleshly parts of our beloved reached the sixth floor of the church! And so, our church was anointed with the blood of the martyrs!"[4]

The congregation erupted into applause and cheers, chanting its refrain: "With our souls, With our blood, We sacrifice for you, O Cross!"

---

2. The popular chanting formula "With our souls, with our blood, we will redeem you, O—! [*Bi-l-rūḥ bi-l-damm, nafdīk yā—!*]" is used in marches and protests throughout the Arab Middle East. Depending on the particular cause of the demonstration, the formula invokes varying objects of address such as nations, movements, or religious faiths. In Coptic protests, the object of address is frequently "The Cross."

3. As of 2017, there are three main satellite television channels dedicated to Coptic Orthodox programming: Aghapy TV, Coptic TV (CTV), and MESat. Founded in 2005, Aghapy TV (Aghabi is "Agape," Arabized Coptic for "love") is the oldest and closely tied to the Coptic Church, headed by Bishop Butrus and broadcast from its headquarters in Heliopolis. For more on Coptic television and film, see Armanios and Amstutz 2013; Heo 2017.

4. Bishop Yu'annis, Eulogy for the Alexandrian Martyrs, January 2, 2011, Aghapy TV. All translations are mine.

Bishop Yuʾannis continued: "As dreadful as the scene of martyrdom [al-mashhad] was, how much more gloriously ascendant was the welcoming of their souls in heaven! And we remember what God said to Cain: 'The blood of your brother screams to me from the ground!'[5] And God listens carefully to the blood of martyrs!"

Again, the crowds overwhelmed the bishop's voice with roaring cheers. The collective memory of violence stirred up the biblical scene of God holding Cain to account for Abel's death, building on fraternal tropes of Christian-Muslim unity in the shared blood of Egyptian nationhood. When the cathedral finally quieted down, Bishop Yuʾannis began to carry out the Coptic Church's more administrative formalities: "We would like to thank our distinguished head of the Republic"—the crowds interrupted in protest, with many men and women standing and waving their hands furiously: "No! No! No! No! No! No! No! No!"

Bishop Yuʾannis signaled for silence. When an acceptable level of quiet was reached, he continued with the names of esteemed guests, reopening fresh wounds: "We would like to thank Alexandria's security forces"—once again, his ceremonial efforts roused deafening chants of rebuke: "No! No! No! No! No! No! No! No!"

Bishop Bakhumius quickly took over presiding duties. Apologizing for Pope Shenouda's absence, he comforted the crowds and spoke about the martyrs in their last moments: "These are the ones who served the Lord in the last night of their lives with praises which reached the rooftops. Where God is, they are there because God loves them."

A new chant began gaining voluminous momentum throughout the pews and balconies. Slowly, the people directed their anger towards the defined target who was present at the funeral, Alexandria's Governor ʿAdil Labib: "Remove the Governor! Remove the Governor! Remove the Governor! [Shīl al-Muḥāfiẓ!]."

As Aghapy TV's cameras zoomed in on him, Governor ʿAdil Labib's steely profile showed his refusal to wilt before the crowds around him. Bishop Bakhumius hurriedly moved to closing the liturgy, pressing ahead: "Where God is, they are there also because they died for his sake! And so, we are comforted that they left us as new martyrs who will intercede on our behalf!!"

Amid cheers and ululating trills, the coffins were hoisted and carried out of the monastery cathedral to the mausoleum outside. Crowds of angry Copts followed the martyrs' bodies, their cries voicing their

5. Genesis 4:10.

collective indictment of the Coptic Church's failure to demand justice from Egyptian state officials for their communal loss.

Most Copts in Egypt and abroad did not make it to St. Menas Monastery, but watched Aghapy TV's live coverage of the martyrs' funeral instead. On January 2, 2011, I was tuned into Aghapy TV with several Copts inside the waiting room of a church in Heliopolis, an affluent suburb in northeast Cairo. We watched the flat-screen monitor together in silence for the most part, with the exception of a few quiet chuckles of satisfaction during the crowds' protests against the governor.

Aghapy TV's coverage closed with additional frames that interspersed visual images from the Two Saints' Church in Alexandria with select shots from *The Passion of the Christ* (2004), Mel Gibson's Hollywood blockbuster that depicts the final twelve hours of Jesus's life. The first frame presented the charred carcass of the bombed car on the streets of Sidi Bishr. The second frame was the bloody scourging of American actor James Caviezel's body. The third frame displayed the black body bags carrying the martyrs' bodies and the blood-splattered mural of Christ on the church's wall. The fourth frame was Caviezel's trembling wrist roped to the cross. The fifth frame featured the wounded bodies of Alexandria's victims in the hospital—bandaged, plaster-cast, scarred, singed, and bedridden.

In the final frames, the television screen turned pitch-black for a brief moment. Then, the luminous Caviezel as Christ reappeared, fully reconstituted into a resurrected whole. Gazing ahead with shining eyes, he appeared to look forward at a triumphant future.

AN INSTITUTION OF MARTYRS

Three weeks after the Alexandrian bombing, the January 25 uprisings launched protests nationwide demanding President Hosni Mubarak's resignation. Chanting for regime change, Christians and Muslims joined hands in their performances of interfaith unity against sectarian division. After the attack on the Two Saints' Church, images of the crescent with the cross had flooded the streets, fostering sympathy for the Copts' tragedy nationwide. The twenty-four deaths in Alexandria signified an attack against not only the Christian community, but also the entire Egyptian nation. The Alexandrian martyrs were one station on the road to Tahrir ("Liberation") Square.

The Coptic Church hierarchy, in support of the Mubarak presidency, prohibited its flock from joining the protests. And yet, as the crowds at

St. Menas Monastery had already indicated, revolutionary sentiments overrode authoritarian alliances between leading bishops, state security forces, and Governor ʿAdil Labib. The calls of Copts for justice and accountability were a stunning rebuke of the church-state entente which had repeatedly failed to protect them over the years. Pope Shenouda's absence at the funeral only attested to this chronic failure. More than anything else, the funeral was a public occasion for Copts to critically reflect on their own vulnerability and the limits of their communal representation in the hands of the Coptic Church's highest power-brokers. To this day, their cries go unanswered; no one has been charged yet for the murders in Alexandria of 2011.

This chapter argues that the Coptic Church is, foremost, an institution of martyrs. The ritual memory of holy deaths serves as the authoritative foundation for the making of the Coptic community and its self-representation. What does it mean to belong to the "community" of Coptic Christians? Who speaks for the Copts, and on what moral and political grounds? The Coptic Church's origin story lies in martyrdom: the martyrdom of its founding apostle and first pope, St. Mark, in Alexandria,[6] and the glorious "Era of the Martyrs" which marks the beginning of the Coptic Calendar at 284 C.E.[7] As historians of Coptic martyrology during Fatimid and Ottoman Islamic rule have shown, ritual narratives and depictions of holy deaths strengthened senses of communal identity and cohesion (Armanios 2011; Swanson 2015; cf. el-Leithy 2005).[8] Currently, the political institution of papal authority and clerical-lay relations continues to crucially hinge on collective acts

6. For a stimulating take on literary representations of "ancient Alexandria" and the colonial discursive production of "cosmopolitan Alexandria" inhabited by Jews, Christians, and Muslims, see Fahmy 2012a and 2012b.

7. The Coptic narrative of its Church origins strikingly differs from widespread histories of the Coptic Orthodox Church that begin at 451 C.E., with its break from the Byzantine Church and the Chalcedonian formula of Christ's two distinct natures, human, and divine, residing in one person and one hypostasis. To little surprise, very few Copts are familiar with the terms of this Christological controversy. Rather, by claiming their church's origins in ancient martyrdom on Egyptian soil, Copts uphold their status as the true "Orthodox" Church and their traditions as uniquely indigenous to Egypt.

8. Of course, the historical settings, causes, and contexts of Coptic martyrdom vary widely across late antiquity and periods of Islamic rule, up until the contemporary present of Muslim-majority nation-states. Referred to as "neomartyrs," Coptic saints who died at the hands of Muslim authorities are distinguished from the ancient martyrs who died under the rule of the pre-Constantinian late Roman Empire. Historian Sidney Griffith importantly observes that, unlike in the world of Roman rule, "Christians were not normally subject to outright persecution in the world of Islam simply by reason of being Christian" (Griffith 2012:148).

of remembering martyrs, old and new. At stake, therefore, in the memory of martyrdom is the possibility for communal self-transformation and the reordering of hierarchy internal to the Church. This possibility for communal self-transformation ultimately implicates the authoritarian politics of the Coptic Church and Egyptian state, a key target of revolutionary critique in Alexandria all the way to Tahrir.

Acts of picturing martyrdom are creative acts of communal self-institution, offering a margin of autonomy from the Coptic Church's more authoritarian impulses. Here, I am borrowing from philosopher Cornelius Castoriadis's notion of "social imaginary significations" that "institute" society, or more precisely, "institute a mode of being of things and of individuals which relate to them" (Castoriadis 1987:364). In its ritually imagined nature, the Coptic Church is reinstituted across each act of remembering scenes of holy suffering and violence. The visual memory of martyrdom organizes the ways in which Copts inhabit their collective past in divine sacrifice, reflect on the ethics of veneration, and evaluate their place in a larger body politic of collective representation. Social imaginaries of martyrdom are the common basis for Coptic communal belonging, promoted by the Coptic Church, even if they also eventually led to a deafening rebuke of its steep hierarchy and its concentration of power in the hands of the few. It was, after all, the high-ranking Bishops Yu'annis and Bakhumius themselves who had declared the potential for "new martyrs who will intercede on our behalf!" Rather than reinscribe a macropolitical model of the Coptic Church as an actor defined by its pope and his inner circle of power-brokers, this chapter aims to highlight the more creative and dynamic components of the Coptic Church's self-institution from below. Understanding the imaginary life of martyrdom as a critical resource for communal accountability is one way to do this.

Collective images of the self are necessary for communal self-transformation. For the theological body politic of the Coptic Church, the chief medium is the Eucharist, which serves as the vehicle of ritual incorporation into the holy community on earth. Martyrs' relics are mimetic representations of Christ's passion and resurrection, mediating the Church's origins through, for example, the "fleshly parts of the beloved" and the "blood of martyrs" from Alexandria of 2011. In moments of tragic violence, today's Copts frequently invoke the old patristic saying, "the blood of the martyrs is the seed of the church."[9]

---

9. Tertullian of Carthage, *Apologeticus*, chapter 50, ca. 150–240 C.E.

The relics of martyrs, ancient and contemporary, ultimately signify the Church's foundational beginnings in remembering death and resurrection, suffering and triumph. This political theology of communal origins and transformation is what organizes relations of past and present, incorporating new martyrs into a sacred realm of commemoration that encompasses Christ, St. Mark the apostle, and all the glorious martyrs from late antiquity to the future. Relics are the media for instituting shrines and disseminating memory, ordering social relations of authority and transmission; they are the constitutive images of a "polity" of blood (cf. "textual polity," in Messick 1993; Anidjar 2014).

Offering collective images of the self, relics structure capacities for communal self-reflection and evaluation. At each scene of remembering death, the holy bodies of martyrs are the media of visualizing the community as a total whole, from a heavenly viewpoint and from the eschatological standpoint of the resurrection. Relics, in other words, are the visual media of envisioning the space and time of "transcendence," or the abstracted site of communal self-objectification from on high. As scholarly literature on the Protestant semiotics of transcendence has shown (Keane 2007; Engelke 2007; also Pietz 1985, 1987),[10] debates around material expressions of divine presence are centered on social and political questions of agency and value. As we will see in this chapter, in the Orthodox semiotics of transcendence, the visual imaginary of parts and whole activates the social institution of relations between the clergy and laity, as well as between the ancient and contemporary martyrs. Visual acts of remembering death and resurrection are the means of reflecting on social relations of belonging and evaluating the powers of the holy priesthood and their ethical limits. Images like the Eucharist and holy relics embody ritual forms of self-representation that powerfully enable acts of communal self-reflection and self-critique. By reinvoking persons and places of holy suffering, martyrs' relics offer the collective possibility for demanding an account of violence and its proper moral response.

Imaginaries of martyrdom are productive, releasing political forms of agency and potential redress. Parallel to other minority communities who suffer violence, Copts are all too often relegated to the "neolachrymose" slot of eternal persecution.[11] As historian of modern Copts Paul

10. Anthropologists of Protestant Christianity have analyzed the material semiosis of the Eucharist to explore larger themes linked to ideologies of "immaterial" transcendence such as belief, language, sincerity, freedom, and globalization.

11. For a critique of the persecution-oriented historiography of Jews in Europe and the Middle East, see Cohen 1994; Nirenberg 1996; cf. Ye'or 1985.

Sedra has emphasized (2011), the main scholarly task at hand is to "restore agency" to the Coptic community, against dominant accounts of its passive victimhood.[12] Ethnographies of martyrdom elsewhere have usefully shown how ritual aesthetics of martyr commemoration advance resistance movements (Khalili 2007; Allen 2013), post–civil war reconstruction (Volk 2010) and minoritarian politics of secular pluralism (Tambar 2014). Exploring visual cultures of Sunni and Shiʿi martyrdom (cf. Ayoub 1987; Aghaie 2004), this literature also suggests overlapping sensibilities with Orthodox and Catholic cults of martyr veneration in the Arab Middle East. Acts of martyr commemoration thus extend the potential of spanning religious and communal boundaries, directing collective forms of agency toward national and international ends. Notably, Egypt's Christians and Muslims who died as "martyrs of Tahrir Square" are explicitly valued as sacrifices for the sake of national unity and revolution.

For the Coptic community, however, the main object of reordering the terms of political agency is the Coptic Church institution. The pope and a handful of bishops continue to function as the de facto spokespeople for the Coptic community and represent Copts within statist horizons of Christian-Muslim nationhood. Rituals of remembering holy deaths offer the power, from within the terms internal to the Orthodox tradition, to disrupt authoritarian rituals of overlooking violence. Relics mediate the authoritative origins of the church body politic, offering resources for collective self-transformation and setting limits on papal authority, clerical hierarchy, and the church-state entente. At the heart of uniting Christians and Muslims are precisely the terms of mediating communal recognition—especially in moments when events of violence place minoritarian belonging to the nation at risk.

This chapter on the politics of martyrdom and memory proceeds in six parts. In the first, I examine the foundational authority of St. Mark's death and the visual techniques that interlink his bodily locus with imaginary scenes of holy violence. The second part turns to the ritual making of popes and their bodily images, focusing on the material transfer of papal authority from St. Mark to Pope Shenouda via relics. In the third and fourth parts, I pay more detailed attention to the Coptic Church's means of self-institution in its mass incorporation of the laity.

---

12. Coptic Church leaders are also aware of their cultural orientation toward self-victimization, what one Coptic church deacon in his interview with me characterized to be a psychological pathology or "martyr-complex" (ʿuqdat al-shuhadāʾ).

To be specific, I delve into the ritual semiotics of clerical-lay relations entailed in the Eucharist and the cinematic aesthetics of envisioning the dynamics of death and resurrection. The chapter closes with a consideration of new martyrs, like the Alexandrian martyrs of 2011, and the ways in which they introduce vistas of communal belonging and intercommunal mediation in Egypt and beyond.

SAINT MARK, FIRST OF THE POPES OF ALEXANDRIA

In the early period of my fieldwork, I spent a fair amount of time in the Patriarchate Cathedral of St. Mark located in ʿAbbasiyya, a neighborhood in Cairo. Since its inaugural opening in June 1968, the Patriarchate is the place where Popes Kyrillos VI (1959–71), Shenouda III (1971–2012) and Tawadros II (2012–) have lived and administered church affairs. The Patriarchate complex, a key site for lay education and civil society programs, bustles with activity throughout its multistory buildings, courtyards, and media centers. The Patriarchate grounds also include several shrines for saints, the most important being its patron St. Mark, the founding apostle of the Coptic Church and First of the Popes of Alexandria.

The holy relics of St. Mark reside in his shrine tucked in the eastern rear of the Patriarchate Cathedral. St. Mark's body mediates the Coptic Church's origins in his apostolic martyrdom in Alexandria. His relics extend the means for visually imagining his death, linking his bodily locus with the creative memory of foundational violence. When Copts remember St. Mark's martyrdom, they enact the imaginary origins of the Coptic Church and its communal institution as a body politic of holy death and resurrection. The Coptic Synaxarium, or "Coptic Lives of the Saints," is a compilation of hagiographic texts that account for all the official Coptic Orthodox saints, especially the martyrs. On his feast day annually in May, the Church's verbal account of his marytrdom is read aloud: "They seized St. Mark, bound him with a thick rope and dragged him in the roads and streets. . . . His flesh was torn and scattered everywhere, and the ground of the city was covered in blood."[13] The ritual memory of St. Mark's bodily violence and passion is the basis for the Coptic Church's capacity for gaining divine recognition and authority.

---

13. Baramouda 30, *The Coptic Synaxarium*. Available online in English at: www .copticchurch.net/synaxarium/08_30.html (accessed May 28, 2018).

In September 2006, while waiting for one of Shenouda's weekly Wednesday meetings, I met Sister ("Tāsūnī") Kiriya. Sister Kiriya was dressed in a plain light brown habit, the attire of a novice training to be a full-fledged "consecrated deaconess," or *al-mukarrasa*. As a result of numerous young, unmarried women seeking to join the holy church orders, Pope Kyrillos had created the new rank of "consecrated deaconess" in 1965. Distinguished from the female monastics (*al-rāhibāt*) who live apart in seclusion, these deaconesses were ordained to serve in the world.[14] In her early to mid-twenties,[15] Kiriya lived nearby at Dayr al-Malak, a convent in Kubri al-Qubba. Having myself experienced one summer living in a dormitory with deaconesses-in-training in Shubra al-Khayma, I could imagine the pressure and competition Kiriya was enduring to achieve official ordination as a deaconess.

We first entered the dimly-lit cupola shrine for St. Mark, separately and solemnly. On that warm autumn afternoon, the fans whirred, the red carpets faintly smelled of stale sweat, and a few people were praying around St. Mark's relics (*al-rufāt, al-ajsād*). St. Mark's relics, hidden from sight, were buried inside a large rectangular sarcophagus, wrapped in red velvet cloth and plastic protective covering. On the walls encircling us was the famous Coptic iconographer Isaac Fanous's portrait mural of two major events which commemorate St. Mark's body (discussed in the next section): St. Mark's martyrdom in Alexandria (68 C.E.) and St. Mark's translation from Venice to Cairo (1968).

At the start of our dialogue, Kiriya was shy and soft-spoken. She gave me lessons on how to pray and effectively address God—or in her words, how to "ask God to hear you." Interceding on behalf of others, in fact, was her assignment at the convent where she was regularly meeting with troubled visitors and receiving letters in mail requesting prayer from the nuns.

---

14. The term *tāsūnī* is a title used to address both a lay "deaconess" (*al-mukarrasa*) (which is what Sister Kiriya is training to be) and an "active nun," both of whom wear bluish-gray habits. A "contemplative nun," on the other hand, is addressed as *umminā* or "our mother" in Arabic, and wears black robes. In Nelly van Doorn-Harder's ethnography on Coptic nuns in the modern Coptic Church (1995), she notes that there are two categories of nuns (*al-rāhibāt*) who are consecrated to the clerical order. The first are the "contemplative nuns" whose forbears are understood to originate as early as the fifth century, in parallel with the Pachomian communal monastics of the desert. The second are the "active nuns" who serve in orphanages, schools, and social service centers.

15. At that time, I was about the same age as Kiriya. That she assumed the didactic role of my instructor was therefore not out of place.

Kiriya began with the relics of St. Mark. "That is the saint's body and we have faith it is his body. We pray so that the saint in heaven will remember us, it's like telling him—don't forget me. The important thing is that you speak the name of the saint. God honors him and wants us to say 'St. Mark, St. Mark, St. Mark,' Because God loves him."

St. Mark's body is the authoritative image of the Coptic Church's self-representation. Establishing the material grounds for communal recognition, holy martyrdom (*al-istishhād*) is an act of divine witness, and its vehicle is the suffering body of the martyr (*al-shahīd*). When one visits the tomb of St. Mark, one visits the place of martyrdom, or the shrine (*al-mashhad* or *al-mazār*). This place of holy death also offers, with its location circumscribed in the martyr's body, the scene or spectacle of witness (*al-mashhad* or *al-manzar*). In this way, the act of visiting St. Mark's relics, or pilgrimage to his shrine, doubles as an act of seeing.

Visiting St. Mark's relics is a visually interactive ritual: the shrine (*al-mashhad*) *is* the spectacle (*al-mashhad*); the locus of the body *is* the visual scene of martyrdom. Nobody can see the fleshly fragments inside the tomb; rather, the act of viewing his holy body requires witnessing the scene of martyrdom again. Relics are therefore not merely holy objects that are circumscribed in space and time. They are also constitutive of a particular style of interactive mediation that links visual acts of imagination to the site and scene of remembered death. In concert with iconography and liturgical text, relics structure visual techniques of re-creating the space of witnessing, thus reinstituting the place of origins.

Inside the shrine, Fanous's panoramic icon painting serves a technical tool for the visual recovery of the martyrdom spectacle (cf. MacCormack 1981). Depicting St. Mark in ropes dragging on the ground, and surrounded by an audience of soldiers and mourners, the icon represents the space and time of his suffering body. The truthful status of the relics crucially pivots on the account of suffering that is rewitnessed. In keeping with the teachings of St. Shenoute of Atripe, the fifth-century monk-warrior who is widely revered in the Coptic tradition, "any account that did *not* recount how the martyr had died under great torments . . . an account [that] could not be authentic, it was a *martyros ñnoudj*, an account of a martyr based on lies" (Brown 2000:7, cf. Brakke and Crislip 2015).

When visitors visualize St. Mark's holy passion, they partake in the saint's powers to intercede. Simply put, remembering martyrs means participating in the church body politic. As historian Elizabeth Castelli has poetically illumined, the power of the martyrdom spectacle lies in its transformation of "the seer into the seen" (Castelli 2004:133; cf. Naguib 1994). Through iconological acts of memory, the martyr's witness is made into an object of witness. Viewers of the martyr's body are able to address God through this visual act of self-mirroring, the church's act of self-imagining its authoritative origins. Moreover, if the martyr's relics offer conduits between heaven and earth, then anyone in principle enjoys the communicative potential for obtaining recognition through them. This potential is exercised in acts of prayer, or intercession.

After Kiriya and I left the shrine of St. Mark, we took a break to reflect on the shrine together underneath the Patriarchate's ivory arcades. Facing the courtyard where people were eating canteen snacks, Kiriya rehearsed the gory details of St. Mark's martyrdom. Although she spoke in a low whisper, the force of her exhortation was not lost on me:

> St. Mark was killed for the sake of Christ, he was persecuted and tortured. Why did our Lord do this? To glorify the name of St. Mark!
>
> Remember what I showed you in the shrine, the picture on the icon. Like I showed you, St. Mark was dragged about when they tied his legs to the horse. He was tortured terribly and he suffered very much. Wasn't he preaching [the message of] Jesus Christ in the beginning? They tied the line to the tail of the horse, and the horse started to run. And so, St. Mark began to follow along on the ground.
>
> Of course, his body was torn, lacerated, shredded—all of it—from being dragged around on the ground! Imagine that there is a person resting on the ground. And his legs are hanging from the tail of the horse. And then, this horse begins to run.
>
> Picture what the scene was like [tit-ṣawwarī al-manẓar biyibʾāʾ izzay]! Of course, it's an awful, awful scene! When someone circles around the city by the tail of a horse, his skin would naturally break open and spill blood. His blood spilled and covered the entire city.
>
> There are films of the lives of saints on video, so you can understand this.

Outside the shrine, Kiriya continued to recall St. Mark's body into her creative imagination. Lingering on the visual details of his tortured flesh—torn into bits, with his blood flowing and staining the streets, she urged me to rewitness the power of his death and re-create the spectacle of violence. Her pace was deliberate, and at once, she was picturing a foundational scene (al-mashhad) and approximating a holy site of witness (al-mashhad). St. Mark's relics and the iconic portraits of his martyrdom are technologies of crafting memory, the technical media of locating his suffering body in space and time. As we will soon see, hagiographic films offer another visual medium for imagining the suffering body.

At one point in our conversation, I asked Kiriya if we could pray without St. Mark or any of the saints in mind. She replied in a matter-of-fact manner, "He's not like us. We are still on earth and haven't done anything yet." Then, Kiriya proceeded to evoke the image of holy sacrifice once again, the ultimate condition for addressing heaven and appealing to the highest tiers of transcendent recognition from above.

REMEMBERING THE POPES' BODIES

Among Copts today, one of the most debated topics is the pope's role in politics. The strongest popes have served as communal arbiters who represent the interests of Copts vis-à-vis the Egyptian state and society. In the context of state authoritarianism, there is a temptation to understand the concentrated investment of communal authority in the hands of popes as a cultural product of the Orthodox tradition. Scholarly literature on Orthodoxy, for instance, has underlined its static-conservatist tendencies and attributed its failures to modernize to its deeply hierarchical structure and its "caesaro-papist" model of power (Pelikan 1977; cf. Hann and Goltz 2010).[16]

The Coptic Orthodox imaginary of the pope, in contrast, suggests a political-theological understanding of mediating authority, spiritual and worldly in nature. All popes ultimately lead to St. Mark and his apostolic authority in martyrdom, the founding moment of the Coptic Church. Each pope, above all, signifies the continuous transmission of Church origins, as "orthodox" or *al-mustaqīm* (also "straight" or "right": see Engelhardt 2014; Luehrmann 2018). It is critical, moreover, to reiterate that the Coptic Orthodox Church was fully independent from its beginnings; its birth did not begin with its belonging to another imperial church (e.g., Eastern Orthodox or Roman Catholic). The Coptic popes were never subordinate to any other popes, in terms of their spiritual authority. Consequently, the Coptic Church's independent identity crucially pivots on its temporal self-propagation as the true Church body that belongs to St. Mark of Alexandria. It is through the commemorative dynamics of imaginary institution that the Coptic popes serve as holy images of collective autonomy.

16. It is worth noting that the Catholic and Orthodox churches adhere to different theologies of the papal authority. In Orthodoxy, there is no doctrine of papal infallibility or supremacy. In the Coptic Church, candidates for the papacy and the bishopric are always monastics (i.e., "unworldly"), in contrast to Coptic priests who "serve in the world."

FIGURE 2. Portait honoring the death of Pope Shenouda III reads: "We will miss you, Our Lordship."

For this reason, remembering the pope's body as a mediating link to St. Mark's body is a necessary ritual of legitimating origins. The material logics of papal representation, as it is conceived from within Orthodoxy, originate in the bodily image of St. Mark's martyrdom. They are also centered on the bodily institution of the holy popes, envisioned as apostolic successors of St. Mark, the First of the Popes of Alexandria.

In March 2012, when Pope Shenouda III died, thousands of Copts went to the Patriarchate Cathedral of St. Mark in ʿAbbasiyya to pay their respects to the late leader of the Coptic community. On the morning after his death, Shenouda's body was on public display for the crowds of visitors. His embalmed corpse (*al-jasad al-muḥannaṭ*) was seated on the Patriarchate throne, fully vested in his papal regalia for three days before the funeral.[17] Cairo's streets were inundated with the wails and tears of his mourning devotees, with cloth banners of his portrait carried on their shoulders.

When Copts beheld Shenouda's dead body on the throne, they witnessed the temporal passage of papal authority at the moment of his death. Shenouda's spectacular corpse on the throne does not carry the same value as St. Mark's hidden relics in the shrine some steps behind his throne. The two holy images, however, are semblances of each other by virtue of their both being images of St. Mark's authority in earthly death and eternal life-in-death. The two images speak to different economies of relic-memory, or remembering via the visual mediation of bodily parts. In the case of the hidden relics, as we learned from Sister Kiriya, St. Mark's body mediates the re-creative act of witnessing as the site and scene of suffering. In the case of Shenouda's dead body on display, the pope embodies the apostolic succession of St. Mark, and at death, the intermediation of his origins from body to body.

In her remarkable work on the "political lives of dead bodies" (1999), Katherine Verdery has argued that dead bodies, such as relics and corpses, have been active in reconfiguring the material politics of space and time. As late as the eighteenth century, the ritual transferal of Coptic papal authority relied on St. Mark's relics to institute its bodily aesthetics of sovereignty and permanence (cf. Bernstein 2013; Yurchak 2015). Newly appointed patriarchs obtained legitimacy through symbolic rites of succession and investiture that tied them to the apostolic lineage of St. Mark. These rites included kneeling and bowing before the head of St. Mark, as well as embracing and kissing it (Pope Shenouda 1975; Atiya 1991).

The material capacity of relics to transmit authority also historically converged on imperial economies of occupation and exchange. Due to its ritual dependence on St. Mark's relics, the sovereign status of the Coptic

---

17. When I use the term "embalmed" (*al-muḥannaṭ*), I mean to designate nothing more than the tradition, arguably of Pharaonic origin, of preserving dead bodies with fragrances and oils. In other contexts, Orthodoxy's association with mummification presented a political problem. See Robert Greene's work on how Bolshevik publicists in Russia deployed mummification as a tool of demystification in "Toppling Saints from their Thrones" (2010). In chapter 2, "Redemption at the Edge," we will further explore the *spatial* dynamics of remembering burial and preservation (*al-taḥnīṭ*).

Church was vulnerable to relic politics of trade and theft. As early as the Council of Chalcedon in 451 C.E., the Byzantine Church dispossessed the Coptic Church of its papal see in Alexandria. In his pamphlet *The Beholder of God: Mark the Evangelist,* Pope Shenouda recounts this era of colonial dispossession by the Byzantine imperial church: "The Roman Melchites [*al-malikīn* or 'imperialists'] confiscated our churches.[18] Many of our Patriarchs never sat in Alexandria" (Pope Shenouda 1975:57).

One of the most legendary accounts of Mediterranean relic theft features the Venetian sailors who stole St. Mark's body (while his head remained in Alexandria) and took it to Italy in 828 C.E. Their goal was to establish regional autonomy from imperial infringements from both sides, with Venice having been situated between the Carolingian West and the Byzantine East.

The Venetians thereby established their own church with its new apostolic patron: St. Mark the apostle. By displacing St. Theodore as the patron saint of Aquileia, St. Mark therefore became identified as a "specifically *Italian* apostle" (Demus 1960:10, italics mine). According to medieval historian Patrick Geary's reading of *Translatio Sancti Marci,* the two custodians of the church of Alexandria were "properly shocked by this suggestion and reminded the Venetians that Mark had been the first apostle to Alexandria" (Geary 2011 [1978]:93). Relic theft, as holy "translation" of a particular kind, gives rise to the contested legitimacy of saints in colonial contexts of trade and dispossession.

Given this historical background, we may revisit St. Mark's shrine and reconsider Isaac Fanous's portrait iconography of St. Mark's translation from Venice to Cairo from a slightly different perspective. To recall the shrine's layout, St. Mark's relics, hidden in his sarcophagus, are surrounded by Fanous's mural, which commemorates St. Mark's martyrdom in 68 C.E. and St. Mark's translation from Venice to Cairo in 1968. In June 1968, the Italian Cardinal Giovanni Urbani had given up a fragment of St. Mark's relics to the Coptic Church in a congratulatory act of friendship. On this joint nineteenth-centennial ecumenical celebration of St. Mark's martyrdom, Roman Catholics referred to the translation of relics as a "gift." Tellingly, Egypt's Copts instead called it a "return" (*al-i'āda*).

The "return" of St. Mark's relics occurred during Pope Kyrillos VI's reign and President Gamal Abdel Nasser's presidency. In a united show of anticolonial nationalism, the Pope and President received St. Mark's

---

18. Currently, the term "Melchites" or "Melkites" (derived from *al-malik,* or "ruler") refers to Byzantine Rite Catholics in communion with Roman Catholicism.

body together at the inauguration of its then-newly built Patriarchate Cathedral in 'Abbasiyya. In this broader context of Egyptian nation-building, relics were instrumental in shoring up the pope-president alliance, a foundational image of church-state authoritarianism after 1952. The politics of papal representation was at the heart of the 1968 return of St. Mark. At last, the two bodily images of St. Mark's authority—Pope Kyrillos the successor of St. Mark and St. Mark the ancient martyr—converged, drawing two temporal iterations of the papacy nearly two millennia apart into the same space and time. Sealed with Nasser's endorsement, the entire spectacular affair also achieved an aura of political consecration, however metaphorical. St. Mark's relics fulfilled the political operation of integrating the spiritual papacy into the worldly realm of government, i.e. the Egyptian nation-state. It is these very relics that are accessible today in the shrines of St. Mark, located at the Patriarchate in 'Abbasiyya and the Alexandrian See of St. Mark.

Currently, the authority of the Coptic pope is central for the communal representation of Copts. As St. Mark's bodily translation in 1968 demonstrates, the historical imaginary of papal authority has been contingent on the material history of relics. The fact that the Catholic Church returned St. Mark's relics long after their theft, and moreover, during Egypt's national period of state-building, played a significant role in shoring up the statist-driven image of the papacy. It was this papal image of spiritual/worldly alliance, enshrined in St. Mark's bodily images, that Shenouda inherited after Kyrillos's death in 1971. As the pope with perhaps the longest reign in all of church history (both Catholic and Orthodox), Shenouda was on the throne for over forty years (1971–2012).

In March 2012, Shenouda's death left a formidable absence in the Coptic community. Shenouda happened to die when Copts were already in the tumultuous thick of political turnover. During his final months, Shenouda witnessed the failure of the Supreme Council of the Armed Forces (SCAF) to protect Copts from terrifying escalations in "sectarian" violence nationwide. In his last days, he even survived to see the Muslim Brotherhood's Freedom and Justice Party rise to power with significant electoral wins in the Parliament. At his death, Shenouda's critics from all corners agreed on one thing: Shenouda had proven to be the single biggest player in the field of Coptic politics spanning several decades. As the first pope to be selected from the ruling bishopric (and not from the monasteries), he quickly obtained a reputation for his political savvy. His public reputation stood in stark contrast to the cult imaginary of his predecessor Pope Kyrillos, who had been cherished as a mystic and miracle-worker averse to worldly politics (for more, see chapter 6, "Hidden Faces").[19] Secularists, Christian and Muslim alike, opposed how Shenouda spoke on behalf of the entire Coptic community on matters, religious and nonreligious. While some blamed Copts for mortgaging out their civic rights to the clerical hierarchy, others diagnosed the problem to be bigger than the Copts or the Church, pointing to the state's tacit support for Shenouda's exclusive management of Coptic affairs.

Throughout his career, Shenouda repeatedly announced that he did not meddle in politics, asserting again and again that he was rather a leader of "spiritual work." In fact, it was his capacity to institute the boundaries of "spiritual work" and to bring the upwardly mobile masses under his political-theological fold that made him the most powerful Coptic figure of his time.

PARTS AND WHOLE I: CLERGY AND LAITY

Pope Shenouda's revivals and reforms were a strategy to govern the explosive growth of the Coptic community from the 1970s on. Under his reign, the Coptic Church assimilated an enormous number of Copts into its orders of sacred government. In this section and the next, I focus on the internal dynamics of the Coptic Church, and more specifically, on the material aesthetics of imagining bodily parts and their constitutive relation to the communal whole. First, we turn to acts of imagining of clerical-lay relations and the body politic of salvation.

The clerical order, or the order of carrying out "spiritual work," is the hierarchy of administering salvation to the communal body politic. As sociologist Dina el-Khawaga has convincingly argued, the laity under Shenouda was "clericalized," or incorporated into the clerical order (el-Khawaga 1997:145). Parallel to the clerical body of bishops, priests, monastics, deacons, and deaconesses, this new diaconal laity corps included teachers, servants, volunteers, counselors, journalists, technicians, and filmmakers who make up the life of churches, seminaries, and monasteries. By serving as its constituent members, Copts were active in making the Coptic Church into the central referent of their communal belonging.

19. During Shenouda's reign, some Copts saw themselves as "of-Kyrillos" rather than "of-Shenouda." For many of them, Kyrillos represented the purely spiritual ascetic leader whose politics were exhibited only through miracles, compared to Shenouda who meddled in political schemes and lacked mystical qualities. I am grateful to Febe Armanios for alerting me to this significant internal divide in the Church.

During my fieldwork, I sought out popular institutions in which Copts were active on a regular basis so that I could better understand how Orthodox Christianity was integrated into their everyday thought and practice. To learn more about popular education programs, for example, I took weekly night classes at the Clerical College (al-Kulliyya al-Iklirikiyya) in the Archdiocese of Qalyubiyya in Shubra al-Khayma for roughly nine months in 2006–7. Founded in 1988, the college in Shubra al-Khayma is one of six Clerical College branches devoted to lay education, the other five based in ʿAbbasiyya, Tanta, Minufiyya, Port Said, and Asyut. Located in a gritty industrial area known for its textile factories and union history (see Beinin and Lockman 1988), the Shubra al-Khayma branch attracted working-class Copts hunting for affordable part-time education courses. Like its sibling branches, it offered a range of class offerings in the study of different languages (e.g., Hebrew, Greek, Coptic, English), theology, history, hymnody, liturgy, and computer literacy.

On one evening, the students in our class lined up to greet one of our teachers, a priest. As is customary for greeting someone from the clerical ranks, each went up to kiss his hand. When I went up, to my surprise, I was not able to follow suit and I instead greeted him with a handshake and sheepish smile. Smiling back, the priest continued on with the next student in line while I returned to my rickety chair, embarrassed that I had not appropriately shown him respect, even though everyone understood that I was just an outsider.

One student named Baligh sat next to me to chat about what had happened. In his mid-forties, Baligh worked as a salesman for the Bible Society of Egypt, a nondenominational organization which supplies bibles and other devotional literature for the Coptic Church. Baligh often gave me insights that pushed me to consider Orthodoxy in new ways, and frequently, with added eloquence and cross-cultural intuition. When I asked him why he kissed the priest's hand, he replied with an astonishing explanation that reflected on the moral limits of clerical power by way of the Eucharist:

> I kiss the priest's hand because it is exactly like the Cross [al-Ṣalīb]. Like the Cross, the wood that carried the Body of Christ [Gasad al-Masīḥ] [historical body of Christ]. The Cross is like the hand of the priest which carries Christ onto the altar [al-haykal] during the holy mass. So that's why we kiss the hand of the priest, because he carries the Body of Christ [the Eucharist] in his hand.
>
> If I had been able to see the wood that carried Christ, I would have kissed it. So it is the same with the priest's hand. The priest takes the Body in his hands—his entire work, his specialty is to carry the Body of Christ [the Eucharist] in service to the Body of Christ [the Coptic Church body].

As for me, well, I've got a lot of jobs. I only go up and take communion, the Body of Christ [the Eucharist] in front of him. As for the priest, his service is to the Body [the Coptic Church body]—in the altar and outside the altar—all of it is dedicated to offer the Body [the Eucharist].

The priest is a normal person like you and like me. For my earthly parents, I kiss and give respect to them. That's just something natural. But as for the priest, I kiss his hand as it is honored because he lifts the Body of Christ [the Eucharist] in his hand. . . .

But if I kiss him as a person [ka-l-insān], then it's better that I don't kiss him at all.

Baligh's meditation on the act of kissing the priest's hand was fundamentally rooted in his understanding of the "Body of Christ" (Gasad al-Masīḥ or Jasad al-Masīḥ).[20] Throughout his reply to me, the "Body of Christ" signified several referents that are all equivalent in value.[21] The Eucharist ("thanksgiving," or al-afkhāristiyā, Arabized Coptic) is the "Body of Christ":[22] in Orthodox theology, the bread and wine are the "real presence" of Christ's body and blood. The Church is also the "Body of Christ":[23] belonging to the Coptic Church means partaking in the Eucharist. The Eucharist, the gift of eternal salvation, is also the collective institution of giving "thanks" for, or ascribing value to, divine sacrifice in death and resurrection.

Through his semiotic analysis of the Eucharist, Baligh emphasizes the proper value of the holy priesthood. Baligh's main point is summed up in his warning: "But if I kiss him as a person, then it's better that I don't kiss him at all." The Coptic Church's principal function is to administer the seven holy "sacraments" (al-sirr, al-asrār, also "mysteries"),[24] the Eucharist holding the highest value among them as the "Crown of Sacraments." In his reflections, Baligh underlines that the priest's vocation

20. The most extraordinary, and to my mind unrivaled, semiotic analysis of the Eucharist's form and function, along with its historical transformations, belongs to Michel de Certeau. For more, see "The New Science" in de Certeau 1992.

21. N.B. Baligh did not use the terms "Eucharist," "the Coptic Church body," and "historical body of Christ" in his monologue. I am the one who added the bracketed explanations, relying on my own interpretation of his multiple invocations.

22. Unlike the Roman Catholic doctrine of "transubstantiation," the Orthodox doctrine of the Eucharist does not specify when the transformation of the bread and wine into Christ's true body occurs. The unknowability is its "mystery."

23. For anthropological work on ritual and linguistic practices of constituting the "Body of Christ," see Handman 2014; Tomlinson 2014.

24. The other six sacraments in the Coptic Orthodox Church are: Baptism, Chrismation, Penance, Anointing of the Sick, Marriage, and the Priesthood.

lies only in his communicative function as a tactile vehicle, or carrying surface, for the Eucharist. Within the larger system of likenesses of the "Body of Christ," the holy value of the priest lies only in iconic relation to the "Cross," the surface which carried the historical body of Christ. The priest is imagined here, not as a "person," but as a mere medium of delivery. As Baligh points out to me (a non-Orthodox student who cannot take the Eucharist), it is better not to kiss the hand of the priest if he is imagined as a person and not in signifying relation to the Eucharist.

At stake in Baligh's explanation is a social ethics of idolatry. Baligh's emphasis lies on the relational dynamics of signifying salvation, placing acts of valuing priests in critical perspective. Just evaluation turns on the proper attribution of value to parts in relation to their whole, for example, the priest's hand in relation to the Body of Christ (the Eucharist). To avoid idolatry, Copts must uphold a distinction between the primary order of "'divine" intercession and the secondary order of "human" intercession.[25] This moral distinction between the divine and the human further correlates to the mimetic, material distinction between the primary medium of Christ's body ("Eucharist") and the secondary media of body parts, like the priest's hand, which bear likeness to Christ's body ("relics").[26] This communicative ethics internal to the Eucharist's institution has significant political implications.

Ritual imaginings of priestly value touch on larger social and political issues associated with clerical-lay relations. Many Copts hold great reverence for their local priests, bishops, and popes, much to the dismay of Coptic secularists who seek to circumscribe the representational authority of the Coptic Church to the realm of spiritual affairs. Many Coptic priests, particularly among the highly educated younger generations, are moreover familiar with widespread critiques of the Coptic

25. In the Coptic Church, there are two holy orders of intercession (al-shafā'a): (1) "propitiatory" (al-kaffariyya) which is unique to Christ, referring to his death and resurrection; and (2) "petitionary" (al-tawassuliyya) which in principle includes all human beings, but most commonly refers to the work of saints.

26. My analysis here on the mimetic relation between the Eucharist and relics in Orthodoxy is inspired by the pathbreaking work of the medievalist Godefridus J. C. Snoek. In *Medieval Piety from Relics to the Eucharist* (1995), he argues that the Eucharist's celebration and relic devotion were activities that took place in "mutual interaction" during the Middle Ages (ca. fifth to fifteenth century). In other words, the Eucharist had not always been an "independent" institution of communicating salvation.

Church's authoritarian character and the problematic devotion of Copts toward their clergy.

Joining Baligh, these self-critical priests also recognize the priest's value, as "a normal person like you and me," and some of them go so far as to ritually enact it for their flock. After my conversation with Baligh, I began to pay more attention to how priests interacted with the laity during my time with church volunteers and especially among youth. As Copts approached them to kiss their hands, many of these priests playfully avoided their kisses by either snapping back their hands or hitting the heads of the youth who tried to greet them. These displays may be understood not only as a performance of humility, but also as a form of moral instruction—even critical commentary—about the priesthood's true value. Baligh, along with a younger generation of priests, are interested in setting moral limits on the ritual authority of the clergy.

To be clear, Baligh is a pious loyalist; he is far from a revolutionary seeking to subvert the Coptic Church's authority in state politics. What he represents, however, is a more subtle trend of communal self-critique that has taken hold among Copts who have experienced the Coptic Church's reforms during its recent decades of rapid growth. Through mass educational programs in Shubra al-Khayma and elsewhere, Copts have become increasingly equipped with the resources and skills to consider the ethics and politics of their ritual traditions. This new clericalized laity upends the reductionist binary—between the "pious" Copts who are active in the Coptic Church and the "secularist" Copts who are not—that often underwrites analyses of the Coptic community's internal politics. The Coptic Church, as a communal image of self-institution, has also become subject to critical reflection on the status of clerical-lay relations from within.

Assessing the proper value of a priest, a bishop, or a pope is a political act of rethinking the proper bounds of "spiritual" (as opposed to "worldly") government (a classic theme in secularism studies). It is also a theological and ethical act of critical self-reflection that is internal to the Coptic Church's imaginary institution. Notably, it was Coptic priests, such as Fathers Mataʾus and Filubatir Gamil of Giza, who were the founding leaders of the secularist youth movements that were the most vocally critical of the Coptic Church's politics leading up to Mubarak's downfall. A new generation of the clericalized laity was recognizing the distinction between serving the "Body of Christ" and supporting the authoritarian regime.

PARTS AND WHOLE II: DEATH AND RESURRECTION

The martyr's body is the mimetic image of the Eucharist's broken body.[27] It is the holy medium through which Copts remember bodily acts of sacrifice and salvation. As we learned in the previous sections, relics serve as the site for visually reenacting the various stages of the martyr's passion. Now, we turn our attention to the other side of witnessing the martyr's body: the resurrection (al-qiyāma). The image of the resurrection is the eschatological whole that represents heavenly transcendence and triumph. It is only in relation to this creatively envisioned whole that martyrs acquire their authority on earth.

Since the 1990s, the Coptic Church has produced films about the lives of the saints. These hagiographic films, regularly availed on Coptic television channels and easily accessed through the internet, provide one of the most popular media for Coptic audiences to revisit scenes of ancient martyrdom and visually experience "sensational" forms of divine power (see also Meyer 2015). I have seen these videos screened in a range of settings: from private homes, orphanages, and hospitals, to buses, monasteries, and shrines. As Sister Kiriya had mentioned at St. Mark's shrine, hagiographic films also offer a useful supplement to ritual readings from the Synaxarium and portrait iconography of martyrdom. Engaging images of death and resurrection availed on video, Copts employ visual techniques of accessing their holy past in suffering and triumph.

In November 2006, I enjoyed the opportunity of interviewing the Coptic filmmaker Magued Tawfik. Since 1987, Tawfik has made over forty low-budget movies to date on the lives and deaths of saints in the Coptic Church. As the first person to make films on Coptic saints, he has set the tone for cinematic depictions of holy death over the pioneering course of his career. Tawfik's films do not spare any of martyrdom's gruesome detail to his audiences. When describing his own commitment for depicting all the details of torture, he said, "It's difficult for the viewer to see [St. Abanub's] stomach come out, but I want people to see that his torture was very difficult."

27. Orthodox Christian relics are fleshly images of vulnerability and their material divisibility is a sign of their subjection to the natural course of decay and death. These relics "suffer" as objects of someone or something else's action. What distinguishes the holy bodies of Christian figures from those of Muslim figures is their material fragmentation. For example, the Prophet Muhammad's hair, nails, and clothing all serve as bodily relics that offer holy presence without violating the whole of his body. For more comparative perspective on holy relics in Islam and Buddhism, see Wheeler 2006; Trainor 2010.

However awful the scenes of torture are, Tawfik's films always end with the visual image of the fully reconstituted saint, as a triumphant whole. At the time of our interview, it had been two years since Mel Gibson's *The Passion of the Christ* (2004) had enjoyed success at Egypt's box offices.[28] I asked Tawfik for his expert opinion on the film. Tawfik expressed reservations to me, "It was okay, but too bloody. It focused too much on Christ's suffering and didn't show enough of God's power." When Tawfik referred to "God's power," he meant the supernatural power of the resurrection to overcome bodily destruction.

One example which showcases Tawfik's style is his popular film *St. Marina the Martyr* (*Al-Shahida Marina*, directed by Tawfik, 1993). Centered on the third-century heroine St. Marina the Martyr, the film takes place during the glorious "Era of Martyrs." A significant portion of the film is dedicated to covering the gruesome details of her torture, rehearsing her various trials in slow, deliberate fashion. The frames alternate between torture and miraculous recovery, creating an imagined cycle of bodily fragmentation and bodily reconstitution. In one cycle, viewers watch St. Marina's face combed with saws, and then become perfectly smooth. In another cycle, St. Marina's body is cut into two halves, and then the halves are rejoined. In yet another cycle, St. Marina is boiling in a pot of water, only to exit the pot without any wounds or scars. In each cycle of spectacular reversal, the emperor and his soldiers express awe at the sight of her new body.[29]

After these repeated cycles of violence and redemption, St. Marina the Martyr is finally beheaded in the end. At the film's last moments, her head returns to her body, newly furbished with a heavenly crown. As St. Marina looks above in prayer, her fully reconstituted body floats into the sky and her stunned executioner confesses Christ while watching her from below.

In Tawfik's films, it is the special materiality of the martyr's body that enacts the creative powers of holy resurrection. The cinematic oscillation between fragmentation and recovery imitates the martyr's immunity to

28. In April 2004, *The Passion of the Christ* opened to mixed audiences of Muslims and Christians in Syria, Lebanon, Jordan, and Egypt. Celebrated in many Arab Christian communities, the film's central focus on the crucifixion, rather than the resurrection, especially resonated with Orthodoxy's liturgical emphasis on Good Friday. Globally, *The Passion* stimulated controversy over its anti-Semitic elements and its heavy aestheticization of torture. For more, see Landres and Berenbaum 2004; Beal and Linafelt 2005; Sobchack 2008.

29. On the gendered nature of this hagiographic imagery, see Armanios and Amstutz 2013.

FIGURE 3. St. Marina's face is lacerated, Video still. Reproduced from *St. Marina the Martyr* (1993), with permission from Magued Tawfik.

FIGURE 4. St. Marina's face is reconstituted, Video still. Reproduced from *St. Marina the Martyr* (1993), with permission from Magued Tawfik.

FIGURE 5. St. Marina's body is sawed in two, Video still. Reproduced from *St. Marina the Martyr* (1993), with permission from Magued Tawfik.

FIGURE 6. St. Marina's body is reconstituted, Video still. Reproduced from *St. Marina the Martyr* (1993), with permission from Magued Tawfik.

death and her body's miraculous capacity to transcend suffering. When Coptic viewers witness St. Marina's trials on film, they see her body regenerate flesh at sites of holy violence—what leading Coptologist Otto Meinardus has referred to as the "human salamander" phenomenon (Meinardus 2002 [1981]). This cinematic aesthetics also imitates the special materiality of martyrs' relics. As Copts often point out at a saint's shrine, the relics do not "decompose" or "fall apart" (*mathalliltsh*). In the case of the Akhmim martyrs, the holy fingernails and hair are believed to grow vigorously, even prompting the shrine's custodians to cut them every once in a while. This bodily aesthetics of extraordinary vitality mediates the power of the resurrection to overcome earthly vulnerability. The martyr's relics "bod[y] forth transcendence and eternity'" (Bynum 2011:256).

At the end of Tawfik's films, viewers are sure to see the martyr's body, transcendent as a whole. The martyr is also visually framed as a spectator of her own body. Throughout her trials of suffering, Tawfik's film portrays St. Marina gazing above in calm, peaceful prayer.[30] This heaven-bound aesthetic resembles the "wonder" that martyrs are described to have felt during their own martyrdom. For example, the fourth-century martyr St. Dativus of present-day Algiers is characterized to have "viewed the ruin of his body all the while like a spectator, rather than feeling its pain" (Maier 1987:72, quoted from Brown 2000:9). The audience of Tawfik's films are also made into spectators of holy martyrdom, assuming the divine, heavenly perspective of witnessing death and resurrection.

Following Tawfik's model, Coptic cinematic aesthetics of martyrdom thus foregrounds the transcendent powers of triumphant resurrection. Recall how Aghapy TV's coverage of the Alexandrian martyrs' funeral in 2011 strategically closed with clips from *The Passion of the Christ.* Splicing frames depicting the victims' bodies from the Alexandrian bombing with frames from *The Passion,* Aghapy TV blended visual images of sectarian violence with visual images of the crucifixion. Aghapy TV's broadcast ended with the same image that closed *The Passion:* the resurrected profile of Christ. By remembering the ultimate ends of martyrdom, Coptic spectators were visually oriented toward the divine promise of salvation and transcendence for the church body

---

30. This visual aesthetic of martyrdom more generally informs a Coptic ethics of illustrating violence for moral and spiritual ends. One Coptic icon-writer in Ma'adi elaborated to me about his martyr iconography, "They should impart peace and strength rather than violence."

politic. The image of future resurrection thus offered an image for communal self-reflection in the present.

Martyrs' bodies are holy fragments which derive their power in envisioned relation to the communal whole of the Church Body. Like the Eucharist, the martyr's relics are imagined as a bodily medium of communal self-transcendence, extending a heavenly vantage point for seeing one's self in the future. Coptic viewers, now accustomed to the cinematic aesthetics of suffering and redemption, anticipate the re-creative and radically transformative elements of martyrdom. Through their visual acts of remembering death and resurrection, they institute and reinstitute the Coptic Church across each incident, or trial, of attack against the community.

BELONGING TO NEW DEATHS

On January 2, the victims of the Alexandrian bombing were declared new martyrs of the Coptic Church, bestowed with the title the "Two Saints' Martyrs" (Shuhada' al-Qiddisin). At their funeral, the martyrs' bodies were hoisted up and carried out to their new mausoleum at St. Menas Monastery. To borrow the words of historian István Rév: "The martyrs were elevated, but it was the executioners who were revealed" (Rév 2005:41).[31] As Egypt headed toward the revolutionary uprisings, new acts of violence against Coptic Christians reoriented their demands for accountability and justice. The commemoration of new deaths was a crucial site of communal self-imagining and reinstitution.

On August 16, 2011, I joined a bus of Copts from Alexandria to St. Menas Monastery to visit the graves of the Two Saints' Martyrs. Only six months after Mubarak's toppling, many of the bus's passengers remained hopeful for justice for the bloodshed in Alexandria. Sophie, who was sitting next to me, was one example. An energetic and vocal woman, she gave me her interpretation of that summer's dramatic course of events: "After [the bombing] in Alexandria, [Pope Shenouda] went on TV and said, 'We will soon find out who did this crime. And when the truth is revealed, this criminal will be punished.' After this, what happened? Tahrir, the Revolution, and now, al-ʿAdli on trial!"

31. In his pathbreaking work *Retroactive Justice* (2005), the Hungarian historian István Rév examines the politics of historical production with a focus on the memory of the dead and their commemorative rituals. In the excerpt that I quoted, the martyrs are those who died in the Hungarian uprisings of 1956 and the elevation of their bodies in 1989 signaled the end of the Soviet era.

During my fieldwork that summer, I had heard other Copts express to me some version of Sophie's narrative of revelation and justice. After the Alexandrian bombing in January 2011, the Tahrir protests led to Egypt's general prosecutor's investigation of the perpetrators behind it in early February. At that time, various news outlets had already reported that Habib al-ʿAdli, Egypt's interior minister and head of security, had engineered the bombing, having expressed his motive to "discipline the Copts" to his hired hand.[32] By early August 2011, Mubarak and al-ʿAdli were both photographed behind caged bars for the entire world to witness.

The public revelation of Egyptian state security's role in the Alexandrian bombing was the public revelation of a betrayal. Copts began to reckon with the very real possibility that the police did not merely fail to protect them, but also actively perpetrated violence against them. Former Interior Minister Habib al-ʿAdli's wish "to discipline the Copts" reflected the fact that Coptic cries for justice had already been placing significant strain on the authoritarian regime months before the Alexandrian bombing. In 2010, the Nag Hammadi shootings and the ʿUmraniyya riots in Giza over an unlicensed church had already exposed the vulnerability of Copts. In 2011, the Alexandrian bombing was regarded as the worst attack on Copts to date (at that time), resulting in a higher death toll than that of the Kosheh murders in 2000, killings that took place in a village near Sohag. Demands for state accountability set the tone for Copts to revisit and remake the meaning of new martyrs and the communal value of their deaths.

Remembering the Two Saints' Martyrs is an act of imagining how new holy deaths relate to older holy deaths. The Two Saints' Martyrs are buried in a mausoleum, a long sarcophagus of white alabaster, outside St. Menas Monastery in the parking lot. Trimmed with flowers and photos of the victims, the gravesite serves as a shrine of commemoration.

As in the case of all holy shrines, there is a placard with lyrics for pilgrims to sing hymnody (*al-madīḥa*) in praise of the martyrs. As an icon does visually, this hymn provides an auditory aid for remembering the scene of holy death. The hymn, composed by a deacon from St. Athanasius Church in Alexandria, also links the new martyrs with other martyrs, ancient and contemporary. Each of its verses is followed with a refrain, the new name conferred to these holy dead, "Martyrs of

32. See Farrag Ismail, "Ex-minister Suspected behind Alex Church Bombing," *al-Arabiya News*, February 7, 2011, www.alarabiya.net/articles/2011/02/07/136723.html (accessed December 19, 2017).

FIGURE 7. Pilgrims read the hymnody in honor of the Two Saints' Martyrs, St. Menas Monastery. Photo by author.

FIGURE 8. Hymnody for the Two Saints' Martyrs, St. Menas Monastery. Photo by author.

the Two Saints' Church" or the "Two Saints' Martyrs" (Shuhada' al-Qiddisin) (translation mine):

> In the Two Saints' Church there are triumphant martyrs, we praise them in all times
> Shuhada' al-Qiddisin (Line 1)

> Our Coptic Church celebrates in Alexandria for the martyrs of Christianity
> Shuhada' al-Qiddisin (Line 2)

> With the beginning of the year, your spirits ascended with peace to the Lord of Creation
> Shuhada' al-Qiddisin (Line 3)

> At that time, St. Mark returned in the beginning of the celebrations with our new martyrs
> Shuhada' al-Qiddisin (Line 4)

> Your blood flowed like streams, as St. Mark the Apostle had in the surrounding streets
> Shuhada' al-Qiddisin (Line 5)

> O children of the martyrs' seal, Heaven has called you, and you answered the call
> Shuhada' al-Qiddisin (Line 6)

> The oppressors killed you, and we ask God, always lifting up prayer
> Shuhada' al-Qiddisin (Line 7)

> Give all comfort, to the families of the martyrs and give us faith and hope
> Shuhada' al-Qiddisin (Line 8)

> With shouts and wailing, Rachel has cried once more over all martyrs in this generation
> Shuhada' al-Qiddisin (Line 9)

> We all mourned throughout the whole country, after the explosions
> Shuhada' al-Qiddisin (Line 10)

> Their limbs flew off, their intestines were also scattered, the bodies of the children
> Shuhada' al-Qiddisin (Line 11)

> You anointed our lands with your blood among us for the sake of our Redeemer
> Shuhada' al-Qiddisin (Line 12)

> We made a record, that we endured the departure, of our martyrs in Iraq
> Shuhada' al-Qiddisin (Line 13)

Nag Hammadi, 'Umraniyya, Kosheh, and Alexandria, Take joy, O Orthodox
Church
　　Shuhada' al-Qiddisin (Line 14)

Our hearts were broken by each beloved witness, Blessed are you, O Children
of Job
　　Shuhada' al-Qiddisin (Line 15)

Your path is sweet and beautiful, we sing it in our hymns, a bouquet of long
remembrance
　　Shuhada' al-Qiddisin (Line 16)

The ritual hymnody for the Two Saints' Martyrs institutes the space and
time of remembering the new martyrs. By evoking the site of Alexandria, it appropriately recounts the Coptic Church's origins in St. Mark
and his "return" to Alexandria on behalf of the new martyrs. By
recounting major incidents of Coptic violence in 2000 and 2010, it also
links the Two Saints' Martyrs to other contemporary martyrs in the
sites of the riots in Kosheh, Nag Hammadi, and 'Umraniyya. Perhaps
the most striking reference in the hymnody are the "martyrs in Iraq,"
the victims of an attack on a Syriac Catholic church by al-Qa'ida. The
al-Qa'ida attack left over fifty Iraqi Christians dead, having occurred
only two months before the Alexandrian bombing in 2011.

Imagined in Alexandria, the Two Saints' Martyrs establish new sites
for accessing the origins of papal representation in St. Mark. As we
learned earlier, the Coptic pope's authority derives from the temporal
transmission of St. Mark's authority through rites of apostolic succession. To the extent that relics mediate this process of transmission, the
dynamics of Orthodox authority are contingent on the materialities of
fragmentation, exchange, theft, and return. The Orthodox institution of
papal authority thus involves the creative reinstitution of origins at each
moment when St. Mark's body is accessed and imagined anew. The Two
Saints' Martyrs, deemed new martyrs out of Alexandria, introduce an
alternative legacy of St. Mark's martyrdom. In the context of the Coptic
Church's failure to demand justice, and of Pope Shenouda's conspicuous
absence at the funeral, the new martyrs offered a new representative
image of authority in the Coptic community. The Two Saints' Martyrs
did not so much displace the Pope, but rather created terms for activating the papal imaginary in relation to their newly remembered value.

Outside the Coptic Church altogether, the Catholic martyrs of Iraq
hail from a different nation and a different faith. After the Alexandrian
bombing, the Egyptian state conjured the image of "foreign terrorists"

seeking to "make civil war [*fitna*],"[33] and Alexandria's Governor ʿAdil Labib specifically accused al-Qaʿida and invoked its recent attack in Iraq. In January 2011, the image of "Christian-Muslim unity" against terrorism was resurrected nationwide—an image that enraged many Copts, who understood this move as a "denial" of Egypt's home-grown problem of sectarianism (Tadros 2011). The inclusion of the Catholic martyrs of Iraq in the commemoration of the Two Saints' Martyrs defies this narrative of Egyptian Christian-Muslim unity. By drawing distant deaths of other Arab Christians into its cast of holy martyrs, the hymnody emphasizes "Christian" ties over "Egyptian" nationhood. Here, the contemporary shared experience of martyrdom overrides nationalist politics of Christian-Muslim brotherhood.

The memory of new martyrs creates possibilities for mediating horizons of communal belonging in Egypt and beyond. The Two Saints' Martyrs prompted reflection on the sacrificial value of their deaths in multiple relation to papal authority, Christian-Muslim unity, and transnational affinity with Christians suffering violence abroad. As vehicles of communal self-imagining, their bodily relics open possibilities for the creative transformation of social ties and hierarchies of belonging constitutive of the Coptic community. The Alexandrian bombing of 2011 was one major event that exposed fractures in the Coptic Church's alliance with the Egyptian state while revealing a growing communal desire for political accountability. New martyrs and their relics extended new forms of self-representation and avenues of mobilizing death toward envisioned justice.

DEMANDS OF MARTYRDOM

One year after the Alexandria bombing in 2011, a group of Copts mounted a face-off with Pope Shenouda at the Patriarchate Cathedral of St. Mark. On January 6, 2012, during Christmas Eve mass, Shenouda began to thank the military officers from the ruling SCAF. Young men and women interrupted Shenouda, crying out from the back rows: "Down, down with the military! Down, down with the military!" (Tadros 2013:172). Challenged in the last months of his papal reign, Shenouda witnessed a younger generation of Copts demonstrate at the

---

33. The state imaginary of Islamic "terrorism" as foreign to Egypt recurs years later with the rise of ISIS after 2011. For more on how this imaginary impacts the national value of Christian martyrs in Egypt, see my epilogue.

Coptic Church's symbolic center of authority. The protests were reminiscent of the dissenting crowds at the funeral for the Two Saints' Martyrs. This time, however, the 'Abbasiyya protests were fueled by acts of violence that were more disturbing than the Alexandrian bombing.

Months prior to the protests, on October 9, 2011, the SCAF attacked Copts marching from Shubra to the Maspero building in Cairo, the headquarters for Egyptian state television and radio. Military tanks chased down and officers opened fire on the demonstrators, killing twenty-eight Copts in less than an hour on one of Cairo's major thoroughfares. In that same period, Egyptian state television announced live that Copts were attacking the army at Maspero, calling on citizens to "protect the army from the Copts." Muslim residents from Bulaq answered the broadcast, descending on the Coptic protestors with weapons. The entire bloody affair is now referred to as "the Maspero Massacre" (Madhbaha Masbiru).

The Maspero Youth Union (al-Ittihad Shabab Masbiru) had organized the march in Maspero to protest the state's dismissal of a church attack in Aswan. Established in the spring of 2011, the Maspero Youth Union is an organization of mainly Coptic youth seeking avenues of communal representation that are independent of the Coptic Church, the pope, and its local clergy. At first, Coptic clergy and laity made up the union's secularist movement. After the military massacre in 2011, numerous Muslims also joined the union in solidarity with activism for Coptic rights. One of the union's leaders, Mina Danyal, who died in the Maspero Massacre, is also notably remembered as a revolutionary symbol, not of the Copts but of Christian-Muslim unity.

This chapter opened with the Two Saints' Church bombing and closes now with the Maspero Massacre, covering the two worst incidents of violence that Copts experienced in 2011. At Alexandria and Maspero, Copts came to terms with the communal limits of their self-representation. Unlike the victims of the church bombing, the victims of the Maspero Massacre were not declared "martyrs" by the Coptic Church. Whereas in Alexandria, the perpetrators had been imagined to be "foreign terrorists," in Maspero, the military tanks and soldiers were captured on video and the state's promotion of sectarian violence was recorded on television. Until now, no one has been held accountable for either incident of violence. Moreover, the Maspero Youth Union, although not entirely disbanded, has significantly weakened since the massacre in 2011.

Martyr commemoration raises questions around the value of any given death and its potential demand for accountability. Throughout this chapter, we examined the Coptic Church as a body politic of remembering holy death and resurrection. From the transmission of papal authority to the moral evaluation of clergy, Copts participate in the active making of communal authority from below. The institution of new martyrs, like the Two Saints' Martyrs, offer horizontal paths of accessing the Church's origins and belonging with other victims in Egypt and elsewhere. Across each ritual of imagining their communal self, Copts envision and evaluate their status in contexts of suffering and violence. As we have seen, it is this collective capacity for self-transformation that enabled Copts to demonstrate against the Coptic Church in Alexandria and 'Abbasiyya in 2011.

The collective forgetting of incidents of violence, like the Maspero Massacre, also attests to the limits of communal self-transformation. The Maspero victims did not die inside a church building, but outside on the streets during public demonstrations for the sake of a church building. Although the Coptic Church did not confer the status of holy martyrs to them, the Maspero victims crucially represent a turning-point in the political dynamics of communal representation. The activists of the Maspero Youth Union—hailing precisely from the clericalized laity and church-organized youth—protested in order to carve a space of communal recognition outside the Coptic Church's channels of holy conferral. The Maspero Massacre is itself evidence that their political ambition posed enough of a threat to authoritarian structures of rule, and especially in the wake of the Tahrir uprisings.

By beginning in Alexandria and ending in Maspero, this chapter also points to that formative window of significant political change in Egypt, the period leading up to the January 25 Revolution and ending with the postrevolutionary installment of interim military rule. The memory of martyrs gave rise to communal acts of challenging authoritarianism at a moment when the nation as a whole was being reimagined. In the epilogue, I revisit these themes of martyrdom and nationhood, exploring the Coptic Church's commemoration of new martyrs after 2014 under the Sisi-led regime. In the next chapter, I provide more historical consideration of the Coptic Church and its making as a "national" church. Whereas this chapter has focused on the internal conditions of communal institution, the next explores the Coptic Church's external borders with other ecumenes and nation-states in order to grasp its identity as "Egyptian."

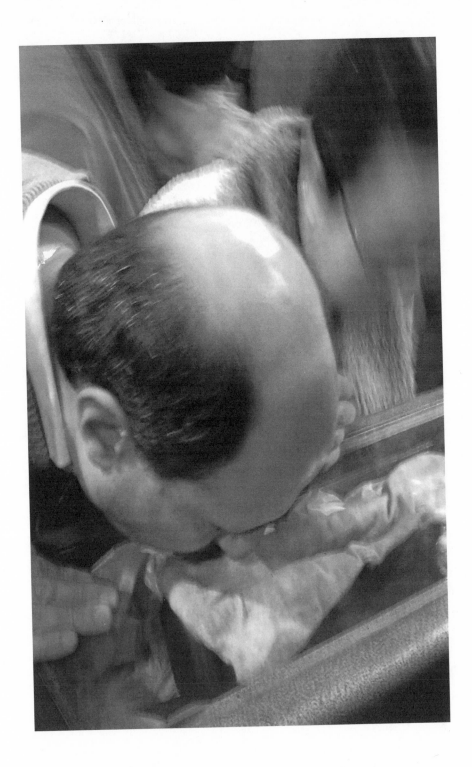

CHAPTER 2

Redemption at the Edge

A universal and exclusive religion, Christianity claimed to
have spread to every region of the known world. In fact,
having spread, it lay around the shrines of saints like pools of
water on a drying surface.

Peter Brown, *The Cult of the Saints*

In time, those Unconscionable Maps no longer satisfied, and
the Cartographers Guilds struck a Map of the Empire whose
size was that of the Empire . . . in all the Land there is no
other Relic of the Disciplines of Geography.

Jorge Luis Borges, "On Exactitude in Science"

BORDERLANDS

Twice a year, in July and again in December, the relic of St. Marina the
Martyr is exhibited for full viewing in Harat al-Rum, the old Greek
quarter in Cairo. On these feast days, her reddish-brown, desiccated
right hand (*al-kaffa*) lies inside a reliquary of transparent glass and
wood. On ordinary days, St. Marina's gnarled hand is wrapped with
layers of protective clothing, but on these special days, it is uncovered,
and a ribbon of pilgrims lines up to see it up-close and take a "holy
blessing" *(baraka)*. With their bodies pressed against the glass, devotees
kiss, press, wipe, and lean their faces and hands toward St. Marina's
body.

FIGURE 9. Taking *baraka* from the relic of St. Marina the Martyr, Church of the Virgin
of Relief, Harat al-Rum. Photo by author.

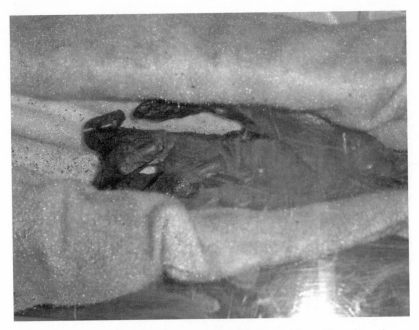

FIGURE 10. Relic of St. Marina the Martyr exposed, Harat al-Rum. Photo by author.

When I visited St. Marina's shrine at the Church of the Virgin of Relief (al-ʿAdhraʾ al-Mughitha) in December 2006,[1] the film *St. Marina the Martyr* (*Al-Shahida Marina*) ran in the background. As pilgrims approached St. Marina's relic, the movie's opening soundtrack blared from the overhanging monitors and filled our ears:

> Fame! I'm gonna make it to heaven, Light up the sky like a flame!
> Fame! I'm gonna live forever. Remember my name . . .

Listening to this song from the American musical film *Fame* (directed by David De Silva, 1980) took my mind to the film's story of New York City's High School of Performing. Instead of dancers gliding past Manhattan's yellow taxi traffic, however, the church's television screens displayed images of a young Coptic girl costumed in bright blue and purple playing the role of the heroine St. Marina. Compared to its bloody end in martyrdom, the film's beginning took off on this upbeat note.

---

1. From 1660 onward, the Church of the Virgin of Relief served as the Holy See of St. Mark and the Seat of the Patriarchate until it later moved in the 1800s to Clot Bey, and then, in 1968, to ʿAbbasiyya.

FIGURE 11. Relic of St. Marina the Martyr concealed, Harat al-Rum. Photo by author.

On her feast days, the line for taking a blessing from St. Marina is long, and on the day I was there, a guard ensured that no one cut to the front or monopolized time with her. Falling into ritual rhythm, pilgrims moved toward her relic, many of them seeking miracles of healing and protection. A few turns ahead of me, a young mother lifted up her toddler to the reliquary and firmly held him in her right arm. She then washed the reliquary's surface with her left hand, transferring whatever was left on it to her son's face and body with generous sweeps. In this kinetic ritual of holy communion, the glassy façade created a tactile site for experiencing redemption at the edge. Open and facing outward, St. Marina's hand appeared to welcome contact from her visitors, further animating desires to be near her. "If I could, I would get even closer," I overheard another woman express after having taken her turn with St. Marina.

St. Marina's relic extends a site of holy contact and sacred territory. Inviting desiring pilgrims into its magnetic realm of power, it generates lively movement toward and around it. Although most of her devotees today are Coptic Orthodox, St. Marina's "fame," or reputation as a powerful saint, has also attracted local Catholics and Muslims in search of miracles of healing. If St. Marina's body offers a site of sacred territory, it also serves as a borderland between various religious groups who are distant and near to one another. As a borderland, it introduces both opportunities for friendship and risks of alienation.

For instance, St. Marina and her bodily duplicates elsewhere reveal ambivalent ties between Egypt's Copts and other Churches.[2] Like St. Mark's body, St. Marina's body is also housed in St. Mark's Square in Venice. A second right hand of St. Marina, known as "St. Margaret of Antioch" in the Roman Catholic Church, is exposed through the glassy window of a gold reliquary in St. Mark's Basilica Treasury. Yet another right hand of hers lies inside a golden arm-reliquary on top of Mount Athos in Greece, within one of the twenty Eastern Orthodox monasteries governed by the Patriarch of Constantinople; there, veneration is accessible to men only. All together, St. Marina's multiple bodies mediate the potential for ecumenism and exclusion across imperial Christendom's East-West divide.

Back in Egypt, St. Marina's location also indexes the Arab Fatimid and Ottoman Turkish rulers who came from outside and conferred Christians and Jews with the status of *ahl al-dhimmī*, or "protected people." St. Marina's shrine is embedded within the labyrinthine area now referred to as "Islamic Cairo," an area with a rich history of interreligious commingling. Only a ten-minute walk from al-Azhar Mosque, this site attests to an era when Copts worshipped next to the most prominent centers of Islamic learning following the Shiite Fatimid Caliphate's establishment of Cairo in 969 as a capital from which they ruled most of North Africa. In a wider alley nearby, the Sultan al-Ghawri funerary

2. To confuse matters even more, there is a second St. Marina, the eighth-century "Marina the Monk" (Marina al-Rahiba), who shares the same shrine with "Marina the Martyr." This Marina is remembered for her lifelong act of cross-dressing as a male to join the monastics in Upper Egypt. Again, Copts are not the only ones to venerate St. Marina for her holy mischief. Lebanese Maronites (Eastern Catholics in communion with Rome) claim that the Holy Valley of Qadisha is the site of her death, not Upper Egypt. This Marina's body remains nowhere to be found.

complex from the early sixteenth century stands in memory of the Mamluk ruler who was also a generous patron of Sufis. In the eighteenth century, the Church of the Virgin of Relief also conducted ritual processions in the open public, at times inciting violence from their Muslim neighbors (Armanios 2011:3–5; cf. al-Damurdashi 1991).

Within Islamic Cairo, Harat al-Rum was once a cosmopolitan neighborhood where religious minorities and ethnic foreigners lived together. By the mid-nineteenth century, trade had brought a sizable number of immigrants to Cairo—Greeks, Armenians, Italians—who later became "Egyptian" (*al-mutamaṣṣirīn*).[3] Harat al-Rum, or "Alley of the Greeks,"[4] was the residential quarter of foreign financiers and businessmen (Raymond 2000:78; Guirguis 2008). In Harat al-Rum, Coptic Orthodox churches neighbored Greek Orthodox and Melkite Catholic churches. Decades later, in the 1950s and 1960s, the rise of Arab nationalism under Gamal Abdel Nasser and the onset of the Arab-Israeli wars led to a significant exodus of Greeks and Jews.[5] At each turn, histories of trade, war and migration have determined the conditions of accessing St. Marina in Harat al-Rum for people outside the Coptic community.

Holy saints like St. Marina index histories of religious coexistence in which sacred territory is entangled with the making of Egypt and its inhabitants. Their holy bodies are sites of blessing, serving as destinations for pilgrimage and creating attachments to their shrines. Saints who have traveled far maintain ties with foreigners outside Egypt who share faint elements of a common heritage. Saints who are embedded in heterogeneous spaces inside Egypt attract neighbors whose desires for miracles blur religious boundaries. Across these geographies of cult expansion, it is relics that mediate contact with sacred territories that define Egypt as Holy Land. In doing so, they also generate new encounters with holiness at Egypt's changing borders and peripheries.

3. The term *al-mutamaṣṣirīn*, or "the Egyptianized," refers to people of foreign origin who had become permanent residents in Egypt. For more, see Beinin 1998; Beinin and Lockman 1988.

4. Literally translated as "the Romans," *al-Rum* is an Arabic term referring to the Byzantine Empire and its adherents in the Greek Orthodox Church of Antioch and the Melkite Greek Catholic Church which is in full communion with the Roman Catholic Church. Under Ottoman Islamic rule, *millat al-Rūm* or "the Roman nation" more generically referred to all ethnic Orthodox Christian minorities including Copts, Syrians, Bulgarians, Albanians, Serbs, and Georgians.

5. For more on the modern history of Jews in Egypt, see Krämer 1989; Beinin 1998; Abdulhaq 2016. For oral histories and personal memoirs, see Dammond 2007; Lagnado 2007; Carasso 2014. For the modern history of Greeks in Egypt, see Dalachanis 2017.

THE TACTILITY OF HOLY LAND

This chapter explores the making of Egypt as Holy Land through spatial imaginaries of contact and movement. The Coptic Church's identity as "Egyptian," or native to Egypt, is rooted in its spatial imagination of Egypt as Holy Land. Rituals of pilgrimage—of approaching saints and taking blessings from them—are creative processes of imagining sites of sacred territory. In places like Harat al-Rum, Copts had once lived in close quarters with Sunni and Shiʻi Muslims as well as Latin and Eastern Catholics. Shrines like St. Marina's exemplify a holy landscape in which Egypt's histories of saintly ecumenes had unfolded alongside frontiers of empire and trade on all its sides (Greene 2002; Ho 2006). The story of Egypt as Holy Land is therefore also a history of common saints who introduce political possibilities of alienation or unity.

My main objective is to understand how the Virgin Mary became the paradigmatic saint of Christian-Muslim unity in Egypt. In May 1968, the Virgin appeared in Zaytun, attracting crowds of Christians and Muslims to northeast Cairo in the wake of the 1967 Arab-Israeli War. In a state of war with Israel, Egyptians were not able to make pilgrimage to the holy sites in Jerusalem. As the headlines of the Coptic newspaper *al-Watany* ("The Nation") reported, "the Virgin visited [us] because we could not visit her."[6] Received as a divine blessing, the Virgin's appearance in 1968 enacted a form of reverse pilgrimage. The Virgin was thus elevated to the status of a "national" saint.

To understand this pivotal event in modern Coptic history, we must first examine the practices entailed in making sacred territory and what these practices do for organizing relations between Christians and Muslims in Egypt. What is Holy Land? What does it look like to inhabit and move through it with others? What does it mean to share in its prohibition and loss? Historians of religion in Egypt have emphasized the centrality of pilgrimage to the making of holy space and landscapes of devotion (Frankfurter 1998b; Gabra 2014). Taking my cue from them, I turn to the social and material practices of pilgrims who imagine Egypt as Holy Land and interact with its topography of holy intercession. Egypt imagined as Holy Land in continuity with other Holy Lands is therefore distinct from Egypt imagined as a territorially bound nation-state. To the extent that Christians and Muslims navigate a common imaginary of holiness, they inhabit a Holy Land together. Collective

6. *Al-Watany*, May 5, 1968.

imaginaries of dispossession, moreover, also generate new means of experiencing unity along the terms of holy blessing.

To grasp the practices involved in the making of Holy Land, I turn to the tactile medium of relics. In this chapter, relics are the body parts of saints (not only martyrs) and their tactile representations, or what are called "contact-relics." Recall the pilgrims in Harat al-Rum, moving in line so they could be as physically close as possible to St. Marina's hand. Acts of tactile contact are integral to pilgrimage and its rituals of mediating proximity and distance. Here, I analyze relics as vehicles of spatial representation, on the order of maps instead of "things" in the world. In his influential writings on social imaginaries of the nation-form, historian Benedict Anderson argues that the map is a medium that transforms Cairo, Mecca, Paris, and Caracas into "indifferently profane and sacred dots" (Anderson 1991:171). Relics, to be distinguished from maps, represent space as dynamically uneven relations of proximity and distance to holy centers. The special value of Holy Land lies in its tactile quality, or the imagining of Egypt as a sacred topography of contact and movement.

Saints' relics are images of miraculous redemption via the sympathetic power of touch. In the last chapter, we caught glimpses of the tactile "edge" of holy body parts: the priest's hand that distributes the Body of salvation, or St. Marina's capacity to regrow bodily flesh like a "human salamander." In this chapter, I further flesh out relics in their resurrective agency, or their "living" and miraculous quality. This power is communicated through holy blessing, or *baraka*, the spiritual currency shared between Christians and Muslims who circulate in the vicinity of shrines. As images that transmit holy power, relics create a living terrain of redemption and mediate a social sense of belonging in the same space. Oriented outward, relics institute a body politic of salvation designed for growth.

Saints' relics are thus also images of reproducibility and expansion; they are the borderlands of empire. As in the case of St. Mark's theft from Alexandria to Venice, relics are reproduced in the portable form of divided fragments. In other instances, they are reproduced in the form of bodily replicates, as in the case of St. Marina's three right hands (and more) which are located in the far-flung sites of Cairo, Venice, and Athens. Historically, relics gave rise to asymmetrical relations of power between Eastern and Western Christendoms. Simply put, they have served as both the cause and medium of conquest. They availed access to imagined sites once touched by Christ, the Virgin, and the holy saints, extending proxies for distant territories. They were desirable objects for imperial powers craving entry into the Holy Land, offering "another Sinai, Bethlehem, Jordan, Jerusalem, Nazareth, Bethany, Galilee, Tiberias."[7] From the perspective of the dispossessed, it is precisely the capacity of relics to offer proxies that also render them an ideal medium for overcoming new states of prohibition and war.

As vehicles of spatial representation, saints' relics are subject to material histories of media and perception. Tactility is a social and cultural technique, not a "natural" physical operation. Moreover, the faculty of touch does not operate in isolation but is rather part of a hierarchical separation and rearrangement of the senses (Taussig 1993; Morris 2000; de la Cruz 2015). In this chapter, I examine how relics mediate a continuum between tactility and visuality, exploring the tactile aspects of seeing and the visual aspects of touch.[8] As I described earlier, relics are at once a site of "visitation" and "witness": seeing is an act of visitation. Whereas in the last chapter we focused more on practices of seeing, in this chapter we shift weight to practices of visitation. As I will show, relics are material technologies that double acts of mobility and vision, mediating acts of movement through tactile acts of seeing. In this way, holy appearances and saintly spectacles also emerge in a spatial economy of pilgrimage.

The making of Egypt as Holy Land ultimately hinges on historical events and conditions of imagining spatial continuities and discontinuities. In the post–World War II context, the tactile dynamics of sacred territory were reconfigured by the historical constitution of nation-states and their changing borders. After the 1967 Arab-Israeli War, Christians and Muslims shared in witnessing the Virgin's appearance—not as a second-order mental reflection of war's material realities, but as itself a material byproduct of territorial occupation and dispossession. By studying the mediating logic of relics, we may gain better insight into how experiences of space and access give rise to images of Christian-Muslim unity like the Virgin of the Apparition. Insofar as it requires Christian-Muslim unity for its success, the Egyptian nation-state crucially relies on such experiences of imagining Egypt as Holy Land.

This chapter moves in six parts. In the first two parts, I examine sacred landscapes and settings of pilgrimage. I trace imaginaries of Holy

7. This quote is taken from the eyewitness account of Nicholas Mesarites, the custodian of the Church of the Pharos after the Fourth Crusade, which had culminated in the siege of Byzantine Constantinople in 1204. For more, see Klein 2006.

8. For cultural studies of touch, see Connor 2004 and Classen 2005. For the tactile nature of visuality, see Lindberg 1976; Taussig 1991, 1993; Pinney 2003; Mitchell 2005a.

Egypt's continuity with holy sites in Israel and illustrate how the Virgin's *baraka* serves as a medium of Christian-Muslim interaction. In the third and fourth parts, I delve into the ritual details of pilgrimage practices, devoting attention to sensory techniques of circulating holiness through the reproduction of relics. More specifically, I explore "virtual" forms of nearing saints' shrines at a distance through practices of tactile sympathy and televisual extension. In the fifth part, I continue to consider the tactile-visual qualities of pilgrimage in Muqattam, an impoverished area that is known for its patron saint who is remembered for saving Copts from the threat of eviction from their land. The sixth part is the culmination of all the previous parts. It describes the coincidence of two major events that signal two holy returns of territorial dispossession: the Roman Catholic Church's return of St. Mark's relics in the wake of Vatican II, and the Virgin's apparition in Zaytun after the 1967 Arab-Israeli War. As I argue it, these two holy returns were central to the consolidation of the Coptic Church's identity as "Arab Egyptian" and the hierarchy of nationhood above Christendom.

THE "TRUE EGYPT"

Egypt's Copts inhabit a geopolitically fraught location between the "Christian West" and "Arab Islam." Like other Christians in the Middle East, Copts have long been tethered to suspect associations with outside imperial Christian powers.[9] Unlike Catholics and Protestants, Coptic Christians claim their native origins in Egypt and Egyptian land.[10]

9. Beginning in 1561, the Roman Catholic Church made several attempts to draw the Coptic Church into its battles against the Protestant Reformation, aiming for a near "union of the Christian world" (Trossen 1948). They were cut short by the abrupt death of Coptic Pope John XIV (1571–85). Later on, during the early to mid-nineteenth century, the Russian Orthodox Church twice invited the Coptic Church under its protection. Although Pope Peter VII (1809–52) had successfully declined the Russian Church's ventures, he encountered more difficulty when it came to the Catholic Church's second round of persuasions, resulting in Muhammad 'Ali's failed attempt "to unite the Church of Egypt with the Church of Rome" (Guirguis and van Doorn-Harder 2011:68). Today's Coptic Catholics, a subcategory of Eastern Catholics in full communion with Rome, are largely an outcome of these negotiations, with its own Patriarchate in Alexandria formally instituted as late as 1895.

10. Coptic Orthodoxy offers a useful point of comparison with Catholicism and Protestantism, Christian traditions that are widely associated with colonialism and globalization. In fact, Copts often lament that they have been dispossessed by other Christians since the Council of Chalcedon in 451 C.E. when they broke away from the imperial church of Constantinople, the predecessor of today's Eastern Orthodox, Catholic, and Protestant Churches.

Copts are indigenous to Egypt, and Coptic Orthodoxy is upheld as an indigenous tradition of Christianity. How Copts imagine Egypt as Holy Land is therefore crucial to their status as "Egyptian" and their relations with other Christians and other Egyptians.

The Virgin Mary is the most important saint for securing Egypt's status as Holy Land. As the "closest" to Christ, she outranks the apostles and martyrs. According to biblical scriptures, the Virgin and the Christ Child had fled from Israel-Judea,[11] and found refuge in Egypt—an itinerary that is referred to as the "Flight of the Holy Family" (*riḥla al-ʿāʾila al-muqaddasa*) or the "Holy Flight" (*riḥla al-muqaddasa*). Following the Coptic Church, the memory of the Holy Flight fulfills the blessed status of Egypt as it had been prophesied in the holy scriptures: "Blessed is my people Egypt" (Isaiah 19:25) and "Out of Egypt I called my son" (Hosea 11:1, also Matthew 2:13). Images of the Virgin and the Christ Child from their flight are foundational traces of holy presence in Egypt. They are the means through which Copts can claim the native status of Coptic Christianity and Christ's presence embedded in Egyptian soil.

Pilgrimage in Holy Egypt follows the journey of the Holy Flight, tracing the routes and sites where the Virgin and the Christ Child traveled, ate, and slept. According to a mix of historical sources and local legends, the Holy Family traveled through Rafah into the Sinai Peninsula and the Delta, then southward along the Nile to Upper Egypt (Meinardus 1962; Mingana 2012). Most pilgrims accomplish only parts of the route, visiting the more popular sites in old Babylon, Matariyya or Musturud near Cairo, and Dayr al-Muharraq or Qusiyya near Asyut. The "True Egypt," or Egypt imagined as Holy Land, is an uneven terrain that is concentrically organized around holy sites.

Itineraries of pilgrimage include sacred loci that are imagined to be in contiguous relation to one another, as sites along the same itinerary. Spatial imaginaries of Holy Land, in other words, link Egypt to other sacred territories elsewhere. For Copts, it is the holy city of Jerusalem (al-Quds) that is the most desirable pilgrimage destination, especially during Passion Week. The Coptic Christian who has achieved pilgrimage to Jerusalem is distinguished by the title *miqaddis* or *miqaddisa* (the Christian counterpart for *ḥājj* or *ḥājja* that distinguishes the Muslim who has made pilgrimage to Mecca). The Coptic Church currently maintains its presence in Jerusalem, upholding its chapel inside the

---

11. "Israel-Judea" is what the Romans later named "Palestine." I am grateful to my colleague Simeon Chavel for providing the accurate term of historical reference.

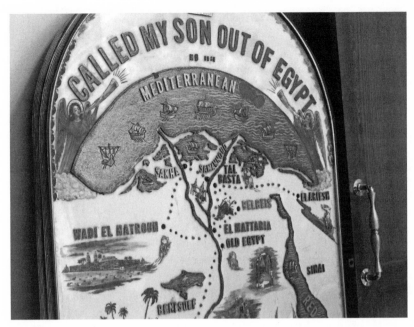

FIGURE 12. Map of the Holy Flight to Egypt, Hanging Church of the Virgin, Old Cairo. Photo courtesy of Marc Dosch.

Church of the Resurrection, also known as the Church of the Holy Sepulchre (Bowman 1993; Cohen 2008).

Imaginings of Egypt as Holy Land rely on spatial relations of contact and continuity. The identity of Coptic Christianity as a "native" tradition also relies on images of holy presences rooted in the land. In the modern era of nationalism and nation-states, imaginaries of sacred territory are subject to the Egyptian nation-state and its territorial borders with other nation-states. Changes in itineraries of holy pilgrimage reflect shifts in geopolitical alliances and territorial ideologies of where Egypt begins and ends. The making of Egypt as Holy Land is therefore deeply implicated in the making of "Egyptian" national identity.

In the 1950s and 1960s, the Coptic Church developed its core identity as an "Arab" Egyptian church. It was during this crucially formative period that the Coptic Church defined its geopolitical location with respect to Europe, Africa, and the Middle East. Under President Nasser's leadership, Egypt was key to promoting Arab nationalism and pan-Arab unity throughout the Middle East. As a result, the Coptic Orthodox Church established its separate identity from other Christian

Churches outside the Arab world, namely in Addis Ababa and in Rome.

In 1959, Pope Kyrillos granted autocephaly to the Ethiopian Orthodox Church, appointing Abune Basilios as its first Patriarch.[12] Before 1959, the Ethiopian Orthodox had belonged to the Ethiopian See of the Coptic Church. Ending an ancient Christian bond, the Coptic-Ethiopian separation occurred during Emperor Haile Selassie's visit with Nasser, when the two discussed Ethiopia's alliance with Israel and the emergence of an Arab-inspired Eritrean movement, among other topics (Erlich 2000). Selassie sought the Ethiopian Church's nationalization and full autonomy. The cleavage led to the Africanization of the Ethiopian Church and the Arabization of the Coptic Church. Decades later in 1998, Pope Shenouda granted autocephaly to the Eritrean Orthodox Church, stirring anger from the Ethiopian Church.

In 1968, Pope Kyrillos also received St. Mark's relics from the Roman Catholic Church. As I pointed out in the previous chapter, the Coptic Church received the relics not as a "gift" but as a "return." After the Second Vatican Council (1962–65), Holy Rome declared its ecumenical aim for the "restoration of unity among all Christians."[13] Years later, the Roman Catholic Church declared that St. Mark the apostle, the common bond between Rome and Alexandria, had improved ecumenical relations between the Churches.[14] The Coptic Church, on the other hand, used the relics to authorize its political alliance with the Egyptian nation-state. Seated next to Nasser, Kyrillos received St. Mark's body at the inauguration of the new Patriarchate Cathedral of St. Mark in 'Abbasiyya. The gigantic Patriarchate complex and the pope-president partnership symbolized the Coptic Church's identity as, above all, an "Egyptian" and "national" church.

Under Nasser and Kyrillos, the 1967 Arab-Israeli War was by far the most definitive event that solidified the "Arab" identity of the Coptic Church. Egypt imagined as Holy Land was also Egypt imagined as Arab national territory. Having lost the Sinai Peninsula, Egypt's Christians and Muslims were united in their state of territorial dispossession. For Arab pilgrims, Christian and Muslim alike, the loss of East Jerusalem

12. For a fascinating study of Ethiopian Orthodoxy and ritual mediation, see Boylston 2018.

13. *Unitatis redintegratio*, www.vatican.va/archive/hist_councils/ii_vatican_council /documents/vat-ii_decree_19641121_unitatis-redintegratio_en.html (accessed May 28, 2018).

14. See Pope Paul VI 1973.

to Israel further deepened their sense of prohibition from their holy sites.

Strikingly, the Coptic Church continues to commemorate the Arab loss of Jerusalem to Israel—and in defiance of the Egyptian nation-state. In 1979, President Sadat normalized relations with Israel, opening travel across the borders of Egypt and Israel. As the fieldworker-novelist Amitav Ghosh has recounted in his book *In an Antique Land* (1992), Jewish pilgrims from Israel began to visit the tomb of the Moroccan Jewish saint Abu Hasira in Damanhur for his annual *mawlid* in December. Copts, by contrast, stayed put. Much to Sadat's fury, Pope Shenouda declared a pilgrimage ban in 1980, shortly after the Israel-Egypt Peace Treaty was signed.[15] Shenouda subsequently earned the nickname "the Arabs' Pope" throughout the Middle East. To this day, the Coptic Church's pilgrimage ban remains in effect.[16]

In this section, I have shown how imaginaries of pilgrimage through Egypt and Israel-Palestine have played a central role in securing the "Arab Egyptian" identity of Coptic Christians and the Coptic Church. The identity of Copts as foremost "Egyptians" is grounded in their status as indigenous and native to the land. By extension, the geopolitical location of Coptic Orthodoxy turns on the various ways in which the Holy Land of Egypt is oriented toward other holy sites in distant cities like Addis Ababa, Rome, and Jerusalem. Papal acts of granting autocephaly, receiving relics, and declaring bans are all political acts of aligning Copts with an Arab vision of Egypt. Moreover, they are all acts of ensuring Christian-Muslim unity under the overarching sign of "Arab Egyptian" identity.

As a brief aside, it is worth mentioning that other Coptic ideologies of nativism have challenged the Arab national identity of Copts, even within the highest ranks of the Coptic Church. Since the turn of the twentieth century, Coptic nationalists have staked their claims to Egypt on the basis of their racial identity, emphasizing their ancestry in the

15. The Coptic Church's ongoing ban on pilgrimage to Israel demonstrates the historical complexities of church-state relations in Egypt. After declaring his ban in 1980, Pope Shenouda further issued a statement to Yasser Arafat in 1982: "The Copts will not be the traitors of the Arabs. Rest assured, brother Arafat, we will not enter Jerusalem unless we are all together, as Arabs, shoulder to shoulder" (Sha'lan 1986).

16. In the last few years, there have been signs of future change. For the first time since 1967, the Coptic pope (Pope Tawadros II) visited Jerusalem in November 2015. In February 2017, the Egyptian court issued a verdict granting Copts the right to take a one-month paid leave to go on pilgrimage to Jerusalem.

ancient pharaohs.[17] In recent years, Copts have also deployed this version of native self-identification through public slogans such as "We are the True Egypt."[18] Perhaps the most inflammatory articulation of Coptic racial nativism was Bishop Bishoy's statement that "Muslims are only guests." Prior to his statement's release in 2010, Bishoy had been known to be one of the closest bishops to Shenouda.

For the most part, however, the Coptic Church has promoted the Arab national identity of Egypt (and as Shenouda once displayed, even to the point of defying the Egyptian nation-state). This identity is currently reactivated through images of the Virgin Mary and imaginaries of the Holy Flight which remember Egypt's blessed status as not only Holy Land, but as "Arab" Holy Land. The Coptic Church's post-1967 claim to the Virgin's status as an "Egyptian" and "Arab" saint further aligns Copts with Arab Islam, severing ties with other centers of Christendom along nationalist lines. Indeed, the shared holy status of the Virgin between Christians and Muslims is a key condition for envisioning Christian-Muslim unity in Egypt. In the next section, I turn to one pilgrimage site on the Holy Flight itinerary to describe Christians and Muslims interacting with the Holy Land of Egypt in shared spaces.

BARAKA WITHOUT BORDERS

In August, the Church of the Virgin in Musturud draws crowds of visitors to its holy grotto. Located along the Ismaʿiliyya Canal, the church sits on the northern rim of Cairo in industrial Qalyubiyya. Every evening for about two weeks, long lines for the crypt curl around the shrine with women and men in separate files. When pilgrims travel to Musturud, their main goal is to access the holy water from its underground well. Since the church is now equipped with modern plumbing, the holy water is accessible with an easy twist of its spigots. On the evening I was there, Coptic teenagers, the church's volunteers or "servants" (al-khuddām), were in charge of filling up plastic bags with holy water, twisting and tossing these slippery wet bundles into bins for distribution. With their

17. For more on Coptic nationalism, see Carter 1986; Shatzmiller 2005; van der Vliet 2009; Ibrahim 2010.

18. In a commemoration march for the Maspero Martyrs held in 2011, Copts wore pharaonic robes and images of ankhs. See Anthony Shenoda, "Public Christianity in a Revolutionary Egypt," Hot Spots, Cultural Anthropology website, May 13, 2013. https://culanth.org/fieldsights/234-public-christianity-in-a-revolutionary-egypt (accessed May 5, 2018).

cuffs rolled up, the laughing teens also passed brightly colored pitchers and cups for pilgrims to drink while waiting in line. The women next to me pointed out that the water tastes "sweet."

The Coptic Feast of the Virgin Mary is held annually in August, honoring the Virgin's assumption into heaven. The Christian (Orthodox and Catholic) and Islamic traditions honor the Virgin Mary and Christ Child, although with different versions of their biographies (Geagea 1984; Haddad and Smith 1989; Schleifer 1998). Whereas Copts refer to the celebrations as al-'īd ("feastday"), Muslims refer to it as al-mawlid ("festival"). In August, a few churches and monasteries in Egypt enjoy a solid track record of attracting thousands of Christians and Muslims to their holy sites evening after evening. Joining the holy well in Musturud, Dayr al-Muharraq in Asyut, Gabal al-Tayr near Minya, and the Virgin's tree in Matariyya are all popular sites of Christian-Muslim veneration. All of them are also sites that commemorate the Holy Flight, composing Egypt's ancient landscape of sacred territories.

In the Church of the Virgin in Musturud, the holy water is felt to be gorged with the Virgin's *baraka*. *Baraka* is translated as a "holy blessing" or "special grace" mediated through holy intercessors, living or dead.[19] To characterize its power to move across communal and ethnic boundaries, the novelist Camilla Gibb penned the image "baraka without borders" (1999), based on her anthropological fieldwork in the fabled Ethiopian city of Harar, the "city of the saints." Both Christians and Muslims in Egypt use the term *baraka* to signify the holy power of saints, prophets, and miracle-workers, and its special capacities to travel beyond ordinary space and time. To describe the fluid movement of *baraka*, ethnographers have used verbs such as "radiate," "channel," and "transmit" (Ewing 1984; Safi 2000). More specifically, *baraka* refers to a spiritual substance conveyed through liquid-like vehicles such as air, dust, light, oil, fragrance or water which have come into contact with saints.

---

19. *Baraka* refers to a spiritual substance of special personhood which conveys efficacy. In the Latin Christian tradition, the word *baraka* correlates roughly to the Latin word *virtus* which is translated into "virtue" or "power" in English: "And the whole multitude sought to touch him, for there went *virtue* out of him, and healed them all" (Luke 6:19, King James Version, emphasis mine). In classic anthropological work on magic, it is perhaps the Polynesian notion of *mana*, a supernatural force found in persons and objects, which best serves as an analog to *baraka* (Firth 1940; Hocart 1914; Mauss 1972 [1902]). In his work on mass society, William Mazzarella has revisited theories of *mana* to advance a critical genealogy of aesthetic autonomy (2017).

For centuries, Christians and Muslims in Egypt have inhabited the same holy landscape for accessing *baraka* (Taylor 1999).[20] Offering traces of the Holy Flight, Holy Egypt is a landscape imprinted with tactile traces of the Virgin and Christ Child's interactions with the land (Lyster, Hulsman, and Davis 2001). Their only relics are contact-relics, or relics that were once physically close to the bodies of holy figures.[21] In Sakha, there is a stone with the Christ Child's footprint. In Gabal al-Tayr, there is the mountain that bears his handprint. In Qussqam, there is the cave that gave shelter to the Holy Family. In Beni Suef, there is the palm tree which al-Maqrizi, the Mamluk-era Sunni historian, described as providing ripe dates for the Virgin (Meinardus 1962). These special landmarks demonstrate where Holy Land exhibits "living" images of holy presence.

Musturud's holy water indexes traces of the Virgin's coexistence in space. The holy water carries *baraka* by virtue of its proximity to the same wellspring that once touched the Holy Family. As a "tertiary relic," the water is valued as holy due to its contact with the "secondary relic," or landscape that had once contacted the Virgin and the Christ Child. Acts of taking *baraka,* in turn, are tactile acts of bodily transmission. Folklorists of the North African Mediterranean have further suggested a cosmological circuit of interconnected senses in which saintly "blessings in the hands" contravened powers of "the evil eye" (el-Aswad 2002; cf. Meri 2002). To take *baraka* from the Virgin's well, people drink its water, wipe it on ailing parts, and wash themselves with it. During my several visits to Musturud, I have also traveled with pilgrims back to their homes where they divided the plastic bags of water among family members who would dab the Virgin's *baraka* on their faces and bodies.

In recent decades, the Virgin's festival celebrations in August have confronted a couple of changes in the mixed composition of its participants. First, Salafist strands of Islamic reform have condemned rituals of venerating holy intercessors, helpers and friends of God (*al-walī,* pl.

---

20. As early as 1916, the Finnish sociologist of Moroccan sainthood Edvard Westermarck published a study entitled *The Moorish Conception of Holiness (Baraka)*. Ethnographers of Islam in North Africa have richly detailed Muslim practices of taking *baraka* at saints' shrines. See Crapanzano 1973; Gilsenan 1973; Geertz 1975; Mittermaier 2011.

21. In the Coptic Orthodox tradition, the Virgin Mary died a natural human death and her body was "assumed" into heaven, or raised up in her full bodily and spiritual existence. Like Christ who was resurrected, the Virgin thus left no fleshly remains behind. For this reason, both of their bodily images availed through contact-relics embedded in the land are all the more prized.

al-ʾawliyāʾ). This critique has extended to *mawālid* which Salafists and other religious reformers have deemed to be false superstitions and human innovations (Schielke 2012). Second, security concerns have led to the Coptic Church's ban of Muslims from attending the Virgin's festivals at churches and monasteries. In August 2017, for example, Dayr al-Muharraq in Asyut suspended its celebrations for the Virgin and limited its yearlong pilgrims to Christians only.

On my last visit to Musturud, in August 2011, the Virgin's holy grotto was ensconced within a bustling festival market filled with sweet shops, art vendors, and tattoo stations. Families took turns riding the enormous ferris wheel at the end of the canal, with its colorful spray of glittering lights spinning against the dusk sky. On my way back home, I took a couple filmy bags of holy water from the Virgin's well with me. Since it was late at night, there were few taxis available and I ended up hopping into one already heading for the Sikka al-Hadid bridge. The other passengers were two older Muslim women, toting plastic bags full of holy water from the Virgin's well: *baraka,* one of them said, making us all aware of what we held in our hands.

PILGRIMAGE I: TACTILE SYMPATHY

In the next two sections, I discuss practical techniques and technologies of taking *baraka* with more detailed attention. Relics serve as media of spatial representation and movement, ordering relations of distance and proximity to holy bodies. They also serve as reproducible media of "virtual" movement.

Inside Coptic shrines, saints' bodies are concealed within reliquaries and glass display cases. To protect them from exposure, Coptic churches keep their relics hidden inside wooden tubes, wrapped with layers of red velvet and white cloths. To take *baraka* from relics, pilgrims approach them as closely as possible. Relics are concrete and fixed objects; taking *baraka* from relics, however, is a tactile dynamic of movement and interaction.

One September evening in 2006, I had a conversation about relics with Father Tuma, one of the younger priests who was serving in one of Cairo's affluent churches, the Churches of Sts. George and Abram in Heliopolis. That day, it also happened to be the "Feast of the Cross." Following Orthodox Christian tradition, the Feast of the Cross commemorates St. Helen's discovery of the "True Cross," or the cross that bore Christ during his crucifixion. St. Helen is the mother of St. Constantine the

Great, the fourth-century ruler of the ancient Roman Empire, and the first emperor to convert to Christianity, making it the official religion of the empire. Both St. Constantine and St. Helen are therefore saints who represent imperial conversion.

The True Cross is a contact-relic. When I asked Father Tuma why Copts take *baraka* from the relics of saints, he described tactile acts of faith including St. Helen's discovery of the True Cross:

> If one has faith [*īmān*], when he takes the aromatic spices [*al-ḥanūṭ*] from the relic [of Bishop St. Abram], it is as if he takes *baraka* from the body of Bishop Abram himself. We have the expression in the Bible that the Prophet Elisha raised the dead, and that the wood of the cross where Christ was crucified raises the dead.
>
> When St. Helen was trying to discover where the cross of Christ was, she found three crosses—one belonging to the thief on the right, the other the thief on the left, and the cross of Christ. To figure out which one it was, she took a dead person from the tomb and put it on the crosses; the first one, he didn't rise, the second one, he didn't again, the third one, he rose. The wood of the cross is made holy by the blood of Christ which fell upon it. So we have the same faith in the wooden tube that touches [*bitlāmis*] the body of the saint.
>
> When I touch the aromatic spices [*al-ḥanūṭ*] that touch the tube, and the tube that touches the body, it becomes *baraka*. To any person. Even if he is not believing. For example, there might be someone who is not baptized. He can say, "I'd like to take *baraka* from St. George," and he goes and takes it.

To explain the material logic of taking *baraka,* Father Tuma drew on the examples of the Prophet Elisha and St. Helen raising the dead. St. Helen's discovery of the True Cross relies on miraculous acts of resurrection through tactile proximity to the blood of Christ. Contact-relics communicate power through touch, by virtue of having touched holy flesh. Analogous to the holy cross of wood that had touched divine blood, reliquary tubes of wood touch the aromatic spices that surround the fleshly parts of holy saints, and the outer layers of red and white cloth touch the outside of the tubes. Relics extend surfaces in tactile contact with other surfaces, transmitting *baraka* through the physical sensation of closing distance.

In his classic work on magic, anthropologist James Frazer introduces the category of "sympathetic magic" and its two principles of reproducing images. The first is "similarity" which relies on resemblance or imitation, giving rise to what he calls "homeopathic magic." The second is "contagion" which relies on the idea that things that had once been in physical contact continue to act on each other from a distance. Frazer further elaborates on the spatial dynamics of sympathy: "Things act on each other at a distance through a secret sympathy, the impulse being transmitted from one to the other by means of what we may conceive as a kind of invisible ether" (Frazer 1998 [1890]:14). The *baraka* of saints, the substance of holiness, circulates through contact and sympathy. The reproducibility of saints' bodies is made possible through contact-relics, new bodily images that mark movement in space. It is through the technique of tactile sympathy that pilgrims can reach the bodies of saints, even when they are buried and hidden from sight.

Father Tuma was emphatic that "any person," even the unbaptized, can take the *baraka* of saints. Faith is important to the transmission of *baraka*, but not believing in Christianity. All those on the peripheral outside of Orthodox expansion—"other" Christians, Roman pagans, Muslims—are imagined to have access. Relics work by drawing potential converts toward its miraculous centers of holy assimilation. They are tactile images of "colonial 'first contact'" (Taussig 1993:251).

After describing the tactility of *baraka*, Father Tuma then further illustrated its power of "travel" with a story of pilgrimage. Coptic churches encourage their parishioners to visit Holy Egypt, organizing inexpensive day trips to the Wadi Natrun monasteries in the Delta for less than 30 Egyptian pounds ($5 US), and overnight trips to Upper Egyptian sites for less than 175 Egyptian pounds ($30 US). Coptic pilgrims frequently seek miracles, traveling to take *baraka* from saints' shrines. Tuma described one woman who was unable to travel:

> One time there was a trip to the Monastery of St. Menas. There was a woman who had cancer. She had faith that if she saw the body of St. Menas and Pope Kyrillos and took *baraka* from them, [she would be healed]. She lived very far away. She came to the church. She found that the bus already left. And she sat on the steps of the church until the bus came back, and waited and cried the whole day long.
>
> The first one who came down from the bus, the organizer or chief of the trip or one of the first ones sitting in the front seats of the bus—she went up to him and took the dust off from his shoe [*al-turāb min gizmithu*]. *From his shoe*. So she took the dust from his shoe and put it on the place where she was ill. And she was healed by her faith.
>
> I want to ask you a question. Was this man . . . ? He could have been in the bathrooms in the monastery. Or maybe he didn't believe, he just went for fun. But she had faith. She believed in the holy intercession of Pope Kyrillos and St. Menas, and she was healed.

In this story of missed pilgrimage, the woman cannot visit St. Menas Monastery. Instead, Pope Kyrillos and St. Menas visit her. As in the case of relics and their layers of wood and cloth, *baraka* is transported through a sequential train of vehicles: first onto dust, second to shoes, and third by bus. The key to grasping the power of *baraka* is to perceive its work "at a distance through a secret sympathy." This felt sensation of distance is what makes faith appear all the more efficacious when miracles are fulfilled.

It is dust that stands in for the distant saints. According to philosopher Charles Peirce, the "virtual" relation indicates an effective substitution: "a virtual X (where X is a common noun) is something, not an X, which has the efficiency (virtus) of an X" (Peirce 1902:763). The dust is not the saint's body, but has the efficiency or *baraka* of the saint's body. Offering a substitute for the saint's body, it is a medium of exchange between the saint's body and the pilgrim. The dust circulates as a medium of "virtual" pilgrimage, or a form of spatial movement that is not pilgrimage but which has the efficiency of pilgrimage.

When relaying the story of the faithful pilgrim, Father Tuma marveled most at the power of otherwise dispensable matter. To repeat his rhetorical question to me: "Was this man . . . ?" That it was lowly dust that saved the woman only serves to further illustrate the redemptive powers of *baraka*. Another example from hagiography helpfully demonstrates this. In one popular film featuring the Coptic saint Ana Simon, the "Queen of the Beasts," a blind nun mistakes a thief in the convent for the holy St. Abram. She decides to wash the thief's feet in a basin. With faith in the *baraka* of St. Abram, she splashes the filthy water on her eyes and discovers that she is healed. The witnessing thief, in turn, converts to Christianity.

Since relics are usually hidden from sight, pilgrims enact faith by touch. For this blind nun, it is tactility that restores her vision. In the next vignette, we continue exploring the tactile-visual circuit of *baraka* by turning to a man with weak sight who was also healed at a tactile distance.

PILGRIMAGE II: TELEVISUAL EXTENSIONS

Travel to Egypt can be arduous and expensive for Copts living abroad (*Aqbāṭ al-mahgar*). Beginning in the 1950s and 1960s, Copts began emigrating to North America, Europe, and Australia, and currently, the Coptic diaspora makes up roughly 10 percent of the total Coptic population worldwide.[22] A sizable number of diaspora visit Egypt and make

---

22. For more on the Coptic diaspora, see McCallum 2012; Sedra 2012; Haddad and Donovan 2013; Hanna 2013.

pilgrimage to saints' shrines, cultivating spiritual attachments to their homeland. I recall one couple from Scotland who had brought their gravely ill daughter with them for their long journey to the Wadi al-Natrun monasteries. Waiting in the bus longer than usual, the other pilgrims agreed to allow them extra time with the body of St. Makarios the Great, knowing how far they had traveled to be with him.

In recent decades, the Coptic Church has become more global and international due to its diasporic growth. As a result of more churches and dioceses abroad, the international profile of adherents to Coptic Orthodoxy has also changed; it is no longer only Copts who are Coptic Orthodox. Through missionization and marriage, foreigners now comprise the Coptic Church's latest batch of converts. This quietly changing demographic was made evident to me during my most surprising fieldwork encounter in the Convent of St. Dimyana. When Bishop Bishoy heard that I wished to better understand Coptic Christianity, he summoned one of the convent's a hundred or so monastics from her prayer cell, Mother Thiyuhibti—a Hong Kongese-Canadian who had converted from Buddhism while studying at the University of Toronto in her mid-twenties. Overlapping immigrant communities (e.g., Egyptian and Chinese in North America) have led to ethnic diversification in the Orthodox churches abroad, and at times, all the way back to the Coptic Church's holiest places in Egypt.

Imaginaries of Egypt as homeland and Holy Land create senses of belonging to faraway sites seemingly out of reach. Recalling the story of the woman who took *baraka* from the dust of St. Menas Monastery, the sympathetic flow of *baraka* extends a "virtual" form of pilgrimage for those who cannot make the journey. In what follows, I explore television as a tactile medium of proximity and distance through which acts of seeing double as acts of traveling. The television screen, similar to reliquaries made of wooden tubes and displayed in glass cases, is a visual-tactile surface that structures styles of interaction, orientation and movement. Here, I analyze the television in material continuity with tactile practices of relic-mediation. The technological domain of mass-mediated visuality is also a religious domain of reproducing images of holiness. Televised images of saints' bodies mediate rituals of moving toward the Holy Land through felt experiences of distance.

According to the filmmaker Magued Tawfik, Coptic hagiographic films enjoy the most success among two Coptic audiences. The first are Upper Egyptians in rural villages where, in his words, "people watch television all day long" (see also Abu-Lughod 2005). The second are the overseas diaspora who use mass media to keep their ties with their Coptic traditions. Tawfik's ultimate professional goal is directed to all viewers of his films: "to bring people closer to God" (*qarrab al-nās 'alā al-rabbinā*).

During one of our interviews back in 2006, Tawfik and I met in his flat next to the Sixth of October Bridge in Ghamra. Over Fanta and fried tilapia, we watched clips from his films and discussed the technical details behind the making of some scenes. Tawfik's high energy personality became especially clear as he spoke about his work and its unexpected outcomes. He asked me, "Have you seen *St. Marina the Martyr?*" I had to confess I had not yet seen it. With excitement Tawfik spoke of how, for the ending of the film and at his insistence, the actual relic was revealed to the camera—a view that few pilgrims could ever share. He had to cajole Father Antunius, the priest of the Church of the Virgin of Relief in Harat al-Rum, where the relic is housed: "And of course, in the film—I know you didn't see the film—there was the relic of the hand [*al-kaffa*] with all its nails in tact. It was there in the [reliquary], and I told Father Antunius, 'Take it out and we will film it.' He didn't want to. He told me that it is 1,750 years old, and if it is held, it will turn into powder. I told him, 'No, Father, we must take it out.' So he took it out with great caution and it didn't fall apart [*mathalliltsh*]. I filmed a very good image of it." The ritual ostentation of St. Marina's hand occurs only on her feast days. Twice a year, her relic is removed from its ordinary layers of wood and cloth, fully bared with the glass case functioning as its sole barrier of protection. Somehow, Tawfik had persuaded Father Antunius to remove St. Marina's body from her usual hiding place for everyone to see. Unlike St. Marina's bodily representations in the rest of the film, this image was the image of her "original" hand, not an artificially-made replicate.

St. Marina the Martyr's last scenes are a spectacular exhibition of her holy body. After viewing the saint's cycles of torture and her final beheading, Tawfik and I watched the film change in genre from hagiography to documentary. In its last frames, the film presents scenes from St. Marina's feast day in Harat al-Rum, capturing Coptic pilgrims lining up and taking *baraka* from her exposed right hand.

In the film's final sequence, Father Antunius approaches the open reliquary and removes St. Marina's hand from its pillowy folds. Then, he kisses the holy relic and elevates it up high. Shot against an acoustic backdrop of suspenseful electronic music, it is then revealed to the film's viewers. The camera spatially approaches the hand on display, as the

FIGURE 13. Father Antunius removes the relic of St. Marina, Video still. Reproduced from *St. Marina the Martyr* (1993), with permission from Magued Tawfik.

FIGURE 14. Close-up shot of the relic of St. Marina, Video still. Reproduced from *St. Marina the Martyr* (1993), with permission from Magued Tawfik.

pilgrim usually does. The reddish, desiccated hand is magnified and rotated outward in slow motion. An image of sympathetic reproducibility,[23] Tawfik's cinematic image of *baraka* is created from the camera's spatial proximity to the relic. By way of ritually tactile mimesis, the camera extends St. Marina's holy hand on the screen.

After watching the end of *St. Marina the Martyr* together, Tawfik told me a story about the film's intervention for a Coptic-Australian viewer. A few years after making the movie, Tawfik went to his niece's baptism at the church in which he made the film. He paid a courtesy visit to Father Antunius and learned about a letter that Antunius had received earlier from a Coptic man in Australia. As many other letters to the church do, this man's letter detailed the miracle St. Marina had performed for him. According to the letter, it was Tawfik's film which had carried her *baraka* to him. In our conversation, Tawfik recounted the letter's account of the miracle:

> And then, the hand appeared [*zaharit*]. This means that [the Coptic-Australian man] came into the room, and the hand was exposed on the television screen [*bita 'rrada 'ala al-shasha*]. And he went to pause the video. He put his eye—his eye was weak, and he had come from the doctor—he put his eye on the television, and he said to St. Marina: "I must travel to Egypt, so that you will heal me."
>
> At that moment, the electricity and the lights went out. After a little bit, the lights came on again and the man's eye healed. Later on, he learned that his younger son had been playing with one of the electricity pads in the house when the lights had been turned on, meaning that [the son] should have died. His son didn't die, even though he had put his hand in the electricity.
>
> The man's eye placed on the screen was healed, and the lights came on [with no harm to the son]. . . . So he sent a letter and said, "I am ready to give any amount of money and chandeliers [*mabaligh wa-nagaf*] to Marina."

The sequence of events reveals a televisual circuit of visual-tactile acts of contact.[24] Hands and eyes are the body parts that figure repeatedly throughout the account. First, St. Marina's hand appears. Second, the Coptic-Australian man sets his eye on the screen and the lights turn off. Third, his son puts his hand into the socket's eyes. Fourth, the Coptic-Australian man's eye is healed and the lights return. The two miracles

23. From the technical perspective of electronic mediation, one could also argue that the moving image of St. Marina's hand is broken and fractured into a series of images in motion—a "serialized iconoclasm"—that endows the relic with a sense of "liveliness" on screen. Here, I draw inspiration from de Abreu 2012.

24. For more on the tactility of cinema, see Benjamin 1969 [1936]; Deleuze 1986; Weber 1996; Marks 2000.

that result are the healing of the man's eye and the protection of his son's hand. Throughout the multiple visual-tactile exchanges, it is electricity and light that connects all the body parts—of St. Marina, the Coptic-Australian man, and his son—together into a contiguous line of transmission. *Baraka,* a kind of "spiritual electricity" (Frazer 1998 [1890]), moves across fragmented bodies, or scattered organs of perception belonging to different persons. The "miracle" is felt as an experience of sensory disorientation.

The televisual relic is an image of St. Marina's hand when it "appeared" (*zaharit*). The relic thus takes the form of an "apparition" (*zuhūr*). As a visual-tactile medium, the relic's appearance combines the visualizable representation of the hand with the camera's movement on screen.

As a "prosthesis of perception" (Buck-Morss 1994), the cinema screen offers a televisual extension of St. Marina's hand.[25] When the Coptic-Australian man pauses the video, he creates a virtual site for taking *baraka* from St. Marina. The tactile site of visiting her relic is extended as a holy appearance. The act of seeing the saint's apparition is therefore itself an act of traveling to the saint's body.

Pilgrimage via televisual extension is certainly not common among Copts in Egypt or in the diaspora. Yet this Coptic-Australian man's miracle illustrates more than a mere ritual-technological variation on taking *baraka*. His story also reveals a mass-mediated sensorium of imagining Holy Land in which visual appearances of saints reproduce tactile sites of holiness. Most notably, these televisual aesthetics of perception are also modes of creating extensions to sacred territory and virtual forms of pilgrimage. Here, diasporic perspectives on pilgrimage are especially instructive because the diaspora are most familiar with the international constraints of traveling back to their homeland. Exposing its contact-relics on camera, Holy Egypt is made virtually accessible.

At the end of Tawfik's story, it is not clear if the Coptic-Australian man made it back to the shrine of St. Marina in Harat al-Rum. In the exchange of appearances for visitations, miracles and gratitude serve as lasting signs of *baraka*. Egypt imagined as Holy Land relies on the circulation of saints and their reputation to work miracles, or their "fame."

25. In her essay "The Cinema Screen as Prosthesis of Perception," the philosopher Susan Buck-Morss points out that the original Orthodox usage of the term "prosthesis" (prósthesis in Greek) indicated the place where the Eucharist table is prepared. Distinguishing the Eucharistic communion from mass communication, she argues that "the religious communal experience is one of bliss" and the "cinematic communal experience is one of shock" (1994:55).

As he had expressed in his letter, the Coptic-Australian man was ready to give "any amount of money and chandeliers" (*mabāligh wa-nagaf*) to St. Marina. In return for her miracle, his promise honors her *baraka*-filled shrine back in Harat al-Rum instead.

TOPOGRAPHIES OF DISPOSSESSION

In late November, feast-day celebrations for St. Simon the Tanner (Samʿan al-Dabbagh) take place in the Cave Churches in Muqattam Hills on Cairo's southeast periphery. Built in the 1990s, the largest of the seven churches is the Church of the Virgin and St. Simon, a stadium-sized auditorium quarried and chiseled out of the limestone cavern.

When I visited for St. Simon's feast day in 2006, the pews and benches were packed with a few thousand Copts for the *taḥnīṭ* ritual. *Taḥnīṭ* is a ritual in which the reliquary containing a saint's relics is opened up to remove a tiny fragment of *ḥanūṭ* and to make more of it for circulation. A gum-like substance, *ḥanūṭ* is a compound of aromatic spices and balms within which the saint's body is kept. Using a tiny fragment of *ḥanūṭ* which had touched the saint's body, the old aromatic bit is mixed into a large blue plastic tub of fresh, aromatic paste for distributing *baraka* to the thousands. This ritual technique is in effect a technology of mass reproduction via the logic of contagion.[26]

To get to the Cave Churches, visitors must wade through stinking beds of garbage in the streets and dodge pick-up trucks filled with plaited bags of trash. In parts of Muqattam Hills and neighboring Man-shiyyat Nasir, the residents are called *al-zabbālīn*, or "the people of the garbage." The vast majority of *zabbālīn* are over thirty thousand Coptic Christians, whose families originally hail from rural Upper Egyptian villages around Asyut. Beginning in the 1930s, waves of impoverished

26. The ritual of *taḥnīṭ* also parallels the ritual of making *mayrūn* ("holy chrism" in Arabized Greek). According to the writings of the fourteenth-century Coptic priest and scholar Abu al-Barakat ibn Kabar (1971), the *mayrūn* originates from oils added to the perfumes which had anointed the body of Christ at his burial; hence, the *mayrūn* is the oil with the highest level of sanctification. Reproduced by bishops following specific rites and recipes (see Swanson 2010:105–6), new batches of *mayrūn* are made according to the Church's need. Used to anoint the newly baptized and consecrate churches and liturgical objects, the quantity of available *mayrūn* also serves as an indexical mark of Coptic Church growth. During the reign of Pope Shenouda III, new *mayrūn* has been made seven times (notably, a significant fraction of the thirty-four total in the history of the Coptic Church).

FIGURE 15. Women sorting through garbage piles, Muqattam. Photo courtesy of Jordi Camí
Caldés.

Copts and Muslims migrated to the cities looking for jobs and better
income. By the late 1960s, many of these rural migrants were forcibly
displaced from Imbaba to the outskirts of Cairo's rapidly developing
centers. For those Copts who landed in Muqattam, garbage collection
became one way to earn a living. Although there are those families who
have earned a comfortable salary over the years, many *zabbālīn* aspire
to leave for more social respectability in other urban neighborhoods.

Almost all *zabbālīn* are Coptic Christians because waste management
effectively means working with pigs, considered "unclean" in Islam and
Judaism. The *zabbālīn* are also called *al-zirraba*, or pig-pen operators.
Intimately raised inside the homes of the *zabbālīn*, pigs eat food scraps
often on a separate floor, where women and children also sort through
trashpiles of bottles, wrappers, syringes, diapers, and so on. Rivaling the
size of wild boars, these pigs are also slaughtered for large sums of money
(up to $300 US each). As of 2014, Muqattam and Manshiyyat Nasir's
pigs totaled 50,000 to 80,000, significantly lower than the 350,000 that
once grazed the garbage villages before 2009. In April 2009, the H1N1

influenza, tragically misnamed the "swine flu," resulted in Mubarak's pig cull and large monetary losses for the zabbālīn.[27]

Muqaṭṭam in Arabic means "cut up" or "broken into pieces." Many Copts believe "Muqattam Mountain" (Gabal al-Muqattam) to be a geological relic of faith, the landscape's trace of holy contact. Signaling its landscape features, the more generally used term muqaṭṭam refers to the topographic division of surrounding hills into three sections. Muqattam's foothills were once part of seventh-century Fustat, the old capital of early Islamic Egypt (Abu-Lughod 1971; Raymond 2000). Today, these same foothills are known as the "City of the Dead," another slum where Cairo's poor once lived and worked in graveyard tombs before the state evicted them. On the opposite side of the valley lies the twelfth-century landmark Salah al-Din's Citadel, the Islamic fortress perched on Muqattam's sister set of hills.

Following Coptic tradition, St. Simon the Tanner is the one-eyed saint who made Muqattam Mountain possible. A tenth-century shoe-maker, St. Simon is remembered for his humble faith, as tanning, involving animal skin and feet, was considered the lowliest job of his time. Obedient to the letter, he is also remembering for gouging out his own eye after lusting for a woman. According to his hagiographic record, St. Simon lived under the Fatimid Caliph al-Muʿizz li-Din Allah, the ruler who conquered Cairo and commissioned the building of al-Azhar Mosque. Legend reports that one of Caliph al-Muʿizz li-Din's hobbies was to convene Muslims, Christian, and Jewish leaders for intellectual debates on religion. When the caliph learned of the Christian teaching that a mustard seed's worth of faith could "move mountains" (Matthew 17:20), he challenged the Coptic Bishop St. Abram to prove it and threatened to evict the Christians from their homes in Muqattam if the bishop failed. The Copts undertook a three-day prayer vigil, and with the guidance of the Virgin, Bishop St. Abram found the person with the right faith—St. Simon. His faith moved the mountain and saved the Coptic community.

During St. Simon's feast day inside the Cave Churches in Muqattam Hills, the head priest Father Samʿan (du Roy 2017) began the taḥnīṭ ritual, assisted with his deacons in white robes. The Church of the

---

27. In the 1990s, the zabbālīn also began to attract widespread international attention for their successful recycling industries. Several Coptic-Americans have made documentary films featuring the zabbālīn as their heroic protagonists including Marina of the Zabbaleen (2008, dir. Wassef) and Garbage Dreams (2009, dir. Iskander) in which former American Vice-President Al Gore makes a cameo appearance.

Virgin and St. Simon, with its open-air design and twenty thousand seating capacity, resembled an evening summer concert hall. Seated in one of the pews, I enjoyed a view of the church's stage from a slightly elevated angle. The surround-sound speakers blared hymns. Flanking the stage on both sides, two white projector screens provided live streaming of the *taḥnīṭ*. Zooming in on the priest's hands in the blue tub of *ḥanūṭ*, the screens captured the material reproduction of St. Simon's contact-relic and the vehicle of his *baraka*.

Some minutes into the *taḥnīṭ* ceremony, the projector screens displayed other spectacular images of St. Simon: an animated color short film of St. Simon's miracle of faith against the scenic backdrop of the mountain. Cartoon drawings of the main characters included: the Caliph al-Muʿizz li-Din on his horse, Bishop St. Abram with his staff, St. Simon the Tanner and his leather bag. On the left wing of the mountain is one audience: Muslim dignitaries in turbans. On the right wing of the mountain is another audience: the Coptic Christians lined up in prayer. In the stadium sanctuary, Copts present at the *taḥnīṭ* joined as spectators of the mass-mediated spectacle at a remove.

While Father Samʿan prayed over the freshly made rust-colored *ḥanūṭ*, the white screens projected a simulation of the miraculous transformation in landscape. *Kiriya Ilaysun, Kiriya Ilaysun, Kiriya Ilaysun!* ("Lord, have mercy!" in Arabized Coptic); with each cry for mercy from St. Simon the Tanner and the Coptic crowds, the mountain jumped up and down three times on the screens. The church hall resounded with simultaneous noises of crashing and singing at once. With a final piercing crack, the spectacular miracle of mountain-moving culminated with the desert landscape splitting into two hills, each finished with rocky edges.

At this point in the evening, the women and children around me in the cave's pews hunted through their purses and pockets, fumbling for personal tokens for the next step of the *taḥnīṭ*. As in all Coptic Orthodox churches, women and men sat on separate sides of the sanctuary. Everyone held a portable item in their hands—paper, cloth, tissue, and photos. The sturdy grandmother in front of me took out a tissue from what seemed to be her underwear beneath her jellabiya robe. When I asked her what she was doing, she explained how she keeps St. Simon's *baraka* close to her chest, to protect her family.

The various Coptic deacons on the stage began to line up for the procession around the sanctuary. They accompanied a middle-aged deacon holding the tub of new *ḥanūṭ*. At first, the procession was orderly and dignified and people waited patiently for their turn at the ends of the aisles, each taking a swipe from the tub with their object of choice. After about a half-hour, however, the people started swiping out of turn. Those who had missed the *baraka* raced after the man with the blue tub while others dove in for a second swipe of *ḥanūṭ*. Panic-stricken, the poor deacon bolted toward the altar lifting the blue tub high. Teenage boys chased him, leaping across the hundreds of steps to the altar. A woman next to me started to faint and asked me to help her escape the cave and its crowds. Avoiding the runners, we surfaced from the cave cathedral, dizzy and short of breath.

Outside the Cave Churches' entrance, a portrait of the Holy Family is carved into the cliffside's rocky relief. Above it is also carved the verse: "Out of Egypt I called my son." Comprising part of the topography of salvation, Muqattam Hills offer an additional geological trace of Egypt's special status. The Coptic *zabbālīn* represent the contemporary analog of St. Simon's faith against the threat of eviction and territorial dispossession. As a result of new construction and development from the 1990s onward, Egyptian state authorities began pressuring the *zabbālīn* to relocate to settlements outside Cairo (Fahmi and Sutton 2013). Currently, Muqattam's upper plateau called "Muqattam City" is a booming upper and middle-class district with high-rise residences, businesses, and production studios like the Christian satellite TV station SAT-7. One consequence of this recent growth of wealthier suburban settlements has been the increased frequency of fatal rockslides in the lower hills where the *zabbālīn* are. Added to the threat of forced eviction, the Egyptian government also began selling annual contracts to Italian and French companies for garbage collection in 2003. Loss of income compounded by forced displacement has forced many *zabbālīn* to move away from Muqattam Hills.

Muqattam's urban topographies of dispossession makes the Cave Churches into a holy site of faith. Before the rural migration of Copts and their development into the *zabbālīn*, Muqattam Hills and its patron St. Simon the Tanner were hardly on the radar of popular memory. Now, the Egyptian version of mountain-moving faith is an internationally widespread one. The Cave Churches currently host ecumenical events like the Global Day of Prayer in which Orthodox, Protestants, and Catholics from various countries convene in the stadium for mass prayer (Armanios 2012).

Carved inside the cavity of Muqattam Mountain, the Cave Churches speak to the special attachment that Copts have with the land. Indices of divine interaction with the landscape, the hills are themselves a contact-relic. Like all other Coptic churches, the relics of their patron saints are ideal for their inauguration. In some accounts, the humble St. Simon had requested to be nameless; in others, he ordered the mountain to land on him so he would not have fame in the world (el-Shamy 1980; Shenoda 2007). In all accounts, he disappeared after mediating the miracle with his prayers. In July 1992, his relics were discovered in the Church of the Virgin in Old Cairo's Babylon. The return of his remains to Muqattam coincided with the opening of several new cave churches in the mid-1990s.

Spectacles of saintly appearance take place in physical landscapes of loss. As exemplified by the *taḥnīṭ* ritual, the desire for holy proximity can generate effects of tactile disorientation and shrinking space. Material returns of patron saints further reactivate the potential for creating new holy sites as well as mass disruption. Both the spatial form and historical context of such returns prove critical to the making of modern Egypt into Holy Land.

TERRITORIAL RETURNS OF WAR

The Virgin's appearance in Zaytun is easily the most widely known, landmark event in modern Coptic history. In May 1968, a figure of light near the dome of the Church of the Virgin in Zaytun made the front-page headlines of major Arab national newspapers including the Egyptian daily *al-Ahram* and the Lebanese daily *al-Anwar*. Evening after evening, tens of thousands of Christians and Muslims traveled to the residential district in northeast Cairo to catch sight of the Virgin's recurring appearances. By June, the miracle in Zaytun had been sanctioned by the Ministry of Tourism and all Egyptian embassies abroad were sent pamphlets narrating the phenomenon (Nelson 1973). Interpreted as a divine sign of collective blessing, the Virgin of Zaytun extended comfort and hope to Egypt and neighboring Arab nations.

The Virgin of Zaytun was a territorial return of war, appearing within a broader historical canvas of geopolitical contest and flux in a post–World War II era of postcolonial nation-states. More specifically, the Virgin of Zaytun was the material nexus between imaginaries of sacred territory and the territorial constitution of new nation-state borders. The Holy Land of Egypt was newly envisioned via a mass spectacle of saintly appearance. Understood to be an image of Christian-Muslim unity, the Virgin of Zaytun was not a "Christian" saint, but Egypt's "Arab national" saint. In a territorial state of war, the Virgin's

FIGURE 16. "Pope Kyrillos Announces:
The Apparition of the Virgin Is True."
Front-page headline of *al-Ahram*,
May 5, 1968.

appearance provided virtual access to Holy Jerusalem in a context when Arab Christians and Muslims could no longer visit their holy sites of pilgrimage. The apparition, an image of blessing across nation-state borders, offered a material extension of Holy Land that was suddenly out of reach.

The Virgin's appearance occurred after the 1967 Arab-Israeli War. The outcome of the 1967 War was significant territorial dispossession for Egypt, Jordan, and Syria. The lost territories included East Jerusalem, the West Bank, the Golan Heights, the Gaza Strip, and the Sinai Peninsula. Taking place at the site of a Coptic church in Cairo, the apparitions were especially consequential to the imagined location of Coptic Christians in the rapidly changing Arab Middle East. The apparitions presented an occasion for establishing the Arab national identity of Egypt's Copts and the Arab Christian identity of the Coptic Orthodox Church.

Prior to the 1967 Arab-Israeli War, President Gamal Abdel Nasser was at the forefront of calling for pan-Arab unity. After Egypt achieved its full freedom from British occupation in 1952, his anticolonial nationalist vision galvanized ties with other Arab nations. Nasser also spearheaded the short-lived United Arab Republic (1958–61), a political union between Egypt, Syria, and Yemen. Leading Egypt during the Cold War, Nasser joined other leaders of the Non-Aligned Movement to maintain its partial independence from developing international blocs. In short, Egypt of the 1950s and 1960s was a period in which the postcolonial terms of Egypt's nationhood and its geopolitical alliances were beginning to crystallize. The 1967 War was critical to defining Egypt's territorial national identity and its stance against foreign occupation.

For Coptic Christians under Nasser, the Arabization of Coptic Orthodoxy required its disassociation from Western Christendom and its alliance with Arab Islam. In an historical context in which national territories were being defined, the imagined status of Egypt as Holy Land was crucial to the geopolitical positioning of Copts. The Coptic imagination of saints and their global ecumenes offered one popular arena for waging holy wars on behalf of the Arab nation-states. Holy images served as political images of friendship or enmity.

In the spring of 1968, Egypt's Copts engaged with two intersecting media of territorial return from two imperial fronts of dispossession: (1) In May, the Virgin's apparitions in Zaytun were interpreted as a holy response to the Arab losses of Holy Lands, and in particular Holy Jerusalem, to Israel. Understood as a "return," the apparition's material presence in Zaytun affirmed the blessed status of Egypt as Holy Land in continuity with Israel, and Zaytun's blessed status as a holy site of pilgrimage in honor of the Holy Flight. (2) In June, St. Mark's relics were gifted from the Roman Catholic Church to the Patriarchate Cathedral of St. Mark in ʿAbbasiyya, Cairo. Understood also to be a "return," the relics from Venice recalled the ninth-century theft of St. Mark's body from Alexandria to imperial Catholic Rome abroad. Coptic Christians saw the convergence of St. Mark's and the Virgin's returns as an interconnected set of blessings from two key patron saints of Egypt. Together in concert, the relics and apparitions served as creatively imagined proxies for two different geographic horizons of dispossession. By way of St. Mark's return, Holy Cairo was linked to Holy Rome; by way of the Virgin's return, Holy Cairo was linked to Holy Jerusalem.

As a token of friendship, the Roman Catholic Pope Paul VI gifted the Coptic Pope Kyrillos VI with the relics in time for the inaugural opening of Cairo's newly built Patriarchate Cathedral of St. Mark in 1968. Following the Second Vatican Council (1962–65), the Catholic Church aimed for the "restoration of unity among all Christians" (*Unitatis redintegratio*, 1964). The Roman Catholic Church later stated that the return of St. Mark to Egypt improved ecumenical relations between the Churches of Rome and Alexandria (Pope Paul VI 1973:299–301). Saints shared between Roman Catholics and Coptic Orthodox (e.g. St. Mark, the Virgin, and many others) attest to some degree of common Christian heritage. Heralding a new international era of ecumenical dialogue, the post–Vatican II Catholic Church advanced mutual ties, common faith, and universal Christian solidarity.

By the time of St. Mark's return in 1968, the Coptic Church had already established its geopolitical distance from Rome. In response to Vatican II's *Nostra Aetate* ("Declaration on the Relation of the Church to non-Christian Religions"), Pope Kyrillos had declared Rome's absolution of Jews from deicide as "an imperialist Zionist plot against the Arab nations and Arab Christians" (Meinardus 2002 [1981]:84). When the Virgin appeared in Zaytun the same spring of St. Mark's return, Pope Kyrillos further announced to the Arab national press: "She is a harbinger of peace and speedy victory . . . the salvage of the Holy Land and the entire Arab Land from the hands of the enemy. We shall triumph in God's Name" (Meinardus 1970:269). Kyrillos's prophetic militarism echoed the words of *al-Anwar,* a leading Lebanese daily supportive of Nasser's pan-Arabism: "The repetition of the Virgin's appearance confirms that the miracle will continue until the return of Arab Jerusalem and its liberation from Zionist terrorism." Oriented toward Jerusalem, and not toward Rome, Egypt's Copts allied its imaginary of Holy Egypt with pan-Arab nationalism rather than postwar Christian ecumenism.

The Arabization of Coptic Orthodoxy in the 1960s therefore resulted in the making of the Virgin Mary into an *Arab national* saint. Common sainthood between Arab Christians and Arab Muslims was emphasized over common sainthood between the Coptic Orthodox Church and the Roman Catholic Church. Although global Marianism had spread far throughout the Mediterranean East and West, anticolonial nationalism resulted in a widening geopolitical divide between the Arab Middle East and the European West. The Arab-Israeli wars and their dispossessive effects for both Arab Christians and Arab Muslims gave rise to shared experiences of holy blessing on the basis of national identity. The fact that the Virgin of Zaytun was valued as a wartime apparition suggests potential continuities with similar apparitions of prophetic military significance. During the 1973 War, for example, when Egypt retook the Sinai, Egyptian soldiers reported visions of angels in the sky as they crossed the Suez Canal to victory (Hoffman 1997; Mittermaier 2012).

The Arabization of Holy Egypt was also a product of shifting territorial materialities at an historical moment when nation-state borders were consolidated through war and technologies of territorial presence. Quoting the Coptic newspaper *al-Watany,* "The Virgin visited [us] because we could not visit her." The Arab-Israeli War of 1967 marked the beginning of the Coptic Church's ongoing ban on pilgrimage to Jerusalem and all holy sites in Israel. The institutional prohibition of access to sacred territory resulted in alternative routes of blessing. Imagined to be contiguous with the territorial effects of war and the shifting institution of nation-state borders, the vision of the Virgin of Zaytun availed the holy presence of a lost Arab Jerusalem to Cairo.

Shifting weight from Israel to Egypt, the Virgin of Zaytun gave rise to new sites of Arab territorial presence. In May and June 1968, two major centers of Coptic Orthodoxy were celebrated: the Patriarchate Cathedral of St. Mark and the Church of the Virgin in Zaytun. Moreover, they were built, funded, and sponsored as Arab Christian churches under the national political partnership of President Nasser and Pope Kyrillos. Conjointly, they commemorate holy returns after losses of sacred territory to the foreign powers of Christendom and Israel: the theft of St. Mark in 828 and the occupation of Holy Jerusalem in 1968. These two churches are currently the largest church buildings by surface area in North Africa and the Arab Middle East.

PART TWO

Apparitions

CHAPTER 3

Territorial Presence

O Heaven and Paradise,
Who carried Jesus Christ,
O Friend of Solomon
O Friend of every one.

From "Hail to You, Mary" ("al-Salamu Laki, Ya Maryam")

Now, the sobering force of self-knowledge is pulling back its
silken wings, and once again we return to the firm ground of
experience and common sense.

Immanuel Kant, "Dreams of a Spirit Seer"

THE VIRGIN APPEARS ALONG THE NILE

On December 11, 2009, the Virgin Mary appeared at the Church of the
Virgin and Archangel Michael in Warraq, a working-class neighborhood in northern Giza. Night after night, for months, thousands came
to the church to witness radiant figures of light around its domes and
steeples. In mid-January 2010, when I was there with a friend, we were
invited to sit next to the bell tower and catch an aerial view of the
impressive gathering while children played around us on the church's
rooftops. Some fifty meters below, the crowds sang their melodious
praises to the Virgin, the timbre of their cymbals floating up the courtyard's chipped ledges. On the other side of the entrance, a blue police
truck was parked outside with a string of guards regulating the foot
traffic in and out of the church building.

FIGURE 17. The Virgin of the Apparition, Church of the Virgin and Archangel
Michael, Warraq. Photo by author.

"Why did she come?" I asked others on the rooftop. "She came to comfort us before Nag Hammadi," one man responded, referring to the drive-by shootings that had occurred days before at another church in Upper Egypt. His wife added that the Virgin appeared during the month of Kiyahk leading up to Christmas when Copts dedicate special honor to her. Another couple nearby chimed in with their opinion: "She came here because Christianity is a religion of love [dīn al-maḥabba], not a religion of domination [dīn al-sayṭara]." Pointing to the towering minarets of the neighboring mosque, they expressed that the Virgin had come to the church, and not to the mosque, to display her heavenly favor.

Surrounding the mosque and church was the familiar scene of concrete homes dotted with shining lights and eroding shutters, with small shops and dirt paths heading toward the main artery of cars, microbuses, and tuk-tuks to the east. In its early beginnings, Warraq served as the location for industries requiring materials from the Nile. Later on, as a result of state efforts to preserve its riverbeds, new factories for textile manufacturing steadily replaced them. Since the 1970s, the number of residents spiked due to heavy waves of rural-to-urban migration, and according to one of the priests serving there, Copts compose an usually high 35 percent of these recent arrivals.

At present in Warraq, divided into Warraq al-Hadar along the Nile and Warraq al-ʿArab inland, there are four Coptic Orthodox churches to serve its exploding Christian population. Hugging the waterfront and bustling corniche, the Church of the Virgin and Archangel Michael is the largest and most accessible among the four.

When news of the Marian apparition hit the streets at the end of 2009, the Coptic Church immediately launched a council of investigation. Led by Bishop Theodosius of Giza, local priests asked witnesses to submit reports of what they had seen. Both Christians and Muslims provided their descriptions, as well as photos and videos recorded on their mobile phones. On December 14, the Archdiocese of Giza released an announcement confirming the fact that the Virgin had truly appeared. On December 20, Pope Shenouda also affirmed the Virgin of Warraq at his Wednesday meeting in the Patriarchate Cathedral, adding that "Muslims love and praise the Virgin more than some of the Protestants."

Shenouda's statement was a reply to televised interfaith debates around the apparitions that had taken place that prior week. As the Coptic Church had been gathering evidence to support its verdict, cameras and journalists for popular Egyptian newspapers also invited ordinary viewers and readers to evaluate the mass-mediated images of bluish-white light around the church in Warraq. Daily television programs like *Cairo Today* (*al-Qahira al-Yawm*, al-Yawm) and *Truth Talk* (*al-Haqiqa*, Dream TV) convened priests, shaykhs, and pastors to offer their opinions on the apparitions. In various roundtables of interreligious dialogue, Coptic priests explained the national significance of the Virgin's blessing and emphasized the fact that both Muslims and Christians saw her. In some of these settings, Coptic Evangelical pastors openly pronounced the apparitions to be false, with some even suggesting them to be "diabolical."

A year later, in December 2010, I returned to the Church of the Virgin and Archangel Michael in Warraq to see if anything had changed. Before heading over the Rod al-Farag bridge from Shubra on taxi, I picked up a university student on the way. A friend of a friend, she was a Copt who also wanted to visit the church on the anniversary of the Virgin's appearance. Sitting in the back seat together, we briefly exchanged some small talk. Curious, I asked our driver where he was from and if he had heard about the Warraq apparition from last year.

The driver answered pointedly that the apparition was not true. He further backed up his opinion with logical reasoning: If the Virgin had truly appeared, she would have come to a "fixed place" at a "fixed time" in the same way that "the moon appears in the sky every night." She would do this so that everyone could know that the light is the Virgin. If she had truly appeared, she would not appear "at a different church every year." He concluded that the hovering lights in the sky were a trick and nothing more than a concocted laser show.

The young passenger surprised me with a prepared, bold retort: "It is impossible for lasers to produce images that moved as quickly as the apparitions had moved." The conversation abruptly closed, and we hurtled along in clipped silence for the rest of the ride. After we were dropped off, the university student continued her train of thought aloud to me. With more bristle in her tone, she drew on what she knew about laser technology: "Lasers also need screens to receive the lights, and, of course, there were no screens. What he said doesn't make any sense at all."

Walking into the church entrance, she and I headed through the narrow foyer to the sanctuary. Quiet and vacant, the church was remarkably different from my rooftop visit one year prior. Resembling a museum, its walls were plastered with cloth banners that displayed magnified photographs of the Marian apparitions. Throughout the mass-replicated images, the Marian apparitions were featured along with the crowds and the church's steeples and domes in the background.

FIGURE 18. Souvenir poster honoring the Warraq apparitions reads: "Blessed are my people Egypt."

In one souvenir poster, handed out as gifts to tourists and pilgrims, the apparitions' images were framed with Egyptian flag colors and the biblical verse: "Blessed are my people Egypt." Made into a site of Marian presence, the Church of the Virgin and Archangel Michael was now part of Egypt's holy territory.

TERRITORIAL PRESENCE: CHURCHES, NATIONHOOD, SECTARIANISM

Egypt is not a homeland that we live in, but a homeland that lives within us.

Pope Shenouda III

In the last chapter, we ended with the Marian apparitions of Zaytun and the Christian-Muslim consolidation of an Arab national identity after the 1967 Arab-Israeli War. As we saw, the Virgin of Zaytun of 1968 also coincided with the return of St. Mark's relics in the wake of the Second

Vatican Council (1962–65) and a new Roman Catholic ethos toward ecumenical reconciliation with other churches. Defining Egypt within world-making contexts of anticolonial nationalism, Nasser and Kyrillos together addressed two geopolitical fronts of dispossession: Christendom and Holy Rome's old theft on one front, and Arab nation-states and their loss of Holy Jerusalem on another. Culminating in two large cathedrals in Cairo, the convergence of St. Mark's relics and the Virgin's apparitions resulted in new holy territories in Egypt. The presence of saints thereby instituted territorial imaginaries of nationhood and religious belonging.

This chapter considers the life of Marian apparitions after 1968, examining how they shape Christian-Muslim relations in subsequent contexts of territorial dispossession. Unlike the Virgin of Zaytun which was championed as a postwar sign of nationhood, the Virgin of Warraq in 2009 took place in an urban neighborhood with a local history of rapid demographic changes and sectarian tensions. The apparition, while having served as a medium of interfaith unity in the past, currently functions as an image of suspicion and animosity among Christians and Muslims, Orthodox and Protestants. What accounts for these slippages in the Marian imaginary from 1968 to 2009? In what ways do apparitions mediate the terms of territorial belonging and exclusion? How do they shed light on the coimbrications of nationhood and sectarianism?

In what follows, I advance two interrelated arguments that help us understand the shifting career of Marian apparitions and its impact on national and religious belonging in Egypt. First, I make the case that apparitions instituted new forms of perceiving presence and new practices of territorial imagination. Beginning in Zaytun up to the present, the church building became an integral element of the apparition-image and its mass-mediated reproductions via print and photography. The visual fixity of this link between church buildings and Marian presence leads us to my second point. Rather than symbolizing "Christian" or "communal" identity, images of churches crucially index the position of Copts vis-à-vis Muslims within different frames of coexistence. For instance, whereas the church in Zaytun was a site of national blessing after war, the church in Warraq was a sign of sectarian competition with the neighborhood mosque. What territorial imaginaries of Marian apparitions illumine are the ways in which churches calibrate senses of coexistence, whether that of Christian-Muslim unity or that of minoritarian discrimination.

Church construction is perhaps the most notoriously battled arena of religious discrimination against Egypt's Copts. Especially in urban

neighborhoods where the numbers of Coptic inhabitants have mush-
roomed in recent decades, the Coptic Church has repeatedly confronted
obstacles to obtaining legal permits for church building and repair. Regulations for building churches are more stringent than those for building
mosques.[1] Following the Interior Ministry's 'Azabi Decree of 1934, permits are granted on the basis of ten conditions, including the religious
composition of the neighborhood, the opinion of Muslims toward the
planned church, the distance between the planned church and neighboring mosques, and the existence of other churches in the neighborhood
(Shukri 1991; Rowe 2007; Elsässer 2014). Since 1934, state leaders have
proposed minor modifications to the old rules; for example, Mubarak
announced in 2005 that provincial governors (instead of the Office of
the President) could approve church repairs, and Sisi in 2016 set up a
committee to legalize all churches without permits. Indeed, there are currently a significant number of churches, as well as mosques, operating
without permits in Egypt. In contrast to mosques without permits, these
"illegal" churches have also incited violence including the church in
'Umraniyya, Giza, which sparked riots with police and state security in
2010, and the church in Marinab, Aswan, which culminated in the
Maspero protests in 2011.

Throughout many neighborhoods like Warraq, churches and
mosques are increasingly embroiled in "visual and sonic competition"
(Mayeur-Jaouen 2012:164). Even after obtaining permits, Warraq's
Coptic priests have also had to negotiate with the local police in times
of church building and repair. In the 1990s, the police had requested
that a wall be erected to conceal the domes and steeples of Warraq's
Church of St. Mark on the island. According to one priest whom I interviewed, the completion of the Church of the Virgin and Archangel
Michael was relatively painless due to outbreaks of sectarian violence in
Upper Egypt; in his words, "In 2000, the government was nervous after
the Kosheh massacres. It let us do whatever we wanted." By 2006, the
neighboring al-Huda Mosque had extended its minarets upward and its
base outward, eating up meters from the public street. "It should have
been illegal," the same priest pointedly observed.

1. Regulations for church building and repair are partially based on the Ottoman
Imperial Reform Edict of 1856 (Islahat Hatt-i Humayunu) which promised non-Muslim
communities civil and political equality, as well as the freedom to practice religion. To
govern religious freedom, the Ottoman sultan granted imperial permits for construction
and repair. Translated into the modern nation-state context, the decree has resulted in the
Egyptian president's direct oversight in affairs concerning places of worship.

FIGURE 19. Street view of the Church of the Virgin and Archangel Michael and al-Huda Mosque, Warraq. Photo by author.

Despite its unrelenting challenges with state authorities, the Coptic Church officially continues to emphasize that its church buildings are "national," and not merely "communal," sites of worship. There is no other moment in modern Egyptian history that recalls the national value of churches with more glory than when the Virgin appeared to Christians and Muslims at the church in Zaytun in a national period of post-1967 war crisis. When the Virgin of Warraq appeared in 2009, the Coptic Church produced and distributed images of the apparitions framed with Egyptian flag colors and biblical verses describing the divinely blessed status of the Egyptian people. Speaking as the Coptic Church's representative, Father Salib, the charismatic priest of Shubra, referred to the Warraq apparitions as "Egyptian, not Christian, events because they belong to all of Egypt. . . . Because the Virgin doesn't appear in the heart of Egypt, but Egypt is in the heart of the Virgin."[2] Subtly invoking Pope Shenouda's famous saying—"Egypt is not a homeland that we live in, but a homeland that lives within us," Salib asserted that Egypt and Egyptians are living within the Virgin's image.

2. *Al-Qahira al-Yawm,* December 23, 2009, al-Yawm Television Channel.

Insofar as it is imagined as a site of Marian presence, the church in War-raq signifies Egypt's status as sacred territory and a holy homeland.

Visual images of church buildings, across repetitions of Marian appearance, represent holy territories of national belonging. Yet, given that their reception changes according to varying contexts of use and imagination, the national meaning of church-images slides easily into sectarian tokens of minoritarian dispossession. In 1968, Nasser and Kyrillos, Christians and Muslims, upheld the church in Zaytun under the sign of Egyptian nationhood, over and against defeat in Jerusalem and Rome's ecumenical overtures. In 2009, the church in Warraq oper-ated within local histories of religious minorities struggling against the state and within different horizons of Christian-Muslim tension where the mosque and its minarets anxiously occupy the territorial skyline of the neighborhood. Commonly touted in ritual repertoires of religious coexistence, the image of "the church and the mosque" thus reveals the tenuous instabilities internal to imaginaries of Christian-Muslim unity. The value of churches, in short, indexes the sectarian terms of Coptic recognition intrinsic to Egyptian nationhood.

Aside from holy apparitions, other territorial imaginaries of churches activate sectarian horizons of suspicion and vulnerability. Throughout neighborhoods and villages, particularly in areas of demographic change, there are Muslims who allege that their Christian neighbors are secretly turning homes into churches (Nikolov 2008), and Christians who allege that their Muslim neighbors are building mosques to prevent new churches from going up in the vicinity, following the state's legal restrictions on church construction and repair. Within such highly charged terrains of competition and suspicion, it is unsurprising that church buildings have also transformed into targets of sectarian attack and fortresses of communal defense. In October 2013, nearly four years after the Virgin's appearance in Warraq, two masked gunmen on a pass-ing motorbike fired at the Church of the Virgin and Archangel Michael, killing four Copts during a wedding. Of course, there is no direct cor-relation between this act of violence and the apparitions that took place beforehand. However, it is crucial to recognize that these acts of vio-lence unfurl within contexts in which apparitions heighten the public visibility of church buildings and construct new sites of minoritarian vulnerability.

To explain why the topic of church-building is so explosive for the Coptic community, it is often said that Copts are "very emotional" about their churches, immediately running to protect them whenever they sense an imminent attack. By examining how Marian apparitions create deeply felt attachments to churches, this chapter delves into the visual imaginaries of territorial presence alive in Warraq today. As we will see, what ultimately lies at the heart of Marian apparitions are visual epistemologies that constitute national and sectarian terrains of belonging and enmity.

GENEALOGIES OF MARIAN APPARITIONS

In the film *The Virgin, the Copts, and Me* (*La Vierge, les Coptes et moi*, 2011), the Coptic-French filmmaker Namir Abdel Messeeh travels from Paris to Upper Egypt to unearth his ethnic and religious roots by making a documentary on the Marian apparitions that took place in Asyut in 2000. The film ends with Abdel Messeeh convening Muslims and Christians in his hometown village for a theatrical and technological re-creation of the Virgin's appearance, complete with a costumed girl hoisted gleefully above with ropes and pulleys.

Marian apparitions are cherished as part of the cultural heritage of Copts, to the degree that the Coptic diaspora in Europe and North America, believing and nonbelieving, are familiar with them. Beginning in Zaytun of 1968, a string of Marian apparitions took place in various locations throughout Egypt, the most prominent among them including: Edfu (1982), Shubra Babadublu (1986), Durunka (1990), Shantana al-Hagar (1997), Asyut (2000), and Warraq (2009). According to Bishop Moussa, the bishop of education and youth, the twentieth century witnessed a surge in Marian apparitions throughout Egypt (Bishop Moussa 2010). To be more specific, after Zaytun of 1968, Marian apparitions in Egypt assumed an objective form of visual appearance: the "mass apparition" or "collective apparition" (*al-ẓuhūr al-gamā'iyya*).[3] For the first time in the world history of holy apparitions, the Virgin appeared as a figure of light at the site of a church building, and in principle, simultaneously visualizable to thousands of witnesses, regardless of faith, ethnicity, age, or gender.

3. Since 1968, the Coptic Church also began to deploy a classificatory distinction between "individual apparitions" (*al-ẓuhūrāt al-fardiyya*) and "mass apparitions" (*al-ẓuhūrāt al-gamā'iyya*). Anthropologist Sandrine Keriakos makes a convincing case that mass apparitions of the Coptic Virgin are a modern twentieth-century phenomenon that shows that divine appearances are "no longer associated with any form of elitism," or privileged access for bishops and other holy persons (Keriakos 2012:177).

The "Virgin of the Apparition" (*'adhrā' al-ẓuhūr*) is now a canonical image that Copts understand to be the way she appears in Egypt.

Strikingly, the irony is that the origins of the Virgin of the Apparition lie elsewhere, in Paris, France. Any tourist of Egypt today may immediately observe that Coptic iconography of the Virgin is the same Roman Catholic iconography of the "Miraculous Mary" (also known as "Our Lady of the Miraculous Medal") of nineteenth-century France.[4] Far more popular than the Theotokos Virgin and the Virgin Hodegetria, the mass print image of the blue and white "Miraculous Mary" is also referred to by Copts as the "Virgin of the Transfiguration" (*'adhrā' al-tagallī*). Throughout modern Catholic Europe, a series of Marian apparitions also took the Miraculous Mary form including the following: La Salette (1846), Lourdes (1858), Marpingen (1876), Fátima (1917), Beauraing (1932), and Medjugorje (1981). As the anthropologist William A. Christian has argued (1972), the popular spread of pilgrimage and sainthood cults beyond the borders of Catholic Europe crucially relied on mass media and migration. Following art historian Monica René, the Miraculous Mary iconography made its way to the Coptic Orthodox via Italian Catholic missionaries and the burgeoning print industry in nineteenth-century Egypt (René 2014; also Burckhardt 1967).

A rich trove of scholarship on Marian apparitions in the modern Catholic world covers an impressive range of topics from clerical and lay church politics to colonial, postcolonial, and global religious movements.[5] On the basis of its aesthetic kinship with Catholic imagery alone, one may certainly argue that Coptic Orthodox Marianism is a phenomenon that is part and parcel of an ecumenical Marian imaginary

---

4. According to historian David Blackbourn, the Miraculous Medal was mass-produced in the millions, serving as a talisman against the anticlericalism of French occupation after the 1789 revolution (1993:22). Blue and white, the Virgin appeared in the colors of royalist France to the nun St. Catherine Labouré just prior to attacks on Notre Dame and Jesuit headquarters in Paris in 1830. Drawing on psychological literature on recognition, anthropologist Monique Scheer (2013) argues that well-known templates like the Miraculous Mary image have led to the global homogenization of Marian imagination after the 1950s.

5. For recently edited collections of historical and ethnographic research on the Virgin and her apparitions, see *Moved by Mary* (Hermkens, Jansen, and Noterman 2009), *The "Vision Thing"* (Christian and Klaniczay 2009), and *Cold War Mary* (Margry forthcoming). To analyze the role of Marian imagination in modern society and politics, scholars have explored apparitions in war-time (Christian 1996, 1998; Claverie 2003; Margry 2009; Scheer 2012; Halemba 2015) and in national and postcolonial contexts (Wolf 1958; Orsi 1985; de la Cruz 2015; Schmidt 2015).

worldwide. However, here I would like to direct my analysis to the ruptures in Marian mediation introduced by the modern Virgin of Egypt
and to the distinguishing traits of mass apparitions in particular.
Unlike Marian apparitions in modern Europe which centered around
privileged seers (e.g., children and women), delivered verbal messages,
and/or came at an appointed time and place,[6] Marian apparitions in
post-1967 Egypt were speechless figures of light which thousands
reportedly saw and described in congruent ways at the domes and steeples of church buildings.

In sum, the Virgin of Egypt appears as an object of light to mixed
crowds at the site of churches. This new apparitional form established
a distinctively new visual relation between the Virgin and the church
building. To provide a historical sense of contrast, let's briefly consider
alternative practices of imagining Marian apparitions and their relation
to churches in the Coptic tradition. In the classic fourth-century Coptic
narrative *The Vision of Theophilus,* for example, the Virgin's private
appearance to the privileged seer Pope Theophilus led to the construction of pilgrimage shrines stretching from the Sinai to the Delta down
the Nile, all erected in memory of the Holy Family's Flight. According
to other accounts in the Coptic tradition, the Virgin appears to political
leaders to save Copts and their churches from violence, to the Abbasid
Caliph Harun al-Rashid, who threatened to destroy a church in Atrib
(present-day Banha), and to Pope Abram who faced threats of church
destruction in Muqattam from the Fatimid Caliph al-Mu'izz li-Din.[7]
Marian apparitions were therefore imagined to be causal agents of
church construction or church protection.

On a more theological register, Coptic Orthodox teachings describe the
church itself as a holy image, an "icon of heaven" linking the earthly to
heavenly realms. Operating in the same visual order of holy appearances,

6. When the Virgin appeared in La Salette (1846) and Lourdes, France (1858), for
example, rural children and women served as privileged seers with divine messages
(Turner and Turner 1978). In other cases, as in Fátima, Portugal (1917) and Knock, Ire-
land (2009), crowds gathered to witness the Virgin's manifestation through solar activity,
what is referred to as the "Miracle of the Dancing Sun."

7. Caliph al-Mu'izz li-Din's threats are not representative of the treatment of Copts
under Fatimid rule. In fact, the period of Fatimid rule in Egypt (969–1171) is regarded as a
period of relative tolerance and flourishing of Coptic churches, church architecture and iconographic art (Skalova and Gabra 2001; cf. Ferré 1991). As architectural historian Peter
Grossman puts it (1991), the "period of the high Middle Ages, roughly contemporary with
the Fatimid period of rule, must rank as the golden age of church building in Egypt."

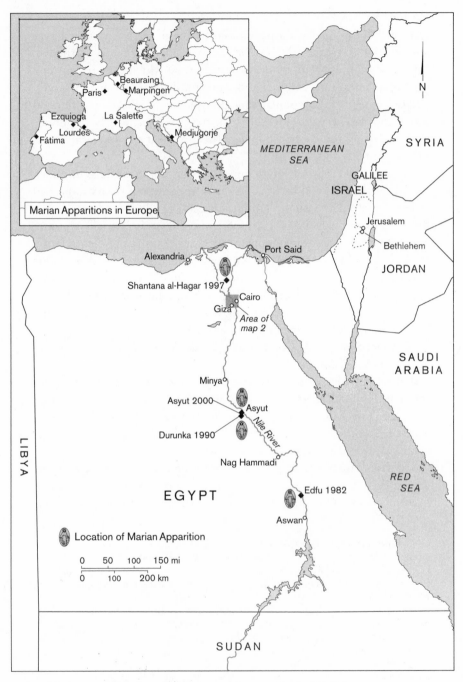

MAP 2. Marian apparitions in modern Egypt and Europe. Map by Bill Nelson.

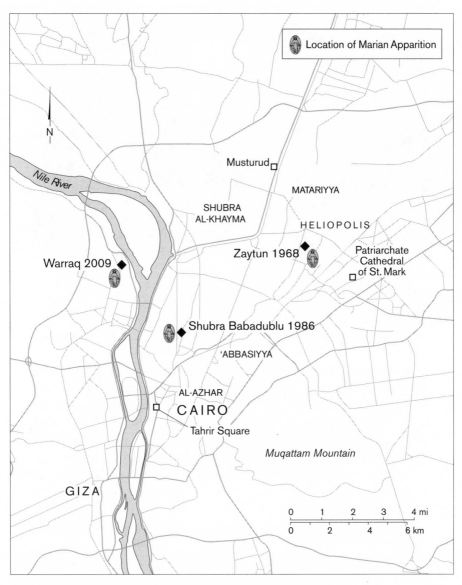

MAP 3. Marian apparitions in Greater Cairo, Egypt. Map by Bill Nelson.

FIGURE 20. A courtyard shrine in honor of the Marian apparitions, Church of the Virgin and Archangel Michael, Warraq. Photo by author.

the Virgin and the church building serve as vehicles of Christ's presence and iconological homologues of each other.[8] In his writings on church architecture, the Coptic monk Father Antunius describes the church's domes as ritual sites of "transfigurational vision [*manzar al-tagallī*]," or human communion with the divine. Antunius describes the church's domes as ritual vehicles of divine presence, the "path by which the vision of one's heart [*baṣīrat qalbhu*] is opened to see heaven" so that one might "enter into participation with the heavens" (Father Antunius 1989:155). In these visual rituals, the church building is not a neutral background of revelation, but a dynamic, active image that effects spiritual work on the inner life of the seer.

In contemporary mass apparitions, by contrast, the church-image functions as a static, objective backdrop for viewing the apparition. Visualizable to everyone, the Virgin also appears regardless of spiritual status. Most significantly, the Virgin of Zaytun in 1968 inaugurated

8. Honored as "Theotokos" (Bearer of God), the Virgin is praised with multiple epithets dedicated to her capacity to carry and convey: Ark of the Covenant, Second Heaven, Burning Bush, Jacob's Ladder, Golden Tower, and many more. During the Coptic month of Kiyahk, these epithets are sung in memory of the Virgin's pregnancy leading up to Christ's fleshly appearance. Church buildings and shrines are also regarded as vessels of heaven that communicate the Body of Christ to the body of believers. Their architectural features, particularly the dome (*al-qubba*), signify priestly altars of heavenly offering.

modern epistemologies of evaluating the "truths" of holy appearances. Mass-mediated through print and photography, mass apparitions circulated in the national public in technologically reproducible form. More than a discrete phenomenon or type of appearance, mass apparitions instituted new visual subjectivities and collective spaces of perception—in short, a "common sense" for determining what is real and what is not. These new public orders of appearance subsequently gave rise to mixed, Christian-Muslim terms of affirming or contesting the apparition's reality and meaning.

Initially in Zaytun, it was the aftermath of the Arab defeat in 1967 which established the territorial significance of the apparition and its visual reproducibility. Egyptian state dailies such as *al-Ahram* and *al-Akhbar* reproduced photographs of the lights at the church on their front pages, proclaiming the truths of the apparition in their leading headlines to the national public.[9] The Lebanese daily *al-Anwar* paired an image of the apparition with a militarist message of recovery: "The repetition of the Virgin's appearance confirms that the miracle will continue until the return of Arab Jerusalem and its liberation from Zionist terrorism."[10] Envisioned from Lebanon, Syria and Jordan, the newspaper images of the floating lights, the church's domes and the crowds heightened a shared sense of pan-Arab nationalism. Relative to the lost Holy Lands, these mass repetitions of the Virgin moreover served as an optical platform for imagining counterattack. Apparition photos served as technological media of territorial imagination and as material links to sacred spaces under conditions of war.

Following from Zaytun, it was the objective lens of the camera which provided the metric for evaluating the status of appearances. After 1968, the Coptic Church began recruiting the use of photos as evidentiary proof that the Virgin had "really" appeared. In addition to collecting verbal reports from firsthand witnesses, the Church compared images of the Virgin's appearance, deploying older images of previous apparitions as visual benchmarks for comparison. Perhaps the most

9. In his lively account of linear perspective (2010), media archaeologist Friedrich Kittler (whom Durham Peters nicknames "the devotee of Mediterranean light") contends that optical media such as the camera obscura and the lanterna magica were at once military and religious technologies of territorial occupation. When accounting for the sixteenth-century spread of the lanterna magica, for example, he turns to Counter-Reformation Jesuit Athanasius Kircher and his deployment of illusory lights to bring Loyolan spiritual exercises out of the cloistered cell into the mass-mediated "outside" of public space (and against the mass vernacular of Protestant scripture).

10. *Al-Anwar*, May 12, 1968.

well-known visual archetype of the Virgin of Egypt is Coptic photographer Wagih Rizk Matta's image for *al-Ahram*'s front-page headline that captures a fuzzy smear of light hovering around the Church of the Virgin in Zaytun.[11] Arguably clearer and sharper than that of the apparition itself, the image of the church building also stands out as a central feature in the photo's backdrop. In effect, what the evidentiary use of photos enables is the visual disassociability of the apparition from its settings and contexts. As repetitions of the Virgin's appearance unfold, the photos of apparitions are reembedded in new contexts of social and political life.

In his writings on nineteenth-century vision and modernity, media theorist Jonathan Crary shows how the status of the "observer" emerged as physiological theories and empirical models of "subjective vision" were developed. Focusing on how optical technologies contributed to the making of visual objectivism, Crary argues that the photographic camera constituted "the position of an interiorized observer to an exterior world" (Crary 1990:34). Individualized and abstracted from the world, modern subjects of visuality were made into "autonomous" observers, distinct and separable from their objective reality. To gauge the enormity of this shift in perception, recall other forms of visuality that we have explored in the previous chapters so far. When interacting with the relics of saints, for example, Copts engage tactile forms of visuality in which seeing sets into motion the sympathetic transmission of power. And similar to practices in the Islamic tradition, Copts also understand that an individual's vision of a saint can be the cause for a new shrine commemorating that vision (*mashhad al-ru'yā*; Taylor 1999; Mittermaier 2011). In all these imaginaries of world-making, visual perception is creatively interlinked with the reality of the saint's presence. This is not the case in the standardization of Marian visuality that occurs with the birth of mass apparitions in Egypt and the convention of a "collective vision" comprised of independent, individual acts of observation.

More broadly, mass apparitions affirmed epistemological shifts definitive of earlier periods of Egyptian modernization. The separation of image and world is emblematic of a political ontology, or a "metaphysics of modernity" (Mitchell 1988:xiii). As political theorist Timothy Mitchell's work on colonial power in Egypt demonstrates, the governance of urban spaces and social hierarchies hinged on the reordering

11. *Al-Ahram*, May 5, 1968.

of appearances in the service of new forms of knowledge. In the same vein, the modern genealogy of Marian apparitions entails those formative practices through which Christians and Muslims understand themselves to be seeing together in the same objectively inhabited space. Christians and Muslims, as well as their churches and mosques, are plotted within a spatial order of reality distinct from the visual appearances and photographic images understood to represent them.

The Coptic Church's sciences of verification introduced a new field that reveals the influence of modern visual ontologies on religious knowledges of holy seership and witness. Conceived for the larger Christian-Muslim public, the Virgin of the Apparition transformed into an image designed to transcend religious identity, and therefore, was subjected to the boundaries of reason.

MASS VISUALITY: MAJORITY FOR THE MINORITY

On December 23, 2009, a couple weeks after the Virgin's appearance in Warraq, the popular television show *Cairo Today* convened a roundtable of two Coptic Orthodox priests, Father Salib of Shubra and Father Bishay of Warraq, and one Coptic Evangelical Pastor Zakariyya. Moderating the interfaith dialogue, the show's two hosts, Amr Adib and Mustafa Sidqi, kicked off the discussion by screening a video clip in slow motion of the bluish-white explosions of light in Warraq. The five participants together observed the objective phenomenon of the Marian apparition.

When asked how the Coptic Church knew that the apparition was "truly the Virgin," Father Salib argued that verification ultimately hinged on numbers. Directly quoting his logic, "When there is one, ten or 100 who say 'no,' and then there is 1,000, 10,000 or 100,000 who say 'yes,' who are you going to believe?" Salib's reasoning echoed the emphasis on numbers from various accounts of Zaytun in 1968, which describe how "millions saw Mary" (Johnston 1982; Zaki 1977), hailing from "different countries, races and religions" (Father ʿAbd al-Masih al-Basit 2010:9). No longer conceived as a crowded swarm of people, the mass visualization of the Virgin amounted to an ordered and countable aggregate of individual viewers. Understood to transcend religious identities, mass apparitions instituted a new sciences of enumerated witnessing.

For the Coptic minority, of course, the apparition's verification requires amassing witnesses from the Muslim majority. This priority of majoritarian recognition reflects a broader minoritarian consciousness across modern national societies—what anthropologist Arjun Appadurai has called an "anxiety of incompleteness" (Appadurai 2006:52). Somewhat of a disputable fact among Copts, Egypt's demographic composition remains a highly charged and contested topic. Any fieldworker of Copts will inevitably encounter wildly fluctuating estimates of Egypt's Coptic percentage, from the 1996 state census data, which report 5 to 6 percent, to Coptic Church reports, which claim up to 15 to 20 percent. As many historical and ethnographic studies have elaborated, enumerative strategies of classification and objectification were effective colonial and state technologies of imposing group identities and distinctions (Cohn 1987; Hacking 1990). Metrics for organizing populations and distributing resources, numbers are materially consequential. As Warraq's priests have described to me, there is a steady record of local state authorities minimizing their estimates of Coptic residents in various neighborhoods to avoid issuing church-building permits. Copts, as a religious minority, are conscious that their communal recognition revolves around their numbers.

On one level, governance by enumeration concerns the terms of minoritarian belonging, that is, the capacity for Copts to seek recognition in their local neighborhoods and state politics. In its search for increased recognition, the Coptic Church focuses on a majoritarian consensus of visuality. This majoritarian orientation leads to its pronounced emphasis on the "Muslim" identity of the apparitions' witnesses. On a broader level, the political logic of numbers is an epistemology of majority-minority difference which relies on abstract notions of equality. The Coptic Church's rationale of the Marian apparitions—a universally perceptible image that transcends religious identities—also borrows from this logic of a countable "majority" of viewers, all of whom have equal access to appearances. The triumph of Marian apparitions, or to be more precise, the mass observability of lights at church buildings, lies in its capacious inclusion of all viewers regardless of religion.

This standardized template of visuality further entails the alignment of religious identity and difference in common space. In her work on religious images and publics in India, art historian Kajri Jain argues that image technologies effect a commensuration between otherwise incommensurate or heterogeneous bodies of "religious" practice (Jain 2017; cf. Asad 1994). What Jain illumines is how the field of religious identity and differences turns on the material leveling of religious practices, in their sensory and spatial complexity, into images and rituals of equivalence and comparison. In the case of Marian apparitions in the Egypt,

Christians and Muslims can evaluate the visions of the Virgin as a "common" image on the condition that they inhabit shared coordinates of perception and space. These shared coordinates are also the public terms of evaluation that underwrite religious identity and difference on a mass scale.

There are two main shifts that emerged out of the institutional logics of a majoritarian consensus based on numbers. First, the leveling of visual subjectivities across the religious divide changed the nature of holy appearances and what it meant to "witness" their truths. When it came to collecting reports for verification, the Coptic Church did not solicit any spiritual confession or personal account of desire and belief from its witnesses. Its reports rather focused on the visually objective facts of observation: how and where the lights moved, at what time and from which visual perspective. This new epistemological orientation was consistent with that of the larger national public: *Cairo Today*'s video-screening of the lights at the church in Warraq served as the a priori grounds for interfaith reflection. Following this abstract form of collective perception, the interior status of visual subjects is irrelevant to the truths of holy presence made into the facts of appearance.

Second, mass visuality changed the ways that apparitions are imagined to appear and reappear, structuring the nature of their repetitions across space and time. The standardization of the Virgin's appearance resulted in a formal distinction between the apparition-image (e.g., lights at a church building) and its spatial-temporal context (e.g., sectarian layout in Warraq versus Arab-Israeli defeat in Zaytun). Repeatable and embeddable, the abstract status of the apparition-image enables the predictability of its re-instantiations. In these territorial imaginaries of lights, the image of church buildings is integral to reappearances as well as the anticipation of future reappearances. Churches, with their domes, steeples, and bell towers, all become enumerable sites of Marian appearances that take place "at a different church every year," to quote the Muslim taxi driver featured in this chapter's opening vignette. I also recall one Coptic student of the Evangelical seminary who joked to me in ʿAbbasiyya, as we walked past an Orthodox church and its neon silhouette of the Virgin *al-tagallī*, "Here in Egypt, the Virgin appears every year."

Both of these homogenizing effects of majoritarian visuality end up also serving as the conditions of sectarian dissent. In the next two sections, we turn to Muslim and Evangelical responses to the Marian apparitions in Warraq, paying attention to how clashing ideologies of communicative form constitute an identitarian terrain of verification and contest. As we will soon see, sectarian disputes over commonly observable signs led to charges of technological deception and mutual suspicion.

"MUSLIM" EYEWITNESSING

Despite how pivotal the Muslim majority is for the Coptic Church's sciences of verification, few Islamic leaders publicly commented on Warraq's apparitions on television programs or newspapers. While there were shaykhs who went on air to affirm the holy status of the Virgin Mary in the Islamic tradition, Muslims were largely imagined to be a silent superaddressee during interfaith debates around the apparitions. In an attempt to gain insight into one Islamic perspective among others, I consulted one imam of the Mosque of Sayyida Hafsa in Ard al-Golf, Heliopolis, for his opinion. Half-blind himself, Muhammad al-Rida offered his reasoning about the Marian apparitions: "First, the teaching of faith itself, first of all. Do [Christians] believe in Christ, peace be upon him, or not? If they believed in Christ, then what is the idea that the Virgin appeared or not? What is the idea? Every once in a while, they say that she appeared. Fine, she appeared. Nobody saw her, except them, so it's not a vision. It's something seen, but it should be that all people saw her—Muslim and non-Muslims, old and young." Following the shaykh, only Christians saw the Virgin in Warraq, and moreover, the very idea of apparitions is problematic in light of their belief in Christ. For the apparitions to qualify as a truly divinely-authored vision, they must have been seen by all, exceeding a "Christian" audience. This logic of a generalizable vision that "all people saw" is entirely compatible with the Coptic Church's ideal of mass visuality.

The point at which Shaykh Muhammad al-Rida and the Coptic Church depart from one another is on the question of whether or not "Muslims" saw the Virgin. Cherished in both the Christian and Islamic traditions, albeit with different biographies, the Virgin Mary is a saint with a robust visual presence in the Arab Middle East; for this reason, the Virgin is often vigorously invoked as a figure of interfaith harmony, particularly in contexts of escalating sectarianism. Yet, the fact of the Virgin's shared status among Christians and Muslims clearly falls short of securing Christian-Muslim unity in public theaters of collective perception. Whereas the Coptic Church asserts that numerous Muslims saw the Virgin in Warraq, the shaykh likely expresses the viewpoint of other Muslims who also believe that "nobody saw her, except them." What does it look like for "all people" to see her?

Beginning from the Zaytun apparitions of 1968, "Muslim guarantors" have played a major role in authenticating the mixed "Christian-Muslim" audience of the Virgin's spectators (Mayeur-Jaouen 2005; Keriakos 2012). Keeping with many scripts of modern mass apparitions in Egypt, the first eyewitnesses are usually Muslim locals near the church building. In Zaytun in 1968, for instance, the first eyewitnesses to spot a lady of light on the church's rooftop ledge were Muslim garage mechanics for the Egyptian Transportation Authority. "Lady, don't jump!" Faruq Muhammad 'Atwa reportedly cried out to her before notifying the church custodians. The Virgin's healing of his gangrenous finger, which 'Atwa used to point at the figure of light, was also reported to be Zaytun's first miracle.

At Warraq in 2009, the first eyewitnesses were the Muslim café owners and patrons who similarly called for church custodians when they caught sight of the frenetic lights vibrating in the vicinity. These first eyewitnesses, moreover, were ordinary Muslims, or to quote one priest's account, the "simple people" (al-busaṭā') of the garages and cafés (Father 'Abd al-Masih al-Basit 2010). Regarded as more trustworthy than religious leaders, Muslim witnesses of the working class are less inclined to devise what they see to meet their communal interest.

What makes a seer identifiably "Muslim"? In Warraq, local Muslim witnesses from the neighborhood gave their eyewitness accounts to the Coptic Church. Their names were enough to secure their identities as "Muslim." Broadcast for Coptic audiences, the television program *Pulse of the Church* (*Nabd al-Kanisa*) aired their reports on the Coptic Church's satellite channel Aghapy TV. The following include a sample of these reports:[12]

> I saw the Virgin at around 11:20 or 11:30 P.M. on top of the big tree and she was still small, she was going to and fro and at around 1:00 A.M., she appeared in full with a white and blue dress in front. (Hasan Muhammad)

> And I was crossing at around 12:30 A.M. and I looked, everyone had come from their houses, I was just rushing home. Then I saw a big light moving on top of the left of the dome and to the right for about two minutes or three minutes. (Muhammad Sayyid)

---

12. *Nabd al-Kanisa*, December 20, 2009, Aghapy TV; *Nabd al-Kanisa*, December 23, 2009, Aghapy TV. All translations are mine.

I was sitting on other side, across the church doing work on my car at around 11:30 P.M. and I found people running, and I said, "Hey! What's going on?" I thought there was a problem at the church, and I ran and I found a big light revolving around the church. (Ahmad Sa'id)

I came to that steeple [pointing], and I found doves flying, two doves and before that, one white dove. A white dove at 2:00 A.M. at night. It was flying toward the church and then came back again. (al-Hajja)

The following are excerpts from church texts distributed at the Church of the Virgin and Archangel Michael in Warraq ('Aziz 2012:35–55; Father 'Abd al-Masih al-Basit 2010:115–18):

We saw light coming out and we ran to the church and found the Virgin on top of the door beside the cross, then we saw doves, then the Virgin was walking between the two crosses and the domes. (al-Hajj Rashad al-'Arabi)

At around 1:00, in the middle of the night, the light gathered around the two steeples at the door of the church, and then the Virgin appeared in the middle of it, complete with white illumined clothing, and she started to move between the steeples and then moved up to the top of the dome of the church. (Sayyid Ahmad)

All these eyewitness accounts describe a figure moving against the backdrop of the church building. Many recount the approximate hour when they saw what was there. Some identify the observed figures as the Virgin or doves, others only identify what they see as light. Architectural features such as the steeples, domes, and crosses further ratify the location of appearance to be the church building.

To be counted among the witnesses, neither Christians nor Muslims were required to confess any belief in the Virgin or any kind of personal transformation after having seen the lights. More significantly for a majoritarian consensus on vision, those witnesses who report seeing lights at the church do not have to identify what they see as "the Virgin." This was made clear to me when I sought a more extended report from Warraq's first eyewitnesses at the café next to the Church of the Virgin and Archangel Michael. The café owner was easy to find, smoking water-pipes outside with other men seated in brightly colored plastic chairs. When I asked if the Virgin had come to the church, he threw up his hands in evasion, "I am no expert on religious things. I just know I saw a bright light and that's all." The patron sitting next to him added with a toothy grin, "It was a laser show! Do you know what lasers are?"

"Muslim" eyewitnessing minimally refers to Muslims who report seeing lights at the church, although without necessarily recognizing those lights to be of divine origin. In fact, as in the case of the café owner who withheld religious judgment or of his customer who alleged technological fabrication, Muslim witnesses can go so far as to deny the Church's identification of the lights with the Virgin. Whether in the form of dubiety or denial, these Muslim witnesses sustain the gap between the factually seen and visual recognition of the Virgin. In a sense, Shaykh Muhammad al-Rida and the Coptic Church are both right: "all people" see the lights, but "all people" do not see the Virgin. The fact that many Muslims thought that lasers were behind the scenes of appearance did little to depreciate the Church's conclusion that the Virgin had truly appeared to Christians and Muslims in Warraq.

PROTESTANTS PROTEST

Days after the Virgin appeared in Warraq, Pastor Sameh Maurice of the well-known Qasr al-Dubbara Evangelical Church in downtown Tahrir posted his congratulations to Orthodox believers on his church's website. In response, the Evangelical Synod of the Nile issued an official rebuke to Pastor Maurice for misrepresenting the Protestant position on holy images. Although Muslim disbelief in the apparitions was more widespread in terms of numbers, the Coptic Evangelical Church was more publicly vocal about what it perceived to be a straightforward deception. As some Orthodox priests confided to me, Protestants were the ones who caused trouble for them, much more so than Muslims.

One clear instance of public Protestant opposition to the Marian apparitions unfolded at the interfaith roundtable on the daily television show *Cairo Today*. After the Orthodox priest Father Salib discussed the Virgin's central place in Egypt and the Church's sciences of numerical verification, the program's hosts, Amr Adib and Mustafa Sidqi, pressed the Synod of the Nile's former secretary, Pastor Zakariyya, for his position. "Do you believe the apparition is true?" Avoiding a direct answer, he responded with an instructive elaboration of the Evangelical Church's teachings on manifestations:

> We distinguish apparitions according to two types. . . . There are apparitions: "divine" [*ilāhī*], when we read the Bible, we find the first apparition was that of an angel of the Lord to Hagar. [In all divine apparitions], there is a goal, and a reason for his coming, and the person who appears says who

he is and the person who sees is certain whom he has seen. . . . The second type is the "deceptive" [kādhiba], it says in the Bible that in the last days, there will be apparitions and prophets that will pretend to be Christ himself.[13]

Drawing on a scriptural precedent from Genesis, Zakariyya outlined the specific image of a person who acts as a divine messenger in perceptible form: to be truthfully seen, the Virgin, like the angel of the Lord, must verbally communicate who she is. The imagined Virgin must speak and identify herself through speech. If these mediating conditions are not met, the apparition is a false pretense, and as Zakariyya suggests in his eschatological reference, of possibly diabolical making. In brief, the Synod's position upheld the speaking angel, not the speechless apparition, as the legitimate prototype of divine revelation.

For some Protestant leaders, like Sameh Maurice of Qasr al-Dubbara Church, public recognition of Marian apparitions was one way to mend an Orthodox-Protestant sectarian past and promote a more ecumenical orientation. For others, like the Evangelical Synod's media chairman, Rifat Fikri, "no truths were worth compromising for the sake of Christian unity." To follow up on the Synod's rebuke of Maurice and how Protestants understood the apparitions, I met with Fikri a few weeks after Cairo Today's interfaith roundtable. In our interview, Fikri emphasized Reformed teachings on the primacy of scripture (al-kalima) over tradition (al-ṭaqs): "If tradition contradicts the Bible, I stand by the Bible; if tradition contradicts Christ, I stand by Christ. In the Bible, apparitions come with messages." Fikri also explained to me that true apparitions arrive not at midnight but during the daytime, as exemplified in the scriptural account of the apostle Paul's blinding encounter on the road to Damascus.

Historians of American and British missionaries in Egypt have shown how Protestant aversion to Orthodox image veneration and the intercession of saints may be traced back to nineteenth-century discourses of modernity (Sharkey 2008; Sedra 2011). Among Coptic Evangelicals, much of this continuing aversion stems from contending semiotic ideologies of communicating truths (Keane 2007). For Zakariyya and Fikri, the individual speaking subject as the locus of truth and identity serves as the model for angels, prophets, and saints to express their

13. Al-Qahira al-Yawm, December 23, 2009, al-Yawm Television Channel.

presence and gain recognition as holy persons. Without a verbal message of words, visual imagery alone is regarded to be an unreliable medium. Extending the question of proper materiality to judgments of truth, Coptic Protestants concluded that the apparitions were irrational phenomena and signs of backward belief. Equating belief in Marian apparitions to acts of "drinking sand to be healed," Fikri concluded that they were nothing more than "a superstition" (al-khurāfa) and the false attribution of agency to mere things. He further insinuated acts of deception linked to the irrationality of miracles and hearsay:

> Let me tell you about what happened when the Virgin came to Minya, maybe a few years ago. There were two Orthodox churches in the village of Qamha—a big one and a small one—and there was tension between the two, they competed with each other. Apparitions took place at the small church and people came from all over [from Alexandria, Cairo, and from everywhere] to visit with all their kids. They ate chips and sweets, bought gifts to take back home, gave donations. . . . They were making good business for the small church!

Reminiscent of old Protestant charges against the Catholic Church, Fikri resurrected the moral problem of clerical enterprise and profit associated with salvation and miracles by way of appearances. Relayed as a parable, Fikri's story conveyed the trademark dangers of economic gain at devotional sites. Following his logic of appearances, manufacturing falsehoods entails the immoral exchange of spiritual images for material gain.

Beyond the relatively small Protestant circles in Egypt, public critique levied against Marian apparitions included proponents of a modern rational divide between the material and spiritual realms. From their inception in Zaytun in 1968, mass apparitions raised questions about the nature of reality, and more specifically, how the miracle of the Virgin's appearance was related to the material realities of territorial loss. In his widely circulated Critique of Religious Thought (Naqd al-Fikr al-Dini, 2003 [1969]), the late Syrian Marxist philosopher Sadiq Jalal al-ʿAzm addressed these questions head-on in his assessment of the Zaytun apparitions as an imaginary illusion. Referring to the Arab national press's coverage of the Virgin as an attempt to divert attention away from military failure, he wrote that "the true miracle was the elimination of the effects of enmity." Al-ʿAzm further elaborated the Kantian limits of reason, characterizing the apparition's ruse as "'the crossing of the material world into spiritual world, and the transformation of the spiritual into the material" (al-ʿAzm 2003

[1969]:102).[14] What al-'Azm's critique placed into the analytic fore-front was the epistemological relationship between visual imagination and the territorial facts of warfare—what he saw to be a transgressive confusion between spiritual and material realities.

From Zaytun in 1968 to Warraq in 2009, allegations of technological fabrication moreover indicated widespread suspicion of human interference in spiritual affairs. In 1968, al-'Azm published his hypotheses that the Arab newspapers were responsible for the public hoax, pointing to significant possibilities of photographic manipulation and mass deception. In Abdel Messeeh's film *The Virgin, the Copts, and Me* (*La Vierge, les Coptes et moi,* 2011), a handful of his Muslim interviewees described Nasser's invention of the apparitions as a strategic method of uniting Christians and Muslims, in contradistinction to his Coptic interviewees who defended their holy truths. In 2009, Muslims and Protestants on the streets hinted at the use of laser technologies, including the first "Muslim eyewitnesses" at the café next to the church. Instead of the Egyptian state or national press, it was the Coptic Church that was imagined to be behind the technological forgery and public fakery.

Throughout all these allegations and negations, it was the image of church buildings that framed suspicions of artificial design. In Fikri's imaginary, it was two Orthodox churches in the village, one small and the other big, which set the imaginary stage for Marian apparitions and a commercial industry of competition. Returning to Warraq, it was the Church of the Virgin and Archangel Michael and its neighboring al-Huda Mosque which activated territorial imaginaries of church-building and minoritarian discrimination. It was within this context that charges of falsehood and technological fabrication presented conditions for developing new genres of church science following from its original sciences of verification.

"THE PROBLEM IS THE CHURCH": A SCIENCE OF DEFENSE

Ordinary Coptic believers in the Warraq apparitions were aware of the significant number of Muslims and Protestants who believed that the

---

14. Sadiq Jalal al-'Azm's critique echoes Kant's model of the "spirit world," as it is formulated in one of his earlier essays, "Dreams of a Spirit Seer" (1992 [1766]). Following the Kantian model, the "human soul" receives impressions of its "immaterial natures" but is "not conscious of them, provided that everything is in good order" (quoted in Andriopoulos 2011:45).

lights seen at the church amounted to nothing more than a laser light show in the sky. In addition to the university student who shared a taxi ride with me in this chapter's opening vignette, I encountered other Copts, from pregnant women chatting in their pajamas to youths surfing internet sites in their basements, who invoked principles of laser light science to debunk their claims. In contrast to the student who directly confronted her Muslim taxi driver, they usually confined circulation of what they knew about lasers and Marian apparitions to within the Coptic community.

Available in churches and bookstores, the slim tract *Apparitions of the Virgin in Egypt: Between Truth and False Allegations* (*Zuhurat al-'Adhra' fi Misr: Bayn al-Haqiqa wa-l-Iddi'a'at al-Kadhiba*, 2010) offers a brief introduction to laser technologies and basic scientific laws of emission and reception. Authored by Father 'Abd al-Masih al-Basit, or "The Simple Servant of Christ" (hereafter, 'Abd al-Masih), the book belongs to a pedagogical genre of Coptic Christian publications called "apologetic theology," or following its literal translation from Arabic, "a theological science of defense" (*'ilm al-lāhūt al-difā'*).[15] Number seventeen in a book series, it also joins a string of apologetic studies that other Coptic priests have written to defend Christianity against, for example, the claims of Dan Brown's *Da Vinci Code* (2003) or of Youssef Ziedan's *Azazeel* (2012; cf. Mahmood 2016). For those Copts who are less inclined to pick up a book to learn why the use of laser technologies was impossible at various churches, the book's lessons are also available as video-taped lectures complete with visual aids. Weeks after the Warraq apparitions, I saw 'Abd al-Masih on two television programs reviewing an abridged version of his proofs using laser science.

Widely reputed for his blunt humor and outspoken style, 'Abd al-Masih is a legendary personality in the Coptic Church. He was among the group of prominent Copts who were placed under monastery arrest along with Pope Shenouda in 1981, when Sadat suspected that they

15. The Coptic Church's contemporary industry of theological apologetics is a relatively new phenomenon. To be sure, Coptic theologians and philosophers have participated in interreligious performances of science, proof, and logic, most famously with their Jewish and Muslim counterparts in the medieval courts of various ruling caliphs. However, Coptic apologetic theology today is intended for popular audiences and develops its arguments based on modern historical reason and evidentiary science. Currently, Father 'Abd al-Masih al-Basit and Bishop Bishoi of Damietta are leading authors of Coptic apologetic print literature. The former host of "Truth Talk" (*al-Haqiqa*, Dream TV) Father Zakariyya Butrus is also regarded as a Coptic apologist notorious for his explicitly anti-Islamic teachings.

were building a separate Coptic nation at a time when sectarian violence was on the rise. After his release under Mubarak, 'Abd al-Masih
began to serve at the Church of Virgin in Musturud, a popular shrine
known for its holy water and a pilgrimage site regarded to be part of the
Holy Family's Flight (see chapter 2, "Redemption at the Edge").

Similar to Warraq, Musturud is a poorer district composed of industrial workers on the outskirts of Cairo, having experienced high levels of
Christian-Muslim tensions over the years. Known for attracting local
Muslims in search of demon exorcisms, the Church of the Virgin of
twelfth-century origin is also a target of suspicion in the neighborhood.
Meters in front of the church's metallic gates, a newly built small mosque
is planted at the edge of the main road hugging the Isma'iliyya Canal.

On Sunday afternoons after mass, 'Abd al-Masih can be found sitting at his desk, juggling multiple conversation strings with all his
parishioners coming in and out of his open office door. While chatting
about the apparitions with me, he managed to give advice about
employment, plan for future baptisms and wedding, and provide
updates on his wife, his children, and his daily battle with diabetes. In
between his dialogues with others, 'Abd al-Masih kept me in his
peripheral view and delivered scandalous declarations to me, such as:
"Islam is a religion of lies [dīn al-kidhb]" and "Muslims are deniers
of truth [mutanakkirīn]." When I later learned that he had received
hate mail for his sermons and writings, I was not so surprised, as
I recalled the offhand style with which he spoke against Islam in his
open office.

In his defense of Marian apparitions, it was clear that "Muslim"
allegations were prominent in 'Abd al-Masih's imagination. After finishing up with his office hours, he reviewed the visual scene of Marian
apparitions in more detail with me. Slowly with rhetorical emphasis, he
directed my attention to local tensions between the church and the
mosque.

> The problem is the church. If the Virgin had come to the mosque, then there
> wouldn't have been any problem. Why do Muslims say that she was pro-
> duced from lasers? Because of what? Because the Virgin appeared at the
> church, and not at the mosque. What did this mean then?
>
> It means that Christianity is right [ṣaḥīḥ] and Islam is wrong [ghalaṭ]. So
> what are Muslims going to say? They are going to say that the apparitions
> are false and they will deny them. . . . They say "lasers," but they don't
> know anything about lasers, so I decided to show them how lasers really
> work.

Following this explanation, it is Warraq's topography of "church versus mosque" that sectarianizes the reception of the Marian apparitions. The visual imaginary of "church versus mosque" stands in for an inter-communal landscape of belonging and division. Consequently, the sectarian divide of "Christianity versus Islam" is isomorphic with a mutually exclusive terrain of religious identity, in which "Muslims" are attached to "Islam" and "Islam" abstractly represents a religion of "domination" or "lies." "Mosque," "Muslim," and "Islam" are all sutured together into generic associations of religious identity, leading to 'Abd al-Masih's conclusion that Muslims must falsify the apparitions if they appear at the church in order to preserve the status of Islam. What 'Abd al-Masih's logic demonstrates is that there can be no imagined church building without the imagined sectarian horizons of "church versus mosque," "Christianity versus Islam," "right versus wrong."

'Abd al-Masih understood his appeal to science, and not to religion, to be a strategy for defending Christianity's truths on the grounds of common perception. Looking out at the church courtyard from his open office door, 'Abd al-Masih pointed to an elderly woman seated on a knobby chair. "You see that old lady sitting over there? I wanted to show that the Virgin was 3-D, exactly like that lady." He explained how he had recruited Coptic physicists in Australia and North America to teach him about laser light science, and more specifically, the restrictions of laser technologies for generating three-dimensional images.

In the final section of *Apparitions of the Virgin in Egypt,* 'Abd al-Masih introduces ten visual exercises or techniques for disproving claims of laser usage. Each exercise exposes a "problem" with the idea of lasers being used at the apparition-site, that is, the church. As hypothetical scenarios to be visualized, each exercise begins with lasers at the site of an imagined church, and then goes on to negate the possibility of laser usage. The negation occurs through contrapositive logic ($X \rightarrow Y$; $\neg Y \rightarrow \neg X$): "If there had been a laser, then Y would have happened; Y did not happen, so there had been no laser." The following sample are problem numbers one, two, seven, and eight, out of a total of ten:

1. If the light had originated from a laser, the apparition would have been so big that it would have covered the entire church. This is due to the law of light: the farther the source of light is from its site of reception, the bigger is the image that it creates.

المشكلة الثانية

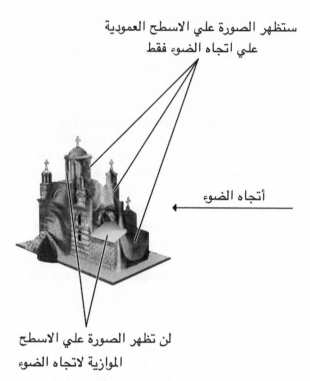

ستظهر الصورة علي الاسطح العمودية
علي اتجاه الضوء فقط

أتجاه الضوء

لن تظهر الصورة علي الاسطح
الموازية لاتجاه الضوء

FIGURE 21. "The Second Problem." A visual exercise for falsifying allegations of laser usage at apparition sites. Image re-created by Dale Mertes.

2. If there had been an external source of light, there also would have been a surface for receiving it. And the apparition in its entirety would not have been received, but only parts of it, not equidistantly and in the direction of the light alone [figure 21].

7. If there had been a screen, it would have been a "dynamic" one which moved from all angles to capture the movement of the Virgin and doves [figure 22].

8. If there had been a screen, one would have been only able to see the image from one side of the church, not all sides of it.

المشكلة السابعة

كيف تتحرك العذراء في الهواء و كيف يطير الحمام في الهواء
و كيف تقترب الاشكال و تبتعد عن الناس؟

سنحتاج اذا الي شاشة ديناميكية
تتحرك في كل اتجاه ممكن
حتى تستقبل الاشعة !!!

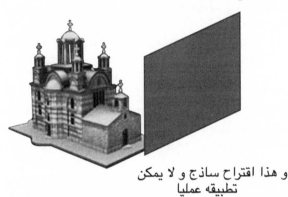

و هذا اقتراح ساذج و لا يمكن
تطبيقه عمليا

FIGURE 22. "The Seventh Problem." A visual exercise for falsifying allegations of laser usage at apparition sites. Image re-created by Dale Mertes.

Through each of these mental exercises, Copts are trained to visualize the scene of allegations and counterallegations. To reveal in stages of imagining that allegations of laser usage are lies, they recall images of the church building over and over again. What effectively recurs is the territorial imagining and reimagining of churches, across visual acts of negation and de-negation. Engaged in tactics of defense, they falsify laser usage in order to falsify imagined attacks on their churches. In principle, these exercises of defense are applicable to the scene and site of all churches where the Virgin appeared.

As a print publication susceptible to circulation outside the Coptic community, 'Abd al-Masih's book does not mention "Muslim denials" or mosques on the horizon. Instead, as in previous church studies of Marian apparitions, it opens with an emphasis on the shared holy status of the Virgin between the Islamic and Christian traditions, drawing on verses from the Qur'an and the Bible. In addition, it continues the majoritarian principle that "Muslim" eyewitnessing is an essential ingredient of verifying the truths of Marian apparitions.

Yet as 'Abd al-Masih's sciences demonstrate, it is clear that shared veneration of the Virgin in Islam and Christianity is insufficient for bridging the sectarian divide. Rather, it is the epistemological framework of common perception that structures the public reception of the Virgin's image, and more significantly, the logics of her differential reception. Here, it is important to recognize that there is no logical contradiction between "Muslim eyewitnessing" and "Muslim denial," according to the Coptic Church's sciences of appearance. The gap between what is reportedly seen in the outer objective world (i.e., "lights at the church") and what is believed in the inner subjective realm (i.e., "it is a laser show") characterizes "Muslim"-specific acts of seeing. This gap preserves the structure of religious difference, enabling a slippage from a visual imaginary of national unity in Zaytun to one of sectarian enmity in Warraq, Musturud, and elsewhere. Put more succinctly, sectarian difference is internal to a modern epistemology of mass apparitions and mixed visuality.

Perhaps more than the apparition's image itself, the image of the church building and the minoritarian imaginary of churches dominated by mosques are what Marian apparitions in Egypt have left behind. Strikingly, the Virgin and her iconic images of light are absent from 'Abd al-Masih's exercises of upholding the divine origins of apparitions. What is foregrounded, rather, is the imagined status of churches, the image of churches under attack through "Muslim" allegations of technological deception. As I previously argued, the mass standardized, abstract rubric of the Virgin *al-tagallī* rendered the apparition re-iterable and re-embeddable across contexts. The envisioned scene of the church building, made into an abstract, generalizable image, is flattened into receiving surfaces of light. The church-image features as a core element in material terrains of Christian-Muslim antagonism, reproduced through print media and ritual exercises of theological apologetics across Egypt's local neighborhoods from Aswan to Alexandria. Set on the imaginary register of "defense," mass apparitions of the Virgin bind churches, Christianity, and Copts together into one sectarian image of territorial presence, thereby shaping the deeply felt attachments of Copts to their churches.

HEIGHTS OF MEMORY

This chapter so far has examined how Marian apparitions shape national and sectarian imaginaries of Christian-Muslim difference, emerging out of territorial contexts in which state borders and neighborhood landscapes were undergoing significant changes. To understand the forms of knowledge that religious institutions have produced about apparitions, I have paid particular attention to priests, pastors, and shaykhs and their epistemological frameworks for understanding holy appearances and mass visuality. Now, I end on an example of visualizing the Virgin that does not quite assimilate into the hegemonic formulations of what it is like for Christians and Muslims to see her together. By hinting at alternative contours of appearance and collective witness, outliers, however rare, are also instructive.

During a visit one year after the apparitions, I discovered the Church of the Virgin and Archangel Michael in Warraq in an unkempt state of affairs. Hemmed in with burlap sacks of concrete, one of its dilapidated steeples was under repair. Next to the church's main entrance, a plot of scraps, empty bottles, and plastic bags sat in a stinking heap of trash. Despite its newly conferred status as a holy site where the Virgin had last appeared in Egypt, the church was also clearly vulnerable to the telltale signs of urban neglect and disrepair.

Wandering the church's halls that afternoon, I studied the cloth banners that captured the Warraq apparitions, their bursts of light and phosphorescent doves around the church's domes. Strolling past me, women from the neighborhood would make small talk with me about their relatives living in America. Office staff sitting in the foyer mentioned the Chinese pilgrims who came to the church some weeks ago. For the most part, I was by myself, but every so often, in between taking notes and photos, I enjoyed a conversation or two with Copts who wished to share what they knew about the Virgin and her appearance last December.

At one point, a construction worker in a paint-splattered jumpsuit caught sight of me from outside the church's entrance and approached me in the halls. Mistaking me for a journalist, Ahmad introduced himself as a local worker who had seen the Virgin last year amid the street crowds which had gathered at the church. After I clarified that I was not a journalist but a researcher, Ahmad offered his eyewitness testimony for my audio recording:

I heard some time ago—I don't follow this—but I heard that sixty years ago in Zaytun, the Virgin appeared. Meaning that after forty years it will have been a century, praise and peace be upon the Prophet Muhammad! . . .
I will describe her form [in Warraq]. She was the expression—forget all that computer and telephone stuff, forget all of that talk! She came from a cloud. Its color was goldish, very close to brown, gold very close to brown, and the cloud came up to her neck. And you found her hair a green color. That's it. There was no, no veil like you always see when they take pictures of her with the head-covering. Her hair was green and her appearance was marvelous, marvelous, marvelous!
My friends yelled, beeping their horns—teet! teet! teet! "The road is blocked! The road is blocked!" I told them, "By God I will not leave this place!" And after, one Christian girl told me, "Take care, don't think that just any person can see her. Your heart must be pure [ṭāhir]." Meaning that three-quarters of the people standing there, maybe they are unclean in their hearts [mudannisīn fī qulūbihum]. She said, "Maybe your heart is pure so our Lord showed you—a lot of us are standing here, a lot of us and not seeing anything."

While Ahmad delivered his testimony in a long-winded ramble, a group of Coptic men and women lingered nearby and eavesdropped on our conversation. Later, I would learn that they had wanted to make sure their new foreigner guest was not being harassed in the church's halls.

With a disheveled look and style, Ahmad was a Muslim who had come inside the space of the church to offer his impression of the Virgin. Rather than the Virgin al-tagallī, or the bluish-white lights reminiscent of Roman Catholic and royalist French origins, Ahmad offered his image of a goldish-green Virgin coming out of a cloud in the sky. He also told me to disregard the photos and video clips I had seen so far, all depictions that happened to visually dominate our surroundings.

After detailing what he had seen, Ahmad continued with an explanation of how he had sought to build a commemorative monument to honor the Virgin of Warraq. Pointing to the stinking trash heap, he described his attempt to go to the owner of the desolate plot of land next to the church and convince him to give him permission to build there:

And after all this, [the two steeples] will become a landmark among landmarks [ma'lam min al-ma'ālim] after time. You will die, and I will die, and all of us will die, and this landmark among landmarks will become a blessing to people who pass by, who will come through the place and will say, "This is where the Virgin appeared."
[The owner] told me, "I'm sorry, but it's enough that our parents gave it to the church." I told him, "Fine, that's no problem." Believe me, I tried.

Because it's important to the extent that you believe—you came here to see if the Virgin appeared, right? Or am I wrong? So does it make sense that you come in and you find this picture of trash? Does it?!

So I told this owner and he didn't want to. If I were a Christian and God gave me this, I swear I would buy it, and if I bought it, I would make a fountain so that it would be a landmark among landmarks—for all time!

Ahmad's eyewitness account of the Virgin clearly departed from the Coptic Church's collection of Christian and Muslim accounts which affirmed approximate images of the Virgin: lights, flying doves, steeples, bluish-white figure. And yet, his impassioned description earned the approval of a "Christian girl," who referred to his "pure heart," and of our Christian eavesdroppers as well. Some minutes after Ahmad had left the church, the men and women in the hallway urged me to include his testimony in my study, one of them going so far as to overlook the straightforward contradiction between the Church's sciences and his vision, "He was wrong . . . but he saw the Virgin!"

Perhaps most strikingly of all, Ahmad sought to build a shrine to venerate the Marian apparitions next to the church building, a "landmark among landmarks—for all time!" Imagining himself to be a "Christian," with the potential to buy from a Christian owner and build next to a Christian place of worship, he was not operating within dominant local horizons of church and mosque competition. Building "a landmark among landmarks" has always been the ultimately desirable endpoint of Marian apparitions in Egypt. The nature of Marian apparitions, however, has also changed as a historical and cultural byproduct of different arrangements of visionary experience and imaginary contexts of belonging. It is Ahmad's desire to remember another version of the Virgin that sheds light on other territorial imaginaries that exist on the margins of nationalism and sectarianism.

CHAPTER 4

Crossovers and Conversions

Whenever some apparition occurs, do not collapse in terror,
but whatever it may be, ask first, bravely, "Who are you and
where do you come from?"

Saint Athanasius, *The Life of Antony*

The only reason God placed sleep in the animate world was
so that everyone might witness the Presence of Imagination
and know that there is another world similar to the sensory
world.

Ibn al-ʿArabi, *The Meccan Illuminations*

SUMMONING ANGELS AND JINN

Packed with perfumes, shampoo, and nail polish, the shelves of Musʿad
ʿAziz's store cater to customers hunting for cosmetic aids and maybe a
little more. In the dust and bustle of Shubra al-Hafziyya, Musʿad's store
sits beneath hanging laundry and between shops for recycled furniture
and car parts. Shubra al-Hafziyya is a subsection of Shubra, one of
Cairo's mixed neighborhoods, known for its high concentration of
Christian families. Within a few blocks of the store, there is a Coptic
church around the corner, and at the time I was visiting, there was a
Muslim Brotherhood branch office a bit further down along the street.

Originally from Qusiyya, a village in Asyut, Musʿad has been living
in Shubra for over forty years with his wife and four children, now

FIGURE 23. Abba Karas the Anchorite, with Jesus, on his deathbed. They are
surrounded by (from left to right): David the Prophet, the seven archangels Sedakiel,
Gabriel, Ananiel, Michael, Suriel, Raphael, Sarathiel, along with Abba Bimwa (left
corner) and Abba Karas's guardian angel (right corner).

fully-grown. By the time I met him in January 2013, he was in his mid-seventies, having established his reputation as the local expert in what some refer to as "magic" (*al-siḥr*) and others as "sciences" (*al-ʿulūm*). On the early evening when I was visiting, Musʿad was attending to a young woman covered with a bright blue and green headscarf. She was consulting Musʿad to know if her latest suitor was serious about following through with marriage.

Tall and bald, with glittering blue eyes and a toothless grin, he handed her a piece of paper with the names of seven angels penned in large, clear handwritten letters. Then, he slowly enunciated the names and recited the formula for invoking them:

> *Taghuriyāʾil. Zinyāʾil. Dahanṭār. Rubyāl. Maḥsūn.*
> Truly, I rely on you, *al-Sayyid Tuwāʾil*
> And truly, *al-Sayyid Mitīṣṭrūn al-Sibʾut.*[1]

Musʿad then instructed the young woman that she must summon the seven angels to appear only at her bedside, after bathing and before falling asleep. Once they appeared to her, she could ask them for details and advice about her suitor. The young woman proceeded to read the seven names aloud for practice, faltering and ending each cycle tongue-tied. "This is in Arabic, my girl!" Musʿad lightly rebuked her. Laughing nervously in reply, she eyed the metal racks of hosiery. Before leaving the store, she finished their exchange by purchasing a stock nude color.

Once she was gone, Musʿad began offering me his full attention and welcome. His cousins had phoned earlier to tell him that I was coming by his store that evening. Earlier that winter, my friend in New York had begun experiencing a series of nightmares and night terrors. After learning of my concern for my friend, Musʿad's cousins suggested I visit Musʿad in Shubra for spiritual help. Expecting a pious intercessor, or some kind of "holy man," I quickly learned that his specialty lay in quite a different realm of knowledge and mediation. Initially confused by his previous dialogue with the young woman, I began to recognize that Musʿad's method was something I had not yet encountered when

---

1. This incantation formula summons the names of relatively obscure angels. The title *al-Sayyid* seems to suggest that these angels hail from the Islamic tradition. In the Coptic Orthodox tradition, the most prominent four archangels are Gabriel, Michael, Raphael, and Suriel (Timbie 2010), and the other three are Sedakiel, Ananiel, Sarathiel. Departing from the rules of transliteration applied in the rest of the book, I retain here the diacritics of my transcriptions, in hopes this might aid future scholarship on angelology in Christianity and Islam.

he requested the names of my friend and my friend's mother. Unlike many other Copts who offer prayers or saintly objects to take home to the ill, Mus'ad used the letters of their names to calculate which Psalms number to pray aloud, and which number of repetitions of prayer. Through these numerological techniques, he worked to cure my friend of his demons and their apparitions.

Mus'ad further explained that his techniques belonged to "science" (al-'ilm) and not to "religion" (al-dīn). When I asked him where he had learned them, Mus'ad pulled out a tattered loose-leaf pamphlet from behind his counter. With his wood-framed portraits of Popes Kyrillos and Shenouda behind him, he proceeded to list and elaborate on five categories of his spiritual sciences: (1) ḥarf (letters); (2) falak (astronomy); (3) raml (sand); (4) taḥḍīr al-arwāḥ (incantation of spirits); (5) siḥr (magic). Beginning in the 1950s, when he was a teenager, Mus'ad made a hobby of experimenting with the spiritual sciences after stumbling on some reference manuals in Asyut like the one he had showed me. Later on, as a university student of trade in Alexandria, he fell in love with one female jinn who regularly appeared to him at night. During his affair with her in the 1960s, he also had the opportunity to meet Pope Kyrillos at the Patriarchate Cathedral of St. Mark. As he described his encounter with Kyrillos to me, in a remarkable show of spiritual clairvoyance (al-shaffāfiyya), the Pope had refused to shake his hand. "I was very, very sad. He knew I was dealing with jinn and he didn't want to greet me," Mus'ad recognized with hindsight.

Every once in a while throughout our discussion, his neighbors wafted in and out of the store with interjections and requests. The shop owner next door overheard us while pouring some boiling water from the rattling kettle buried in one of Mus'ad's cabinets. "He is going to hell!" he solemnly warned me, wagging his figure at Mus'ad's face. Mus'ad grinned in reply. Some minutes later, a boy about eight to nine years old popped in and requested gray contact lenses for his older sister. Taking the five pounds from him, Mus'ad asked in a playful tone, "You gonna be Salafi?!" Shyly shaking his head and suppressing a laugh, the boy skipped off with the lenses in his clutches.

Mus'ad's humorous reference to the Salafis in the neighborhood was somewhat timely. At that moment when I was visiting in 2013, President Mohamed Morsi and the Freedom and Justice Party had been in elected power for a half-year. What surprised many Egyptians was the success of the Brotherhood's rival the Nur Party in the elections, with newly politicized Salafis opposing the inclusion of non-Muslims in positions of government leadership. Like most other Copts, Mus'ad objected to the rise of Salafism in Egypt. However, unlike most other Copts, his stance toward the Brotherhood was more ambiguous. In Mus'ad's intimate circle of family and friends, there was Ashraf, his eldest son's best friend from childhood. An active member of the local Brotherhood branch, Ashraf also made an appearance that evening in Mus'ad's store. Slinging his arm around Mus'ad's neck, Ashraf announced proudly in a bold voice to me and others in the store, "This man is my father. He raised me." There was no doubt that Ashraf knew about Mus'ad's practice of divination, and despite this, he publicly claimed him as one of his most respected kin.

In addition to the Salafists and the Muslim Brotherhood, the Coptic Church and al-Azhar regard magic and other spiritual sciences as a heretical departure from orthodox teachings of religion. Moreover, Egyptian state law is clear that any semblance of chicanery (al-sha'wadha) for monetary gain makes enough grounds for arrest. Yet, Mus'ad was making no attempt at hiding his side-practice, and enough people openly consulted him for solutions to their life problems.

As he walked me to the Coptic church a couple corners away from his store, past the fleet of trees and cars, I asked Mus'ad if the priest knew about his spiritual business.

> Father is not pleased that I am doing this, because I am working as a magician and I am using Satan and not God. He told me, "Shame on you. If you do it again, I will be angry with you. If you have a problem with something, you are supposed to solve it with prayer and God will take care of your problem. You are not supposed to work with Satan and angels, your relationship is between you and God." So this is a transgression when it comes to religion. I consider myself a transgressor, I consider this a mistake. Satan tempts people and deceives me. I'm supposed to be committed to religion and the church prohibits this.

And he added a plea for my understanding: "But I don't use these sciences to oppose people."

CROSSOVERS AND CONVERSIONS

Despite the Coptic Church's attempts to prohibit them, Copts like Mus'ad who engage worlds of magic, jinn curings, and angelic invocations attest to more heterodox spaces of communicative overlap between Christians and Muslims in Egypt today. Outside the institutionally sanctioned landscape of churches and mosques, an array of marginalized practices takes place in homes, stores, clinics, markets, and bazaars. Widely regarded by Copts and Muslims to be "transgressions" (*al-mukhālafāt*) and "superstitions" (*al-khurāfāt*), such practices raise questions about the nature of religious authority and tradition, as well as the deep histories of clandestine expertise and mediation that escape their disciplinary purview. Musʿad's ambivalence about his magical arts reflected his personal bind between his "sciences" that he uses to help people, and his "religion" which deems his version of help to be sinful temptation. Aside from the Coptic Church, Musʿad was also most likely negotiating the moral value of his work against the growing tides of Salafist Islam and its prohibition of spiritual intercession, not only of jinn and angels but also of saints, shaykhs, and healers more broadly.

This chapter examines the fragmented and open nature of religious traditions, paying attention to the ways in which the boundaries of Christianity and Islam are defined and elaborated in relation to each other. From the standpoint of modern reformists and their correlates in the Coptic Church and al-Azhar, Musʿad is squarely located on the heretical peripheries of both traditions. From another angle, however, he is precisely straddled between Christian and Islamic traditions of knowledge and embodied experience at their more unsettled, dubious margins. Learning from old pamphlets of the spiritual sciences, Musʿad prescribes the names of extremely obscure angels (and likely of Islamic origin) to a Muslim customer, and brings his love affair with a female jinn into the institutionally authoritative presence of Pope Kyrillos at the Patriarchate. He is a communicative vehicle of spirit-worlds between Christians and Muslims.

Rather than regarding Musʿad's practices to be outside orthodoxy and its doctrinally prescribed norms, I draw here on a more distributed and diffuse notion of tradition and authority. Composed of embodied practices of mediation, discursive reason, and moral judgment, religious traditions derive authority in their everyday forms of expression, activity, and effects. Traditions, in their aspiration for coherence, are creative and subject to transformation. To quote the anthropologist Talal Asad, "in principle tradition can accommodate rupture, recuperation, reorientation and splitting—as well as continuity" (Asad 2015:169). Seen in this light, Musʿad's practices of numerology and dealing with jinn may be understood as experimenting with the limits of the Christian and Islamic traditions, rather than resisting or subverting them (Doostdar 2018). Drawing on the untidy fragments of traditions, Musʿad and his clientele participate in an open-ended inquiry of what spiritual terms and practices can be shared, circulated, and exchanged among Christians and Muslims. They interact in the interstitial spaces between orthodoxies often taken to be separate and distinct.

In what follows, I look at the crossovers and conversions that ensue from horizontal nodes of overlap, particularly in mixed settings of Christian-Muslim interaction. By "crossovers," I refer to practices of traversing boundaries and stretching the limits of various traditions of knowledge and mediation (as Mus'ad does). Crossovers include movement across the boundaries not only of Christianity and Islam, but also of "religion" and "science" as well as of "popular" and "elite." By "conversions," I refer to a person's reorientation to new horizons of moral imagination, often catalyzed by an experience of divine revelation. In this sense, a conversion may be considered a subcategory of crossover to the extent that a Christian's alignment with new Islamic figures and media (or vice versa) involves a passage from the ends of one tradition to another.

Crossovers often occur in settings where Christians and Muslims consult specialists for cures, personal messages, and solutions. On the more institutionally sanctioned front, there are select priests and shaykhs who communicate with otherworldly presences such as prophets, demons, and saints. Exchanges with these spiritual intercessors may take place openly in churches, mosques, and shrines. In comparison, across more subterranean locales such as stores, clinics, and homes, there are the holy men of the villages, Qur'anic healers, jinn curers, seers, and magicians who exercise expertise for their clientele. When any such spiritual specialist is found to earn monetary profit, he or she is potentially subject to being arrested on charges of public deception and trickery—in sum, "false knowledge." At the heart of the modern state's intervention is a moral distinction between legitimate and illegitimate religious authority, the latter associated with the popular underclasses and irrational superstition. Following my argument concerning religious traditions and the internal conditions of extending their boundaries, it is crucial to recognize that this distinction is more a reflection of an ideological evaluation of what "religion" should or should not be, than it is an accurate approximation of what a religious tradition actually entails in modern societies. As anthropologists of Islam have persuasively argued, dichotomies between "Salafism" and "Qur'anic healing" (Vinea 2015), "reason" and "irrational superstition" (Mittermaier 2011), "popular" and "scriptural" authority (Spadola 2009), are misleading inasmuch that healers, dreamers, and curers craft their practices and sensibilities in relation to contemporary forms of reason, hermeneutics, and textuality. Various tiers of religious and spiritual mediation, in other words, do not occupy spheres of categorical distinction, but emerge instead out of the same modernizing elements of knowledge and communication.

Crossovers between religious traditions (e.g., Christianity and Islam) therefore also intersect with crossovers between institutionally separated disciplines of knowledge—namely that of "religion" and "science." At the same time that he is chastised for his heterodox departure from religion, Mus'ad expressly defended his techniques as "scientific" in nature. As much classic anthropological work on Islam in North Africa clearly demonstrates, the work of jinn curers, seers, exorcists, and trance specialists is regarded as paradigmatic of the "occult sciences" (*'ulūm al-gharība*) or the "science of spirituality" (*'ulūm al-rūḥāniyya*) (Westermarck 1968 [1926]; Geertz 1968; Crapanzano 1980; Pandolfo 1997; el-Aswad 2002). Throughout the Mediterranean in rural and insular Greece, anthropologists have also examined demonology and divination practices such as "the evil eye" in relation to standard Orthodox Christian ideas of the devil (Stewart 1991; Seremetakis 1991, 2009). Venturing further into their ancient and medieval roots, we might also surmise that such geographically proximate, Christian and Islamic worlds of occult science flourished not so much in parallel, but in historically contiguous relationship to each other (Magdalino and Mavroudi 2006). Scholars of ancient Egypt, in fact, have argued that early Christianization was a culturally "syncretic" or "hybrid" process of combining ancient Egyptian pagan magic with new ideas of holiness and sanctity (Brakke 2011; van der Vliet 2014; Frankfurter 2017). My point here can be distilled into a simple claim: both the Christian and Islamic traditions have established the core and peripheries of "religion" in negotiation with the far-reaching activity of the "spiritual sciences." Consequently, although Mus'ad's expertise with jinn may be safely categorized as "Islamic" occult science, it is also highly probable that many of his techniques are owed to ancient epistemologies of Egyptian, Greco-Roman, Persian, or Byzantine influence that have also made their way into Coptic Christian techniques of exorcism and spiritual healing. Situated on the boundary between "religion" and "science," Mus'ad therefore bridges the overlapping edges of Christianity and Islam.

Conversions are a particular type of crossover movement toward a religious tradition, following the classic connotation of a "conversion" to be a "turn" or "reorientation" (James 1982 [1902]); Hefner 1993; Buckser and Glazier 2003). To be sure, the term "conversion" often implies a relatively durable change in one's religious identity (legal or confessional), or at the least, a transformation in one's personal commitment to a set of beliefs and practices. By expanding the meaning of conversion to more minor acts of spiritual and moral alignment, I do not mean to discount these interpretations; rather, I seek to include the fair number of Christians and Muslims in Egypt who adopt beliefs and practices outside their traditions, in fragmented measure and to varying degrees of self-consciousness. Moreover, there are those individuals who do so covertly, still others more openly, and many without significant consequences for one's personal identity or relationships to family members. In such cases, these partial acts of conversion are not acts of radical "cultural change" which signal a moral repudiation of old structures of meaning toward the adoption of new ones (Robbins 2004a; cf. Sahlins 1976). For example, religious conversions from Islam to Christianity are not of the same order as, say, conversions from Confucian ancestral veneration or Yucatec Mayan shamanism to Christianity. This difference is largely due, I would argue, to the declared kinship between Christianity and Islam as traditions that are at once distinct and ambivalently folded into one another.

As is widely rehearsed in the Muslim world, the Islamic tradition specially recognizes Jews and Christians as "People of the Book" (*ahl al-kitāb*), acknowledging a degree of inclusive continuity among the monotheistic faiths. This inclusion proceeds in one direction only and with qualifications, with the Torah and the Gospels valued as discursive forerunners to the Qur'an, the endpoint of scriptural revelation. Features held in common between the Christian and Islamic traditions speak, not only to social histories of their interactions, but also to the fragmentary overlaps internal to the traditions of divine revelation themselves. Aside from holy figures such as the Virgin, Jesus, Aaron, Moses, John the Baptist, and many more, Christians and Muslims believe in the revealed existence of Satan and the angels (with differing conceptions of their cosmological origins and moral status). There are many Copts who fear the work of jinn, and fewer, like Musʿad, who partake in intimate, at times dangerous, friendships with them as Muslims from Morocco to Pakistan also do (Crapanzano 1980; Khan 2006).[2] In addition to a common cast of figures, Christians and Muslims also recognize similar

2. According to Islamic teachings, jinn are created, intelligent beings made of vapor or flame who are capable of appearing under different forms. Their relation to Satan and demons is not clear. Although Church teachings reject the existence of jinn, there are some Copts in practice who interact with them as if they were "angels" or "demons" in Christianity. For more, see "Djinn," *Encyclopedia of Islam*, 2nd ed., P. Bearman, Th. Bianquis, C.E.Bosworth, E. van Donzel, W.P. Heinrichs, eds., Brill Online Reference Works.

practices of communication that authorize acts of otherworldly revelation, messengership, and prophecy. At the heart of each tradition of scriptural revelation, for instance, there are visionary experiences of light, as well as other sensory perceptions of holy appearance.

It is perhaps unsurprising, then, that Christian and Islamic conversions are often spurred by visionary encounters with holy appearances. Following the individual narratives detailed in this chapter, such encounters are experienced as revelations, resulting in a person's spiritual reorientation to new moral horizons. Visions reveal unknown saints and prophets, as well as relay personal messages for the aim of self-transformation. So far, I have been referring to crossovers and conversions between the boundaries of the Christian and Islamic traditions, without problematizing the vast variety internal to each of them. It is worth reemphasizing that they are not monolithic, contained wholes, and that differences internal to a tradition can be greater than those across traditions, particularly on the monotheistic problem of intercession. For instance, the Coptic Orthodox pantheon of saints may be more unfamiliar to a Coptic Protestant than to a Sufi Muslim ensconced in the world of saints' festivals and shrines. Apart from the teachings and practices of religion, moreover, there are those Christian and Muslim believers who are not piously devout, and for whom personal revelations are experienced as divine signs toward spiritual and moral transformation in the broadest sense.

To be clear, crossovers and conversions are not representative of the majority of Christian-Muslim interactions. As I have mentioned throughout this book, it is more often than not the regulated separation and insulation of Copts and Coptic Christianity that has limited the exchange of religious practices between Christians and Muslims in Egypt today. Nonetheless, this chapter draws attention to the apparitional experiences which attest to those fragments and strands of religious life at the margins of state-sanctioned institutions of communal belonging. In doing so, I hope to shed light on the ways in which individual, personal experiences of interacting with otherworldly presences exhibit movements within and between traditions that resist easy assimilation into contemporary logics of religious identity and difference.

VISIONS, MESSAGES, MIRACLES

What is at stake in the visual nature of a holy appearance? How do various forms and practices of visuality enable crossovers and conversions between Christians and Muslims? At the end of the previous chapter on collective apparitions, we finished with Ahmad and his idiosyncratic vision of the Virgin as a goldish-green figure, at odds with the bluish-white figure reported by the Coptic Church's witnesses. Ahmad does not see the same way as other individuals do. Furthermore, his personal reply to the apparition's message differed from both the state-sanctioned message of national unity and the minoritarian sign of defending church buildings. On his own, Ahmad alternatively wished to build a monument to the Virgin out of the trash heaps next to the church in Warraq.

Individual apparitions frequently communicate messages and miracles on a personal basis. In keeping with the scriptural orthodoxies of Christianity and Islam, visual encounters with saints, prophets, and angels serve as vehicles of revelation and prophecy. Additionally, in everyday practice, ordinary people encounter apparitions, receiving them as signs of comfort or commands to repentance and conversion. Such encounters are not marginal, outlier practices, but rather common and central to the religious experiences of many Christians and Muslims in Egypt.

Here, it is useful to point out strikingly instructive overlaps between Coptic and Islamic grammars of visuality. For both Christians and Muslims, apparitions may take material, perceptual form through dreams and waking visions, troubling the dichotomy between "inner" and "outer" vision that defines realist epistemologies of visual objectivism. In her richly detailed account of Sufi dreaming practices in Egypt, anthropologist Amira Mittermaier provides a helpful lexicon of types of vision (Mittermaier 2011:84–111). Copts, like Muslims, also use the Egyptian colloquial *shaff/yashuff* ("to see") for both physical and spiritual sight, and draw on the metaphor of visions as "visitations" (*al-ziyārāt*) through expressions such as "he came to me" (*gā'-lī*) or "she visited me" (*zāritnī*). For both Copts and Muslims, holy appearances are movements originating from the beyond, with the domain of sleep offering a specially designated bridge or "threshold" for anyone to experience revelations through dreams (Pandolfo 1997). Differences in Coptic and Islamic taxonomies of apparitional experiences are also worthy of mention. Whereas Muslims use the term "dream" (*al-ḥulm*) and "dream-vision" (*al-ru'yā*) to refer to visual experiences of holy presences, Copts more frequently use the term "apparitions" or "manifestations" (*al-ẓuhūrāt*), with dreams featuring as one subcategory of apparitions. In addition, while both Copts and Muslims refer to phenomenal manifestations as *al-ẓāhir*, Copts, unlike Muslims, do not acknowledge its "hidden" correlate as *al-bāṭin*.

From a more comparative historical perspective, dream interpretation and dream cultures have flourished since late antiquity, before the advent of Christianity and Islam (Miller 1994; Shulman and Stroumsa 1999). From the early Christian period until now, dream interpretation has long been suspected to be a species of divination, as opposed to Islam that has enjoyed a more vibrant tradition of transmitting techniques and manuals of *tafsīr* (Lamoreaux 2002; Mavroudi 2002). In Greco-Roman Egypt, rituals of dream incubation attracted pilgrims to sleep in specially designated shrines for cures from illness and divinely inspired guidance (Patton 2004; Graf 2008; Macalister 2012). Traversing spiritual and medicinal realms, sleeping visions continue to offer a medium for messages and miracles in modern versions of incubation. Scholars of Islam in North Africa and South Asia have described rituals of *istikhāra*, when Muslims invite God's guidance through prayer, and induce answers through dreams (Ewing 1984; Green 2003; Mittermaier 2011). In similar fashion, Copts also seek guidance through dream-visions, often accompanied by miraculous healings and signs of personal direction.

Individual apparitions turn on styles of special visuality that mark thresholds of bodily transformation by way of sight. Given how central dreaming practices are in Christianity and Islam, holy encounters often involve practices of seeing that occur "inside" the seer's eye. In addition to sleeping visions, miraculous accounts of blind seers regaining sight through their encounters with apparitions include Christians and Muslims. What visionary spaces of sleep and blindness share is a style of visuality that takes place within the highly personalized domain of the individual seer.

Revisiting the Marian apparitions in Warraq in 2009 and Zaytun in 1968, there are several cases that illustrate the variety of visualities that Copts and Muslims reported in their accounts. As we saw in the last chapter, the Coptic Church's procedures for verifying apparitions relied on visual epistemologies of objective perception. Aside from these procedures, the Coptic Church also circulated individual accounts that highlighted transformations in capacities of sight as a result of "seeing" the Virgin in extraordinary ways. One of the most widely disseminated miracles from Warraq features a Coptic woman, Kawkib Munir Shahata, afflicted with partial blindness. After traveling to the apparition site, she reported how she saw the Virgin from "inside" her eye: "At first, I felt a terrible sensation. . . . But the pain increased and I felt something hitting my eye, in my eye from inside. Afterward, I found the wife of my brother and her daughter [before me]—and I could *see* them and I told them: 'I see you! And I am staring into your eyes!'" (*Nabd al-Kanisa*, December 20, 2009).

In the Coptic Church's report of the Zaytun apparition, there is a Muslim eyewitness named Madiha Muhammad Sa'id whose experience of visual encounter resembles that of Kawkib. Like Kawkib, she had felt a "terrible sensation" before experiencing the miraculous recovery of her sight.

> Miss Madiha Mohammed Said (20 years old)—Teacher's Institute, Helmeh [Cairo] had lost sight [and speech] through a psychic attack. . . . On the 4th of June 1968, Madiha was taken by her two brothers, Mahmud and Ahmad Sa'id to the Coptic Orthodox Church at [Zaytun, who] prayed for their beloved sister. . . . They even asked the priest to pray for their sister. A terrible sensation had been felt by Madiha Mohammad before being miraculously cured. She could see that she was in a church and could feel her presence in front of a Coptic priest. . . . Madiha says that she then saw the apparition of the Virgin of the Blessed Virgin right in front of her, then she cried in a loud voice: "The Virgin—the Virgin." (Bishop Gregorious 1968:21–25)

The similarity between Kawkib's and Madiha's individual experiences (as visually impaired seers) shows that "inner" styles of seeing occur among Christians and Muslims alike. Significantly, it is the Coptic Church that highlights the possibility that Muslims value churches as holy sites for seeking cures and guidance, and apparitional visions as the means for miraculous transformations.

Another style of special visuality involves seeing within the liminally somatic zone between waking and sleeping. Often in these cases, it is the bedside, rather than the church or shrine, which serves as the setting for apparitions. Envisioned as personal visitations from the other world, saints and prophets appear between an individual's inner and outer visions. In the Coptic tradition, a visual ontology of revelational manifestations at the waking/sleeping boundary has been a long-standing one. For example, Ibn Katib Qaysar, the thirteenth-century Coptic theologian who authored a commentary on the Book of Revelation, described a spectrum of visionary states that spanned various bodily states of wakefulness and sleep (Davis 2008b). The bedside where angels arrive at the threshold of death, moreover, represents the site of crossing, not only from the waking world into slumber but also from earthly life into life in the hereafter.

During my fieldwork, as I was collecting individual accounts of visions, I noticed that a number of Coptic Christians also signaled a form of visuality that oscillated between full and indistinct planes of awareness. Some of them likened their sensational state at the time of experiencing their visions to that felt while under "anesthesia" (*bing*). In the following narrative, a Copt named Girgis describes his vision at the state hospital Qasr al-'Ayni in Cairo, where he had undergone brain surgery in his early twenties:

> And the doctor did really really bad work on me. Why? Because it was a bad hospital, and this doctor thought of all us sick people as "just cases" for teaching, not human beings. . . . When I was laid down on the stretcher—it was a very dirty stretcher by the way, I thought I was at the butcher—I felt that I saw the [biblical] verse across my head: "Do not be afraid, I am with you [*Lā takhaf, anā ma'ak*]." I just closed my eyes when the doctor was giving me anesthesia. And I felt as if I was hearing in my ears and seeing it, like when you close your eyes and when you think about something.

Again, it is the personal bedside where Girgis's encounter with a divine message occurred, and more specifically, the scene of the questionable hospital stretcher. At once visual and auditory in its mode of transmission, Girgis's textual vision unfolded just as he is medically put under anesthesia. In the next narrative, another Copt named Nivin also highlights the bedside and her anesthetic state of hazy suspension. In Nivin's case, her experience watching a film of another woman's dream preceded her own encounter with a saintly apparition later on:

> I'll also tell you something that happened. One time I was watching a video and there was a [woman in the video] who had breast cancer. So the Lady Virgin went and performed surgery on her, and took out the tumor from her breast. And afterwards, the woman grabbed the hand of the Virgin. So, I insisted that I would grab the hand of the Virgin Mother. At that time, I was about twenty years old. I said, "I will not sleep, I want to see. And afterwards, to take her hand."
>
> I insisted, I didn't hesitate. I continued to sit on the bed until very late at night. And in the end, I felt . . . have you ever gone inside the surgery room before? Have you ever taken anesthesia? I have gone many times. I had my tonsils taken out, and my appendix [also]. Anyways, so afterward, I felt that, in that very moment when I was sitting on the bed, I felt as if I had taken anesthesia. And I found the Virgin standing next to the bed. She took my hand and pushed me, sitting me down on the bed. In the same moment, I woke up and I couldn't find her anymore.

Nivin's desire to see the Virgin began with the cinematic image of dream incubation in which the Virgin appears as a surgeon who cures her patient of breast cancer. Desiring to repeat elements of the scene, she also envisions the Virgin's appearance at her bedside while swaying into an anesthetic stupor the instant before sleep. For both Girgis and Nivin, we can see how ancient elements of ritual incubation, combining the medicinal with the miraculously divine, continue on in contemporary contexts of dreaming in the hospital, cinema, and home.

Ultimately, what dreams and waking visions enable are forms and practices of visuality that are highly personalized, felt as divine visitations on an individual basis. In contrast to the collective apparitions that are objectively perceived as bursts of light at a public site of worship, individual apparitions may occur via interior acts of seeing, within the intimate settings of bedrooms and private homes. Such special visualities enable the "blind" to experience visions and link an act of watching a video to the mimetic space of dreaming. Upending distinctions between inner/outer, sleeping/waking, real/imagined, they offer the ocular potential for revelatory encounter. Conveying messages of comfort and rebuke, at times to miraculous effects, visions may also spur conversions and spiritual transformations.

So far in this section, all the visual practices and accounts that I have detailed fit squarely within the orthodox teachings of the Coptic Church. At the same time, as I hope to show in the next sections, they also introduce possibilities of more heterodox, outlier forms of otherworldly apparitions that expose the sanctioned limits of religious authority. Recall Mus'ad's directions to his Muslim client to summon the seven angels at her bedside. Or Ahmad's response to the Virgin's appearance through his offer to build a shrine in her honor. Resembling orthodox forms of bedside visitation or building churches and mosques, these visual practices also draw on overlaps between Christian and Islamic traditions of visual revelation and holy place-making. In the next sections, we turn to hybrid settings of Christian-Muslim interaction and biographical scenes of Muslim-to-Christian conversion to understand how marginal practices of visuality can straddle the boundaries of religious difference.

DEMON EXORCISM

On Friday and Sunday evenings, the pews of the old Cathedral of St. Mark in Azbakiyya are normally filled with up to five hundred to six hundred people. It is a unique attraction for a couple reasons. The former seat of the Coptic Patriarchate before it moved to 'Abbasiyya in 1968, the historic cathedral is where the Coptic popes led under Ottoman rule until Nasser's presidency. Centrally located on Ramses Square, a few blocks away from al-Fatah Mosque, the grandiose cathedral has also acquired a reputation for drawing numerous Muslims to its central location. The Patriarchate cathedral offers both a symbol of the highest clerical authority and a site where peripheral crossovers between Christians and Muslims take place.

Father Makari Yunan, the head priest in his late-seventies, is famous for his spiritual gift of demon exorcism (*ikhrāj al-shayṭān, ṭard al-shirīr*). Hailing from a village in Sohag, Makari Yunan speaks in a strong Upper Egyptian accent with a brusque, vibrantly forthright personality. Until a generation or two ago, especially in rural villages of Upper Egypt and the Delta, Muslims consulted Coptic priests when seeking exorcism. Following anthropologist Catherine Mayeur-Jaouen's study on exorcism at the shrine of St. George in Mit Damsis, Muslims have traditionally regarded Coptic priests as sorcerers because they are "closer to nature" (Mayeur-Jaouen 2012:161). Aside from priests, villages often included a "holy man," often a Coptic man with spiritual gifts who is neither a saint nor clergy. Currently, in the more urban environs of Cairo, a handful of charismatic priests are known to exorcise demons, such as Father ʿAbd al-Masih of Musturud's holy well of the Virgin and Father Samaʿn of Muqattam's Cave Churches (see chapter 2, "Redemption at the Edge"). Drawing Christians and Muslims hunting for solutions to their afflictions, these priests and their churches become sites for interconfessional commingling.

A typical evening gathering with Makari Yunan opens with singing devotional songs and listening to his sermon. On one Friday summer night in 2011, when I was there, he also read aloud a selection of folded notes passed to him from the pews. Written anonymously, the notes sought his advice about confession, divorce, drug addiction, and conversion to Christianity. After addressing the questions in about a half-hour, he proceeded around the sanctuary to bless everyone with holy water, and heal some from demon possession.

Makari Yunan is a spiritual specialist among others, including Qurʾanic healers, jinn curers, shaykhs, and saints throughout Egypt (Hoffman 1995; Vinea 2015). Dealing with manifestations of evil or other agents requires skills of spiritual discernment and rapport. Priests with the gift of exorcism often also have the gift of "clairvoyance" or "second sight" (*al-shaffāfiyya*), the capacity to see into a person's past and future. The mixed scene of demon exorcism also interweaves different ontological orders of otherworldly beings. For instance, what Muslims may recognize as appearances of jinn or angels are what Christians may recognize as those of demons and devils.

FIGURE 24. Father Makari Yunan casts out a demon, Cathedral of St. Mark, Azbakiyya. Photo by author.

As Makari Yunan passed through the aisles, camera operators followed him while live images of his interactions were displayed on the overhanging television monitors. Exorcism is a ritually staged performance.[3] With his wooden cross in one hand and a pitcher of holy water in the other, Makari Yunan applied his techniques to individuals in the pews. Interacting with one youth, he set the cross on his head and loudly roared, "In the name of Jesus Christ [*bism Yasū' al-Masīḥ*]!" After the youth trembled, Makari Yunan threw more holy water into his face, as the two men beside him elevated his arms in victory while surrounding viewers clapped and wept. Elsewhere, a woman began to writhe as Makari Yunan approached her, throwing back her head and eyes. "Stop the wars [*Baṭṭal al-muḥārrabāt*]!" he yelled, commanding the spiritual presences to lie on the ground. Engaging in dialogical rapport with the patient and the spirits possessing her, he dove into a lengthy series of questions: "Who is doing this? . . . Are you alone, how many are there? . . . Do you know who Christ is? Who is he? . . . How long have you been here?"

Strikingly, Father Makari Yunan identified scenarios where his expertise was not relevant. In one of the back rows, a man sat with his family,

3. Father Makari Yunan has a website which live-streams video coverage of his Sunday and Friday gatherings including his exorcisms. For more, see Father Makari Yunan's website, www.fathermakary.net (accessed May 6, 2018).

nervously curled with his hands balled into his chest. After quietly asking questions to his family, Makari Yunan pronounced that he needed to go to a doctor for his "psychological problem" and prayed over them. Toward the end of his rounds about the sanctuary, a few mothers brought their disabled children to him in search for cures. Cutting them short and sending them off, Makari Yunan declared with some exasperation, "I am not special, you can be healed by your own faith!"

As Coptologist Otto Meinardus described from his fieldwork in the 1950s and 1960s, the Coptic exorcist once served as a "physician" at saint festivals, or *mawālid* (Meinardus 2002 [1981]: 102–3; Schielke 2012). Until a few decades ago, Christians and Muslims visited the Coptic priest or holy man for cures, afflicted by diseases (e.g., epilepsy, paralysis, speech loss) often attributed to jinns or demons. For more routine ailments, Muslims also went to churches for healing, and Copts left notes for Sufi saints like Shaykh al-Badawi on the street.[4] With the advent of modern psychiatry in Egypt, exorcism rituals have become more scarce, and it is highly possible that priests themselves are developing distinctions between their spiritual expertise and the medical sciences (see Vinea 2015).

News of the many Muslims attending Friday and Sunday meetings at the old Patriarchate Cathedral has stirred suspicions of secret baptisms and Muslim conversions, especially of women. As with its other few popular, charismatic priests, the Coptic Church warily keeps a close eye on Makari Yunan to make sure his activity does not cause too much trouble. Back in 2006, when the police requested that the cathedral monitor its gates to prevent Muslims from entering, Makari Yunan was recorded for his refusal: "The church is open to everyone."[5] By the time of my most recent visit in 2014, a new guard had been posted at the gates to check ID cards and ensure the cathedral's status as an exclusively Christian space. Facing post-Mubarak instability after 2011, churches increased security at their entrances, and in the case of St. Mark's in Azbakiyya, the pro-Morsi Brotherhood protests and outbreaks of violence in 2013 occurred at al-Fatah Mosque in close

4. The thirteenth-century saint al-Sayyid al-Badawi is the founder of the Badawiyya order of Sufism and is regarded as one of Egypt's most popular saints. His tomb lies in Tanta as a major pilgrimage site. I am grateful to Alan Mikhail for alerting me to Copts seeking al-Badawi's intercession.

5. Dina Sulayman and Hani Ahmad Rizq, "Father Makary Younan Is Accused of Convincing Muslim Women to Embrace Christianity," *Arab West Report*, August 28, 2006.

proximity. This change at the cathedral's gates might therefore be only partly owed to threats of conversion.

ENCOUNTERING THE ANGEL GABRIEL: A CONVERSION NARRATIVE

Very few Egyptian individuals legally convert, from either Islam to Christianity or Christianity to Islam. Despite their small percentage, cases of legal conversion continue to catalyze public controversy over religious freedom and communal autonomy (Oraby 2015; Mahmood 2016).[6] Occasionally during my fieldwork in Coptic churches via diaconal networks, I encountered a handful of converts openly serving as church volunteers, one even training to be a preacher. For reasons of legal complication and family disruption, however, I learned that the majority of converts choose to hide their change in religious affiliation whether on their ID cards or through their devotional practices. Beyond the issue of religious identity, these covert conversions raise questions about what constitutes a change in religion, and whether or not converts may belong simultaneously to the worlds of Christianity and Islam.

In the next subsections, we look at the conversion narrative of a man I will call "Khalid," whom I met through a mutual acquaintance in Shubra al-Khayma. Chatting behind closed doors in a friend's flat in Ghamra, Khalid showed me his ID card: "Khalid Muhammad Sayyid." In his mid-seventies when I met him in 2010, he was living in an impoverished part of Giza called Kunuyyisa and scraping by with temporary office jobs. Belonging to an older generation of Cairo's migrants from Upper Egypt's villages, Khalid originally hails from a village in Beni Suef, a governorate seventy miles south of Cairo. When he was in his mid-forties in Beni Suef of the 1980s, he experienced a series of visions of the angel Gabriel, interpreting them as a divine message to explore Christianity. Like the Virgin, the angel Gabriel is a shared figure in the

6. Religious conversions in Egypt are controversial for a variety of reasons. First, the Egyptian state and social norms make it extremely difficult for a Muslim to convert to Christianity, whereas conversions from Christianity to Islam occur with comparative ease (Mahmood 2016:135–41). Second, in recent years, a number of Coptic converts to Islam (or their children) have sought to reconvert back to Christianity. The Fatwa Council of al-Azhar has long been recognized as the administrative body competent to certify a born Copt's exit from Coptic Orthodoxy. Today, the Coptic pope may confer membership in the Coptic Church by issuing a Certificate of Return, but only to Copts who were previously affiliated with the Church. For more on the complex legal conditions authorizing re-conversions in Egypt, see Oraby 2015.

Christian and Islamic traditions, with different biographies and slightly different names. In Islam, Gabriel or "Jibril" (Arabic) is the messenger who relayed the Qur'anic revelation to the Prophet Muhammad. In Orthodox Christianity, Gabriel or "Jibra'il" or "Ghubrayyal" (Arabized Coptic) is an archangel and saint who foretold the births of Jesus and John the Baptist to the Virgin.

Khalid's narrative of his turn to Christianity suggests the formal ambiguities of conversion, exceeding a delimited model of conversion as an election in one's religious status. As we will see, overlapping tropes in Sufi and Orthodox visionary experience give rise to "Christianized" counterparts of Islamic figures. In the villages a few decades earlier, moreover, various spiritual authorities—shaykhs, holy men, exorcists, curers—offered crossover spaces for Christians and Muslims to interact more openly in matters of religious belonging. For Khalid, it was a Coptic holy man with the gift of clairvoyance who directed him to read from the Christian scriptures.

Divided into three subsections, the following account is partially a transcription of Khalid's recorded narrative, and partially my summary of it. Each subsection corresponds to a different scene of Khalid's encounter with the angel Gabriel, all of them cumulatively resulting in his conversion. The first scene of encounter occurs while Khalid performs his *dhikr* prayers when he was a Sufi novice in Beni Suef. The second takes place in a bazaar in Cairo's 'Ataba Square. The third unfolds at the holy man's home in Biba, one of Beni Suef's small cities.

A Pair of Crosses

Before 1982, I was nothing but Muslim [*Muslim baht*]. It never occurred to me that I would question religion at all. I was a very religious Muslim and that's it. I prayed, went to mosque and after some time, I joined the Burhamiyya [Sufi] order,[7] and I felt that they were pleasant people—not aggressive or anything like that.

Chain-smoking while recollecting aloud, Khalid frequently broke his descriptions with pauses of heavy thought or light laughter. His story began with undesirable intrusions during his practices of solitary

---

7. *Burhamiyya* is a vernacular Upper Egyptian term for the Ibrahimiyya Sufi path founded by Ibrahim al-Dasuqi (d. 1288). Burhamiyya is not be confused with the Burhaniyya Sufi path founded by the contemporary Sudanese Shaykh Burhani (d. 1982). For histories and ethnographies of Sufism in Egypt, see Gilsenan 1973; Hofer 2011; Mittermaier 2011.

meditation (*al-khalwa*). For ten months, he had trained under the guidance of a Sufi shaykh in Beni Suef to cultivate his mind toward sustaining an uninterrupted remembrance of God (*al-dhikr*).

Passing two or three hours alone in a small dark room, Khalid's initial bouts in his spiritual disciplines were difficult, his nomadic mind generating "thought giving birth to thought, like bacteria." By the third month, he was able to maintain focus for longer periods of time, repeating the name of God in tick-tock tempo and closing his repetitions with two cycles of prayer. When he joined his other cohort members for meetings with the shaykh, he would recall and listen to others recall what was presented to them in their solitude—about events and meetings from the future, about hidden depths of the self (*aghwār al-nafs*) and lights honoring other worlds.

Khalid's turning point began with violent apparitions, a pair of illumined crosses in the dimmed space of his solitary meditations.

> I was about to witness to the Prophet, and then I found one cross which came up illumined [*ṣalīb rāḥ-munawwar*] on my right-hand side. And it came from the floor [*baṭn al-arḍ*]. . . . It was a very very strong light, my heart beat hard and I was afraid. I saw on my left-hand side that another one was coming out again. This light was not any ordinary light, like anything I had ever seen before, in my meditation room or any other place, this light was extremely terrifying! And I screamed and yelled, got up running from the dark room.

Anticipating that the crosses would upset him, Khalid gingerly ventured a brief description of his vision when his shaykh called for it. "It is Satan who lit up the crosses," Khalid cited the shaykh's reply, gleefully recounting the shock on the faces of his guide and brothers. "Did you know what the crosses were?" I asked Khalid. "Of course, I didn't understand anything, I was very foolish." To avoid seeing other "demonic" appearances, he stopped doing meditation and eventually stopped going to the Sufi-order meetings altogether.

In the Bazaar

Shifting to his next encounter with an apparition, Khalid described the rowdy markets of 'Ataba Square in Cairo. Some months after having seen the two crosses, he traveled to the bazaar to trade old coins in one of the coffeehouses. Collecting coins was a past-time that he frequently enjoyed, exchanging embossed portraits of the great singer Umm Kulthum, Princes Faruq and Fu'ad, Presidents Sadat and Nasser.

So that day, I was sitting in the café. I found a youth coming to me, with long hair, about this length [pointing to his neck] with a handsome face. And he was wearing a jellabiya and shoes, worn and tattered but clean. He was holding a rusty piece of tin in his hand. It was so rusty and corroded that rust was on his hands. He went to me, coming directly at me.

I told him, "What is this? This is tin!"
He said, "I know."
"This doesn't sell."
"Yeah, but I want to sell it."
"Fine, go sell it."
"You are the one who is going to buy it from me."

We went on like this for a while. And then, I realized that God was seizing my conscience from inside. I looked at him, and it seemed to me, "This person has dignity. He is respectful, he doesn't want to beg and ask anyone for money. So, he is wrangling over this piece of tin because he needs to eat."

After buying the tin scrap from the boy, Khalid showed it to other coin collectors in the bazaar. As one of them handled it, he felt that there was something underneath the tin's superficial composition. Rubbing off its residual patina against the concrete pavement, he surprised the others with an image.

An image of an angel [ṣūrat malak]. His two arms, winged, were lifted up. Each of his hands was holding a cross emerging from it. So, the angel was holding two crosses, one in each hand. And written in the middle of the tin: "The Angel Gabriel [al-Malak Jibra'il]."

Iqra'!

Khalid laughed, remembering how he had so quickly ignored the coin and its revelatory portrait.

But God doesn't leave people who don't understand, God had to finish the message. So the Lord sent me my cousin, the daughter of my maternal uncle, who came from Cairo. Her son was with her, he was afflicted by the devil. My cousin took her son to see one of my friends, and my friend took one look at that boy. The boy spoke to him with terrible words, cursing him and hitting him. My friend said, "That boy has an impure spirit. Take this piece of paper and go to the holy man [miqaddis]."[8]

8. The title *miqaddis* (*miqaddis* in Upper Egyptian dialect) was originally given to a Christian who completed pilgrimage to Jerusalem (al-Quds), similar to the Muslim title *ḥājj* (see chapter 2, "Redemption at the Edge"). More frequently heard in villages than cities among the older generation, the term *miqaddis* is used to convey respect for elders and spiritual figures.

Strict and stern, the holy man reminded Khalid of a police officer who rustled his visitors with questions and orders. In the mornings outside his spacious house, people would line up to consult him, women on one side, men on the other. When Khalid brought his cousin's son to him, the holy man told the boy to stand aside and turned to Khalid for questioning.

"What's Christ doing with you these days?"

"What's Christ doing with me?"

"Yeah."

I told him everything that happened, I told him how I saw two illumined crosses, and how someone sold me a piece of tin with an angel with two crosses. He said to me, "That [boy who sold you the tin] is the angel who lit up those two crosses for you. The Angel Gabriel is the one who lit up those crosses for you, and he is also the one who sold you the tin."

I told him, "What?!" I didn't believe him at all. Okay, so something angelic lit up the crosses for me in meditation?! Big deal, fine. But did the Angel Gabriel meet me at the café and sell me tin?!

I laughed. When I laughed, he felt that I was mocking him. He looked at me with one eye, squinting, and then with the other.

I thought to myself, "This man is crazy." And I said to him, "No, I'm sorry."

"I want you to believe that all that happened to you is by the hand of the Angel Gabriel!! He is the one you lit up the crosses and he is the one who sold you the tin! Go over there!"

On top of the cabinet at the far end of the next room, there was a Bible. The holy man ordered Khalid to pick it up before sitting down on the carpet. Khalid sat with the Bible, with its back facing the holy man

"Read [*Iqra'*]!"

"Read what?"

"Read anything!"

I was stubborn, my mind was resistant. I thought, "I am going to do the exact opposite. Instead of reading from the right, I am going to read from the left; instead of reading from the top, I am going to read from the bottom." Meaning, I was going to read from the end of the page, from the bottom and the left.[9] And what did I read aloud?

---

9. Bibliomancy, or "divination by books, or by verses of scripture" is a heterodox practice found among Christians, Jews, and Muslims. Originating from the ancient Roman ritual of sortes, scriptural divination relies on passages being selected and read at random.

FIGURE 25. Panoramic view of Biba, Beni Suef. Photo courtesy of Phil Jackson.

"And suddenly, the angel of the Lord appeared to them. And the glory of the Lord shone around them, and they were terrified."[10]

Truly, the light had been very strong and terrifying. Was it possible that the holy man had planned for me to read this verse, when I had decided to read from the left, not from the right, from the bottom not from the top, back to front? Of course not. My body shivered, it began to shake. I cried, tears flowing from my eyes. I gave that man respect, the one who became a saint in front of me.

Vehicles of revelation, visions communicate not only messages and miracles, but also new messengers, prophets, wonderworkers, and saints. Previously unknown, such unfamiliar figures initiate visionaries into new traditions or expose the fragmentary overlaps and fissures across different traditions. The process of discovering the apparition's identity often entails material repetitions through sensory modes of mediation.

Khalid's conversion narrative depicts a journey of discovering the angel Gabriel, and more notably, the "Christian" Gabriel with two crosses. Across visual styles of revelatory repetitions, Khalid encountered Gabriel through a variety of images and settings: as illumined crosses in solitary meditation, as a waking vision of a boy in the bazaar, as the hidden underneath of a coin's surface. His narrative culminates in a scene that bears a shadowy semblance to Islam's foundational moment of revelation: Gabriel's command to the prophet Muhammad

10. Luke 2:9 refers to the angel's sudden appearance to field shepherds and the acclamation of Christ's birth in Bethlehem.

to "recite [*Iqra'*]!" Stemming from the same triliteral root (*q-r-'*), the "Qur'an" are scriptures that are recited via aural and oral faculties of transmission, with the ear serving as the privileged organ of the Islamic textual habitus (Messick 1993; Hirschkind 2006). In a striking variation on the same theme, the village holy man exhibited the double meaning of the Arabic term *iqra'*—"recite" and "read"—by commanding Khalid to "take and read" the scriptures, a shadowy semblance to yet another scene of revelation: St. Augustine's conversion. And like Augustine, Khalid opened the Bible and read the first words on which his eyes first fell to be a divinely, personal message pointing to Gabriel.

Khalid's conversion narrative also sheds light on continuities between and at the limits of tradition—Christian and Islamic, orthodox and heterodox. Although it is felt as a rupture of the "new," the revelation of an unknown figure is often prefigured by familiar tropes and forms of sensory mediation. For instance, Khalid's Sufi vision of illumined crosses appearing out of the earth's *baṭn* suggests an Islamic visual regime which features lights and illumined figures and centers around an ontology of hidden and manifest worlds. Moreover, his recognition of the "Christian" angel Gabriel was in part owing to his familiarity with his "Islamic" crossover counterpart. Significantly, these slight variations in Khalid's imaginary are heterodox aberrations, "demonic" from the perspective of the shaykh or in the unsanctioned hands of a "holy man" from the perspective of the clergy. The point is that the visual elements of revelation are often not altogether sudden or originating from a radical elsewhere (despite their narration as such).

In the next two brief portraits of conversion, we focus on a Coptic Protestant and a nondevout Muslim who experience personal revelations of strange and unfamiliar figures. Unlike Khalid, these two individuals had little previous exposure to spiritual visuality; like Khalid, their apparitional encounters are cumulative, resulting in their newfound orientation to a visual imaginary of intercession.

Hilda is a Coptic woman in her fifties who grew up in Sohag in an ardently Evangelical family who distinguished themselves from Orthodox "superstitions." In Hilda's account to me, she conveyed how a dream changed her perspective toward Orthodoxy and the power of saints:

> So one time, I was sleeping and I dreamt I was in one of the houses of my husband's siblings. We were sitting and watching television. Suddenly, there was a small youth—I didn't know him and I'd never seen him before—who entered the room.

My sister-in-law said, "Turn off the television, St. Menas is here." I had never even heard of St. Menas at all, I knew nothing about him to begin with. So St. Menas came and prayed over each of our heads, and he came to me and asked me, "What do you want?" I told him, "I'd like a little boy." So he told me, "Not the next year, but the year following, you will have a baby boy named Menas."

I didn't know who St. Menas was, but after my dream, I wanted to know "who is St. Menas?" I knew the prominent saints, Pope Kyrillos and St. George for example, or the Virgin Mary, those saints I had heard a lot about. So I went to the Orthodox church—all this happened around 1982 or 1983. I went to the Orthodox church, and I saw the icon picture of St. Menas. "This is the one whom I dreamt, but I don't know him."

Although Hilda did not "convert" to Orthodoxy per se, her visual encounter with an unknown figure and his prophetic message encouraged a new moral orientation toward the authoritative intercession of saints. Spurred by the revelatory contents of her dream, she visited Orthodox churches and used an icon to match a name with the face she had seen.[11] As a medium of material repetition, the visual image of the icon portrait offered another instantiation of the unknown figure. At the time I recorded her account in 2006, Hilda's last son Menas was a dental student who had returned to Cairo after finishing up his studies abroad in Los Angeles.

The next narrative features a Muslim engineer in his early sixties named Badr, who, unlike Khalid or Hilda, had neither interest nor exposure to spiritual matters before his revelatory vision. To the extent that he had been exclusively preoccupied with work (a "workaholic" was the English term he invoked for me), his account of Muslim-to-Christian conversion placed little weight on the "Muslim" aspects of his prior self. Badr elaborated to me how shaken up he was when he discovered his dream of an unknown setting with unknown characters coming true in "real" life:

This was the first time I ever went into church. I mustered up the courage, and went inside with [my neighbors]. Even though I had never gone inside a church before, I found the vision from my dream-vision [al-ru'yā] before me, exactly as it was in the dream. I found monks wearing strange clothes, and singing strange music, I found that they were playing cymbals. And they were singing in Coptic. That is, of course, language I didn't understand and music I hadn't heard. Plus, the brightness which had been inside the church, caused me fear. Like the fear that I had in the dream.

11. The use of icons to verify the identity of apparitions is common within the Coptic tradition. For a similar example during the Ottoman period, see "A Female Martyr Cult in the Nile Delta" in Armanios 2011.

> So as soon as I stepped into the church, I left the church. And I sat down [next to the road] and asked myself questions: "What was that I saw? What does it mean that I saw that? Why I did see those things?" From that point, it was the beginning of the road to God.

Having rarely remembered his dreams, Badr found himself flooded with anxiety when he reexperienced his vision during his first visit at a church in one of Minya's villages. Dropping off his Coptic neighbors at the local church, he had entered out of politeness at their invitation. Using the Islamic term *al-ru'yā* ("dream-vision") to refer to what he had seen, Badr took his revelation of the Christian liturgy and church's interior to be the "beginning of the road to God." According to his self-account, this revelation is what catalyzed his decision to learn more about a faith entirely foreign to him, leading to his baptism several years later.

An individual's account of conversion exceeds his or her vision account, consisting of his or her biographical details, background, motives, personality, and so on. Far from providing a holistic picture of the factors that shape an individual's spiritual transformations, I have focused more on the visual form of revelatory encounter, especially in contexts where a subject is envisioning figures and settings which are entirely alien, unfamiliar, and disruptive. Indeed, in each of these two narratives, the emphasis lies on the unknown: Hilda underscores several times that she "didn't know" but "wanted to know" the saint's identity, and Badr repeats that elements of his vision were "strange." Like Khalid, who was alternately surprised and forgetful of Gabriel's various apparitions, Hilda and Badr made sense of the visions as personal prophecies about their futures. With its origins perceived as external to the self, the dream is a divinely authored message to be realized in the dreamer's unfolding life.

Inciting shifts in moral and spiritual alignment, revelations of the unknown generate new horizons of conversion. Beyond a change in religious identity (from "Muslim" to "Christian"), conversions may also entail smaller-scale shifts such as becoming acquainted with a new saint, engaging a holy man or walking into a foreign place of worship. One mediating venue into the interior imaginary of the individual, a saintly apparition breaks paths to other worlds and one's possible future in them.

VISIONARY AMBIGUITIES

Whereas the previous chapter investigated how Marian apparitions ordered Christian-Muslim difference according to national-sectarian logics, this one explored how saints, angels, demons, and jinn appear to individuals in mixed settings with more porous transactions between Christians and Muslims. In addition to the visual epistemologies of objective realism heralded by the onset of collective apparitions, Christians and Muslims in Egypt also experience divine revelations through more unwieldy, ephemeral forms of seeing that are less subject to the disciplinary governance of religious institutions. Across Christianity and Islam, visual ontologies that upend dichotomies of waking/sleeping and inner/outer realms of perception release possibilities for crossovers and conversions. While immersed in Islamic tropes of revelation, a Sufi may interact with Christian figures and images, and Protestants and nonbelievers may change their lives as a result of personal messages, prophecies, and commands felt to be from elsewhere.

Many of the apparitional encounters described in this chapter were mediated by waking visions and dreams experienced on an individual basis that can escape institutional sanction. This is not to suggest that these forms of appearance are radically asocial, or that they stand outside histories of custom and rituals of communication. On the contrary, my attention to the material sensibilities of saintly manifestation, shared among Christians and Muslims, suggests that the social life of visions may travel farther than dream narratives and its interpretive contents. How might we think of dreams, in their intimately personal register, going into public circulation? How do visions achieve force in the social realm beyond the bounded interiority of the individual seer? Turning dreams inside out, the material afterlives of visions further extend their capacity to move through the media of objects and technologies. These material transmissions create the potential for new problems and challenges across the Christian-Muslim divide.

PART THREE

Icons

CHAPTER 5

Public Order

Whenever you contemplate icons, do not stop at the boundaries of painted color or wood or aesthetic beauty, in its
nothingness, but lift up your thoughts to the one who is behind
the color and material, to the person who is their owner.

Father Matta al-Miskin, *The Life of Orthodox Prayer* (*Hayat
al-Salat al-Urthuduksiyya*)

The empire was undergoing a political crisis; therefore it was
thought necessary to furnish a political explanation for it. . . .
But what if this political crisis was precisely a crisis of
iconicity?

Marie-José Mondzain, *Image, Icon, Economy*

THE MIRACLE ICON IN PORT SAID

The miracle icon of the Virgin Mary in Port Said is celebrated for exuding holy oil in abundance. Housed inside the Church of St. Bishoi the
Great, the icon is a mass print poster of the "Virgin of the Apparition"
(*'adhrā' al-ẓuhūr*) or the "Virgin of the Transfiguration" (*'adhrā'
al-tagallī*). The icon's bottom half is visibly drenched in oil. At its foot,
there is a large vinyl canopy designed to catch the oil as it trickles down
the poster. Fragrant and viscous, the oil is then distributed in finger-
sized plastic vials as a holy blessing, or *baraka*.

Built in the 1860s, Port Said is a coastal city in northern Egypt where
the Suez Canal meets the Mediterranean Sea. During my first visit in

FIGURE 26. Miracle icon of the Virgin, Church of St. Bishoi the Great, Port Said. Photo
by author.

2007, it did not take long for me to realize that I had been spending too much time in Cairo. With its seagulls and salty breezes, fresh fish and slower pace, Port Said was a welcome reprieve from big-city headaches like traffic and desert dust mixed with pollution. Located in central Manshiyya Square, with its Omar Effendi department store and major banks, the Church of St. Bishoi is less than a ten-minute stroll to the Suez Canal. Manshiyya Square is also a historic site of collective protest, where Egyptians had once gathered to claim their national rights to the Suez against the British and French in the 1950s. In February 2012, the square also held protests against the military for the Port Said Stadium massacre, when over seventy soccer fans were killed and hundreds injured.[1]

I first traveled to Port Said on February 20, 2007, the date considered to be the icon's feast day and when it exudes oil most vigorously. Several Copts in Cairo had advised that I visit the icon when they learned of my interest in Marian apparitions. From my conversations, I inferred that the Virgin's icon in Port Said most probably follows the Virgin of Zaytun as the second most popular and well-known Marian image in Egypt; indeed, they are the same image.

Entering the Church of St. Bishoi, I found myself among middle-school children who had traveled to Port Said from Upper Egypt on an organized field trip. With mild fidgeting in the pews, they were listening to the priest Father Bula Sa'd tell the story behind the icon. An engaging and skilled storyteller, Father Bula rehearsed the story in all its complex detail without skipping a beat, as if repeating it for the nth time. In his early fifties when I saw him, he had been telling it for nearly twenty years, and multiple times a day every February during the icon's heavy pilgrimage season.

The story of the Virgin's icon in Port Said opens with a Coptic woman named Samya Yusif Basiliyus and her path to repentance. In 1988, Samya was a thirty-eight-year-old widow and working single mother, living in Port Fouad, on the other side of the canal. She had no interest in going to church, a place she perceived to be rife with hypocrisy and gossip. At the ceaseless prodding of her daughter Violet to give church a try, she finally decided to go. Moved by the liturgy, Samya began pursuing her spiritual journey for the next two years under the pastoral

1. In 2011 and 2012, the ruling SCAF (Supreme Council of the Armed Forces) organized attacks against the Ultras Ahlawy, a soccer fan club who had been active in protests against the police and military. The Port Said massacre resulted in charges against nine police officers including the former Port Said security director.

guidance of Father Bula at the Church of St. Bishoi. Samya's life changed as a result: she wept profusely during her first communion, dropped chain-smoking full stop, and volunteered janitorial services for the church in her spare time.

On February 20, 1990, a dramatic miracle happened to Samya, while she was sleeping at around 1:30 A.M. Having been diagnosed with breast cancer, she was scheduled to travel to Cairo later that morning to remove her tumor. Instead, the Virgin Mary appeared to Samya in her dream and performed the surgery. Accompanying the Virgin were three other figures: an elderly man, an elderly woman, and a child.

In her dream, the Virgin robed in blue and white, declared, "Get up, I am going to perform the surgery for you [anā ḥa 'amilik al- 'amiliyya]."

Samya protested, "No—are you going to remove my breast?"

The Virgin replied, "Don't be afraid, I will be the one to do the surgery for you." Samya felt a jolt of hot, searing pain surge across her chest.

When she woke up from her dream, Samya was completely healed from cancer. Underneath her blood-soaked nightgown, she found her white gauze bandages dotted with red crosses. She also discovered her physical tumor wrapped in bandages and resting outside her chest. After reexamination, Samya's physicians in Cairo confirmed that her cancer had disappeared.

Within days, it was everyday gossip that set Samya's miracle on a more openly public course. News about the miracle traveled quickly among Christians and Muslims in Port Said. As to be expected, friction ensued between believers and enthusiasts on one side, and skeptics and naysayers on the other. Samya's body ended up itself as the answer to the public's confusion. Confirming the divine truthfulness of her dream, her right hand began to exude oil (bitnazzil zayt).

About a month after her fateful healing, Samya retreated from the public eye. On March 25, 1990, Pope Shenouda consecrated Samya into the clerical order of deaconesses. With her new name "Sister Alisabat," she resided first in the Convent of St. Dimyana in Bilbays, and then in the Convent of the Good Shepherd in Port Fouad, where she spent the remainder of her life under the Coptic Church. As Father Bula phrased it in his talk for the church's visitors, Pope Shenouda consecrated her "so that she would not return again to the world."

During the brief period when Samya was living at the Convent of St. Dimyana, her hand stopped producing oil. In its place, the print poster of the Virgin in her cell began to exude oil. It is this poster which is regarded as the miracle icon of the Virgin Mary in Port Said. It is also widely understood that the icon produces the greatest volumes of oil every February 20, the date of Samya's miraculous dream. In this way, the miracle icon and its oils are a reminder, or *dhikrā,* of the Virgin's surgery for Samya.

At the end of telling the story of the Virgin's icon, Father Bula gave out ampoules of oil for the children from Upper Egypt to take back home. Nearly word for word, his narrative synchronized with all the church-published accounts I could find. Having recorded his talk, I compared it with the pamphlets, videos, and handwritten descriptions in the hallway display. Together, they made for a uniform, inviolable report endorsed by Bishop Tadros of Port Said and Pope Shenouda. In short, the story I have rehearsed so far is a ritual narrative reproduced by Coptic Church author-ities. At the center of this story are two major witnesses to Samya's repent-ance and the Virgin's miracles: Samya and Father Bula. Father Bula was not only a storyteller, but also himself a key character in the story. As Samya's confessional priest, he had supervised Samya's spiritual growth and seen her first after she woke healed from her dream. He was also intimately familiar with the public effects of her miracles.

Each winter between 2007 and 2010, I visited the Church of St. Bishoi in Port Said. Each time I interviewed Father Bula, he described the peo-ple who had flocked to the icon in the previous twenty years. Early on, he made it clear to me that Muslims in the neighborhood had also come to the church to see the icon and take a blessing from the Virgin.

During my last visit, on December 27, 2010, I conducted a private interview with Father Bula in which he disclosed further details behind the icon's story that are absent from the Church's official narrative. Fol-lowing his firsthand account, both the local police and national state security officials had been actively involved in managing how Samya's miracles were publicized. As Father Bula put it, they had intervened in order to prevent problems between Christians and Muslims—namely problems of "disquiet" or "confusion" (*al-balbala*). As a result, there are few Muslims visiting the icon today.

As for finding Samya, or Sister Alisabat, I only learned of the mystery behind the Port Said icon when she was gravely ill and back in her old home in Port Fouad. Although I enjoyed the chance to meet her grand-children and greet her briefly on the phone, Samya had already fallen too weak for a longer conversation with a foreign stranger. In 2012, Samya passed away in Hayat Hospital in Cairo.

To my knowledge, not many Copts these days express interest in what happened to Samya after she entered the convent. Rather, it is the

FIGURE 27. Muslim women looking at the miracle icon of the Virgin in the Church of
St. Bishoi the Great, Port Said. Photo courtesy of Father Bula Sa'd.

miracle icon of the Virgin and its oils that serve as the principal attraction of the Church of St. Bishoi in Port Said. Toted back to homes in vials, the oils are famed for their miraculous healing properties. As *dhikrā*, the icon and its oils are media of remembering the Virgin's miracle.

But what exactly *was* the miracle that happened back in 1990? And how and why does it differ from what is publicly remembered about it some twenty years later?

PUBLIC ORDER

A core function of the Egyptian state is to uphold public order (*al-niẓām al-ʿāmm*), including order between religious communities. What public order entails is the regulation of public expressions of religion such as speech, published teachings, and ritual phenomena. The state's authority to determine which religious forms and practices require regulation characterizes its sovereign nature (Agrama 2012) and the political conditions of religious freedom (Mahmood 2016). As Christianity and Islam have both gained influence in the everyday lives of Egyptians in recent decades, state-backed institutions such as the Coptic Church and al-Azhar have played a key role in defining the public limits of religion. For the Coptic Church in particular, maintaining public order often means promoting harmony between Christians and Muslims, in addition to preventing sectarian conflict.

The Virgin's icon in Port Said is a cult image. To the extent that it is openly accessible, the icon is also a public image. This chapter entertains the possibility that the Virgin's icon—and more precisely, the "owner" (al-ṣāḥib) behind it—posed a challenge to public order. Rather than serving as an exclusively "Christian" image, the miracle icon had once attracted Muslims as well as Christians to the Church of St. Bishoi. In what follows, I argue that the mystery of the icon in Port Said lies in the strategic reconfiguration of public memory. I investigate the icon and its material nature in order to grasp the political regulation of religion in the public sphere and its transformative effects. As I further suggest, these transformative effects are in line with a widespread Egyptian state strategy of separating and insulating the Coptic community from its surrounding Muslim society.

Port Said provides a special setting for analyzing the risks and precedents associated with Christian-Muslim interactions. Like other port cities under colonial rule, Port Said was where Western Europeans brought Christian institutions of reform and social service, as well as more objectionable elements such as brothels and alcohol. Belonging to the Suez Canal region, Port Said is less than an hour's drive north from Ismaʿiliyya, where the Muslim Brotherhood was first founded in 1928. This combination of foreign activity and growing Islamist activism gave rise to a climate of mutual suspicion between Christians and Muslims. As historian Beth Baron expertly details (2014), for example, the religious battle for orphaned girls' souls in Port Said eventually spawned antimissionary movements which swept Egypt in the early twentieth century. Of course, the Coptic community is not the same as Swedish, British, and American Protestants, and the nature of tensions between Coptic Christians and Muslims differ as a result. Such events, however, speak to the broader history of interreligious controversy in Port Said, as well as the institutional techniques of installing public order that developed in their wake.

There is a gap, in other words, between the official narrative of the Virgin's icon in Port Said and one single account which offers an alternative perspective on what happened. At the outset, my ethnographic analysis thus concedes a sobering methodological limitation. Based on the firsthand testimony of one speaker, Father Bula Sa'd of the Church of St. Bishoi, it defies the standard of the ideal account as one which represents as many voices and viewpoints as possible. Nor does it present Father Bula's testimony in the biographical genre, as a narrative lens onto his individual experiences and personal worldviews. Rather, I argue that Father Bula's counternarrative has meaningful implications for how we understand the public status of images, which should be taken seriously. Privileging his anomalous account of a public image and its history, I raise the prospect that the ritual narrative embraced by so many Copts today is a product of the church's collusion with the state—and all for the sake of public order. That there currently exists only one voice providing an alternative to the official ritual narrative might itself be yet another possible sign of the politics of this collusion.

Composed in the subjunctive mood, or "in the modality of the maybe" (Caduff 2015), this chapter thus advances the possibility that state security intervened in the public expression of one Coptic woman's miracles. What if the image caused sectarian disputes between Christians and Muslims? If the police and Coptic Church did get involved, then what are the implications for how we understand icons and their threats? More than anything else, my intention in describing an outlier (and possibly repressed) account is to stretch our scholarly imagination of what the politics of a holy image, including its endangering potential in the public, practically entails in real-life contexts. To an outsider hailing from a disenchanted universe, the idea that a laywoman's dream of the Virgin could cause such public controversy might appear to be a bit incredible. Perhaps more unbelievable is the notion that Samya and her seemingly obscure hand would draw the attention of state security officials all the way out to their headquarters in Cairo.

From a slightly different angle, if the Coptic Church and the Egyptian state had indeed paid attention to a Coptic woman's impact on sectarian relations, their direct interventions into Samya's public visibility would be entirely consistent with their recent activity. Since the early 2000s, disputes over the religious status of several Coptic women have caused tensions, and at times, outbreaks of violence. The conversion scandals of Wafa' Qustantin and Kamilya Shahata, for example, sparked riots between Christians and Muslims nationwide (see the introduction). The case of Samya and her miracles in Port Said is similar to those of the alleged converts in two significant respects. First, it is notable that Samya, like Qustantin and Shahata (both wives of Coptic priests), is a Coptic laywoman who was at once external and very close to the clerical order. Second, the fact that Samya became a consecrated deaconess only serves to corroborate the Church's regular tactic of hiding controversial women behind its monastery walls. Authorized by state security forces, the Church has since established a track record of keeping high-profile women under its custodial surveillance for the cause of upholding order between Christians and Muslims. Such tactics have further incited public outcry against the state's denial of these women's individual rights and the repressive mechanisms entailed in policing religious boundaries.

My point in raising the similarities between these conversion scandals and Father Bula's account of state intervention is to exercise our analytic sensibility of Samya and her miracle icon within a currently existing and active field of political operations. What I further push to consider here is the deeply transformative intersection of religious practices with security statecraft. In other words, my study of public order does not merely concern individual and exceptional events of public disruption (i.e., one woman's miracle), but also the lasting impact of church and state intervention on the the everyday aspects of religious mediation in Port Said (i.e., the ongoing memory of the icon).

Entering into the politics of the Virgin's icon involves analyzing the holy image as an institution of memory. Such an analysis requires considering the icon beyond its status as a circumscribed portrait or bounded object, considering it instead through its linkages to other miracles and events in its past. It is only through these signifying linkages that the icon carries holy value as a *dhikrā,* or token of memory. As I aim to show, by way of the contested narratives behind the Virgin's icon in Port Said, what is implicated in these relations of signification is the very public nature of sainthood. The public nature of the icon is fundamentally governed through acts of defining, disciplining, and transfiguring the terms of common access. The terms of the public "common world" (Arendt 1998 [1958]) include the communicative conditions of recognizing a holy person and his or her images. To the extent that Christians and Muslims have mixed sensibilities of what a saint or wonderworker does and looks like, they thus compose a shared religious public. This mixed character of public sainthood across communal lines introduces a potential threat to public order.

As it stands now, the miracle icon in Port Said is an image that belongs unequivocally to the Christian community. Contained within the church's confines, it attests to the institutional separation between

Christian and Muslim spheres of Marian devotion. By entertaining the image's potential to exceed communal limits of ownership, what follows raises the specter of repressed public arrangements from the past.

ICONS, ANICONISM, AND ICONOCLASM

According to Orthodox teachings, the holy icon depicts a holy person. As a ritual medium, the icon serves as a visual tool of memory. In the words of the late Coptic monk Matta al-Miskin (or "Matthew the Poor"), one should "lift up [his or her] thoughts to the one who is behind the color and the material, to the person who is their owner [*ilā shakhṣ ṣāḥibha*]" (Father Matta al-Miskin 1952:576). The ritual end of the icon's mediation is one's identification of the image with the hidden saint, or its "owner" to whom it refers.

From a historical perspective, controversies broke out over the visual representation of holy persons at various moments in both Christianity and Islam.[2] For all the theological significance that the Coptic Church assigns to icon usage, for example, there have been modern reformers such as Pope Cyril IV (1854–61) who destroyed images in public burnings in Cairo and Asyut to prevent popular idolatry (Butler 1884; Meinardus 2002 [1981]:70). Against essentializing dichotomies of "aniconic Islam'" versus "iconophilic Orthodoxy," it is therefore necessary to analyze the specific contexts which frame religious institutions and their respective politics of material imagination. Such an analysis demands considering the holy icon as something more and other than a superficial proxy of contending sociopolitical actors. As scholars of eighth- and ninth-century Byzantine iconoclasm have shown, the icon's form is not simply contested by preexisting religious or political authorities; rather, the icon *mediates* religious and political authority in the first place (Elsner 1988; Pelikan 1990; Mondzain 2002; Brubaker and Haldon 2011). Iconoclasm, in other words, must not be approached merely through the lens of opposing actors (e.g., emperor vs. clergy, Protestants vs. Catholics, Salafis vs. secularists, etc.), utilizing images

---

2. Art historian Finbarr Barry Flood puts it best in his argument for the necessity for proper historical analysis on iconoclasm in Islam: "The conception of a monolithic and pathologically Muslim response to the image, which substitutes essentialist tropes for historical analysis, elides the distinction between different types of cultural practices. It not only obscures any variation, complexity or sophistication in Muslim responses to the image but also a priori precludes the possibility of iconoclastic 'moments' in Islamic history, which might shed light on these complex responses" (Flood 2002:641).

for their own motives and ends. At stake in the defense and destruction of images is the very imaginary institution of divine authority.

With this in mind, it is crucial to approach the holy icon as itself a total institution of signifying linkages. In the case of the Virgin's icon in Port Said, such linkages connect the print portrait to a laywoman's dream, and later to her own oil-emitting body. Contests over these linkages concern the imaginary politics of authority such as the religious authority of a spiritual novice, or the state's authority to intervene in extraordinary matters. The holy icon is therefore not simply the bounded portrait image, but, rather, the image in relation to the larger organizational complex of signs within which it is embedded. Following Charles Peirce's (1955) schema of signs, the "icon" signifies by virtue of its "likeness" or "similarity" to the signified. The signifying potential of the icon ultimately derives from the force of convention and the regulation of custom. Inasmuch that different people share signifying linkages between any given image and its ritual value, they belong to a common realm of imagination.

To grasp the politics of the icon and its impact on Christian-Muslim relations in particular, there are two points to examine in more depth. Both concern the public nature of sainthood. The first is the representation of the holy person, or what Matta al-Miskin referred to as the icon's "owner" (al-ṣāḥib). The second is the hidden world of divine manifestation, or what liturgists refer to as the icon's "mystery" (al-sirr). A closer examination of these two points provides a useful gauge for assessing the potentials and threats associated with images.

A holy man or woman can be a saint, prophet, wonderworker, or messenger. As fieldworkers have richly described, Christians, Jews, and Muslims in Egypt share the notion of a holy contemporary, or the saint who lives among us (Ghosh 1992; Hoffman 1995). To the extent that a contemporary holy person figures in the imagination, he or she is a "living icon" (Brown 1971). The mediation of saints, moreover, has caused disputes within and internal to religious traditions as they have developed in late modern Egypt: Salafis and Sufis disagree on the legitimacy of saints, as do Coptic Orthodox and Coptic Evangelicals. What is common among believers in saints—Muslim and Christian alike—is the practice of recognizing holy contemporaries through his or her miracles or wonders (al-muʿgizāt for Christians, al-karāmāt for Muslims). In other words, it is the signifying linkage between any given holy sign and its "owner," which is essential to the common recognition of saints. It is also this linkage between a sign and its author which introduces the possibility of religious engagement across faiths.

Standing in for its owner, the holy icon functions as a holy person does. Miracle icons are those special icons attributed with human, life-like qualities such as bleeding, weeping, and sweating. In the place of the saint whom it represents, the icon enacts miracles with the ultimate effect of converting unbelief into faith. An excerpt from a tenth-century Coptic manuscript helps illustrate the icon's miraculous agency and purpose:

> When the workman picked up the basket, blood flowed continually from the basket which contained the icon of the Virgin, which [the unbeliever] had destroyed. . . . Thereupon when they had come to me I brought up, out of the basket, the tablet of wood upon which the picture of the Virgin as drawn. Believe me, my brothers, I gazed at the face of the picture—I and the bishops who were with me—we saw its countenance to be sad, as if weeping tears of blood. . . .
>
> The icon remains ever unto now, and it shall remain world without end. And every man that is in various diseases and those that are possessed of devils, and those who writhe—in a word, anyone that has any disease—if they salute this icon of the Virgin in faith, will obtain good health and restoration. (Attributed to Patriarch Theophilus 384–412 C.E., quoted from Skalova and Gabra 2001:33)

In this manuscript's account, the Virgin's icon overcomes iconoclastic attempts to destroy it. As the medium of worldly salvation, its presence is described as endless, or "without end." Accessible to everyone in principle, the icon's miraculous power circulates widely for all who recognize it with faith. Functioning also as a relic that transmits the saint's power through tactile sympathy, the icon propagates *baraka* across boundaries via fluid substances such as blood, oil, and water. Distributing the fame of the saint, the icon advances belief, the ultimate mark of spiritual conversion.

The holy icon is not only public image in the sense that it is commonly accessible. It is also public in the sense that it provides an outward, visible manifestation of its invisible owner—a link between two separate worlds of earth and heaven. For this reason, Coptic teachings refer to the icon as a "mystery" (Bishop Mettaous 1996) and other Orthodox teachings refer to it as a "window" or an "opening" (Florensky 2000 [1922]; Bishop Kallistos Ware 1979). Revealing its hidden owner, the icon links the believer to "the one who is behind the color and material," to repeat the words of Matta al-Miskin.

The icon's role as a revelatory medium must be situated in relation to the larger visual culture of manifestations in which it is embedded. As the previous chapter demonstrated, Christians and Muslims in Egypt today share an active realm of dreaming through which saints make appearances from the hidden world. Here, it is worth briefly noting that a definition of "aniconism" (often attributed to Islam) that is narrowly fixated on the icon as portrait art fails to account for the icon's relationship to this rich, lived dimension of visual figurations. Linked to dream-images that cross the boundary between worlds (Pandolfo 1997; Crapanzano 2004), the icon provides another ritual interface for communicating messages and miracles. For example, I have listened to several Copts tell me how a saint appeared in a waking vision by way of his or her icon, in addition to others who have used icons to resuscitate their visual encounters with a given saint. Icons and dreams may, in short, reveal hidden presences across a series of interconnected images. The meaning of icons therefore must be approached within this larger context of mimetic images and their locally understood linkages.

In Christianity and Islam, the realm of dreams provides a common world of miracles and wonders. In late ancient Mediterranean Egypt (before the historical advent of Christianity and Islam), Greco-Roman rituals of dream incubation attracted people of various social strata looking for fertility, remedies from illnesses, and general guidance from the other world (Frankfurter 1998a). The Arabic language of a saint "performing surgery" (ʿamal ʿamiliyya) in one's sleep hints at the historically doubled role of gods like Asclepius as both temple priests and medical physicians who were understood to frequently cure his clientele with the help of his assistants (Miller 1994; cf. Lang 1977). For contemporary Muslims, the ritual of istikhāra continues as a vibrant practice of seeking divine guidance, wherein dreams are a key venue of signs and miracles (Ewing 1997; Edgar and Henig 2010; Mittermaier 2011; Hamdy 2012). As is the case with all holy signs, the religious authority of prophets and saints hinges on people recognizing them as their authors. For both Christians and Muslims, dreams are one key means to secure the linkage between a miraculous sign and its owner.

To sum up, the holy icon belongs to a larger system of signs that shape the visually public nature of the holy saint. As such, the politics of the icon does not concern the portrait image in isolation, but rather the entire network of accessing signifying linkages that endow the icon with its meaning and force. In this analytic vein, acts of iconoclasm exceed delimited acts of physical destruction. Iconoclasm also includes acts of intervention and disruption into those crucial linkages between images and their owners—linkages that reveal the icon's mystery. Such acts can foreclose the possibility for holy icons to effect conversion and manifestation across religious lines.

"MUSLIM VIRGIN" VERSUS "CHRISTIAN VIRGIN"

On the face of it, it is clear that the owner (al-ṣāḥib) behind the miracle icon in Port Said is the Virgin Mary. More enigmatic, however, is what the icon and its oil-exuding activity remember about the Virgin. The story of the miracle icon is a story about how the Virgin's authority is made public. Accounting for different versions of the story requires unearthing the linkages between the acts attributed to the Virgin and what they are perceived to manifest or reveal.

Let us first rehearse the details of the church's official narrative of the icon's origins in a dream event. In the dark early morning hours of February 20, 1990, the Virgin Mary visited Samya Yusif Basiliyus in her dream and healed her of breast cancer. News of the miracle spread like wildfire. Only a day later, on Wednesday, February 21, 1990, the Egyptian national daily al-Ahram published an article with the headline: "Citizen of Port Said Alleges That the Virgin Mary Came and Performed Surgical Excision of a Cancerous Tumor for Her in Her Sleep." By Thursday, other major newspapers such as Ruz al-Yusif and al-Akhbar circulated their reports. The verb "allege" (tadda'ī) and the article's placement in al-Ahram's section "Events . . . and Issues" (rather than "Local News," for example) cast doubt on Samya's account of the Virgin's miracle for her. If there was any public controversy on the streets that the mass media had sparked, it concerned Samya's account of the Virgin as a reliable one. In keeping with the official church narrative, Samya herself began to exude oil on March 17. The Virgin made Samya's right hand exude oil, as the narrative goes, so that people would not doubt Samya's account any longer.

In what follows, I focus on what might have occurred during the brief window of time between the mass media's announcements of Samya's dream (February 21) and Samya's hand exuding oil (March 17). Following her confessional priest Father Bula's alternate narrative, the full plot of the Virgin's icon unfolds during this period when significant public "disorder" or "confusion" broke out over the dream's contents. Nothing in Father Bula's story counters the church's official narrative; rather, it only reveals significant omissions. These omissions are what I further engage here, by first revisiting the details of Samya's miracle on February 20.

According to her officially documented account,[3] Samya's dream opens with a mysterious cast of characters:

I slept and I found that the Virgin Mary came—she was very very beautiful, I cannot describe her beauty—and her color was as bright as a neon light and her eyes were very very blue. She was wearing a light blue robe and a white dress, just like how she is dressed in pictures of the [Zaytun] apparition.

And then she said to me, "Get up, I am going to perform the surgery for you." I said to her, "No, are you going to remove my breast?" She said, "Don't be afraid, I will be the one to do the surgery for you."

We walked to this place where there was a beautiful, very big garden. And after, as we were walking, we saw a church and there was an elderly man [*ragul kabīr*] sitting in there. There was also an elderly lady [*sitt kabīra*] with him, and I had seen this woman before [in my dreams.] And I asked the Virgin and the two, "Take me with you, please take me with you."

And we walked through the garden, they weren't walking with their feet touching the ground. They were walking as if on smoke. We walked right through the doors, and we found a beautiful, very beautiful room. And we found a bed there.

They laid me down on that bed. I told her, "I am afraid." She said, "Don't be afraid." And then, a small child [*ṭifl ṣughayyar*] came down from above and stood next to the Virgin.

Then, they took my hands and stretched me out on the bed. And after, I found the elderly man grabbing one hand—I didn't know him—and the elderly lady grabbing the other hand. And I saw the young boy give the Virgin something, but I didn't know what it was. Then I felt heat and an intense pain, and heat. And because of that pain and heat, I pulled back my hand and grabbed my breast. That's why when I woke up there was a lot of blood in my hand.

The Virgin looked at me with intensity, with her blue eyes. I found that they were holding me down strong, so strong that I cried a lot. And then the elderly man took my hand and began to pat it gently. When he did that, I asked the Virgin, "Who is he?" She said, "That is the guardian of your church."

And then suddenly, none of [the three] were there in front of me any more—they disappeared. It was just me and the Virgin.

In this drama of her dream, there were a total of four figures at the surgeon's bed. In addition to the Virgin, three of her assistants were present: "an elderly man," "an elderly lady," and "a small child." In her official account, Samya also identifies the "elderly man" to be "St. Bishoi the Great" and the "small child" to be "St. Abanub the Martyr" (both are

---

3. Samya's oral testimony is available on the following websites: (in Arabic) https://youtu.be/FNlPwibzY1U; (with English subtitles) https://youtu.be/e9DcW-w4ZDw (accessed May 28, 2018).

fourth-century Coptic Orthodox saints). When I interviewed Father Bula privately, on December 27, 2010, he provided additional details about how the identities of these three unknown figures had been revealed to Samya. Immediately after she awoke from her dream, Samya used the church's icons to link the faces she saw in her dream to the portrait pictures of St. Bishoi and St. Abanub. However, she could not locate the icon of the "elderly lady," unable to link her face with a name.

According to Father Bula, it was the unknown identity of this lady—whom he referred to as "the fourth" (al-rābi')—which caused a problem. To this day, "the fourth" remains curiously unidentified in Samya's recorded account: Who was "the fourth"?

Father Bula further elaborated on how "the fourth" rapidly became an open sign for public speculation. Within a couple days of the newspaper reports on Samya's dream, one interpretation reached residents in Port Said. Father Bula explained to me what had occurred on Friday, February 23, after Samya's miracle on Tuesday, February 20 (not part of the official church narrative).

> On Friday—and here is the important part—on Friday, the mosques in Port Said got involved. They said, "Everyone! Sayyida 'A'isha [the wife of the Prophet Muhammad] did a miracle with Sittina Maryam [Islamic title for the Virgin Mary] to a woman and they healed her."
>
> When they said this, it caused disorder [balbala] among the Christians. "We want to know who this lady [the fourth] is."

When Father Bula described to me the controversy over "the fourth," he lingered a bit on the word balbala. The Arabic term balbala translates into several English terms such as "disorder," "confusion," or "chaos." An onomatopoetic word, bal-bal-a mimetically captures the sound of "disquiet" or "jumble." Muslim pronouncements that the authors of Samya's miracle were Sayyida 'A'isha and the Virgin Mary incited balbala among Coptic Christians in Port Said. Copts sought a definitive answer: Who was "the fourth"?

> So she slept and saw a vision. Samya slept on the night of that Friday. And she saw a vision of the Virgin with the elderly lady who came to her. She already knew St. Bishoi and Abanub the Martyr. She said to [the Virgin], "Who is this fourth?" [The Virgin] said to her, "Ask her."
>
> She asked [the fourth], "What is your name?" [The fourth] said to her, "My name is Alisabat." She said to her, "We don't have your icon." [The fourth] said to her, "But you have an icon of my son John the Baptist [Yuhanna al-Ma'madan]."

Samya's second dream, on the evening of Friday, February 23, revealed "the fourth" to be St. Elizabeth (or "al-Qiddisa Alisabat" in Arabic). To allay the *balbala* in the public, the Virgin reappeared to Samya to resolve the mystery of the elderly lady who had assisted in her miraculous healing. The anxious Coptic community received Samya's message as the Virgin's response to the Muslim community's broadcasts at the mosques on Friday morning.

In the official church account, there is no mention of Muslims in Port Said exerting any impact on the public course of divine revelations. The ritual narrative of Samya's encounter with the Virgin is rather confined to the communal space of Christian interpretation. Father Bula's account, by contrast, draws on aspects of the larger national and religiously mixed public to explain exactly how and why *balbala* materialized. Public disorder—*al-balbala*—was one outcome of Samya's dream, having been shaped by the public particularities of sainthood. What I mean to argue here is the way in which Christians and Muslims share enough in common to make for a significant public controversy over a woman's dream. The potentials and risks associated with saints are defined by the specific media and modes of communicating divine messages to people. It was only because there were enough commonly held signs and communicative practices (particularly between Christians and Muslims in Port Said) that *balbala* could even happen in the first instance.

On one register of the Christian-Muslim public, there is the common cast of holy persons whether they are saints, prophets, miracle-workers, angels, messengers, and so on. The Virgin Mary, as we saw in the previous chapters, is the most popular and widespread example of a holy figure venerated in both Christianity and Islam. The fact that Christians and Muslims share the Virgin gave rise to the potential for common recognition of Samya's miracle. At the same time, the empty signifier of "the fourth" also introduced the risk for Christian-Muslim difference: Was "the fourth" Sayyida 'A'isha or St. Elizabeth? Was the Virgin in Samya's dream the "Muslim Virgin" or the "Christian Virgin"? As the wife of the Prophet Muhammad, Sayyida 'A'isha is cherished in the Sunni tradition (and despised in the Shi'i tradition for leading a war against Imam 'Ali). As the mother of St. John the Baptist, St. Elizabeth is honored in the Coptic Church, but with arguably less popularity relative to other saints. Following Islamic tradition, John the Baptist and Elizabeth are also venerated; however in practice, they are much more so among Christians. During that brief period when the Virgin was collectively imagined to have performed surgery with a mysteriously unidentified woman, Christians and Muslims took avid interest in talking about her and speculating on "the fourth." The condition of possibility for this communicative activity was the common imagining of the Virgin Mary across communal lines.

On another register of the Christian-Muslim public, there is the entire complex of communicative practices that structure the circulation and exchange of news, images, hearsay, and revelations. Beyond a cast of common characters, Christians and Muslims believe in the visual manifestation of hidden figures, and in the miracles and wonders that confirm their authority. Even the dream-incubation genre of the Virgin "performing surgery" is recognizable for members of both communities. Within days of Samya's miracle on February 20, the national dailies introduced news of an imaginary encounter between the Virgin and a "citizen of Port Said" (religious identity is unmarked). The plot of Marian revelations continued to unfold across a chain of events that took place between Christians and Muslims: Muslims learned about the "elderly lady" from Christians, Christians overheard the mosques' announcements. Composed of linked causes and effects, the popular imagination was mixed and reciprocal across time and space. The potential for *balbala* thus emerged out of a particular cultural public of Christian-Muslim interactions.

In reply to the *balbala,* Samya's second dream presented the identity of her miracle's author: "the Christian Virgin." By revealing "the fourth" as St. Elizabeth, her dream confirmed Christian ownership over the miracle in a moment of public disorder and confusion. Samya's dream was authoritative, however, only to the extent that Christians and Muslims recognized Samya's authority to see saints and represent them. As the church's official narrative also recounts, there were also many people who still thought she was lying.

THREATS OF CONVERSION

At this point, it was Samya's hand—an image of holy contact—that intervened in the controversy. On March 17, 1990, Samya Yusif Basiliyus's body began to exude oil and continued exuding for a significant period of time. During a women's meeting at the church, her right hand started dripping oil from its pores with such volume that it could be visibly collected in cups. In the words of Bishop Tadros of Port Said, the

Virgin gave this sign so that it would be "so clear that God has accepted Samya and her repentance." Unlike the interior and private space of dreaming, her hand emitted oil "so that everyone could see with their own eyes." Seen in this light, her body's new miracle was directed toward dispelling confusion, or *balbala*, with regard to her mediating authority.

In fact, what ended up happening was quite the opposite. Samya's oil-manifesting hand generated new types of *balbala*. Was Samya herself a saint and wonderworker? In March 1990, Samya was a forty-year-old, uneducated, ordinary store owner who had only joined the Church two years prior. Speaking in throaty dialect and dressed in a bright orange jellabiya with a purple headscarf, she was far from the image of a quiet monastic nun in a neutral-colored habit. We can easily imagine what kind of threat she might have posed for the Coptic Church and within the Coptic community. In the Christian Middle East more broadly, female visionaries have been subject to popular suspicion and clerical control, from the eighteenth-century Hindiyya al-ʿUjaymi of Mount Lebanon (Makdisi 2008; Khater 2011) to the contemporary stigmatic Myrna Akhras of Damascus (Bandak 2013). In my conversation with one prominent Coptic bishop in September 2010, I was told that popular attention to Samya's oil-exuding oil would be of no "spiritual benefit" to Samya; if it had truly been a miracle, she could "simply keep the miracle to herself." This bishop also explained that "the people are simple" (*al-nās basīṭa*) and they would be "confused" by her. In his view, Samya's miraculous hand posed a moral and spiritual threat to communal order.

Outside the Coptic community, there was also the additional threat of Christian-Muslim *balbala*, or the confusion of religious identities. Samya's miraculous body was a potential attraction for any Egyptian who believed in saints. From a secular-critical perspective, a description that "the people are simple" is the same as that of "gullible masses" (cf. Le Bon 2002; Tarde 1989). As the classic subject of manipulation, "the masses" are imagined to be susceptible to irrational belief and conversion. For Egypt in particular, the cult of saints—with its rowdy, crowded street festivals or *mawālid*—suffers from a reputation of disorderliness, entertainment, and superstition. For example, anthropologists of Sufism have shown how British colonial authorities banned these festivals as they were viewed as classic occasions for "mob formation" (Gilsenan 2000), and how the Egyptian police under the Mubarak regime used street festivals to inculcate public order through new practices of civil spatial organization (Schielke 2008). If Samya had already been gaining significant mass-mediated interest, it would have been highly possible that her newly active hand was attracting increasingly more attention from both Christians and Muslims in her neighborhood.

Following Father Bula's firsthand account to me, Samya's oil-exuding hand had attracted enough public attention for the local police in Port Said to get involved shortly after March 17. After inspection in Port Said, Samya, Father Bula and another priest from St. Bishoi Church were requested to travel to the national headquarters of the Ministry of the Interior in Cairo.[4] There, one chief official of state security also examined Samya's hand with her two priests and about ten to twelve officers present in the inspection room: "This was in front of him and other officers, in his office. They all saw the oil and some of them were afraid of her. They said, 'She is doing this so that Muslims will believe.' He said, 'Where are you going, Father?' 'We are going to the monastery.' 'Fine. It would be best if you stayed there a little bit and don't go home now. If you go home, it will make disorder [al-balbala] between Muslims and Christians.'" The preceding excerpt is a priest's verbal account of state security's encounter with a holy sign. As such, it opens with a familiar, hagiological tone. Skeptics of Father Bula's account might raise the following questions: "Did this really happen?" "Why would Egyptian state security possibly want to intervene in a phenomenon as strange as one woman's alleged miracle?" In reply to these questions motivated by doubt, I pose a related question from a slightly different direction: "Given its record of policing the public activity of citizens, what is unbelievable about Egyptian state security intervening in one woman's alleged miracle?" Apart from whether or not the officers had been actually shaken up by the miracle, their intervention is only another example of how the state's regulatory powers extend to the public expression of divine authority.

Samya's visit to state security headquarters in Cairo ended with her staying put behind monastery walls for five years. In contexts of managing Christian-Muslim *balbala,* the Coptic Church and the Egyptian state have a widely known record of institutional collusion. Signaling the transgression of communal boundaries, acts of conversion have historically sparked sectarian unrest between Christians and Muslims for

---

4. In the Tahrir protests of 2011, the Ministry of the Interior building was partially destroyed. In April 2016, Sisi opened its new headquarters in New Cairo inside the National Police Academy.

a variety of reasons. If Samya had been perceived as attempting to convert others, she would have been considered on the order of a proselytizer of Christianity to Muslims. One Coptic employee of a nongovernmental organization with extensive fieldwork experience developing peace-building projects with priests and shaykhs in the Delta offered another hypothesis. When I told him about Samya and the possibility of police involvement in her publicity, he suggested that the Coptic Church might have also placed her under its guardianship for her own physical safety from unruly crowds or religious extremists. Due to threats of conversion and/or violence, it would have been highly probable that state security officials charged the Coptic Church with subjecting her to close surveillance.

The tactics of hiding women behind monastery walls in the name of Christian-Muslim order is relatively routine. On a regular basis, the Coptic Church functions as the institutional patron of communal rights in ways that problematically subordinate the individual rights of Coptic women. As I mentioned earlier in this chapter, the Egyptian state and Coptic Church have worked together to hide Coptic women who have allegedly converted to Islam behind monastery walls. In this context of managing *balbala* between Christians and Muslims, the Egyptian state has authorized the Coptic Church to bring these women under its custodial discipline and without their consent. However, the *balbala* linked to Samya's public visibility was of an entirely different nature than that ignited by the converts. She was not a disputed subject of conversion who had ignited Christian-Muslim uproar around rights to religious freedom. Rather, Samya and her oil-exuding hand catalyzed Christian-Muslim confusion in the field of wonders, miracles, and the transmission of divine authority. As a holy image herself, Samya presented a threat to religious and political institutions of representing the highest rungs of power.

To understand the nature and effects of Samya's arrest behind monastery walls, I therefore shift our analytic frame to the institutional politics of public imagination. More specifically, I propose considering the state's intervention into the common realm of miracles on the order of "iconoclasm." To reiterate, iconoclasm is not so much about physical acts of image destruction, as it is about disruptions in communicative linkages between an image and its holy owner. At stake in Samya's separation and exclusion from the public domain is the communication of holy authority. Here, I find the work of philosopher Marie-José Mondzain on the politics of the Byzantine imaginary useful for analyzing the institutional transformations entailed in Samya's monastery arrest. In her approach to iconoclasm, Mondzain rejects the widespread notion that Byzantine debates around the holy image were a "doctrinal screen" in secondary relation to the political realities of the Byzantine empire and its crisis of authority. Charting a different line of inquiry, she asks: "But what if this political crisis was precisely a crisis of iconicity?" (Mondzain 2002:2).

The public nature of sainthood is based on the holy icon and its mediation of authority. At the heart of the politics of sainthood is the legitimate institution of "holiness." Mondzain further argues that Byzantine iconoclastic controversies centered around two competing orders of "holiness": the *hiéron* and the *hagion*. Building on the work on the structural linguist Émile Benveniste, she explores the implications of the distinction between *hiéron* and *hagion* (Greek terms used in eighth-century theological debates over the icon):

> In respect to the Greek material, Benveniste concentrates specifically on *hiéron* and *hagion,* the sacred and the holy. The sacred—*hiéron*—occurs in relation to the terminology of sacrifice and venerated places or people. . . . On the other hand, *hagion* indicates rather "that the object is not allowed to be violated in any way." [The] definition of the *hagion protects it from any human contact* . . . [on the contrary], the *hiéron* comes into contact easily with the profane by means of sacrifice and human legitimation (Mondzain 2002:118, emphasis mine).

According to Mondzain's argument, Byzantium's defenders of image veneration relied on the concept of *hiéron,* opposing iconoclasts who advanced the concept of *hagion.* The distinction between *hiéron* and *hagion* is a distinction between two communicative orders of "holiness."

The *hiéron* is the public emanation of holiness through human sensory interaction. Consider the icon's capacity to circulate the saint's power outward to any potential beneficiary of the saint's *baraka:* "blood flowed continually from the basket which contained the icon of the Virgin" (Skalova and Gabra 2001:33). By contrast, the *hagion* is the public institution of holiness through the sovereign act of prohibition. The concept *hagion* is captured by the biblical image of the "holy of holies," the sanctuary "set apart" to be the sacred domain of inviolability or taboo.

In the name of public order, Samya and her hand were secluded from public visibility. In effect, the result of the state security's elimination of *balbala* was a total reconfiguration in the communicative nature of holiness. Rather than circulating in a Christian-Muslim world of divine signs and revelations, Samya's oil-exuding hand was stripped of its manifestational function. Relegated to the monastery's confines, her hand also lost its potential to move freely across communal lines and produce conversions. From the perspective of some Copts today, there is even precedent for the Egyptian state's interventions in public signs of sainthood: during my fieldwork, I have also heard rumors of the police asking bishops to put away holy men and women in the monastery to prevent *balbala*.[5] Once placed under clerical purview, such public signs of sainthood are assimilated into the Coptic Church's hierarchical order of holiness. Once placed inside the monastery, Samya and her hand thus belonged to the consecrated order of priesthood. As such, the public manifestations of her miracle also became subject to the regulatory powers of the Church.

Following Mondzain's analytic approach and argument, Samya's monastery arrest can be grasped as an act of iconoclasm. The police's ban on her holy hand—a "living icon" (Brown 1971)—is grounded in the prohibitive notion of holiness, the *hagion*. From a slightly different angle, Samya's arrest can also be approached as a violation of her human rights. Here, political philosophers of state sovereignty may recognize how Giorgio Agamben's *Homo Sacer* (1998) also draws on Émile Benveniste's distinction between the *hiéron* and the *hagion*. The one who can be killed yet not sacrificed is the "homo sacer," or the "sacred man" who occupies the space of *hagion*. Excluded from the domain of human law and recognition, the *homo sacer* stands for the "separation of life" from "the world of the living" (1998:66).

On March 25, 1990, Pope Shenouda III ordained Samya Yusif Basiliyus into the order of consecrated deaconesses. Following the ritual logic of consecrating all monastics in the Coptic Church, he did this "so that she would not return again to the world" (Father Bula Sa'd 2009). About a week after her hand had first begun exuding oil, she went to the Monastery of St. Bishoi in Wadi al-Natrun, later moving to the Convent

5. For example, there are rumors of Father Fanus of Beni Suef and his light-radiating hand, a saint likened to the Russian mystic Rasputin and reputed to have "a spiritual intelligence of the higher world [*l'intelligence du monde d'en-haut*]" (Mayeur-Jaouen 1998:148). It is further rumored that his hand had incited enough *balbala* that the police asked the Coptic Church to hide him in the Red Sea Monastery of St. Paul. As of 2014, he takes appointments there on Thursday mornings to see visitors.

FIGURE 28. Photograph of Sister Alisabat squeezing oil from her right hand into a cup, Church of St. Bishoi the Great, Port Said. Photo by author.

of St. Dimyana in Bilbays. With her newly consecrated status, Shenouda also gave Samya her new name: "Sister Alisabat."

MIRACLE OR TRICK?

At some point during her monastery confinement, Samya noticed that oil was exuding from her icon of the Virgin Mary. Located inside her cell, the icon was a print portrait of the Virgin of the Apparition—the image of the Virgin that Samya had dreamt during her miraculous surgery. When the Virgin's portrait began to exude oil, Samya's hand stopped exuding. When I asked Father Bula why her hand stopped exuding, he answered: "The icon exudes oil so then why would her hand exude oil? It is settled [khalāṣ]." Freed by the print portrait, Samya was moved to the Convent of the Good Shepherd in Port Fouad, where she could be closer to her family and home.

Now housed in the Church of St. Bishoi in Port Said, this portrait of the Virgin is venerated as a miracle icon. A "living" image, its public activity is sweating trails of oil from its paper pores. In the place of Samya's hand, the Virgin's icon and its humanlike quality is the focus of

FIGURE 29. Close-up of the bottom half of the miracle icon of the Virgin, Church of St. Bishoi the Great, Port Said. Photo by author.

cult attention. To catch the fragrant oil as it trickles down the skin of the icon, there is a plastic vinyl canopy which lines the foot of the image. It is the excessive production of oil that the icon's enthusiasts promote most. "Buckets and buckets of oil!" is how one friend's nephew had described it, showing me his keychain replica of the icon. Visitors to Port Said often record video clips of the icon's oil-exuding action with their mobile phones. On one of my visits, I also spotted a television in the church's courtyard that was broadcasting live images of the icon and its shimmering beads of oil.

In his book *Art and Agency* (1998), anthropologist Alfred Gell examines the ways in which people interact with art as living agents in the world (see also Freedberg 1989). Exploring what he refers to as the "art nexus," Gell argues for studying the agency of art through the network of social relations in which any given art-object is embedded. As I have argued so far, the holy authority of the Virgin's icon is situated within the larger manifestational context of its signifying linkages to other images and events. Imagined as an agent of the Virgin's power, the icon is an indexical connection to the Virgin and her capacity to act in the world. According to the church's ritual narrative which links the icon to

Samya's encounter with the Virgin, the person behind the icon is ultimately its "owner": the Virgin Mary. Following the narrative, the miracle icon's agency indicates the Virgin's displacement of Samya's hand with the print portrait. The oil-exuding icon provides another sign among signs, in memory of Marian acts for its viewers.

However, there are not many viewers of the Virgin's miracle icon who know about Samya, her dreams, and her hand. From my conversations about the icon with Copts back in Cairo, for example, I learned that most had limited and vague knowledge about the Virgin's miracle for a woman in Port Said. What rather captivated the most public interest was the icon's unnatural production of oil: Is the oil "human" or "divine" in origin? Is the icon a "miracle" (al-mu'giza) or a "trick" (al-khidā')? This new direction of public inquiry, which focused on the icon's spectacular manufacture of oil, removed the icon from its social relations to other signs and messages in the past. Consequently, the icon-object entered into another nexus of perceiving and evaluating its activity.

In the neighborhood surrounding the Church of St. Bishoi in Port Said, there were a number of people who characterized the icon as a "trick" (khidā'). Roaming around in Manshiyya Square and its side streets, I popped in and out of stores to learn what Muslim local residents thought about the Virgin's icon. For those who did know about the icon (and not many knew of it, actually), their immediate reaction was to explain its oil-exuding activity in terms of human illusion and technical fabrication. In my interview with him, Father Bula had also pulled out his personal archive of newspaper clippings that documented the various investigative journalists who had visited the icon over the previous twenty years. Many of these journalists were hunting for the "real cause" behind the icon's apparent production of oil. Were priests refilling the vinyl canopy with oil when no one was looking? Were there hidden tubes and ducts that connected the icon to its true supply of oil? In some of the clippings' photographs, these journalists are searching behind the Virgin's print portrait for possible explanations to its oily surface. Aiming to expose the secret behind the icon's extraordinary agency, the news industry presented its account through the prism of technological artifice.

There was relatively little attention, all told, paid to the icon in Port Said outside the Coptic community. When there has been public interest in the icon, however, the icon has been primarily framed as a technology of deception. These public tropes of disillusionment and mystification suggests some family resemblance to the icon's ritual language of revelation and mystery. Instead of approaching them as categorical opposites, the "miracle" and the "trick" may also be considered as two sides of the same coin. Borrowing the words of philosopher Hent de Vries, the "special effect should be understood against the backdrop of the religious tradition, in particular, the miracle . . . the miracle has always been characterized by a certain mechanicity or technicity" (de Vries 2001:28). The icon's miraculous agency, in other words, may be regarded to be itself a technical effect of tradition.

Aside from public discourse on its status as a "trick," indifference to the icon altogether was expressed. In this perspective, the icon was not relevant to "true belief" even if its oils were not human-produced. To give an example, I invoke the reply of one older Muslim man to my question if he had heard of the oil-exuding icon of the Virgin in Port Said. After Father Bula had informed me about the mosques' Friday announcements about Samya's dream, I tried to learn more by visiting the popular al-Abbasid Mosque a few hundred meters inland from the Church of St. Bishoi. Inside its side entrance, over a table of enormous shrimp, the mosque's custodian explained that neither dreams nor icons were essential to faith. Building on a Qur'anic reference, he replied: "They said, 'Show us God in public signs,' but we in Islam, we believe in God, whether or not anybody saw him. That's why the Prophet said, 'My companions are those who believe in me without seeing me.'"

The custodian's caution against signs and wonders was not exclusive to Muslims in the neighborhood. Shortly after my visit to the mosque, I rode the green-painted ferry over the Suez Canal to Port Fouad in an attempt to find Samya at the Convent of the Good Shepherd. One younger nun who met me at the convent expressed a kindred tone of caution. As I showed her my plastic ampoules of oil from the miracle icon, she soberly noted: "The true miracle is that Samya repented and came to Christ." Against popular trends toward sensationalism, this nun's rebuke is directed toward the excessive focus on saints' miracles instead of the greater moral message of the saints and their exemplary lives.

The public value of the Virgin's icon in Port Said hinges on what truth (or falsity) its oil-exuding activity is perceived to signify. Currently bound to the binary opposition of "miracle" versus "trick," contestations over the icon's agency are delimited to whether or not it is a by-product of "divine" or "human" design. And yet, the icon's value as a *dhikrā*, or token of memory, is elided in the process. The material memory of the icon consists of the temporal sequence of causes and effects which gave rise to its signifying power. It also consists of the narrative linkages between Samya's various encounters with the Virgin. Once alienated from its history of social interactions, the icon's terms of mystery and revelation were radically transformed. Simply put, the question of what the icon remembers, or what it is supposed to recall for open reflection, has been entirely forgotten.

Before the icon's displacement of Samya's hand, the public controversy over authorship (al-ṣāḥib) had centered around which saints had been present in Samya's miraculous dream. Recuperating this memory behind the icon risks retrieving the repressed threat of Christian-Muslim balbala. As far as I can tell, there are only two traces of this repressed memory currently in public circulation. The first is Samya's new name in the convent, "Alisabat." The second is the icon's oil, the active secretions that recollect the secret of Samya's arrest.

SECURITY AND SECRECY

After hearing that the local police and state security had once taken interest in Samya's oil-exuding hand, I immediately embarked on a hunt for concrete evidence. Was it true that the state had been involved in regulating the miracle? If so, what were the exact reasons for removing Samya from public sight? For obvious reasons, I did not have access to state security files, nor did I wish to draw unwanted attention to my questions from the police or state authorities. As is the case with all ethnographic accounts, I accepted that mine would also have to remain incomplete, penned in the Frazerian spirit of an "anthropological detective purveying both clues and answers" (Munn 1996:446).

Toward the end of my fieldwork in Port Said in 2010, a conversation with one inquisitive woman got me thinking that I might have been asking the wrong questions all along. In my quest for an account full of as many points of view that I could possibly gather, I had been wandering around the church in an attempt to find local Muslim residents who could remember any talk of Marian miracles from twenty years ago. Veiled and clothed in business attire, a middle-aged woman noticed me popping in and out of doors. She approached me on the street and invited me to share an afternoon tea in her office. A manager at the National Bank of Egypt, she worked in an impressive corner office which commanded a glorious vista of Manshiyya Square. Sipping hot sugary black tea, we sat next to her office window, which overlooked the square's fountain, the kiosks, and shops, in addition to the Church of St. Bishoi.

Introducing myself to her, I explained that I was an anthropologist interested in the miracle icon of the Virgin in the Church of St. Bishoi. She asked, "Did you see it with your own eyes?" I nodded, pulling out the plastic vials of oil from my bag. Opening each one, she peered inside and sniffed its fragrances. At this point in our dialogue, she said something that caught me by surprise: "Christians do most of their activities inside the church. I don't know what goes on inside there."

In this chapter so far, I have stayed close to the story behind the Virgin's icon in Port Said, beginning with the public life of dream incubation and the confusion that it stirred between Christians and Muslims. Analyzing the mediating specificity of dreams, icons, and saintly authority, I focused on points at which Christian and Islamic traditions overlapped and diverged. What this bank manager directed my attention toward is the plain fact that Christian activities are cordoned off from the mixed public at large: the miracle icon is simply not accessible to Muslims. More than this, her reply that she doesn't know "what goes on inside there" betrayed her sense of curiosity and prohibition. The idea that Copts conduct their activities in mysterious seclusion further serves to affirm the ongoing stereotype of Copts as "devious and secretive," along with the deeply troubling sociological conclusion that their secretiveness is due to a "natural desire for self-preservation" (Pennington 1982:178). The secret status of the miracle icon adds merely another element to the broader, public sense that Copts are hiding something from Muslims.

The Coptic Church's tactics of secrecy are productive, fueling suspicions and new types of threats. Rather than verifying if something did occur in secret, it is thus also imperative to examine what the *effects* of secrecy are (whether or not there is a secret to begin with). In Port Said, there is a long-standing history of Muslims perceiving and suspecting Christians to be carrying out criminal activities. Most recently, for instance, the prominent Islamist intellectual Muhammad Salim al-ʿAwa suggested in a television interview that churches in Port Said are stockpiled with weapons transported from cargo ships from abroad.[6] Newspaper cartoons have also featured churches and monasteries as crusader fortresses behind which missionary activity and plans for foreign influ-

6. *Al-Jazeera*, September 23, 2010. Salim al-ʿAwa was specifically referring to news reports about a Copt-owned ship allegedly loaded with explosives that had arrived in Port Said from Israel in August 2010. See "Rising Tensions between Muslims, Christians in Egypt," Middle East Media Research Institute, November 15, 2010, www.memri.org /reports/rising-tensions-between-muslims-christians-egypt#_edn7 (accessed May 28, 2018).

ence develop (Baron 2014:154). Strategies of walling people out of visibility or preventing the open circulation of activity can also shore up public perceptions of Copts and their churches.

By directing attention to the detrimental effects of secrecy, I am not suggesting that the threats perceived by the Coptic Church and Coptic community are unwarranted. The rise of militant Islam and Salafi extremism from Aswan to Alexandria has certainly advanced a climate of violence and antagonism toward Christians overall. Keeping things quiet in order to prevent *balbala* between Christians and Muslims remains a proven strategy for maintaining communal security. At the same time, however, it is precisely the Church's history of secret-keeping which has transformed it into a target of suspicion and even violence. Perhaps the most widely known example of this highly problematic outcome are the mass-circulated threats of violence by ISIS and al-Qaʿida, levied against the Coptic Church for holding women hostage inside their churches. In natural response to these publicized threats, churches emphasize the urgent necessity for more security—and more secrecy.

In this way, security and secrecy are enmeshed in a cyclical feedback loop through which the very mechanisms of security create suspicions and threats anew. Consequently, the Egyptian state-security apparatus (*amn al-dawla*) shores up its legitimacy toward the exercise and expansion of authoritarian rule (Guirguis 2016). The Coptic community is vocal about its fears and anxieties of political Islam and sectarian disorder. Harnessing these Coptic fears, the security state has increased police regulation and intervention in alliance with the Coptic Church. The Coptic Church, in turn, has insulated the Coptic community from its surrounding Muslim society, containing its religious activities within its ghettoizing confines. Following anthropologist Joseph Masco's characterization of state counterterrorist tactics, this strategy of securitization exemplifies "the ability of officials to manage the public/secret divide through the mobilization of threat" (Masco 2010:433). Currently, the entrances of Coptic churches throughout Egypt are fortified with hired guards, new security devices, and monitoring techniques such as ID checks and required inspections.

Such structures of prohibition have a significant impact on the everyday public life of Christian-Muslim interactions. Despite her daily panoramic view of the Church of St. Bishoi on Manshiyya Square—kitty-corner and steps away from her office—the Muslim bank manager expressed that she has no idea what Christians are doing inside of it. And yet, in my dialogue about the Virgin's icon with her, I could also hear traces of her shared public sensibility with those very Christians she cannot engage. Her question to me, "Did you see it with your own eyes?" mirrored Father Bula's refrain to me, "So that everyone could see for themselves." Unlike the space of dreams, Samya's hand and the icon were controversial precisely due to their potential accessibility to all. As Father Bula showed me with his archive of photos, there was a brief period when other Muslim women had also come to the church and seen the icon's miraculous activity with their own eyes. The icon remains the sole image through which Muslims in Port Said are able to access the past of a Christian woman in the neighborhood.

SECTARIANIZING THE PUBLIC

In December 2015, five years after my last fieldwork trip to Port Said, I was back in Cairo looking for popular hagiographic literature. I went to the bookstore inside the Church of St. Mark in Heliopolis, known among Coptic bookworms for its well-stocked inventory. The clerk was an older gentleman with an unusual knack for retrieving available texts and sermon recordings. After we chatted some about saints and miracles, he handed me a Christmas card from the previous year with a handwritten greeting in English from Bishop Tadros of Port Said.

The Christmas card was also a twenty-fifth anniversary souvenir for the miracle icon in Port Said. The clerk also gave me a few plastic vials of oil, explaining how the Virgin's image had exuded enormous amounts of oil since 1990. Then, for the first time since my interview with Father Bula, he told me about the police's past involvement in Port Said. In a casual and friendly manner, he mentioned how *balbala* had transpired between Christians and Muslims, and how the police had to intervene as a result.

A lot had happened since December 2010. Aside from Samya's death in 2012, Egypt's revolutionary spirit in 2011 met its tragic end with the brutal reinvigoration of the state-security apparatus under Sisi in 2013. Against this political backdrop of increased surveillance and repression, what is possible to remember from the past? When this bookstore clerk spoke about the icon's origin in *balbala* and state regulation, he hinted at an account that has been repressed as a secret. Still, its origin is a secret that clearly lives on as one to be retold—even through the Coptic Church's bookstores.

Today, the Virgin's icon in Port Said and its mass-replicated souvenirs are largely treated as communal images within and for the Coptic

FIGURE 30. "25 Years of Oil." 2015 Christmas card from Bishop Tadros.

FIGURE 31. Ampoules of oil from the miracle icon of the Virgin, Church of St. Bishoi the Great, Port Said. Photo by author.

Christian community. The sectarianizing divide of the Egyptian public sphere has given rise to two separate publics: the "Christian public" and the "Muslim public." Egypt's Copts have their own bookstores and libraries, television and radio stations, and shops for religious paraphernalia. Egypt's Muslims have the same, and as the religious majority, with greater volume and influence. The fact that the miracle icon is housed inside a Coptic church and valued as a sign of a Coptic woman's path to repentance makes it a "Christian" image. Like any other form of Coptic media (pamphlet, video, audio recording, etc.), it travels as an exclusively communal artifact in Coptic bookstores and churches. In doing so, it attests to the broader sectarianization of Christians and Muslims into two distinct and segregated spheres of religious coexistence.

Against the widely held presumption that "religious difference" is the basis for the sectarianization of the public, the icon's backstory of *balbala* suggests that the Egyptian security state played a large role in consolidating the Christian-Muslim divide in Port Said. In other words, the sectarian divide is owed, not to essential, irreconcilable differences between Christianity and Islam, but to common points of overlap between Christian and Muslim practices of visual mediation and saintly manifestation that enabled public disorder—*balbala*. Circulated through national newspapers and mixed hearsay across churches and mosques, a woman's dream of the Virgin traveled across and throughout the mixed public. The icon was the by-product of an emergent, inchoate chain of images that brought Sayyida ʿAʾisha and St. Elizabeth into the same space of imagination. Moreover, the icon attracted Muslim women to the church and to the story of a Coptic woman's spiritual journey.

Indeed, it was the common elements between Christians and Muslims that introduced enough potential for crossover, confusion, even conversion. It was this very commonness that raised enough alarm with state security to the degree that it would intervene in the public imagination. And finally, it was the capacity of the Virgin to circulate within and across religious communities that presented a threat to public order. Sectarianizing the public is one key tactic for governing Christian-Muslim interactions. As the case of Samya's icon reveals, regulating the intercommunal divide means arresting the circulation of signs and limiting access to spaces and memories. The result is the transformation of the miracle icon into a communal image.

Rather than re-rehearsing the official church narrative of the icon, there are those very few Copts like the bookstore clerk in Heliopolis who openly recall its potential for Christian-Muslim *balbala*. In his bookstore, the ampoules of oil and its excessive abundance serve as *dhikrā* for miracles as well as for secrets.

CHAPTER 6

Hidden Faces

Humility is the life one lives between himself and God, in
which he feels he is nothing, even less than nothing, and
whatever good or righteousness he has is from God, and
without God he is but dust, darkness and evil.

Bishop Youanis of al-Gharbiya, "Humility," from
Paradise of the Spirit

Perhaps the main principle of ritual order is not justice
but face . . .

Erving Goffman, "On Face-work"

"ROBBED BY VAINGLORY"

Mornings in the Upper Egyptian village of Manahra open with the
orange-pink crawl of sunrise over its lush green fields of wheat and date
trees. One nippy morning in January 2013, I enjoyed a breakfast of
fresh curdled cheese, durra bread, and hot tea with Mahir and his family in his brick home. A farmer with deep family roots in Manahra,
Mahir worked with his mother, sister, and wife in the fields nearby.
While his sister and wife shelled dried cobs of corn in the hallway,
Mahir and his mother, Suzan, sat and chatted with me in their family
sitting room.

Upper Egypt is the great stretch of land from south of Cairo to the
Sudanese border. Manahra is located in the Mataiy district along the
Ibrahimiyya Canal, forty kilometers north of Minya, one of Upper

FIGURE 32. Photographic iconography of St. Pope Kyrillos VI, Hanging Church of the
Virgin, Old Cairo. Photo courtesy of Marc Dosch.

Egypt's largest cities. Composed of three hundred to four hundred households, Manahra is distinguished for its unusually high proportion of Coptic Christians, who currently make up about 70 percent of the village. Historically, Upper Egypt is also a region reputed for its higher concentration of Copts in comparison with the rest of Egypt. For this reason, many Coptic migrants currently living in Cairo or abroad often trace their family lineages to villages around Minya, Asyut or Sohag.

Having arrived in Manahra from Cairo the evening before, I had stayed overnight in the village's Church of the Virgin. The reason I had come to Manahra was the same reason that many Copts from Cairo and elsewhere come to Manahra: to visit the shrine of ʿAbd al-Masih al-Manahri (1892–1963, hereafter ʿAbd al-Masih). When he was alive, Christians and Muslims from Minya and its surrounding villages recognized ʿAbd al-Masih as a holy monk and wonderworker. Today, pilgrims travel to the Church of the Virgin in Manahra to take blessings from the cavelike hut where he had once performed miracles.

In addition to visiting the shrine, I also went to Manahra to learn more about the category of "the contemporary saint" (al-qiddīs al-muʿāṣir), or the holy man or woman who lived in recent instead of ancient times. Similar to the Catholic Church's revival of the "saints among us," the Coptic Church established this new category, directing attention to the continuing, living presence of holiness in the modern era (cf. Woodward 1996; Meltzer and Elsner 2011). What struck my curiosity most was the role that ordinary people played in disseminating the contemporary saint's public image after their death. Given ʿAbd al-Masih's death in 1963, the people in the last generation who had interacted with him when he was alive were most likely past their sixties at the time of my visit. How had this generation of villagers recognized his holiness? How do the people who had once lived with ʿAbd al-Masih in-the-flesh now tell stories of his sainthood to others?

When the village priest Father Istifanus heard that a foreigner had arrived in Manahra with an interest in the local saint, he immediately called on Mahir to give me a tour. At the crack of dawn, Mahir and I started our stroll through the village as its inhabitants set out to work, roused from their sleepy quiet. Sturdy women hauled ladders to their homes, carpenters pounded away in their workshops, and girls scattered feed to their ducks, chickens, and cows. After finishing our tour, Mahir invited me to meet his mother, Suzan, who used to cook food for ʿAbd al-Masih as a young girl.

FIGURE 33. From left to right: Mahir's sister, Mahir's wife, Suzan (Mahir's mother), and Mahir in Manahra. Photo by author.

On short notice, Suzan prepared us breakfast, and after eating our fill, we began to chat about the saint. Suzan described an incident when she once caught 'Abd al-Masih conversing with angels, appearing to him as flickering bursts of light, in one of the bedrooms across the hall. Suzan further described how 'Abd al-Masih told her that the lights she had noticed were not angels, but rather cars passing in the night. Mahir elaborated on his mother's final point on 'Abd al-Masih's attempt to keep his extraordinary spiritual activities a secret from others. He continued with an illustration of how one Muslim girl in a neighboring village, Na'ima Husayn, also concealed the late saint's holy powers:

> Father 'Abd al-Masih al-Manahri was a very simple man—simplicity [al-basāṭa] from the old days. He used to escape, to avoid all people in roundabout ways [biydārī al-nās].
> There was one little girl named Na'ima Husayn. She was crippled and unable to move. He used to go to her from time to time, and then one time, he healed her without going to her house to see her. He said, "Get up." And she got up, and walked in the streets. She began to play and jump, she was very happy. She said, "Father 'Abd al-Masih healed me."

So of course, the shaykh went to her and said, "Is 'Abd al-Masih a second Lord [*rabbinā al-tānī*]?" He went and made her sit down in her bed again, as she was before, and then left her. Some days passed, and the shaykh asked her, "Tell me. Who healed you? 'Abd al-Masih or the Virgin?" She said to him, "I will not say."

Mahir's account of 'Abd al-Masih, Na'ima Husayn, and the shaykh reflected a world in which saints and healers worked miracles for Christians and Muslims behind the scene.[1] His narrative closed with Na'ima evading the shaykh's question about the author of her miracle. I asked Mahir why Na'ima had refused to answer the shaykh. Replying to me, he further explained:

> Because of the wars of the people.
> "Holy virtue appeared and was robbed by vainglory [*Inna al-faḍīla ẓaharit wa-suriqit min al-magd al-bāṭil*]."
> Vainglory is something of the world. Saints don't want glory or veneration from the people. The only thing they want is heaven. After 'Abd al-Masih died, everything appeared [*ẓaharit*]. In that way, he went to heaven which was what he aimed to do. But the world, and the earth, he didn't want any of it.

Mahir invoked an image of "the people" to explain why Na'ima hid 'Abd al-Masih's identity from the shaykh. On one level, "the wars of the people" referred to Christian and Muslim contests over religious authority in the villages: whose saint is behind the miracle? On another, perhaps more primary level, "the people" introduce a source of moral peril for the saint who stands at risk of losing his salvation in exchange for worldly popularity. Drawing on an old Coptic proverb, Mahir identified "vainglory" (*al-magd al-bāṭil*) as the key reason that 'Abd al-Masih had consistently deflected credit for his miracles. For both Christians and Muslims, the act of ascribing divine value to a human being is a sin, an endangering form of false recognition. Seen in this light, 'Abd al-Masih's priority during his lifetime was to preserve, or at the very least perform, the virtue of all virtues—humility.

After our breakfast and conversation in his home, Mahir and I headed back over to the Church of the Virgin to see 'Abd al-Masih's shrine. Located behind the church, "the cave" (*al-kahf*) is where 'Abd al-Masih used to eat, sleep, and receive visitors when he was alive. Invoking the early monastics who had preferred to live in desert seclusion, the cave signaled the late saint's desire to run away from the people

---

1. Mahir's account of Na'ima Husayn's miracle can be found in roughly similar form in Coptic Church pamphlets on the life of 'Abd al-Masih al-Manahri and his miracles.

FIGURE 34. Iconography of St. ʿAbd al-Masih al-Manahri inside his cave shrine, Manahra. Photo by author.

who sought him out. ʿAbd al-Masih's tactics of escape were a key element of his legendary personality. Wearing tattered rags (now relics on display), he played the role of the wandering beggar. Cursing visitors and yelling bursts of nonsense, he feigned insanity. To this day, Manahra's villagers who remember ʿAbd al-Masih recognize this dissimulative behavior as constitutive of his holy persona.

Inside the cave, the walls are plastered with portrait icons of the late saint. Almost all of them are based on the same image—an old black-and-white photo of ʿAbd al-Masih from the late 1950s. The photo captures the late saint posing with his brows furrowed and his eyes mildly crossed. Befitting his public role, he is looking away from the camera.

MYSTICAL PUBLICITY

This chapter examines popular imaginaries of saint-making, driven by an interest in their social and political effects on Christian-Muslim interactions. Like other cult celebrities such as entertainers, politicians, and intellectuals, holy saints rely entirely on their public recognition for their canonical value. Joining 'Abd al-Masih al-Manahri and other contemporaries, Popes Kyrillos VI (1902–71) and Shenouda III (1923–2012) have also been promoted as holy exemplars through two new museums that were opened in 2014–15 and dedicated in their honor. The Coptic explosion of "contemporary saints" only further attests to the increasing prominence of charismatic publicity.[2] Through moral styles of social imagining, popular images of saintly personae are made public in accord with particular communicative genres of circulation. In what follows, I aim to show how these genres of saint-making emerge in covert, shadowy relation to the sectarian and national publics which are more hegemonic in Egypt today.

To do this, I explore what I call "mystical publicity," a communicative genre that is distinguished by its core paradox: to be visible, holiness must be invisible; to be revealed, holiness must be hidden. Mystical publicity relies on techniques and technologies that mediate practices of holiness "becoming public." Saint-making presents a particular challenge of public relations, requiring acts of holy disclosure by means of acts of renunciation, hiding, escape, and dissimulation. These ascetic performances of withdrawal originate from Egypt's founding traditions of monasticism, as exemplified by the legendary desert fathers and cave-dwelling hermits of late antiquity (Gruber 2003; Schroeder 2007). Publicizing asceticism, however asocial it may appear to be, hinges on the social circulation of holiness—what anthropologist William Mazzarella has referred to in another context of icon-making as the "substance of its collective truth" (2010:23). The collective recognition of sainthood involves social acts of hiding that serve as holy images of self-revelation.

Contemporary saints further offer the potential to exceed the intercommunal framework of national public. Scholars have usefully proposed that Coptic saints, and their miracles on behalf of Muslim elites in particular, provide communal signs of assertion in light of the marginalized status of

2. Referred to as "twentieth century jewels" (gawāhir al-qarn al-'ashrīn), the Coptic Church's contemporary saints include the following sample: Bishop Abram of Fayyum (1829–1914), Father Mikha'il al-Bahayri (1848–1923), Father Falta'us al-Suryani (1922–2010), Father 'Abd al-Masih al-Habashi (1898–1973), Father Yustus al-Antuni (1906–76), and Father Andrawus al-Samu'ili (d. 1988). There are also a handful of females in the saintly ranks including the caregiver Umm al-Ghalaba ("Mother of the Poor," 1910–92), and the late abbess of the Convent of St. Abu Sayfayn, Tamav Irini (1936–2006) (Mayeur-Jaouen 2010). Coptic contemporary saints are mostly monastic males, to the overwhelming exclusion of women.

Copts (Shenoda 2012). Here, I suggest that mystical publicity is a communicative order of image circulation that percolates beneath and against the Christian-Muslim divide. From the village fool to the papal head, the saint performs otherworldly acts for everyone and all, eliminating the tenuous distinction between "Christian" and "Muslim." Acts of mystical publicity signify holy power in ways that both ameliorate and override sectarianizing structures of the national public sphere.

As recounted in the previous chapter, Christians and Muslims occupy separate and unequal enclaves of religious belonging. In national theaters of engagement, priests and shaykhs periodically enact interfaith unity and pronouncements against sectarian violence. Beyond these performances of unity, the Egyptian national public is more accurately understood as several publics that organize different styles and subjects of communication. In his work on the Islamic revival, for example, anthropologist Charles Hirschkind uses the term "counterpublic" to refer to the ethical forms of affective reason that stand in complementary and oppositional relation to the national public sphere (Hirschkind 2006; cf. Fraser 1990; Warner 2002). Majoritarian and minoritarian publics of religious mediation are additionally uneven and unequal in volume and effect. In many urban settings, the mosques, daily calls to prayer, and Islamic sermons disseminated via loudspeakers can often overshadow churches. From street stalls and microbuses to national television and print media, Islamic paraphernalia are abundantly accessible compared to Christian materials which are largely confined to Coptic neighborhoods or bookstores inside churches.

The effects of sectarian segregation and insulation are generative: communal secrets amplify suspicions and threats. At the same time, there are forms of concealment and covert practices of circulation—that is, mystical publicity—that are constitutive of public imaginaries of holy personhood and their open manifestations. If Coptic Christians must keep quiet about their saints and their miracles, then what work do their acts and discourses on hiding accomplish? What does it look like to "publish" a saint into wider circulation?

To answer these questions, I analyze mystical publicity as a coextensive supplement to the mixed national public and its unevenly repressive character. The repression of holiness is, in fact, what animates the social imaginary of the wonderworking underground. The contemporary saint is foremost a "hidden icon." As a "hidden icon," he or she sets into motion a paradox of secrecy and disclosure, refusal and revelation. Secrecy is therefore intrinsic to mystical publicity. To be more precise, mystical publicity sets into motion a communicative dynamic in which "secrecy must itself be performed in a public fashion in order to be understood to exist" (Herzfeld 2009:135). The contemporary saint relies on the social collusion, or "intimacy," of others who manage his or her holy image in secret. The public making of sainthood thus creates social spheres of inclusion and exclusion that revolve around maintaining holy virtue.

Ethical imperatives of upholding holy virtue further override religious boundaries between Christians and Muslims. Mystical publicity is anchored in the ontological divide between life-on-earth (ephemeral) and life-after-death (eternal), captured in the temporal gap between *I will not say* and *everything appeared* in our opening fieldwork vignette. Such temporal frames of circulation also index the crucial boundary between the "human" and the "divine,"[3] an ethical limit signaled by "vainglory" in Christianity and "false association with the divine" (*al-shirk*) in Islam. Consider the shaykh's question to Na'ima Husayn: "Is 'Abd al-Masih a second lord [*rabbinā al-tānī*]?" To the extent that Christianity and Islam meet in the moral management of the human-divine divide, mystical publicity registers the potential to supersede the Christian-Muslim divide. This ethical intersection of religious traditions, moreover, enables the imagined ritual complicity of Muslims like Na'ima Husayn in keeping Coptic charisma safe in salvation.

By engaging the ethical dynamics of icon circulation, this chapter may also be read as an addendum to my previous chapter's focus on the state's regulation of the icon's miracles in Port Said for the sake of public order. Here, I see myself taking up one curious fragment (with the bishop's admonition ringing in my ears): Samya should "keep the miracle to herself" because "the people are *simple*" (emphasis mine). Similar to the Coptic Church, Russian clerical authorities under Soviet state rule were also known to invoke the Orthodox trope of the "simple people" (Greene 2010; Kormina 2013; Keane 2014). Instead of approaching the "simple people" as a political rationale for intervention, how does the virtue of "simpleness" (*al- basāṭa*) limit or prevent "wars of the people"? Aside from "simple-mindedness," simpleness connotes purity and guilelessness, or a "simple-hearted" lack of self-interest and ostentation. A variant of simpleness, the value of humility (*al-tawāḍu'*) is essential to

3. In Orthodox traditions of saintly intercession, there is a robust discussion of saints partaking in the divine essence—what is called "theosis" or "deification of the human" (*ta'līh al-insān*). However, like Copts themselves, I exercise caution when referring to saints as "divine" in contrast to my more liberal use of the term "holy." For a discussion of contemporary Coptic debates on theosis, see Davis 2008a and Heo 2013c.

maintaining the contemporary saint's public persona. Again, the moral virtue of simpleness transcends the Christian-Muslim sectarian divide, and if anything, conjures more to mind a geographic imaginary of rural villagers in Upper Egypt and the Delta than it does a religious or communal identity. More than the saint him- or herself, it is the iconic image of the "simple people" that plays a role in fixing this persona with the proper dispositions and at the right time. The "simple people" are therefore a constitutive element and effect of mystical publicity.

This chapter proceeds through several sections, first introducing the mediating logics of contemporary sainthood and then moving to their implications for Christian-Muslim sectarianism and the covert, underground forms of publicity that exceed it. Ultimately, my focus lies on the generative convergences between two moral and political economies of secrecy: (1) mystical publicity, the heart of which lies its ascetic iconology of hiddenness and revelation; and (2) communal enclaving, perhaps best symbolized by the monastery as a sacred space of exclusion from the world, and the performative mystery of its popes. All of this is to consider further the communicative horizons of exclusion that operate against, and in shadowy parallel to, the national public of religious coexistence.

HIDDEN FACES

On June 20, 2013, the Holy Synod declared the holy sainthood of St. Pope Kyrillos VI.[4] For the first time, on March 9, 2014, his annual feast-day was held on the date of his death in 1971. A year later on March 9, 2015, the inaugural opening of the Museum of St. Pope Kyrillos took place in the old Cathedral of St. Mark in Azbakiyya. Frontally facing guests at its entrance is his icon. A gold-embossed portrait with heavy black contours and geometrically simple features, the icon of St. Kyrillos is written in the hallmark style of neo-Coptic iconography pioneered by the late Isaac Fanous. To my knowledge, this icon is the first consecrated portrait painting of St. Kyrillos. Even while he had been alive, the ubiquitous presence of his visual photography indexed his status as one of the most popular saints. However, it was only after his death, and his canonization some forty years later, that this museum icon confirmed his special status in heaven.

---

4. In this chapter's description of his canonization and miraculous activity, I refer to Pope Kyrillos as "St. Pope Kyrillos." In the remainder of the book, when describing him as a political actor, I refer to him as "Pope Kyrillos."

FIGURE 35. Icon of St. Pope Kyrillos VI, Museum of St. Pope
Kyrillos VI, Azbakiyya. Photo by author.

The icon is the touchstone medium of declaring a holy person's death
and safe passage into eternal life. Intrinsically temporal in nature, the
icon is therefore a technology that institutes a divide between earthly,
worldly transience and heavenly, eternal permanence. According to art
historians Zuzana Skalova and Gawdat Gabra, the icon's progenitor
was the "mummy-portrait" or death-mask wrapped around the corpse
which was designed to signal the dead's place in the eternal realm

(Skalova and Gabra 2001:48–50; Florensky 2000 [1922]; cf. Bazin 1960). According to the theological grammar of Orthodoxy, the icon captures the contemporaneous existence of the human with the divine enabled by Christ's incarnation—what is referred to as the "hypostasis."[5] In his essay "The Meaning and Language of Icons," Russian theologian Léonid Ouspensky (to whom Pope Kyrillos had sent Isaac Fanous to study iconography in 1960s Paris) elaborates the icon's special dynamic of mediation: "Thus the icon is not a representation of the Deity, but an indication of the participation of a given person in Divine life" (Ouspensky 1999:36). As a medium of divine participation, the icon therefore serves as an instrument of prayer, a means for ordinary people to reach the saints in the other world. The metaphors of "window," "passage," "door," and "threshold" are commonly invoked to relay the unique status of the icon and the kinds of seeing associated with it.

The icon is the ritual equivalent of the holy person; the saint *is* a "living icon" (Brown 1971). The saint is a living image of extraordinary limits that transgress ordinary space and time. Seen in this light, he or she also embodies the special temporality of the icon by enacting visual exchanges between life and death. In Coptic practices of visualizing the moment of a saint's death, the saint's death is immediately followed by the substitution of a holy image in his or her place. In his film *St. Marina the Martyr,*[6] for instance, Magued Tawfik depicts St. Marina's final departure, first with the actress receding into the sky with crowns, and then with the closing image of her holy icon portrait emerging on the screen. Rather than fictional cinema, the following example belongs to the genre of miracle-images (e.g., photos or cell phone videos of Marian apparitions). During my fieldwork, a few Copts alerted me to a video that documented the spectacular death of the late saint Bishop Makarios of Qena (1923–91) while he was preparing the Eucharist.[7] The video

5. The semiotic imaginary of the "hypostasis" (the person of Christ which combines divine and human natures) lies at the knotty core of theological controversies over image veneration. Both iconophiles and iconoclasts uphold the ontological distinction between "human" and "divine" natures, but differ in their understanding of the relationship between "image" and "identity." Ouspensky elaborates: "For the Orthodox outlook, the possibility of being at the same time identical and different is quite evident—*hypostatically different, yet in nature identical* (the Holy Trinity), *and hypostatically identical, yet in nature different* (the holy icons)" (Ouspensky 1999:32, emphasis his).

6. For more on this film, see chapter 1, "Remembering Martyrs," and chapter 2, "Redemption at the Edge."

7. The video clip is available on the internet: https://youtu.be/mIkg2V5U8Xw (accessed May 5, 2018).

is perceived to reveal how the Eucharist in his hands climbed up to the altar at the moment the bishop dropped to the floor. In this visual exchange of the saint's excursus into death for the presentation of Christ's body, the video captured the mediating logics of the icon. The holy person's withdrawal is the condition for the icon's existence.

For all saints, living or dead, the icon economy provides the visual infrastructure for his or her publicity. For the contemporary saint, in particular, gaining mass visibility in the public introduces moral dangers associated with popularity, excess, and idolatry. What forms of circulation and social practices of interaction does the icon medium enable? What difference, in other words, does the mediational specificity of the icon make for the formation of cult publicity? By asking these questions, I draw attention to mystical publicity and its distinctively temporal dynamics of suspending recognition of extraordinary personhood. We can see its particular temporality in two key respects: first, in the institutional logics of canonization; and second, in the interactive techniques of covert imagination that follow from them.

Canonization is a temporal institution that foregrounds the event of death and the waiting period before canonization. In the Coptic Orthodox Church, as in the Roman Catholic Church, a candidate is eligible for canonization once a minimum duration of fifty years has elapsed after his or her death.[8] The principle behind this rule is that the moral truth of "sanctity" (al-qadāsa)—not of "popularity" (al-sha'biyya)—establishes the canonical status of the saint. At the same time, however, the Coptic Holy Synod's decision to canonize a person is based precisely on popular input, or the aggregate account of a given candidate's miracles. Again, as in the case of verifying Marian apparitions, numbers matter. Saint-making, in short, crucially hinges on the prolific publication of their acts and the moral regulation of when to publicize them. Ultimately, all acts of accounting are geared toward the most authoritative medium of saintly publication: the icon, that is, the consecrated portrait image. The icon serves as the revelation of a forever, eternal, perpetual status. Copts deploy metaphors of engraving through verbs such as "insert" or "inlay"

8. In the absence of formal legalized procedures for naming saints, the Eastern Orthodox Churches do not technically use the term "canonization," instead using the term "glorification." I use "canonization" as shorthand for what the Coptic Church refers to as the Holy Synod's 'recognition of sanctity' (i'tirāf al-qadāsa). As in the Roman Catholic Church, the Coptic Orthodox fifty-year period of waiting is not a fixed, but a flexible criterion. It is highly likely that this condition is a modern modification in Coptic Church procedures of verifying sainthood.

(*nazzala fī al-Siniksār*) when referring to a saint's written inclusion in the Holy Lives of the Saints, or the Coptic Synaxarium. Canonization is, in effect, the written inscription and eternal fixation of a holy identity.

In the interlude of waiting before his or her death, the saint exists in a temporal zone of social jeopardy. At risk is the icon's fatal transformation into an idol. A "hidden icon," the saint has the future-oriented potential to become canonized. In his or her time on earth, the saint must manifest abundant signs of holiness in order to be canonized, while necessarily avoiding popular recognition out of proper time. What this means in practice is the performance of a public secret: everyone knows he or she is a saint, but no one is saying it (or one is only saying it secretly). This social drama of covert imagination is known to make for some legendary theatrics, façades, and charades. One well-known example that comes to mind is the late saint Yustus al-Antuni (1906–76), the Red Sea monk whose signature act was frequently asking aloud, "What time is it?" Further posing this question in ways that made him appear "crazy," Yustus al-Antuni is remembered for his double-sided trick of orienting the attention of others toward death while deflecting their excessive reverence away from him. Of course, the people are not so easily fooled. Aware of the necessity of postponing recognition, the people also mirror the saint's theatrical acts of deferral and refusal. Their acts include maintaining silence about a miracle or withholding its author's name from suspecting others. Following the ethics of mystical publicity, perishing happens before publishing.

HOLY FOOLERY AND SIMPLE PEOPLE

"People invent stories, I get very nervous when I hear something that is not exact," Tasuni Injil expressed to a group of women visiting her in her flat in March 2007. Tasuni Injil Bassili, a silver-haired, petite woman who spoke with vibrant charisma, lived alone in the Alexandrian district of Sporting, named after the neighborhood sports club. The widow of the late contemporary saint Father Bishoi Kamil (1931–79),[9] Tasuni

---

9. Celibate marriage is an example of holy foolery (or "holy folly"), one strategy for escaping promotion to the bishopric or papacy, or the higher clerical positions available only to monastics. Like Bishoi Kamil, ʿAbd al-Masih al-Manahri is also described as invoking marriage in an attempt to dodge clerical promotion: "So he went to [the Diocese Headquarters] and yelled, 'You are married to my mother! He could see heaven and everything in it because he made himself into a stupid fool (*al-ʿabīṭ*)'" (audio-recordings of Metropolitan Menas of Girga, January 25, 1981).

Injil was often consulted about the intimate details of his biography
since she had been his closest witness during his life.

Another woman from Cairo named Ranya had heard anecdotes
about Father Bishoi Kamil by word of mouth and sought to verify them
with Tasuni Injil. She asked, "Did Father really give Jesus a ride to the
monastery in his car?"

"For twenty-three years, I didn't believe this story at all," Tasuni Injil
began to answer with a preface. Describing how she had once directly
confronted her husband to ask him whether or not it was true, she reca-
pitulated Father Bishoi Kamil's reply: "Oh, our people are simple people. Maybe they were thinking about St. Bishoi the Hermit who carried
Jesus on his shoulders, and they thought, 'how could Father Bishoi
Kamil carry Christ?' So they reasoned that I took him in the car." Bishoi
Kamil invoked the stock image of the "simple people" and inserted its
polyvalent possibilities into circulation. Representing the fine line
between piety and gullibility, between the pure and the prone to make-
believe, the "simple people" provided him with an alibi. Injil was also
alert to the people's capacity to deceive and mislead, unwittingly puffing
up a saint's cult with the dangers of hearsay.

The "holy fool" is the counterpart-image of the "simple people." An
ancient figure discovered across religious traditions, the "holy fool"
(al-ʿabīṭ, al-ʿubāṭ) is famous for avoiding recognition, engaging in dramatic exercises of escapism and antisociality.[10] An intrinsically social
figure, the holy fool only makes sense if there is an audience of people
who present the threat of vain celebrity. The following is a hagiographic
account of a fourth-century Egyptian hermit, feigning demonic possession to comedic effect:

> He ran into his house, saying "come out and meet the recluse." And when
> from a distance the holy man saw them coming out with lamps, he guessed
> the reason, and he took off his clothes and threw them into the river and
> began to wash them as he stood there naked. On seeing this the disciple was
> embarrassed and said to the people, "turn back, for the holy man has gone
> out of his mind" . . . And he went up to him and asked, "Father, why have
> you done this? Everybody said that you were possessed by a demon." And

---

10. In addition to Copts in Egypt, contemporary traditions of holy foolery thrive
among Russian Orthodox Christians (Kormina and Shtyrkov 2011) and South
Asian Muslims (Green 2009; Pamment 2017). For literature on holy foolery in Orthodoxy and Catholicism, see Saward 1980; Rydén 1983; Krueger 1996; Bishop Kallistos
Ware 2004.

he replied, "That is what I wanted to hear." (Nau 1907, quoted in Ivanov 2006:30–31)[11]

Recounting a theatrically flamboyant face-off between the saint and the people, this narrative establishes a trope for performative enactments of holiness. Rehearsed in hagiographic film, for example, holy foolery is captured when the actor playing 'Abd al-Masih al-Manahri bolts for the church doors with the crowds chasing him hot on his heels. The crowds are doubly figured as little devils or saboteurs on the one hand, and sources of mystical insight on the other. In the public imaginary of final revelation and vindication, they are the ones who end up knowing who he "really" is. Imagined as unassuming stewards of virtue, the "simple people" are typically those capable of seeing the truth.

In his well-known essay "On Face-work," sociologist Erving Goffman defines the term "face" as "the positive social value a person effectively claims for himself by the line others assume he has taken during a particular contact" (1974 [1955]:224). According to Goffman's framework of interaction, it is the social "line" that one is expected to perform which is the principle behind ritual order, rather than the correspondence between the self's outer and inner forms.[12] Holy foolery is a mode of face-to-face interaction involving two key participant actors: "the saint" (al-qiddīs) and "the people" (al-nās). Much of their social interactions are further staged around a mystical tactics of disguise in order to shield the saint from false self-valuation and the people from idolatrous transgressions. To begin with the theatrical faces of holy foolery enables thinking of the saint and the people as preeminently social actors engaged in acts of presentation and recognition, rather than as literary figures of the hagiographical archive.

From yet another slightly different angle, the "simple people" is a communicative *effect* of saint-making. In recent theorizations of crowds and populism, anthropologists have analyzed how processes of mass mediation give rise to representations of "the people" (Rafael 2003;

11. According to historian Sergey Ivanov, the surface-level theatrics of holy foolery is partially derivative from ancient Greek Cynicism (Ivanov 2006; cf. Sloterdijk 1988).

12. Critics of Goffman find his model of social performance ethically questionable for what they take to be a morally groundless self beneath the surface play of face-work. For example, moral philosopher Alasdair MacIntyre argues that, "Goffman's is a sociology which by intention deflates the pretensions of appearance to be anything more than appearance" (MacIntyre 1984:116).

Tambar 2009; Sánchez 2016). Cultural images of the public are, in other words, unstable creations of publicity. In this sense, the image of the "simple people" reflects more a communicative style of circulation, than it does a real, existing character. Mystical publicity obfuscates and discloses the status of its characters over time. It attaches holiness to "the saint" and "the people" across various moments of re-narrating and reflecting on their interactions from the past. The "simple people," envisioned as an image of holy recognition, is itself an icon of virtue.

To hide himself, Bishoi Kamil further invoked another saint's icon into circulation: the fourth-century St. Bishoi the Hermit, a desert father and founding figure of monastic antiquity. St. Bishoi the Hermit is the saint known for his hospitable virtue toward the imagined figure of the "stranger", whether washing his feet or carrying him up the mountain; in all the accounts, the "stranger" ends up revealing himself as Jesus. Invoking his namesake patron saint, the late Bishoi Kamil suggested that the "simple people" confused the idea that he gave Jesus a ride in his car, with St. Bishoi the Hermit's signature act of carrying Jesus up the mountain. He did this by concealing himself behind his name. Not incidentally, one of Bishoi Kamil's most popular nicknames is "Bearer of the Cross" (Hamil al-Salib).

It is only through the special mediation of the icon-form that the name "St. Bishoi" can serve as a vehicle of dissimulation. A portrait icon is a unity of two elements that signify the saint's identity: a face and a name. For most icons, there are additional signifying elements such as miracles or holy sites from the saint's hagiography; however, at minimum, the icon must depict both a face and a name. For this reason, Copts use the icon as an instrument of revealing the names of unknown saints: recall how Hilda (chapter 4, "Crossovers and Conversions") and Samya (chapter 5, "Public Order") used icons to pin down the identity of the apparitions they had dreamt. Bishoi Kamil unfastened and disassembled his face from the name of "Bishoi" in the popular image of "Bishoi carrying Jesus." To avoid being elevated into a holy icon out of proper time, he thus disassociated himself from the narrative, withdrawing his identity from the imagined act. It was only after his death that Injil reconsidered Bishoi's reply beyond its initial face value.

Tasuni Injil described to us how she eventually realized that Bishoi Kamil had been hiding secrets from her all along. Years after his death, she consulted one of his spiritual mentors who confirmed that Bishoi Kamil had indeed given Jesus a ride in his car. On one level, the authoritative chain of transmission was what finally confirmed the story for Injil. On another level, the recirculation of the story, and its posthumous layer of ratification, only served to confirm the status of the "simple people." In keeping with the performative script, Injil explained to the small audience in her flat that the people, in the guise of being "simple," ending up being the bearers of truth. Mirrors of one another, the saint and the people generate an entire imaginary of underground, covert signs of virtue that are ascribed to them after a period of time.

Toward the end of our visit in her flat in Sporting, the women gathered together with Tasuni Injil for a group photo in front of Bishoi Kamil's icons of Sts. Domitius and Maximus, the two brothers who renounced the fourth-century imperial elite world for the then-emerging monastic path. Later in the day when I checked my camera to review my photos, I noticed something interesting. While everyone else was facing forward for the shot, Tasuni Injil was looking slightly down with her tilted head turned away from the lens. Like many other monastics I encountered, she had staged on camera her own small publicity act of withdrawal.

NAMING STRANGERS

"If wandering is the liberation from every given point in space, and thus the conceptional opposite to fixation at such a point, the sociological form of the *stranger* presents the unity, as it were, of these two characteristics" (Simmel 1950 [1908]:402). Sociologist Georg Simmel's classic essay opens by characterizing the "stranger"-form by a special type of mobility in space and time. On the remote peripheries of the village or town, the stranger at once embodies nearness and distance, perceived to be in the social order but not of it. Unlike the temporal horizon of the wanderer who always ends up leaving, the stranger comes today and "stays tomorrow."

Inside Coptic imaginaries of sainthood, everyday interactions with mysterious presences are enhanced through face-to-face encounters with strangers. Moreover, these fleeting copresences are imagined to occur while on the road, within the transient and transitory spaces of mobility and travel. Consider again the story of Bishoi Kamil giving Jesus a lift in his car, a story modeled after Bishoi the Hermit carrying a stranger on the side of the road who turns into Jesus. Another iconic figure of estrangement in spaces of traveling is the "anchorite" or "tourist" (*al-sā'iḥ, al-suwwāḥ*).[13] Journeying long distances in a matter of seconds, the anchorite is a special kind of ascetic who magically exits and reenters normative orders of space and time. When I have asked what anchorites look like when they are traveling, a number of Copts described them as black birds that "fly" (*ṭīr, ṭayyār*), with their monastic black habits soaring like distant dots visible in the sky.

In his writings on publics and counterpublics, literary scholar Michael Warner proposes that stranger-relationality, or stranger sociality, is a constitutive aspect of the mass public. Against Simmel's exotic "stranger" of an earlier social order, he argues that the impersonal "stranger" of the public is "unremarkable, even necessary" to the nature of modern polities (Warner 2002:56 n. 3). Although his focus primarily lies in print circulation and textual mediation, Warner's emphasis on a normative horizon of indefinite, abstract others also applies to cultural publics of transit. In a global era of mass mobility and transportation, megacities like Cairo and Alexandria run on multiple railway and underground metro lines, buses and microbuses on regular routes, taxis and private cars along homes and highways. These technologies standardize orders of time and contemporaneity (Barak 2013), as well as propel social fascinations with speed and solitude (Augé 2002; Virilio 2006). With everyone on the move without fixed location, all passengers are strangers to one another. On a national scale of circulation, this collective imaginary of transit presents a mass of passing faces without names.

This transient orientation activates a conjunction between normative stranger-relationality and covert fields of interacting with estranged figures along routes of travel. As the following accounts from my fieldwork show, spaces of mass transit are common sites where strangers are made into "saints":

> One time, I was taking my necklace with the cross from my workplace in Garden City. And then afterward, I lost it on the microbus. After I got off, there was somebody from the corner who came to me and told me, "Young lady, there was a woman who told me to tell you to take this." It was my

13. The term "anchorite" derives from the Greek *anakhoretes* meaning "to withdraw" or "to retire," and the Arabic translation into *al-sā'iḥ* (plural, *al-suwwāḥ*) conveys the additional meaning of "to tour" or "to wander." A Coptic anchorite is also distinguished by his or her capacity for miraculous self-transport, or "flying" at high speeds. This saintly movement may be likened to "bilocation" in the Roman Catholic tradition, or *ṭayy al-arḍ* ("folding up of the earth") in the Islamic tradition (Goldziher 1971; Doostdar 2018).

gold cross. Believe me! Who was the lady who told him? Of course, the Virgin! (Woman, Matariyya, Cairo)

When I was young, I went to the Monastery of St. Menas and thought I had bought a round-trip ticket from Alexandria. But I hadn't. I needed only two piasters more. I saw the bus and I thought, "Oh my God, where can I get the two piasters?" I found someone calling my name and didn't pay attention to who the man was. "Mark, here are two piasters, take the bus." [Later on], I realized that the man was St. Menas. (Man, Sporting, Alexandria)

You know St. George is a soldier ['askarī], right? We were driving once from St. George's shrine in Mit Damsis [near Tanta] and we got lost on our way there. We saw a policeman [dābiṭ] on the side of the road and asked him how to get there, and he climbed into the car and directed us to the place. He was very polite and quietly left us when we arrived. That man was not a policeman, he was St. George the soldier. (Married couple, 'Ayn al-Shams, Cairo)

Each of these narratives foregrounds a peripheral figure located at the margins of transit—on the side of the road, around the corner, at the bus stop. In between spaces of travel, this figure appears and offers a gift via a face-to-face interaction. Significantly, the figure is an empty avatar of presence, anonymous until the protagonist gives him or her a name. The saint's face, in sum, is iconologically unified with his or her name. In keeping with the temporal ethics of visualizing holy personhood, these figures are recognized to be saints only in that window after they have already departed from the social scene. Naming strangers further enchants the modern public with contemporary presences from elsewhere.

Social theorists of the public sphere have pointed out the mediational specificities that give rise to differential subjects, addressees and stranger-relationalities. Warner's claims are specific, for example, to textually and discursively-mediated publics in which "space and physical presence do not make much difference" (Warner 2002:53). What difference does the icon imaginary make for a common imaginary of anonymous consociates? Representing a negative identity of belonging, normative stranger-relationality unites strangers through public participation alone, rather than through the positive content of identity, territory, or belief. The living saint offers an intersecting frame of strangerhood; as a "hidden icon," he or she is formally emptied of content. The hidden icon oriented toward death also signals a presence, at once uncannily familiar and otherworldly distant. A vehicle of anonymity, it complements the abstract quality of stranger-relationality while also offering a portal of ephemeral potential. As an anchorite does, it appears and disappears according to extraordinary spatial and temporal coordinates that exceed the ordinary face-to-face encounter.

The stranger's face, in its abstract portability, is also repeatable and translatable into textual form. Substituted and re-placed into circulation, latent presences on the road are given names only in their lurking absences. Constitutive of secrecy and potential, interactions with strangers create social modes of address and recognition. The imagined saint results from the circulation of a stranger in exchange for a face and a name: the icon. The living icon's condition of possibility is therefore a social imaginary of unknown others who are, in theory, indefinite and strangely intimate.

COVERT POLITICS OF SECTARIANISM

In the last two sections, we focused on the icon's materiality and its mediation of mystical publicity. As I have shown so far, the icon is a medium which orders social relations of hiddenness and revelation, constituting a cult imaginary of saint-making. Now in the next two sections, we further consider icon imaginaries to understand its effects on Christian-Muslim relations. To be precise, I examine the shadowy dynamics between national and sectarian publics, in the ways that national imaginaries of Christian-Muslim unity intersect with the visual politics of sectarianism.

A politician and a saint, Pope Kyrillos is a modular icon of national and sectarian imagination. On the face of it, Kyrillos was the key communal figure under Gamal Abdel Nasser whose inaugural vision of national unity entailed the entire remake of Christian and Muslim orders of authority. It was under Kyrillos's papal reign (and notably, not Shenouda's), for instance, that the lay council of secular elites was dissolved and reconstituted with pious church servants. To reiterate, the Virgin of 1968 was a key vehicle of publicizing Christian-Muslim unity under the sign of Arab nationalism, with Nasser and Kyrillos pictured hand-in-hand. More significantly, Marian apparitions after 1968 demonstrated the formal continuity between national and sectarian orders of imagination; hence, my invocation of the hyphenated term "national-sectarianism." Kyrillos established the "national" character of the Coptic Church and the Coptic community, as an integral element of the Egyptian state order of "Christian-Muslim unity."

Beneath this national persona, however, Copts remember St. Kyrillos to have ultimately wielded extraordinary power over Nasser. As with other contemporary saints, St. Kyrillos is imagined to be more than a "Christian" saint; he was an extraordinary figure, a "solitary hermit" (*al-mutawaḥḥid* or *al-taqashshuf*) who had lived apart from everyone and all. Represented as "the people's saint," there are many written, published accounts of the miracles he had performed for Muslims (Voile 2004). Above all, it was St. Kyrillos's special relationship with Nasser, one marked by "affection" (*al-ʿāṭifa*) and "trust" (*al-ṣadāqa*), that set him apart from the other popes. To convey Nasser's deep respect, even fear and trembling, of St. Kyrillos's spiritual authority, I have heard several, different Coptic devotees recount similar stories of his miracles.[14] According to one version, Nasser mocked St. Kyrillos's prayer staff, only to be chastened by St. Kyrillos's miraculous intervention in the serious illness of his son. As another variation would have it, Nasser himself was healed of heart disease by St. Kyrillos. All the stories I had heard of St. Kyrillos's miracles for Nasser were verbal, despite my efforts to find print accounts in various bookstores throughout Cairo.

It was later divulged to me why I had trouble finding them. One summer morning, a few weeks after his canonization was formally announced, I traveled to St. Kyrillos's Windmill (al-Tahuna) on the eastern side of Muqattam Hills where he had lived in the 1950s. An abandoned artifact of grain milling, its sail-less cylindrical base now serves as one of the most popular Coptic shrines and pilgrimage sites. A bit out of the way, the Windmill is perched at the crest of a rocky, desert landscape under extensive development. To get up there, pilgrims commonly ride microbuses lined up at the Zahra' metro station for pick-ups and drop-offs.

Near the metro station, the Church of St. Menas and its bookstore attracts a few pilgrims on their way up or down. After having failed to find any booklet or recording which described any of St. Kyrillos's miracles for Nasser, I asked the clerk if he knew where I could get one. As we stood in an aisle filled with St. Kyrillos paraphernalia, he replied to me: "There isn't a book like that because it would create *fitna* with Muslims. Muslims will get upset if they found out that the Christians are saying these things. Yes, everyone knows that Kyrillos healed Nasser and that Nasser was afraid of Kyrillos, but we have to keep it quiet so there are no problems." In his explanation, the bookstore clerk raised the political

14. Miracles are imagined to be one domain of transaction between Coptic mystics and Egyptian state authorities at the highest ranks. Similar to St. Kyrillos on behalf of Nasser, Tamav Irini is believed to have performed miraculous healings in secret on behalf of former First Lady Suzanne Mubarak (Shenoda 2012).

possibility of *fitna*, a term that loosely translates into "civil strife" or "disruption" that breeds sectarian schism within a polity. In the context of publicizing St. Kyrillos's miracles for Nasser, *fitna* concerned the outbreak of sectarian tension between Christians and Muslims over authority figures in Egypt. What would it imply if Pope Kyrillos had commanded any sway over Nasser? Following this clerk's logic, the solution to such an imagined threat is for Copts to regulate the accounts of his miracles, circulating within Christians and concealing from Muslims.

The clerk's explanation brings us back to a set of familiar themes concerning miracles and the threat of their public circulation across the Christian-Muslim divide. As we learned from the regulation of the miracle icon in Port Said, the security state upholds public order by containing Christian practices within churches, sequestering them from their surrounding Muslim environs. Enclaved behind walls and enshrouded in suspicion, Copts are consequently made into a community insulated by secrecy. What this clerk further offers is insight into how this national formula of divide-and-rule invigorates mechanisms of secret-keeping internal to the Coptic community. Copts are ethically obliged to monitor the publicity of saints against idolatry. The force of this obligation is redoubled once the image of *fitna* comes into play. Establishing a line between what Copts can know, and what Muslims should not know, the Coptic imaginary of saint-making is made into a covert imaginary.

It is no secret that relations between the Muslim majority and Coptic minority are unequal, and that this national inequality is reflected in the differential presence of their religious publics. Whereas Islamic print literature and sermon recordings can be readily found in open street stalls, their Christian counterparts are cordoned-off to church bookstores or neighborhood sections such as parts of Shubra which have a high concentration of Copts. This imbalance is owed neither to "Islam" nor to "Christianity"; rather, it is intrinsic to majority-minority relations across modern nation-states. This Christian-Muslim inequality, moreover, shapes Coptic caution regarding the kinds of religious material that might potentially offend Muslims and lead to sectarian trouble.

Yet, it is also critical to distinguish between the fact of Christian-Muslim inequality and the larger governing structure of national authority which orders sectarian difference. The core problem with circulating St. Kyrillos's miracles for Nasser stems not so much from the threat that "Christian" saints are healing "Muslim" patients. In fact, there are many print publications of various Coptic saints (e.g., 'Abd al-Masih al-Manahri) performing miracles for Muslims (e.g., Na'ima

Husayn). The problem derives from the idea that St. Kyrillos, and the mystical realm of spiritual power which he represents, has authority over Nasser, thus disrupting the hierarchy of authority integral to the national imaginary. In the national imaginary, Pope Kyrillos's proper location is as a "communal icon," a figurehead intelligible within the Egyptian grid of Christian-Muslim unity. The official public sphere, in other words, circumscribes the sign of Christian miracles always within the disciplinary realm of nationhood. The potential for Christian miracles to overturn this national hierarchy of power signals a threat not so much to Islam, but to the state's authority over all religious authorities.

SECLUSION TACTICS

On December 8, 2004, Pope Shenouda retreated behind the walls of St. Bishoi Monastery in Wadi al-Natrun to gain visibility in the national public. Covering his retreat, the news' headlines reported: "The top Coptic cleric has withdrawn to a desert monastery to draw attention to grievances among Egyptian Christians." Quoting the rationale issued by Shenouda's secretary, the international press further reported: "The seclusion of His Holiness the Pope will continue until he reaches a solution [with the government] that satisfies his conscience to the problems related to the Copts."[15]

Shenouda's seclusion tactics ended up being effective with the Egyptian state. In the heat of sectarian upheaval, his publicity act occurred in the thick of a scandal involving a Coptic priest's wife named Wafa' Qustantin and her allegedly forced conversion to Islam (see the introduction). Escalating Coptic riots at the Patriarchate Cathedral, his retreat into the desert monasteries led to a theatrical standoff with the police back in Cairo. At the end of the public demonstrations, state security forces located Qustantin and handed her over to clerical authorities.

Throughout his forty-year papal tenure, Shenouda managed his national image as both a savvy political actor and a holy spiritual leader. Engaged in a nebulous balancing act, Shenouda frequently announced to the national newspapers that "the church did not meddle in political affairs" while also asserting his responsibility to "care after his flock." In contrast to Kyrillos whose public persona reflected a solitary mystic and wonderworker, Shenouda's moniker, the "learned one" (*al-muta'allim*),

---

15. "Egyptian Pope Goes into Seclusion," BBC News, December 20, 2004.

reflected a more worldly image than that of his predecessor.[16] At the same time, Shenouda's political currency revolved around his communal headship as a spiritual figure of holiness, that is, the pope of the Coptic Church. Theatrical strategies of monastic seclusion offered one means of drawing public attention to his holy status, thereby strengthening his position for registering discontent and demanding concessions on behalf of the Coptic community. Notably, Shenouda's tactics have been passed onto his successor Pope Tawadros, who also announced that he would go into seclusion to protest attacks on the Patriarchate Cathedral in April 7, 2013.

As this chapter has examined so far, mystical publicity enlists a monastic repertoire of renunciation through acts of hiddenness and revelation. Crafted in virtuous coordination with holy fools and anchorites, Shenouda's exit from the public eye heightened his communal authority as a holy figure. Retreating from politics into the space of prayer, he established his iconic visibility within an ascetic imaginary of otherworldly intercession. Strategic and efficacious, his mystical performance was not one of ecstatic removal into a space of alterity (de Certeau 1992; cf. Napolitano and Pratten 2007; Hollywood 2012). Rather, his public image as an intercessor on behalf of the Coptic community* was squarely assimilated into an authoritarian choreography of patronage and intervention.

Against the political background of church-state arbitrations from the past, Shenouda's publicity maneuvers may also be understood within a historical context of subversion and repression.[17] In 1980, he had provoked Sadat by banning Easter celebrations and summoning the Holy Synod to retire to their desert monasteries during Holy Week as an expression of the "desperate plight of the Copts in Egypt" (Watson 2002:96–97). Attracting international levels of publicity to un-redressed incidents of sectarian violence and rising trends of Islamic militancy in Egypt, his demonstrations undermined Sadat's image, especially vis-à-vis the United States. Consequently, Sadat placed Shenouda and over one hundred clerical hierarchs under monastery arrest, exiling them to the Wadi al-Natrun desert compound until 1981. Shenouda's forced

16. It is possible that St. Pope Kyrillos would have been canonized earlier had it not been for Pope Shenouda's tacit rivalry with him and his robust reputation as a wonderworker even after his death. I am grateful to Reader 1 for alerting me to this insight in his/her review of this manuscript.

17. For an interesting comparison, see sociologist Malika Zeghal's work on sainthood and the authoritarian politics of critique in Morocco (Zeghal 2009).

seclusion was a disciplinary act that transformed the monastery into an imagined site of state power and surveillance. Following Sadat's assassination and Mubarak's inauguration, Shenouda's political persona transformed from one of subversive dissidence to docile allegiance.

Toward the final years of Mubarak's presidency, Shenouda reinitiated his seclusion tactics as acts of protest and appeal. His monastery retreats communicated a position of public leverage in the performative theater of church-state relations. To the dismay of Egyptian secularists, Christians and Muslims alike, Shenouda's theatrics were at once too political and bad politics. The Coptic Church's top hierarch's publicity in conversion scandals and outbreaks of sectarian violence endowed too much political power to religious authorities. The fact that Shenouda was, moreover, the mediating vehicle through which a Coptic woman was delivered back into the hands of the Church was a violation of individual rights to religious freedom and the state's obligation to protect its nationals from clerical infringements. Seen in this light, Shenouda's withdrawal into the monastery is a dissimulative performance of intervention.

What Shenouda's appeal to an imagined monastic persona ignited was an array of political responses that unfurled around his image and its mediating capacity. In national arenas of Christian-Muslim conflict, his withdrawals enacted his status as an image of sacred value, retired from the realm of sectarian dissent. As a site of repressive arrest and a sanctuary of exclusion, the monastery space further consolidated the Church's subordination to the state regime at its holiest margins. In line with the paradoxes of mystical publicity, Shenouda's seclusion tactics, forced and voluntary, staged his iconic image as the representative leader of Egypt's Copts.

SHRINES OF POWER

Popes Kyrillos and Shenouda are the two pivotal actors in the national imaginary who, as many scholars have argued, cemented the governing formula of the Coptic Church's partnership with the state regime after the 1952 revolution. As is the case with other charismatic figures and cult personalities across the Middle East, their visual iconography inspires loyalties and ambiguous attachments (Wedeen 1999; Özyürek 2006; Haugbølle and Kuzmanovic 2015). Publicizing Coptic authority, their images are the media for picturing the political relationship between spiritual and state powers, sainthood and nationhood.

Nowhere else is this political relationship more prominently enshrined than in the portrait gallery of popes and presidents in Old Cairo. Beginning with Pope Yusab II and King Farouk, and closing with Pope Tawadros and President Sisi, the gallery is a visual symposium of ruling pairs corresponding to successive eras of alliance. Following the classic rubric of political-theological rule (Kantorowicz 1957), the unbroken lineage of popes and presidents signifies the reproduction of permanence. In photo after photo, the gallery presents the diplomatic profile of a pope shaking hands and exchanging smiles with a president. Of all the pope-president pairs in modern Egyptian history, the hallmark alliances are those of Pope Kyrillos-President Nasser and Pope Shenouda-President Mubarak. Toward the tail-end of the gallery, the revolutionary signs of high turnover after 2011 begin to show. A photo of Shenouda with SCAF Field Marshal Tantawi is followed by another of Tawadros and President Mohamed Morsi (eliminated from the gallery in 2015), and then another of Tawadros and Interim President 'Adli Mansur. Yet even amid tumult, the visual display's structure produces the aura of church-state stability.

Analogous to a state museum, the gallery of popes and presidents offers an iconographic representation of modern communal history in the official national public sphere. Outsiders and visitors seeking to learn more about Copts and Christian-Muslim relations often make their first stop here. Located inside the foyer of the Hanging Church, the gallery is housed in one of the world's oldest churches, a destination for tourists worldwide. The gallery is also ensconced in a historic part of Old Cairo, an area which symbolizes the early medieval coexistence of Christians, Jews, and Muslims through the proximity of the Hanging Church with its neighboring Ben Ezra Synagogue and Amr ibn al-'As Mosque. Propping up portraits of pope-president pairs, the gallery affirms that contemporary Christian-Muslim relations are primarily mediated through the church-state alliance. In the hegemonic public, the portrait images celebrate and honor cardinal personalities like Nasser and his ties with communal dignitaries like Kyrillos.

Lingering behind the gallery, along the racks of wood and wire, are postcard portraits of Kyrillos and Shenouda amid the faces of saintly contemporaries including the Red Sea monk Yustus al-Antuni and St. Abu Sayfayn Convent's late abbess Tamav Irini. In one iconic photo of the desert mystic, Kyrillos is carrying his prayer staff in one hand, his cross clasped in the other. In another of the regal leader, Shenouda's corpse is seated on his throne the morning after his death. Whereas the gallery's focus lies on the role of spiritual leaders as state functionaries, this

FIGURE 36. Portrait of Pope Kyrillos VI and President Gamal Abdel Nasser, Hanging Church of the Virgin, Old Cairo. Photo courtesy of Vivian Ibrahim.

iconographic backdrop captures an alternative imaginary of life and death that commemorates the hidden qualities of elusiveness and eternal glory.

Parallel to the foreign tourists and national officials who pay homage to the visual halls of authority, there are those Copts who go to the Hanging Church and remember Kyrillos and Shenouda foremost as holy personalities. In this chapter, I have elaborated some of the social and ethical rubrics that situate Kyrillos and Shenouda within the iconological universe of saint-making, alongside characters like 'Abd al-Masih al-Manahri from the rural horizons of the Upper Egyptian village, and Bishoi Kamil of Alexandria, whose mark of fame was his self-effacing humility. What would it look like to regard Kyrillos and Shenouda, less as authoritarian partners with Nasser and Mubarak, and more as personalities on the ascetic path to sainthood? If the icon imaginary exceeds the bounded portrait image, then which visual economies of extraordinary personhood assign which values to leaders and saints? Making Kyrillos and Shenouda into saints activates an entire style of publicity. There are the portrait images of popes and presidents in the state-sanctioned national public. Behind them, there also lies an imagined enclave of lurking and transient potentials: Kyrillos as Nasser's secret wonderworker or Shenouda as Sadat's monastic dissident. Organizing temporal relations of deferral and disguise, imaginaries of potential icons also create popular genres of covert communication. Figured as the "simple people," witnesses of power also become icons of enchantment and revelation, as well as of *fitna* and unwitting sabotage.

These two spheres of publicity—national and mystical—offer two distinctive modes of visualizing charismatic power. Yet they are not separate spheres, but rather deeply interconnected insofar that the underground world of saints flourishes in supplemental relation to the official realm of communal autonomy. To be sure, Copts cannot speak about saints, and about Coptic Christian leaders as saints, on publicly equal terms with Muslims. Given their minoritarian position in the national public, Copts sit at the margins of sectarian segregation and communal sanction. As a corollary of their enclaved location, it would seem logical to characterize the mystical imaginary of Coptic saints as a "communal" phenomenon. Against this naturalized analytic impulse, I have alternatively considered covert performances of holy power as sites of transcending intercommunal, Christian-Muslim difference. Exceeding cult performances of church-state mediation, mystical publicity recruits Muslims into the image of "simple people," and Muslim collaborators into the making of a shadowy, fragmented canvas of saintly operations. At stake is how shrines of power are envisioned in ways that exceed distinctions between the national and religious, secular and sacred, Christian and Muslim.

Epilogue

Martyrs of the new covenant
Their blood was renewed
And their remembrance became a feast day
Martyrs of Egypt in Libya

Then the permit was given
By the decision of the agreeable judge
To build a church to the martyrs of Christ
Martyrs of Egypt in Libya

Hymnody excerpt from *Clouds of Light* (*Sahabat al-Nuraniyya*),
Archdiocese of Samalut

It is true that we love martyrdom but we also love life . . . we
don't hate life on earth. God is here with us on earth because
we live, not because we die.

Bishop Rafa 'il's Facebook post after the Palm Sunday bombings
of 2017[1]

Tiriza lost her twenty-three-year-old son Yusif Shukri Yunan to the
Islamic State of Iraq and Syria (ISIS) on February 15, 2015. Months later,
in December, I sat with her on a long cotton sofa in her home, surrounded
by bright turquoise, pockmarked walls of brick and concrete. Dressed in
a black, heavy wool jellabiya and headscarf, she recounted in her strong
and hoarse voice how her son Yusif had recently appeared in her dreams.

---

1. Cairo Downtown Churches, April 10, 2017, Facebook post.

FIGURE 37. Icon of the Libya Martyrs, Church of the Virgin, 'Aur. Photo by author.

"His face shone light, and he was holding the keys to heaven in his hands. He was holding them out to me."

"Mama, she doesn't want to hear about your visions of heaven." Listening in on our conversation, her other son quietly interrupted from the wooden table where he was eating spoonfuls of chicken and rice. Evidently, they had experienced their share of international journalists coming into their home and running through their stock list of questions.

I shook my head, in hopes of assuring her. "No, no, I want to hear more about your dream and what Yusif looked like."

But Tiriza had already moved on. "Because of the video, everyone could see that they were slaughtered for their faith. That's why the Church could announce that they are holy martyrs. Because of what the video showed us."

Since their husbands and sons were killed, widows and mothers like Tiriza were thrown into the center of global attention, their lives forever transformed in ʿAur, an impoverished village near the city of Samalut in the Minya governorate. While working as migrant laborers in Sirte, Libya, twenty-one Christians were kidnapped and then executed by ISIS, twenty of them Copts and fifteen hailing from ʿAur.[2] ISIS uploaded gruesome footage of their beheadings on the internet, adding to its expanding archive of execution videos of Muslims, minorities, foreigners, refugees, fighters, and children. The day after the video's release, President Sisi dispatched air strikes against ISIS targets in Libya, positioning himself as a key leader in the international war against "radical Islamic terrorism." A week later, Pope Tawadros declared the holy martyrdom of the twenty-one victims, naming them the "Libya Martyrs" (Shuhadaʾ Libya).

In the village of ʿAur today, it is the ISIS video that is credited for bringing glory to the village's deaths. Banners, cards, portraits, calendars feature still-clips of the twenty-one hostages in orange jumpsuits, kneeling before a row of masked black-clad ISIS fighters on the Mediterranean beachfront. Converted into saintly iconography, the chilling

2. Of the twenty-one ISIS victims, fifteen hailed from ʿAur, five from other villages in Samalut, and one from sub-Saharan Africa. Matthew Ayariga is the only non-Copt and non-Orthodox of the Libya Martyrs. Referred to as "Matthew the African" (Mathiyu al-Ifriqi), Matthew was a migrant laborer in Libya like the others, likely from Ghana or Chad. Despite his foreigner status, the Coptic Church counts him in their roster of holy martyrs: "We don't know where or when Matthew was born, but all we know of him is that he is a child of heaven in Libya with our honored martyrs, and that our hearts are tied to him, and that he rose to be one among us because he became a martyr of Christ partaking in glory" (Archdiocese of Samalut 2015:20).

scenes of terrorist violence are now elements of holy repertoire that captures the sacrificial threshold between life and death. New shrines furnished with shiny alabaster floors and wooden bureaus were erected inside the mourning homes of the deceased. Visitors to 'Aur walk into these homes where mothers and widows greet them at their open doors, handing out photographic iconography of their lost ones crowned with gold and clothed in white robes and red sashes.

By far, the biggest sign of recognition was the enormous church under construction along the road leading up to the mouth of the village. Financed by the state, its completion was due that following spring of 2016. A large banner was hanging outside the construction site. Embossed with the seal of the Ministry of Defense, its endorsement was clear:

> We the Egyptian Armed Forces
>
> Build the Church of the Martyrs of the Faith and of the Nation (Shuhada' al-Iman wa-l-Watan).

. . .

Four years after the Arab uprisings, the Libya Martyrs symbolized the challenges facing Egypt, including its soaring levels of poverty and its unstable surroundings in the aftermath of toppled dictatorships. The tragic deaths of the twenty-one migrant laborers, aged twenty-five to forty-four, were a reminder of the cruel socioeconomic vulnerabilities marking an upcoming generation of youth forced to look for income elsewhere.[3] Eclipsing the quotidian problem of survival, their deaths at the hands of ISIS also registered alarm at the growing presence of Islamic militancy at Egypt's border zones. In addition to killing soldiers in the Sinai Peninsula, ISIS was establishing bases in post-Qaddafi Libya and attracting youth from war-torn Sudan (see Salomon 2016). President Abdel Fattah al-Sisi, in turn assuming the mantle of regional leadership, stepped up his counterterrorist operations in a new era of militarization and securitization.

In ISIS's video of their beheadings, the Libya Martyrs were launched into the limelight of a war waged along the transnational lines of

---

3. Since President Sadat's market liberalization policies in the 1970s, Egypt's economy has relied significantly on migrant labor in Libya and the Gulf, and remittance economies. Due to its proximity and open-border policies, Libya ranks on top of the list of destinations for Egypt's unemployed and underemployed youth. Most of Egypt's migrant youth in Libya come from the rural Delta, with a significant fraction also from rural Upper Egypt. See Gerasimos Tsourapas, "The Politics of Egyptian Migration to Libya," *Middle East Research and Information Project*, March 17, 2015.

religious faith.[4] Reinstating an ongoing geopolitical divide between Christianity and Islam, ISIS disseminated global images of Coptic Christians as members of "the Nation of the Cross" and of the "hostile Egyptian Church" as an enemy of Islam. The execution video declared ISIS's aim to "conquer Rome," signaling the civilizational-historical center of European Christendom across Libya's Mediterranean shores. In addition to targeting the Roman Catholic Church, ISIS's magazine *Dabiq* described the Coptic beheadings as "revenge for Kamilya Shahata, Wafa' Qustantin, and other sisters who were tortured and murdered by the Coptic Church in Egypt."[5] The headlines referred to the infamous conversion scandals involving Coptic priests' wives in 2004 and 2010 that ended in Pope Shenouda's vilification throughout the Islamic world in Africa, the Middle East, and Asia. Collapsing European Catholicism and its crusader history with the Coptic Church's tarnished reputation from the recent past, ISIS thus framed its Coptic victims as casualties of Christianity's timeless war against Islam worldwide.

Yet collective imaginaries of Christian-Muslim violence exceed discrete acts of kidnapping and murder, as well as rhetorical declarations at the grandest levels of civilizational warfare. In the village of 'Aur, the ISIS video and its grisly terror found a visual afterlife via the mass-mediated iconography of sainthood in the public. As Tiriza attributed to it, the ISIS video was the reason that the Coptic Church could bypass the normal fifty-year waiting period of establishing sainthood and immediately confer her son Yusif with the holy status of "martyr." By capturing the twenty-one victims as each mouthed "O My Lord Jesus" or "Jesus help me," it served as a crucial piece of evidence that confirmed their steadfast confession of faith in their final moments. As some villagers also expressed to me, the ISIS video was also what ultimately pushed Sisi to dispatch his military planes and bombs into Libya, after weeks during which they had appealed for government support, to no avail, to locate their missing family members. Aside from processes of canonization and militarization, Tiriza and other residents of 'Aur

4. "ISIS Sets Sights on Europe in Latest Beheading Video," *Time*, February 16, 2015, http://time.com/3711022/isis-libya-copts (accessed May 28, 2018); "Al-Qaeda Threat on Iraq Christians Linked to Egypt," *al-Arabiya News*, December 26, 2010, www.alarabiya.net/articles/2010/12/26/131037.html (accessed May 28, 2018); "A Closer Look at Egyptian Kidnappings in Libya," Tahrir Institute for Middle East Policy, January 29, 2015, https://timep.org/commentary/a-closer-look-at-egyptian-kidnappings-in-libya (accessed May 28, 2018).

5. "Revenge for the Muslimat persecuted by the Coptic Crusaders in Egypt," *Dabiq*, no. 7 (Rabi' al-Akhir 1436 [January 2015]): 30–32.

experienced their wounded mournings in the intimate detail of their dreaming experiences and their personal transformations of earthly loss into divine glory.

Throughout this book, I have explored the political lives of saints, tracing how traditions of Orthodox intercession shape senses of community, territory, and security. As jarring as their images of violence are, the Libya Martyrs and the ISIS video attest to familiar rituals of imagining holiness that invite us to consider the more ordinary histories and contexts in which scenes of murder, devastation, and fear unfold on the ground. As we learned earlier, acts of remembering martyrs' bodies are central to the making of communal authority, and visual practices of dreaming set into motion processes of canonizing contemporaries into cult glory. Adorned with ISIS-produced iconography, the new Church of the Libya Martyrs stands in steadfast honor of the old post-1952 alliance between the Coptic Church and the Egyptian military state. The Libya Martyrs are "martyrs of the faith and of the nation," and the Church of the Libya Martyrs is a territorial sign of minoritarian identity and military protection.

In the previous chapters, I have further examined how imaginaries of sainthood have organized Christians and Muslims under the hierarchy of nationhood over religious difference. A ubiquitous image throughout Egypt, the Virgin of the Apparition offers an ever-present reminder of the slippery slope between national unity and sectarian tension. Whereas in 1968, the image had served as the medium of the Coptic Church's "Arab Egyptian" identity after the 1967 Arab-Israeli War, by 2009, it had already become a sign of majority-minority inequality in landscapes rife with churches and mosques in competition. Although Christians and Muslims carry out their religious activities in separate spheres, and by the Egyptian state's design, I have also drawn our attention to the more unwieldy afterlives of the shared Virgin—the clues of her disruption and the police's reply in Port Said, as well as the overlooked desires of a Muslim to build a shrine in her honor with Christians in Giza. Now in ʿAur, a village on the outskirts of Egyptian epicenters of power, it is martyr memorials and church buildings again that urge a reconsideration of Copts in Egypt, their imagined links with Christian Rome and Arab Islam, and their post-2013 vulnerabilities after the Muslim Brotherhood and in the time of Sisi-led militarization.

In this epilogue, I now step out from the intricacies of religious mediation and offer some final thoughts on violence in a new post–Arab Spring era in which "terrorism" is gaining more prominence in global imaginaries of Christian persecution in Egypt. On December 11, 2016, twenty-seven Copts, nearly all women and children, died in the bombing of St. Peter and St. Paul's Church within the Patriarchate Cathedral complex in Cairo, the symbolic epicenter of Coptic Church authority. On April 9, 2017, fifty-six Copts died in the bombing of two churches, St. George's Church in Tanta and St. Mark's Cathedral in Alexandria, during Palm Sunday celebrations. And the attacks have not only been directed at Christians. On November 26, 2017, over three hundred Muslims were bombed and gunned down during Friday morning prayers at al-Rawdah Mosque, a Sufi mosque of Bir al-Abed in the northern Sinai.

All the incidents bore hallmarks of ISIS attacks, advancing a new era of violence in which bombs are now taken inside churches and mosques. For the first time, ISIS affiliates in Egypt also began targeting civilians, Christians and Muslims, after months of attacking the police and military. Given the unprecedented nature of violence and the foreign elements involved, the bombings galvanized support for the Sisi regime's escalating "war on terrorism" and legitimized its brutal exercise of violence nationwide. This war includes an ongoing, criminalized ban of the largest opposition group, the Muslim Brotherhood, deeming it a terrorist organization and pointing to its extranational ties to Qatar, Turkey, and Sudan.

In this current climate of fear and anxiety, Egypt's Copts and Coptic victims are consequently caught up in the thick of threats leveraged into Sisi's enlargement of the military and police. Joining many of Egypt's Muslims in the grip of postrevolution fatigue, the vast majority of Copts see state militarization as a fate necessary for advancing the country's path to social and economic stability. Sisi's heightened focus on terrorism and counterterrorism raises questions that resonate with many themes that this book has explored so far. How are Coptic victims of terrorism—the victims of the Palm Sunday bombings in 2017 (Shuhada' Ahad al-Sha'anin, or "Palm Sunday Martyrs"), the victims of Cathedral bombing in 2016 (Shuhada' al-Butrusiyya, or "St. Peter's Martyrs"), and the victims of the Libya executions in 2015 (Shuhada' Libya, or the "Libya Martyrs")—remembered as deaths on behalf "of the faith and of the nation"? What is the value of Christian deaths and what horizons of Christian-Muslim belonging do they calibrate and foreclose? How do different categories of recognition—"national," "sectarian," and now "terrorist"—result in different responses to attacks directed at Copts?

To address these questions, I draw on philosopher Judith Butler's writings on what she calls the "frames of war," or "the ways of selectively carving up experience as essential to the conduct of war" and "to the perpetually crafted *animus* of that material reality" (Butler 2009:26). Penned during the Bush administration after the American invasion of Iraq, her essays analyze how the politics of war are continuous with sexual and immigration politics, pushing beyond established frameworks of multiculturalism and minorities' recognition in light of newly divisive contexts of violence. Here, I would like to extend Butler's insights to consider how Coptic Christians and their felt experiences of violence and threat are framed in service to the material realities of Sisi's war on terrorism. Repeatedly identified as besieged religious minorities in the past, Copts and the spectacular visibility of their deaths are now conscripted into the military's counterterrorism efforts at home and abroad. In these frames of war, holy martyrs are enlisted on behalf of the state's regulation of commemorating some deaths over others—what Butler refers to as the "differential grievability of lives." This regulation includes determining which Christian deaths count and which Christian-Muslim rubrics of belonging shape Egypt's future of nationhood.

The remainder of my epilogue is divided into two short sections that explore how frames of "Sisi's war on terrorism" give rise to the differential valuation of deaths and of Christian-Muslim violence. In the first section, I review the roster of major attacks on Copts between 2011 and 2016, beginning with the Alexandrian bombing of 2011 that opened this book, and ending with the cathedral bombing of 2016. By revisiting the terms of revolution and counter-revolution, I examine how the Egyptian state and Coptic Church have remembered some acts of violence and overlooked others under the weight of their authoritarian alliance. In the second section, I turn our attention to the villagers of ʿAur and the material realities that cross-border migration and memories of terrorist violence create at the local level. Closing this book with an ethnographic eye, I hope to offer some on-the-ground perspective on the ways in which the Egyptian military's consecration of the Libya Martyrs amplifies Coptic vulnerabilities and generates new settings of Christian-Muslim tension.

. . .

After the Alexandrian bombing on New Year's Eve of 2011, Egyptian public discourse had swirled around the specter of "terrorism." Immediately following the church attack, President Mubarak announced that "foreign elements" would not divide the nation, and Alexandrian Governor ʿAdil Labib directed his blame at al-Qaʿida affiliates. Deemed a national tragedy, the bombing rejuvenated displays of Christian-Muslim solidarity including the Muslim Brotherhood's condemnation and its call for Muslims to protect churches. Such rehearsals of national unity served as precursors to the Tahrir uprisings that unfolded weeks later. At the time of this writing, in 2018, the mastermind behind the attack on the Copts remains unidentified.

Contending narratives of revolution and counterrevolution in Egypt are inextricably intertwined with accounts of violence, security and the military. Attacks on Copts, to the extent that they register cracks in nationhood, have proven significant for legitimating the overthrow of leaders, including Mubarak in 2011 and Morsi in 2013. The Alexandrian bombing of 2011, the Libya executions of 2015, and the Cathedral of St. Mark bombing of 2016 have all been recognized as national tragedies by virtue of their imagined terrorist authors, whether domestic or international.

Yet these imaginings are unstable and subject to revision. For instance, although the Alexandrian bombing is now remembered as a strike against foreign terrorism, there had been a significant window leading up to Mubarak's downfall, when his Ministry of Interior was under investigation for engineering the attack in order "to discipline the Copts." Examining how dissent and threat are framed is thus critical for grasping the ways in which Coptic incidents of violence are bound up with securitization and militarization.

The distinction between "sectarian" and "terrorist" violence is significant for determining the value of Coptic deaths under the sign of Egyptian nationhood. Cases of sectarian violence occur with more frequency and are caused by local conflicts of a "personal" nature, such as feuds and vendettas. Cases of terrorist violence result in innocent victims targeted for their faith whose deaths are framed as "attacks on the nation." On the ground, however, the distinction between "sectarianism" and "terrorism" is murkier, both involving the same methods of violence (bombs, torchings), targets (churches, homes), and the innocent status of victims (civilians, worshippers, wedding attendees, etc.). Sectarianism functions as more of an elastic, umbrella term, encompassing any act of "Muslim" violence toward a "Christian," and vice versa. Terrorism, on the other hand, critically turns on the state's identification of the perpetrators as "terrorists" and threats to national security. For Copts, however similar experiences of sectarian and terrorist attacks are felt to be, their distinction from one another is vastly consequential, resulting in national heroes of commemoration on the one hand, and failures in obtaining legal enforcement or punishment on the other.

Given that the Egyptian state decides which acts of violence are "terrorist" and which not, Coptic victims of violence are also framed as threats and perpetrators of attack against the nation. The bloodiest example of this misrecognition is the Maspero Massacre of October 2011 (Madhbaha Masbiru). As I briefly mentioned in chapter 1, the Maspero Massacre was the Armed Forces' massacre of twenty-eight Copts during their peaceful march to Egyptian state television headquarters. Organized by the Maspero Youth Union, the march encapsulated a growing movement of Copts seeking to advance communal means of self-representation independent of the Coptic Church. Simultaneous with the military's attack on the demonstrators, state-owned channels broadcast messages to the national public: "Urgent: Army under attack by Copts" (Guirguis 2016). The channels also called on "all honorable citizens" to defend the army during the week of national holiday commemorations of the Arab-Israeli War of 1973. Although the interim ruling Supreme Council of the Armed Forces later vindicated the Maspero protestors, the damage had already been done.

What is striking today about the Maspero Massacre is the deafening silence that continues to surround its victims at the military's hands. In contrast to the deaths in Alexandria, Libya, and the Patriarchate Cathedral, the Maspero deaths are not currently counted among the Coptic Church's official roster of holy martyrs. Their omission from communal memory indexes the vulnerabilities attached to those Copts searching for a sense of Christian-Muslim belonging unyoked to religious institutions. Months after Mubarak's downfall, the Maspero demonstration was a continuation of the Tahrir protests against authoritarianism, redirected against military rule. Under the Sisi regime, such calls for the military's accountability have been effectively extinguished.

In the post-2011 revolutionary period leading up to the Sisi presidency, the differential grievability of deaths sets into motion particular horizons of Christian-Muslim solidarity and forecloses others. Compared with Alexandria's victims who are seen as precursors to Tahrir's interfaith unity, the victims of the Maspero Massacre are largely forgotten, their deaths unredressed. As in the case of Maspero, the Raba'a Massacre that followed Sisi's coup in 2013 occurred during an interim period of army-led government. Parallel to Maspero's erasure, the memory of the Raba'a Massacre, the military's slaughter of over a thousand Muslim Brotherhood protestors, is repressed in the national public. In both incidents, the military legitimated its excessive acts of violence by marking the protestors as "threats" to national security. Insofar that the

Maspero and Rabaʿa demonstrations posed a challenge to military authority, their deaths are excluded from narratives of national revolution and sacrifice. Each massacre with its body of deaths is counted separately as a "communal" tragedy—Maspero to the Copts and Rabaʿa to the Islamists.

It is no secret that Copts oppose Brotherhood rule, in sheer view of Morsi's chaotic experiment with the presidency and the Brotherhood's plan for political Islamization at the expense of Christians. By drawing similarities between Maspero and Rabaʿa, I do not mean to suggest that Copts would be better off under the Brotherhood or to justify the Brotherhood's violence against Copts. Rather, I wish to gesture to alternative horizons of mourning victims, by placing the memory of Maspero and Rabaʿa into the same overall frame of war in which the Egyptian army is a shared perpetrator of gross violence. This commemorative act of reframing offers the potential to foster cross-communal sympathy for deaths—Muslims for Copts in Maspero and Copts for Muslims in Rabaʿa. At a moment when fear and vitriolic retribution loom large, sectarian narratives of violence overshadow these glimmers of Christian-Muslim solidarity in the wake of the Egyptian military's atrocities. As the memory of Maspero recedes, Copts also increasingly overlook the hard reality that it was the army who had once pitted its tanks and guns against them only a few years ago.

Under Sisi's rule from August 2013 onward, the Egyptian state has equated the Brotherhood with "terrorism" and leveraged this equation toward reviving old formulas of church-state partnership. During the coup, Pope Tawadros declared his anti-Brotherhood stance, issuing several statements in support of the incoming military regime. The Coptic Church's clear vote of support for Morsi's ouster was an act that turned Copts into pawns in Sisi's war on terrorism. Immediately after the Rabaʿa Massacre, over forty Orthodox, Protestant, and Catholic churches were looted and torched by Brotherhood sympathizers in their nationwide retaliation against Tawadros and Coptic Christians writ large.[6] Referred

6. Following the evidence collected by human rights organizations, witnesses in Minya reported hearing signs of Brotherhood support prior to church violence. For example, one witness heard men say "Go help your brothers in Rabaʿa" and "Islamic [state], Islamic [state] [*Islāmiyya, Islāmiyya*]," before breaking the doors of Sts. Mary and Abram Church. Other witnesses reported the crowds chanting slogans "Tawadros, you are a coward for the Americans" and "Tawadros, you coward, get your dogs out of the square," referring to the pope and Coptic Christian demonstrations in support of Morsi's ouster. See "Egypt: Mass Attacks on Churches," Human Rights Watch, August 21, 2013, www.hrw.org/news/2013/08/21/egypt-mass-attacks-churches (accessed May 28, 2018).

to as "love offerings" (*qurbān*) by Tawadros, these churches and their destruction gained sacred value under an emerging national narrative of second revolutionary overthrow. The military, in turn, pledged to finance and reconstruct the destroyed church buildings, transforming them into fresh signs of church-military alliance in a post-Morsi era of threat and securitization.

Material edifices of religious memory are deeply intertwined with political imaginaries of violence and enhanced militarization. The army's construction of the Church of the Libya Martyrs and the military funeral held for the St. Peter's Martyrs in Nasr City introduced unprecedented forms of state presence in Coptic Christianity.[7] Subject to national and global orders of recognition, Coptic victims of "terrorism" find themselves confronting new sectarian vulnerabilities in their neighborhoods, villages, and homes.

. . .

"No, they are poor people, they are too simple to even come up with the idea of torching a church."

As he was driving me from Samalut to 'Aur in a white Lada, Mishal entertained my questions about 'Aur. When I asked if there had been any violence in the village after Sisi's coup two and half years earlier, he and his friend Abram in the passenger seat elaborated on what villagers and village life were like.

Abram illustrated rural poverty with a sense of humor. "Do you know what kids do around here to play? They just pick up dirt from the ground and throw it at each other. *Wooosh!*" Mimicking the game, he threw balls of air at Mishal with sound effects.

Mishal and Abram were twenty-something-year-olds from another village nearby, but spent most of their time in the city of Samalut located thirty kilometers north of Minya. Both Minya and Samalut have witnessed growing Muslim Brotherhood influence, confirming a general trend in all Upper Egypt's cities over the past decade. When Brotherhood supporters attacked Copts in retaliation for Morsi's ouster, Minya's largest churches, including Amir Tadrus and Anba Musa, were destroyed, and Samalut suffered some property damage and lootings.

---

7. After the Coptic Church's funeral for the St. Peter's Martyrs, each of the martyrs' coffins were wrapped in an Egyptian flag and transported to the Unknown Soldier Memorial site in Nasr City for a separate military funeral. For more details, see http://en.wataninet .com/coptic-affairs-coptic-affairs/sectarian/church-and-military-funeral-for-boutrossiya-blast-victims/18226 (accessed May 28, 2018).

Nothing happened in 'Aur; as Mishal summed up me, "the people are too simple."

The Coptic Church's Archdiocese in Samalut is responsible for taking care of 'Aur, a small village of three hundred families with a relatively even distribution of 40 percent Christians and 60 percent Muslims. My contact there Father Girgis used to be the village priest, having raised many of the ISIS victims into their faith as elementary school boys. Before sending me off with Mishal and Abram to see 'Aur, Father Girgis gave me a more human portrait of its residents—industrious farmers and laborers who have earned their local reputation as a "dawn-to-dusk village." He also noted that some of its Muslim inhabitants were helping to build the new church in honor of their Christian brothers.

As our car crept up to the village, I began to see the new Church of the Libya Martyrs and the military's banner declaring support for "martyrs of the faith and of the nation." A block compound walled with brick and concrete, the enormous construction site appeared a bit obtrusive within a landscape of vivid green fields and dark rows of tilled soil. Mishal and Abram pointed out to me where 'Aur was, about a kilometer or so away from the site.

Earlier that year, church construction initially unfolded in a more central location at 'Aur's main entrance. In late February 2015, shortly after the ISIS executions, Sisi granted a legal permit and military financial support to begin building at the village's mouth. By mid-March, the construction, and its conspicuous location in particular, flared controversy between Christian and Muslim residents of 'Aur. On Friday March 28, a forty-day commemorative mass for the Libya Martyrs was held at the new church site. During the mass, a mob of Muslim youth mounted a rally against its construction. On that same evening, a smaller group attacked the site with molotov cocktails, leaving seven people injured and a car in flames. According to several witnesses, the aggressors were connected to local Muslim Brotherhood branches and to outsiders to 'Aur. Others reported that Samalut's police had delayed arrival at the scene on purpose, a veiled charge of state collusion with the assailants.[8]

8. "Muslims, Christians Clash over 'Martyrs' Church' Construction," *al-Monitor*, May 13, 2015, www.al-monitor.com/pulse/en/originals/2015/05/egypt-christians-muslims-churches-law-reconciliation-session.html (accessed May 28, 2018); "Coptic 'Church of the Martyrs of Libya' Attacked after First Stone Laid," *The Tablet*, April 8, 2015, www.thetablet.co.uk/news/1960/0/coptic-church-of-the-martyrs-of-libya-attacked-after-first-stone-laid (accessed May 28, 2018); "The Martyr's Church: Islamic State Massacre

Belying its official stamp of endorsement, the Sisi regime failed to safeguard the church's construction and ʿAur's Copts during worship. After assuming power in 2013, Sisi had appointed local authorities to hold "reconciliation sessions" (*jalsāt al-sulḥ*) and resolve matters of sectarian conflict among Christians and Muslims, particularly in Upper Egypt and the Delta. In practice, these extrajudicial meetings have forced Copts to negotiate with powerful families and leaders of religious organizations, without legal recourse, protection, or enforcement. Often, perpetrators of violence end up walking away without punishment. This is, in fact, what happened in ʿAur. The reconciliation sessions amounted to the church's relocation from the village's entrance to the agricultural fields about a kilometer away, as well as the release of seven arrested Muslims directly involved in the attacks.

Months from completion, due that following spring, the Church of the Libya Martyrs was not yet functional. Mishal and Abram dropped me off inside the village's center at the old Church of the Virgin. There, Father had arranged for two village guides to wait for me. Seated at a table in front of the church, two police officers from Samalut stopped Mishal, asking for my information and making several phone calls to confirm my identity and purpose. After about an hour, I was allowed inside the church to begin my guided tour, provided that the two officers escort us for our entire itinerary.

Maryam and Maryann, teenagers born and raised in ʿAur, were polite, shy, and sisterlike with each other in every way. Keeping a watchful distance from the rifle-toting officers behind us, the girls and I gradually warmed up to each other and got into a rhythm. It quickly became clear that Maryam and Maryann had already taken several guests on a relatively established route through the alleys, waterwheels, and animal pens. Embarking on a pilgrimage, we visited the homes of the fifteen martyrs of ʿAur, one by one, each regarded as a holy shrine to be paid honor.

The widows and mothers waited at their open doors, dressed in black with many wearing medallions engraved with their martyrs' faces around their necks. Only a few years older than Maryam and Maryann, some women carried infants in their arms. Ushering us inside their homes, while the police officers waited outside, the widows and mothers

in Libya Casts Sectarian Shadow on a Village in Egypt," *The Intercept*, June 15, 2015, https://theintercept.com/2015/06/15/martyrs-church-islamic-state-massacre-libya-casts-sectarian-shadow-village-egypt (accessed May 28, 2018).

showed us how dramatically their lives had transformed as a result of their family's personal encounter with ISIS. On one level, they faced higher tiers of vulnerability now with incomes lost at the deaths of their primary breadwinners. On another level, they had never before experienced such an unexpected shock of gifts, financial aid, and international exposure.

In the earliest days of 'Aur's tragedy, Christians and Muslims gathered together in a show of solidarity with the ISIS victims. A number of Muslims in the village had worked in Libya with the Coptic victims, living in the same shared dormitories for migrant laborers. When ISIS fighters came to their flats on their hunt, they sifted the Christians from the Muslims using their national ID cards. After having watched their childhood companions kidnapped away, the Muslim laborers immediately returned to 'Aur to convey the heartbreaking news to the victims' families. According to Father Girgis, they were also the first to offer as much as they could spare in order to support relatives of the missing. For several nerve-wracking weeks, the villagers appealed to state authorities for help without receiving any answers.

The villagers' world turned upside-down the moment ISIS uploaded its video of its executions. In addition to financing the new Church of the Libya Martyrs, Sisi issued a decree granting monthly pensions for life to the families victimized by terrorism. The Coptic Church also gave money to the widows and mothers so that they could convert their living rooms and bedrooms into shrines dedicated to their sons and husbands. Filled with portrait photos and personal relics, the shrines were newly furnished with alabaster and bureau cabinets, even adjoining bathrooms and hallways with freshly painted walls. Flush with the flow of outside funds, the homes of these women were simply standing out more distinguished compared to those of their neighbors. In ritual coordination with Maryam and Maryann, the widows and mothers had also become familiar with the routine of political leaders, journalists, pilgrims, and fieldworkers offering their consolations and gifts.

After finishing our tour, we returned to the old Church of the Virgin, where I waited for Mishal and Abram to pick me up. Bathed with winter sunshine, its courtyard was decorated with banner iconography repicturing scenes from the ISIS beheadings. At the front entrance of the small education building, where I heard children singing and playing inside, there was an impressive image of Jesus photoshopped onto rows of ISIS fighters, holding down the bowed necks of their Coptic captives. Another banner next to the sanctuary's doors presented a magnified portrait of 'Aur's villagers dressed in iconic orange jumpsuits, the new scene of their holy passion and saintly suffering conjuring older scenes of violence exercised in American detention camps in Guantánamo Bay (cf. Caton 2006).

While I was seated on the church's steps, a man approached me to shake my hand. As we exchanged introductions, I recognized his name and his story from news reports and satellite television. Bashir Kamil had been hit twice by ISIS, losing two of his younger brothers, Bishoi and Samu'il. With a heavy shawl draped around his angular face, Bashir spoke about the great pride and joy that his brothers brought to him and his family.

Bashir's pride went so far as to openly express gratitude to ISIS for releasing its execution video. In his opinion, the video was the most powerful proclamation to the whole world that his brothers had been faithful to Christianity in the face of death. With the knowledge of my American citizenship, Bashir added that American visitors from the Evangelical churches were scheduled to honor the village's fifteen martyrs sometime next month after Christmas. If 'Aur had signified Egypt's most neglected margins in the past, its current place at the center of international counterterrorism and ecumenical solidarity meant nothing less than a radical reorientation toward more global horizons—and all because of ISIS's video.

. . .

"Of the faith and of the nation," Coptic Christians are now forced to reckon with new geopolitical coordinates of recognition, caught between ISIS's war on "Rome" and "the Nation of the Cross" at one end, and the international war on "radical Islamic terrorism" at the other. Aur's Christian families received condolences from the Roman Catholic Church and Christian pilgrims from Europe and North America expressing sympathy for victims of religious persecution. Fueling a conflict beyond nation-state borders and denominational lines, the recalcitrant image of a "Christianity versus Islam" divide was rearing its head once again.

However globally oriented its discourses may be, the concrete effects of terrorism and counterterrorism are firmly entrenched within the politics of the nation-state. For Copts in post-2013 Egypt, it is Sisi's brutal crackdown on the Muslim Brotherhood that frames their national value as honored deaths. For example, in the Cathedral bombing of 2016, despite ISIS's claim of responsibility for the attack, Sisi pinned the blame squarely on the Brotherhood. The public memory of these Coptic deaths, in turn, is imprinted with seals of military authority. Conscripted as allies of the military state, Copts confront new risks and threats in the guise of retribution. Against the backdrop of Sisi's ongoing war on terrorism, the state's pledge to rebuild destroyed churches reopens old wounds bound up with Morsi's ouster and the state's criminalization of Brotherhood opposition.

In lived contexts of Christian-Muslim interaction, the slippery slide from "terrorism" into "sectarianism" amounts to devastating consequences on an everyday scale. As we saw in ʿAur, the military's outward support for church construction invited outsiders rumored to hold ties with Minya's underground Brotherhood branches. Protests at the construction site eventually descended into another local incident of "sectarian" violence. State and foreign funds funneled to the victims' families and the Coptic Church, in addition to increased international attention to ʿAur's Copts, all served to advance the Christian-Muslim divide in a village whose inhabitants used to be more equally poor and "simple."

The point at which Christian-Muslim tensions are read as "sectarian" is also the point at which national heroes lapse into the shadows of state neglect. Having reaped the benefits and liabilities of state honor, ʿAur's Copts in the wreckage of village violence faced the dark fact that they were subject to reconciliation sessions and the mercy of local authorities like everyone else. According to the Egyptian Initiative for Personal Rights, there have been at least seventy-seven cases of sectarian attacks on Copts between 2011 and 2016 in the governorate of Minya alone. By a far distance, there are more recorded incidents of violence that occur in the quotidian settings of homes, stores, and streets than internationally publicized acts of terrorism such as church bombings or execution videos. In cases of sectarian violence, Sisi's deferral of state responsibility has resulted in the depreciated enforcement of law and justice in ordinary spheres of Christian-Muslim coexistence.

Perhaps the most punishing contradiction for the vast majority of Coptic victims lies in the fact that local arbiters operate in villages and cities where Brotherhood sympathy is strong and widespread, even if covert in the repressive wake of the military coup. Recently, the Coptic Church has reported a national surge of attacks on Copts averaging about once a month since 2013. This worrying trend has mobilized mounting criticism of Pope Tawadros and his fidelity to the military state at the expense of Coptic rights and safety. The criticism is breaking from within the Church's highest ranks: in his repeated acts of resistance, Bishop Makarius of Minya has boycotted numerous reconciliation sessions.[9]

Across Egypt nationwide, Copts now confront new yet familiar binds of minoritarian vulnerability. ʿAur, a village on the neglected periphery, exemplifies the fraught dynamics that have unfolded among Christians and Muslims whose local frames of coexistence have been shaped by pan-Islamic militants across Egypt's borders and Muslim Brotherhood supporters behind the scenes. Reconciliation sessions and heightened military security have consistently been the state's solutions for curtailing conflict and violence. All the while, across each new incident of violence, Copts revisit tired scripts of failed protection and reconsider the risks and threats that are tied to the Coptic Church's subordination to the authoritarian regime. They reckon with the limits of a persecution narrative that pits Christians against Muslims when facing the fact that Christians and Muslims are slaughtered by the same actors, whether by the military (Maspero and Rabaʿa Mosque massacres) or by ISIS (Libya/Butrusiyya Martyrs and Sufi mosque victims in Sinai). These limits also extend windows of possibility for forging sympathies across sectarian lines.

Despite the urgency and paralysis that often accompanies violence, the situation of Copts in Egypt invites us to consider the more ordinary terms of inhabiting life in its wake. It encourages us to consider what a mourning mother's dream means for the public memory of her son, what the transformation of church buildings into security zones entails for a village, and who the victims and victors are after all the fleeting sensationalism of violence has gone. Saints—the Virgin after the 1967 War, martyrs "of the faith and of the nation," freshly canonized communal leaders—embody histories of a Christian-Muslim nation at stake and the creative potential for their remaking. The terrible atrocities of violence that Copts experience are neither aberrant examples of exceptional tragedy nor re-articulations of eternal suffering. Activating the memory of saints and martyrs, their appeal to millennia-long traditions point not to an anachronism from an ancient world, but to a set of deeply engrained sensibilities and landscapes that can retool horizons of memory, action, and hope toward common flourishing.

9. "How Egypt's Copts Fell Out of Love with President Sisi," *Foreign Policy,* December 9, 2016, http://foreignpolicy.com/2016/12/09/how-egypts-copts-fell-out-of-love-with-president-sisi (accessed May 28, 2018).

Bibliography

FILMOGRAPHY

Abdel Messeeh, Namir, dir. 2011. *La Vierge, les Coptes et moi.* Boulogne-Billancourt: Oweda Films.

De Silva, David, dir. 1980. *Fame: The Musical.* Los Angeles: MGM Studios.

Gibson, Mel, dir. 2004. *The Passion of the Christ.* Los Angeles: Twentieth Century Fox Home Entertainment.

Iskander, Mai, dir. 2009. *Garbage Dreams.* Brooklyn: Iskander Films.

Tawfik, Magued, dir. 1993. *Al-Shahida Marina.* Cairo: Sharikat Jun Film al-Intaj wa-l-Tawzi'.

Wassef, Engi, dir. 2008. *Marina of the Zabbaleen.* Brooklyn: Torch Films.

TELEVISION SOURCES

Al-Qahira al-Yawm, December 23, 2009, al-Yawm Television Channel.

Nabd al-Kanisa, December 20 and December 23, 2009, Aghapy TV Television Channel.

ARTICLES AND BOOKS IN ARABIC

Abu al-Barakat ibn Kabar. 1971 [1296–1332]. *Misbah al-Zulma fi al-Idah al-Khidma.*

'Aziz, Latif. 2012. *Tajalliyat wa-l-Zuhurat: Kulliyyat al-Tahar wa-l-Batul bi-l-Warraq wa-Mu'jizatha.* Cairo: al-Mahabba.

Al-'Azm, Sadiq Jalal. 2003 [1969]. *Naqd al-Fikr al-Dini.* Beirut: Dar al-Tali'a.

Archdiocese of Samalut. 2015. *Sahabat al-Nuraniyya: Shuhada' al-Iman wa-l-Watan.* Samalut: Orthodox Diocese.

Bahr, Samira. 1979. *Al-Aqbat fi al-Hayat al-Siyasiyya al-Misriyya*. Cairo: Maktabat al-Anjlu al-Misriyya.

Bishop Sawiris ibn al-Muqaffa'. 1999. *Tartib al-Kahanut*. Cairo: Nashrat al-Anba Samu'il.

———. 1975. *Misbah al-'Aql*. Trans. Rifaat Y. Ebeid and M. J. Young. Corpus Scriptorum Christianorum Orientalium. Louvain: Impremerie Orientaliste.

Al-Bishri, Tariq. 1981. *Al-Muslimun wa-l-Aqbat fi Itar al-Jama'a al-Wataniyya*. Cairo: al-Hay'a al-Misriyya al-'Amma li-l-Kitab.

Pope Shenouda III. 2006. *Ta'lih al-Insan*. Cairo: al-Kulliyya al-Iklirikiyya bi-l-'Abbasiyya.

Father 'Abd al-Masih al-Basit abu al-Khayr. 2010. *Zuhurat al-'Adhra' fi Misr: Bayn al-Haqiqa wa-l-Iddi'a'at al-Kadhiba*. Cairo: Egyptian Publishing in Ain Shams.

Father Antunius al-Baramusi. 1989. *Ayqunat al-Sama'*. Cairo: Dar Nubar.

Father Bula Sa'd. 2009. *Mu'jizat al-Sayyida al-'Adhra' Maryam bi-Bur Sa'id: Tuba wa-Shifa'*. 4th ed. Cairo: Inter-Egypt.

Father Matta al-Miskin [Matthew the Poor]. 1952. *Hayat al-Salat al-Urthuduksiyya*. Wadi al-Natrun: Dayr Abu Maqar Press.

Hanna, Milad. 1980. *Na'am Aqbat, Lakin Misriyyun*. Cairo: Maktabat Madbuli.

Juzif, Mikhail. 2009. *Kun Mutma'innan*. Cairo: al-Mu'allif.

Mothers of the Convent of Amir Tadrus in Harat al-Rum. 2011. *Sirat al-Shahid al-'Azim al-Amir Tadrus al-Shatbi*. Cairo: Art Group.

Shukri, Ghali. 1991. *Al-Aqbat fi Watan Mutaghayyir*. Cairo: Dar al-Shuruq.

ARTICLES AND BOOKS IN ENGLISH

Abdulhaq, Najat. 2016. *Jewish and Greek Communities in Egypt: Entrepreneurship and Business before Nasser*. London: I. B. Tauris.

Abu el-Haj, Nadia. 2001. *Facts on the Ground: Archaeological Practice and Territorial Self-Fashioning in Israeli Society*. Chicago: University of Chicago Press.

Abu-Lughod, Janet L. 1971. *Cairo: 1001 Years of the City Victorious*. Princeton, NJ: Princeton University Press.

Abu-Lughod, Lila. 2005. *Dramas of Nationhood: The Politics of Television in Egypt*. Chicago: University of Chicago Press.

Agamben, Giorgio. 1998. *Homo Sacer: Sovereign Power and Bare Life*. Trans. Daniel Heller-Roazen. Stanford, CA: Stanford University Press.

Aghaie, Kamran Scot. 2004. *The Martyrs of Karbala: Shi'i Symbols and Rituals in Modern Iran*. Seattle: University of Washington Press.

Agrama, Hussein Ali. 2012. *Questioning Secularism: Islam, Sovereignty, and the Rule of Law in Modern Egypt*. Chicago: University of Chicago Press.

Albera, Dionigi, and Maria Couroucli, eds. 2012. *Sharing Sacred Spaces in the Mediterranean: Christians, Muslims, and Jews at Shrines and Sanctuaries*. Bloomington: Indiana University Press.

Albera, Dionigi, and Benoit Fliche. 2012. "Muslim Devotional Practices in Christian Shrines: The Case of Istanbul." In *Sharing Sacred Spaces in the Mediterranean: Christians, Muslims, and Jews at Shrines and Sanctuaries*, ed. Dionigi Albera and Maria Couroucli, 94–117. Bloomington: Indiana University Press.

Allen, Lori. 2013. *The Rise and Fall of Human Rights: Cynicism and Politics in Occupied Palestine.* Stanford, CA: Stanford University Press.

Altorki, Soraya, ed. 2015. *A Companion to the Anthropology of the Middle East.* New York: John Wiley & Sons.

el-Amrani, Issandr. April 28, 2006. "The Emergence of a 'Coptic Question' in Egypt." In *Middle East Research and Information Project,* www.merip.org /mero/mero042806 (accessed May 5, 2018).

Anderson, Benedict. 1991. *Imagined Communities: Reflections on the Origin and Spread of Nationalism.* New York: Verso.

Andriopoulos, Stefan. 2011. "Kant's Magic Lantern: Historical Epistemology and Media Archaeology." *Representations* 115(1): 42–70.

Anidjar, Gil. 2014. *Blood: A Critique of Christianity.* New York: Columbia University Press.

Appadurai, Arjun. 2006. *Fear of Small Numbers.* Durham, NC: Duke University Press.

———. 1993. "Number in the Colonial Imagination." In *Orientalism and the Postcolonial Predicament: Perspectives on South Asia,* ed. Carol A. Breckenridge and Peter van der Veer, 314–40. Philadelphia: University of Pennsylvania Press.

———, ed. 1986. *The Social Life of Things: Commodities in Cultural Perspective.* Cambridge: Cambridge University Press.

Arendt, Hannah. 1998 [1958]. *The Human Condition.* Chicago: University of Chicago Press.

———. 1966. *The Origins of Totalitarianism.* New York: Harcourt.

Armanios, Febe. 2012. "The Coptic Charismatic Renewal in Egypt: Historical Roots and Recent Developments." Paper presented at International Association of Coptic Studies Congress, Rome, September 17–22, 2012.

———. 2011. *Coptic Christianity in Ottoman Egypt.* New York: Oxford University Press.

———. 2002. "The Virtuous Woman: Images of Gender in Modern Coptic Society." *Middle Eastern Studies* 38(1): 110–30.

Armanios, Febe, and Andrew Amstutz. 2013. "Emerging Christian Media in Egypt: Clerical Authority and the Visualization of Women in Coptic Video Films." *International Journal of Middle East Studies* 45: 513–33.

Asad, Talal. 2015. "Thinking about Tradition, Religion, and Politics in Egypt Today." *Critical Inquiry* 42(1): 166–214.

———. 2012. "Fear and the Ruptured State: Reflections on Egypt after Mubarak." *Social Research* 79(2): 271–98.

———. 2007. *On Suicide Bombing.* New York: Columbia University Press.

———. 2003. *Formations of the Secular: Christianity, Islam, Modernity.* Stanford, CA: Stanford University Press.

———. 1994. "Ethnographic Representation, Statistics, and Modern Power." *Social Research* 61(2): 55–88.

———. 1986. *The Idea of an Anthropology of Islam.* Washington, DC: Center for Contemporary Arab Studies.

el-Aswad, el Sayed. 2002. *Religion and Folk Cosmology: Scenarios of the Visible and Invisible in Rural Egypt.* Westport, CT: Praeger.

Atiya, Aziz Surya. 1991. "Saint Mark." In *The Coptic Encyclopedia,* vol. 5, ed. Aziz S. Atiya, 1528–1533. New York: Macmillan.

Augé, Marc. 2002. *In the Metro.* Trans. Tom Conley. Minneapolis: University of Minnesota Press.

Ayalon, Ami. 1999. "Egypt's Coptic Pandora's Box." In *Minorities and the State in the Arab World,* ed. Ofra Bengio and Gabriel Ben-Dor, 53–72. Boulder, CO: Lynne Rienner Publishers.

Ayoub, Mahmoud. 2007. *A Muslim View of Christianity: Essays on Dialogue.* Ed. Ifran A. Omar. Maryknoll, NY: Orbis Books.

———. 1987. "Martyrdom in Christianity and Islam." In *Religious Resurgence: Contemporary Cases in Islam, Christianity, and Judaism,* ed. Richard T. Antoun and Mary Elaine Hegland, 67–77. Syracuse, NY: Syracuse University Press.

Bagnall, Roger S. 2007. *Egypt in the Byzantine World, 300–700.* Cambridge: Cambridge University Press.

———. 1993. *Egypt in Late Antiquity.* Princeton, NJ: Princeton University Press.

Baker, Raymond William. 1978. *Egypt's Uncertain Revolution under Nasser and Sadat.* Cambridge, MA: Harvard University Press.

Bakhtin, M.M. 1990 [1919]. *Art and Answerability: Early Philosophical Essays.* Ed. Michael Holquist and Vadim Liapunov. Austin: University of Texas Press.

Bandak, Andreas. 2014. "Of Refrains and Rhythms in Contemporary Damascus: Urban Space and Christian-Muslim Coexistence." *Current Anthropology* 55 (S10): 248–61.

———. 2013. "Our Lady of Soufanieh: On Knowledge, Ignorance, and Indifference among the Christians of Damascus." In *Politics of Worship in the Contemporary Middle East: Sainthood in Fragile States,* ed. Andreas Bandak and Mikkel Bille, 129–55. Leiden: Brill.

Bandak, Andreas, and Tom Boylston. 2014. "The 'Orthodoxy' of Orthodoxy: On Moral Imperfection, Correctness, and Deferral in Religious Worlds." *Religion and Society: Advances in Research* 5: 25–46.

Barak, On. 2013. *On Time: Technology and Temporality in Modern Egypt.* Berkeley: University of California Press.

Baron, Beth. 2014. *The Orphan Scandal: Christian Missionaries and the Rise of the Muslim Brotherhood.* Stanford, CA: Stanford University Press.

Bashkin, Orit. 2012. *New Babylonians: A History of Jews in Modern Iraq.* Stanford, CA: Stanford University Press.

———. 2008. *The Other Iraq: Pluralism and Culture in Hashemite Iraq.* Stanford, CA: Stanford University Press.

Bazin, André. 1960. "The Ontology of the Photographic Image." *Film Quarterly* 13 (4): 4–9.

Beal, Timothy K., and Tod Linafelt, eds. 2005. *Religion, Popular Culture, and "The Passion of the Christ."* Chicago: University of Chicago Press.

Beinin, Joel. 1998. *The Dispersion of Egyptian Jewry: Culture, Politics, and the Formation of a Modern Diaspora*. Berkeley: University of California Press.

Beinin, Joel, and Zachary Lockman. 1998. *Workers on the Nile: Nationalism, Communism, Islam, and the Egyptian Working Class, 1882–1954*. Princeton, NJ: Princeton University Press.

Benedict, Philip, et al. 2007. "AHR Conversation: Religious Identities and Violence." *American Historical Review* 112: 1433–79.

Bengio, Ofra, and Gabriel Ben-Dor, eds. 1999. *Minorities and the State in the Arab World*. Boulder, CO: Lynne Rienner Press.

Benjamin, Walter. 1969 [1936]. "The Work of Art in the Age of Mechanical Reproduction." In *Illuminations*, ed. Hannah Arendt, trans. Harry Zohn, 217–51. New York: Schocken.

Bernstein, Anya. 2013. *Religious Bodies Politic: Rituals of Sovereignty in Buryat Buddhism*. Chicago: University of Chicago Press.

Bianchi, Robert. 1989. *Unruly Corporatism: Associational Life in Twentieth-Century Egypt*. Oxford: Oxford University Press.

Bialecki, Jon. 2014. "After the Denominozoic: Evolution, Differentiation, Denominationalism." *Current Anthropology* 55: S193–S204.

———. 2011. "Beyond Logos: Extensions of the Language Ideology Paradigm in the Study of Global Christianity(-ies)." *Anthropological Quarterly* 84(3): 575–93.

Biehl, João. 2005. *Vita: Life in a Zone of Social Abandonment*. Berkeley: University of California Press.

Bishop Gregorious. 1968. *The Virgin in Zeitoun*. Official Report drafted by Papal Commission. Cairo: Coptic Orthodox Patriarchate.

Bishop Kallistos Ware. 2004. *The Collected Works*. Vol. 1. Crestwood, NY: St. Vladimir's Seminary Press.

———. 1979. "The Spirituality of the Icon." In *A History of Christian Doctrine*, ed. H. Cunliffe-Jones and B. Drewery, 195–98. Edinburgh: T & T Clark.

Bishop Mettaous. 1996. "Sacramental Rites in the Coptic Orthodox Church, 2nd Edition." Coptic Orthodox Church Network, www.copticchurch.net/topics/thecopticchurch/sacraments (accessed May 5, 2018).

Bishop Moussa. 2010. *Saint Mary, the Theotokos*. My Coptic Church 2. Bishopric of Youth: Abbassia, Cairo.

Bishop Youanis of al-Gharbiya. 2009 [1960]. "Humility." In *Paradise of the Spirit*, vol. 1, 95–136. Trans. St. Mark Coptic Orthodox Church of Chicago. Burr Ridge, IL: St. Mark Coptic Orthodox Church of Chicago.

Blackbourn, David. 1993. *Marpingen: Apparitions of the Virgin Mary in Nineteenth-Century Germany*. Oxford: Clarendon Press.

Bolman, Elizabeth S., ed. 2016. *The Red Monastery Church: Beauty and Asceticism in Upper Egypt*. New Haven, CT: Yale University Press.

———, ed. 2002. *Monastic Visions: Wall Paintings in the Monastery of St. Antony at the Red Sea*. New Haven, CT: Yale University Press.

Borges, Jorge Luis. 1975. "On Exactitude in Science (Del rigor en la ciencia, 1946)." In *A Universal History of Infamy*, trans. Jorge Luis Borges and Norman Thomas de Giovanni, 131–32. London: Penguin Books.

Bourdieu, Pierre. 1993. *Language and Symbolic Power.* Ed. John Thompson. Trans. Gino Raymond and Matthew Adamson. Cambridge, MA: Harvard University Press.

Bowman, Glenn, ed. 2012. *Sharing the Sacra: the Poltics and Pragmatics of Intercommunal Relations around Holy Places.* Oxford: Berghahn.

———. 1993. "Nationalising the Sacred: Shrines and Shifting Identities in the Israeli-Occupied Territories." *Journal of the Royal Anthropological Institute* 38 (3): 431–60.

Boylston, Tom. 2018. *The Stranger at the Feast: Prohibition and Mediation in an Ethiopian Orthodox Christian Community.* Berkeley: University of California Press.

Brakke, David. 2011. *The Gnostics: Myth, Ritual, and Diversity in Early Christianity.* Cambridge, MA: Harvard University Press.

———. 2006. *Demons and the Making of the Monk: Spiritual Combat in Early Christianity.* Cambridge, MA: Harvard University Press.

———. 1995. *Athanasius and the Politics of Asceticism.* Oxford: Clarendon.

Brakke, David, and Andrew Crislip, trans. 2015. *Selected Discourses of Shenoute the Great: Community, Theology, and Social Conflict in Late Antique Egypt.* Cambridge: Cambridge University Press.

Brown, Peter. 2000. "Enjoying the Saints in Late Antiquity." *Early Medieval Europe* 9: 1–24.

———. 1983. "The Saint as Exemplar in Late Antiquity." *Representations* 2: 1–25.

———. 1981. *The Cult of the Saints: Its Rise and Function in Latin Christianity.* Chicago: University of Chicago Press.

———. 1971. "The Rise and Function of the Holy Man in Late Antiquity." *Journal of Roman Studies* 61: 80–101.

Brown, Dan. 2003. *The Da Vinci Code.* New York: Bantam Press.

Brubaker, Leslie, and John Haldon. 2011. *Byzantium in the Iconoclast Era, c. 680–850: A History.* Cambridge: Cambridge University Press.

Buck-Morss, Susan. 1994. "The Cinema Screen as Prosthesis of Perception: A Historical Account." In *The Senses Still: Perception and Memory as Material Culture in Modernity,* ed. C. Nadia Seremetakis, 45–62. Chicago: University of Chicago Press.

Buckser, Andrew, and Stephen D. Glazier eds. 2003. *The Anthropology of Religious Conversion.* Lanham, MD: Rowman & Littlefield.

Burckhardt, Titus. 1967. *Sacred Art in East and West: Its Principles and Methods.* Trans. Lord Northbourne. Bedfont, Middlesex: Perennial Books.

Butcher, Edith Louisa. 1897. *The Story of the Church of Egypt: Being an Outline of the History of the Egyptians under Their Successive Masters from the Roman Conquest until Now.* London: Smith, Elder.

Butler, Alfred Joshua. 1884. *The Ancient Coptic Churches of Egypt.* Oxford: Clarendon.

Butler, Judith. 2009. *Frames of War: When Is Life Grievable?* New York: Verso.

Bynum, Caroline Walker. 2011. *Christian Materiality: An Essay on Religion in Late Medieval Europe.* Cambridge, MA: MIT Press.

Caduff, Carlo. 2015. *The Pandemic Perhaps: Dramatic Events in a Public Culture of Danger*. Berkeley: University of California Press.

Calhoun, Craig. 1992. *Habermas and the Public Sphere*. Cambridge, MA: MIT Press.

Calhoun, Craig, Mark Juergensmeyer, and Jonathan van Antwerpen, eds. 2011. *Rethinking Secularism*. Oxford: Oxford University Press.

Campos, Michelle. 2010. *Ottoman Brothers: Muslims, Christians, and Jews in Early Twentieth-Century Palestine*. Stanford, CA: Stanford University Press.

Canetti, Elias. 1984. *Crowds and Power*. New York: Farrar, Straus & Giroux.

Cannell, Fenella, ed. 2006. *The Anthropology of Christianity*. Durham, NC: Duke University Press.

Carasso, Lucienne. 2014. *Growing Up Jewish in Alexandria: The Story of a Sephardic Family's Exodus from Egypt*. New York: Interactive International.

Carter, Barbara Lynn. 1986. *The Copts in Egyptian Politics, 1918–1952*. New York: Routledge & Keegan Paul.

Casanova, José. 1994. *Public Religions in the Modern World*. Chicago: University of Chicago Press.

Castelli, Elizabeth. 2006. "Praying for the Persecuted Church: US Christian Activism in the Global Arena." *Journal of Human Rights* 4 (3): 321–51.

———. 2004. *Martyrdom and Memory: Early Christian Culture Making*. New York: Columbia University Press.

Castoriadis, Cornelius. 1987. *The Imaginary Institution of Society*. Trans. Kathleen Blamey. Cambridge, MA: MIT Press.

Caton, Steven C. 2006. "Coetzee, Agamben, and the Passion of Abu Ghraib." *American Anthropologist* 108(1): 114–23.

Chakrabarty, Dipesh. 2000. *Provincializing Europe: Postcolonial Thought and Historical Difference*. Princeton, NJ: Princeton University Press.

Chatterjee, Partha. 1993. *The Nation and Its Fragments: Colonial and Postcolonial Histories*. Princeton, NJ: Princeton University Press.

Christian, William A. 1998. "Six Hundred Years of Visionaries in Spain: Those Believed and Those Ignored." In *Challenging Authority: The Historical Study of Contentious Politics*, ed. M.P. Hanagan, L.P. Moch and W. Te Brake, 107–19. Minneapolis: University of Minnesota Press.

———. 1996. *Visionaries: The Spanish Republic and the Reign of Christ*. Berkeley: University of California Press.

———. 1972. *Person and God in a Spanish Valley*. New York: Seminar Press.

Christian, William A., and Gábor Klaniczay eds. 2009. *The "Vision Thing": Studying Divine Intervention*. Budapest: Collegium Budapest.

Classen, Constance. 2014. *A Cultural History of the Senses in the Age of Empire, 1800–1920*. London: Bloomsbury.

———, ed. 2005. *The Book of Touch*. New York: Berg.

Claverie, Elizabeth. 2003. *Les guerres de la Vierge: Une anthropologie des apparitions*. Paris: Gallimard.

Cody, Francis. 2013. *The Light of Knowledge: Literacy Activism and the Politics of Writing in South India*. Ithaca, NY: Cornell University Press.

———. 2011. "Publics and Politics." *Annual Review of Anthropology* 40: 37–52.

Cohen, Mark R. 1994. *Under Crescent and Cross: The Jews in the Middle Ages.* Princeton, NJ: Princeton University Press.

Cohen, Raymond. 2008. *Saving the Holy Sepulchre: How Rival Christians Came Together to Rescue Their Holiest Shrine.* Oxford: Oxford University Press.

Cohn, Bernard. 1987. "The Census, Social Structure, and Objectification in South Asia." In *An Anthropologist among the Historians and Other Essays.* Delhi: Oxford University Press.

Comaroff, Jean. 2007. "Beyond Bare Life: AIDS, (Bio)Politics, and the Neoliberal Order." *Public Culture* 19(1): 197–219.

Comaroff, Jean, and John Comaroff. 1991. *Of Revelation and Revolution: Christianity, Colonialism, and Consciousness in South Africa.* Vol. 1. Chicago: University of Chicago Press.

Connor, Steven. 2004. *The Book of Skin.* Ithaca, NY: Cornell University Press.

Cornell, Vincent. 1998. *Realm of the Saint: Power and Authority in Moroccan Sufism.* Austin: University of Texas Press.

Crapanzano, Vincent. 2004. *Imaginative Horizons: An Essay in Literary-Philosophical Anthropology.* Chicago: University of Chicago Press.

———. 1980. *Tuhami: Portrait of a Moroccan.* Chicago: University of Chicago Press.

———. 1973. *The Hamadsha: A Study in Moroccan Ethnopsychiatry.* Berkeley: University of California Press.

Crary, Jonathan. 1990. *Techniques of the Observer: On Vision and Modernity in the Nineteenth Century.* Cambridge, MA: MIT Press.

Cuffel, Alexandra. 2005. "From Practice to Polemic: Shared Saints and Festivals as in the Medieval Mediterranean." *Bulletin of the School of Oriental and African Studies* 68(3): 401–19.

Dalachanis, Angelos. 2017. *The Greek Exodus from Egypt: Diaspora Politics and Emigration, 1937–1962.* New York: Berghahn.

Dammond, Liliane S. 2007. *The Lost World of the Egyptian Jews: First-Person Accounts from Egypt's Jewish Community in the Twentieth Century.* New York: iUniverse.

al-Damurdashi. 1991. *Al-Damurdashi's Chronicle of Egypt, 1688–1755.* Trans. Daniel Crecelius and 'Abd al-Wahhab Bakr. Leiden: Brill.

Davis, Stephen J. 2008a. *Coptic Christology in Practice: Incarnation and Divine Participation in Late Antique and Medieval Egypt.* Oxford: Oxford University Press.

———. 2008b. "Introducing an Arabic Commentary on the Apocalypse: Ibn Kātib Qayṣar on Revelation." *Harvard Theological Review* 101(1): 77–96.

———. 2004. *The Early Coptic Papacy: The Egyptian Church and Its Leadership in Late Antiquity.* Cairo: American University in Cairo Press.

———. 2001. *The Cult of St. Thecla: A Tradition of Women's Piety in Late Antiquity.* Oxford: Oxford University Press.

de Abreu, Maria José Alves. 2012. "The FedEx Saints: Patrons of Mobility and Speed in a Neoliberal City." In *Things: Religion and the Question of Materiality,* ed. Dick Houtman and Birgit Meyer, 321–38. New York: Fordham University Press.

———. 2002. "On Charisma, Mediation, and Broken Screens." *Etnofoor* 15 (1–2): 240–58.

de Certeau, Michel. 1992. *The Mystic Fable: The Sixteenth and Seventeenth Centuries.* Chicago: University of Chicago Press.

———. 1984. *The Practice of Everyday Life.* Berkeley: University of California Press.

de la Cruz, Deirdre. 2015. *Mother Figured: Marian Apparitions and the Making of a Filipino Universal.* Chicago: University of Chicago Press.

de Vries, Hent. 2001. "In Media Res: Global Religion, Public Spheres, and the Task of Contemporary Comparative Religious Studies." In *Religion and Media,* ed. Hent de Vries and Samuel Weber, 23–29. Stanford, CA: Stanford University Press.

de Vries, Hent, and Samuel Weber, eds. 2001. *Religion and Media.* Stanford, CA: Stanford University Press.

Deleuze, Gilles. 1986. *Cinema 1: The Movement-Image.* Trans. H. Tomlinson and B. Habberjam. Minneapolis: University of Minnesota Press.

Demus, Otto. 1960. *The Church of San Marco in Venice: History, Architecture, Sculpture.* Washington, DC: Dumbarton Oaks Library and Collection.

Dobrowolska, Agnieszka, and Khaled Fahmy. 2004. *Muhammad 'Ali Pasha and His Sabil.* Cairo: American University in Cairo Press.

Doostdar, Alireza. 2018. *The Iranian Metaphysicals: Explorations in Science, Islam, and the Uncanny.* Princeton, NJ: Princeton University Press.

Dubisch, Jill. 1995. *In a Different Place: Pilgrimage, Gender, and Politics at a Greek Island Shrine.* Princeton, NJ: Princeton University Press

du Bourguet, Pierre. 1991. "Historiography of Coptic Art." In *Claremont Coptic Encyclopedia,* ed. Karen J. Torjesen and Gawdat Gabra, http://ccdl.libraries .claremont.edu/cdm/ref/collection/cce/id/250 (accessed May 5, 2018).

du Roy, Gaétan. 2017. "Abûnâ Sam'ân and the 'Charismatic Trend' within the Coptic Church." In *Copts in Context: Negotiating Identity, Tradition, and Modernity,* ed. Nelly van Doorn Harder, 66–79. Columbia: University of South Carolina Press.

———. 2014. "Le prêtre des chiffonniers ou la construction d'une autorité religieuse au Caire entre charisme, tradition et clientélisme (1974–2014)." Ph.D. diss., Université Catholique de Louvain.

Edgar, Iain, and David Henig. 2010. "*Istikhara:* The Guidance and Practice of Islamic Dream Incubation through Ethnographic Comparison." *History and Anthropology* 21(3): 251–62.

Eisenlohr, Patrick. 2012. "Media and Religious Diversity." *Annual Review of Anthropology* 41: 37–55.

Elsässer, Sebastian. 2014. *The Coptic Question in the Mubarak Era.* Oxford: Oxford University Press.

Elsner, Jas. 1988. "Image and Iconoclasm in Byzantium." *Art History* 1(4): 477–81.

Emmel, Stephen. 2004. *Shenoute's Literary Corpus.* Vols. 1 and 2. Leuven: Peeters.

Engelhardt, Jeffers. 2014. *Singing the Right Way: Orthodox Christians and Secular Enchantment in Estonia.* Oxford: Oxford University Press.

Engelke, Matthew. 2013. *God's Agents: Biblical Publicity in Contemporary England*. Berkeley: University of California Press.

———. 2010. "Religion and the Media Turn: A Review Essay." *American Ethnologist* 37(2): 371–79.

———. 2008. "The Objects of Evidence." *Journal of the Royal Anthropological Institute* 14(1): S1-S21.

———. 2007. *A Problem of Presence: Beyond Scripture in an African Church*. Berkeley: University of California Press.

Erlich, Haggai. 2000. "Identity and Church: Ethiopian: Egyptian Dialogue, 1924–59." *International Journal of Middle East Studies* 32 (1): 23–46.

Ewing, Katherine Pratt. 1997. *Arguing Sainthood: Modernity, Psychoanalysis, and Islam*. Durham, NC: Duke University Press.

———. 1984. "The Sufi as Saint, Curer, and Exorcist in Modern Pakistan." *Contributions to Asian Studies* 18: 106–14.

Fahmi, Wael, and Keith Sutton. 2013. *Cairo's Contested Waste: The Zabaleen's Local Practices and Privatisation Policies*. Bristol, England: Policy Press.

Fahmy, Khaled. 2012a. "The Essence of Alexandria." Part 1. *Manifesta Journal* 14: 64–72.

———. 2012b. "The Essence of Alexandria." Part 2. *Manifesta Journal* 16: 22–27.

Farag, Lois M., ed. 2013. *The Coptic Christian Heritage: History, Faith and Culture*. New York: Routledge.

Fargues, Philippe, and Youssef Courbage. 1997. *Christians and Jews under Islam*. New York: I. B. Tauris.

Fernando, Mayanthi. 2014. *The Republic Unsettled: Muslim French and the Contradictions of Secularism*. Durham, NC: Duke University Press.

Ferré, André. 1991. "Fatimids and the Copts." In *The Coptic Encyclopedia*, vol. 4, ed. Aziz S. Atiya, 1097–1100. New York: Macmillan.

Finnestad, Ragnhild Bjerre. 1996. "Images as Messengers of Coptic Identity: An Example from Contemporary Egypt." Special issue of *Scripta Instituti Donneriani Aboensis* 16: 91–110.

———. 1994. "Apparitions, Icons, and Photos: A Study of Modern Coptic Visions of the Holy World." *Temenos* 30: 7–34.

Firth, Raymond. 1940. "The Analysis of Mana: An Empirical Approach." *Journal of the Polynesian Society* 49: 483–510.

Flood, Finbarr Barry. 2002. "Between Cult and Culture: Bamiyan, Islamic Iconoclasm, and the Museum." *Art Bulletin* 84(4): 641–59.

Florensky, Pavel. 2000 [1922]. *Iconostasis*. Trans. Donald Sheehan and Olga Andrejev. Crestwood: St. Vladimir's Seminary Press.

Florovsky, Georges. 1972. *Collected Works*. Vol. 1. Belmont, MA: Nordland Publishing.

Foster, Hal, ed. 1999. *Vision and Visuality*. New York: New Press.

Frankfurter, David. 2017. *Christianizing Egypt: Syncretism and Local Worlds in Late Antiquity*. Princeton, NJ: Princeton University Press.

———. 1998a. *Religion in Roman Egypt: Assimilation and Resistance*. Princeton, NJ: Princeton University Press.

———. 1998b. *Pilgrimage and Holy Space in Late Antique Egypt*. Leiden: Brill.

———. 1993. *Elijah in Upper Egypt: The Apocalypse of Elijah and Early Egyptian Christianity.* Minneapolis: Fortress Press.

Fraser, Nancy. 1990. "Rethinking the Public Sphere: A Contribution to the Critique of Actually Existing Democracy." *Social Text* 25–26: 56–80.

Frazer, James. 1998 [1890]. *The Golden Bough: A Study in Comparative Religion.* Oxford: Oxford University Press.

Freedberg, David. 1989. *The Power of Images: Studies in the History and Theory of Response.* Chicago: University of Chicago Press.

Freud, Sigmund. 1965. *The Interpretation of Dreams.* Trans. James Strachey. New York: Avon Books.

Gabra, Gawdat, ed. 2014. *Coptic Civilization: Two Thousand Years of Christianity in Egypt.* Cairo: American University in Cairo Press.

Gaonkar, Dilip, and Elizabeth Povinelli. 2003. "Technologies of Public Forms: Circulation, Transfiguration, Recognition." *Public Culture* 15(3): 385–97.

el-Gawhary, Karim. 1996. "Copts in the 'Egyptian Fabric.'" *Middle East Report* 200: 21–22.

Geagea, Nilo. 1984. *Mary of the Koran: A Meeting Point between Christianity and Islam.* Trans. L. T. Fares. New York: Philosophical Library.

Geary, Patrick. 2011 [1978]. *Furta Sacra: Thefts of Relics in the Central Middle Ages.* Princeton, NJ: Princeton University Press.

———. 1986. *Sacred Commodities: The Circulation of Medieval Relics.* Cambridge: Cambridge University Press.

Geertz, Clifford. 1968. *Islam Observed: Religious Development in Morocco and Indonesia.* Chicago: University of Chicago Press.

Gell, Alfred. 1998. *Art and Agency: An Anthropological Theory.* Oxford: Clarendon.

el-Ghobashy, Mona. 2011. "The Praxis of the Egyptian Revolution." *Middle East Report and Information Project* 41(258): 2–13.

Ghosh, Amitav. 1992. *In an Antique Land: History in the Guise of a Traveler's Tale.* New York: Knopf.

Gibb, Camilla C. T. 1999. "Baraka without Borders: Integrating Communities in the City of Saints." *Journal of Religion in Africa* 29: 88–108.

Gilsenan, Michael. 2000. "Signs of Truth: Enchantment, Modernity, and the Dreams of Peasant Women." *Journal of the Royal Anthropological Institute* 6(4): 597–615.

———. 1973. *Saint and Sufi in Modern Egypt: An Essay in the Sociology of Religion.* Oxford: Clarendon Press.

Ginsburg, Faye D., Lila Abu-Lughod, and Brian Larkin, eds. 2002. *Media Worlds: Anthropology in a New Terrain.* Berkeley: University of California Press.

Goffman, Erving. 1974 [1955]. "On Face-work: An Analysis of Ritual Elements in Social Interaction." In *Language, Culture, and Society: A Book of Readings,* ed. Ben G. Blount, 224–49. Cambridge, MA: Winthrop Publishers.

Goldziher, Ignác. 1971. "Veneration of Saints in Islam." In *Muslim Studies,* trans. C. R. Barber and S. M. Stern, vol. 2, 255–341. London: Allen & Unwin.

Graf, Fritz. 2008. "Incubation." In *New Pauly,* ed. H. Cancik and H. Schneider. Brill Online.

Green, Nile. 2009. "Transgressions of a Holy Fool: A Majzub in Colonial India." In *Islam in South Asia in Practice,* ed. Barbara D. Metcalf, 173–86. Princeton, NJ: Princeton University Press.

———. 2003. "The Religious and Cultural Roles of Dreams and Visions in Islam." *Journal of the Royal Asiatic Society* 13: 287–313.

Greene, Molly. 2002. *A Shared World: Christians and Muslims in the Early Modern Mediterranean.* Princeton, NJ: Princeton University Press.

Greene, Robert H. 2010. *Bodies Like Bright Stars: Saints and Relics in Orthodox Russia.* DeKalb: Northern Illinois University Press.

Griffith, Sidney. 2012. *The Church in the Shadow of the Mosque: Christians and Muslims in the World of Islam.* Princeton, NJ: Princeton University Press.

Grossman, Peter. 1991. "Church Architecture in Egypt." In *The Coptic Encyclopedia,* vol. 2, ed. Aziz S. Atiya, 552–55. New York: Macmillan.

Gruber, Mark. 2003. *Sacrifice in the Desert: A Study of an Egyptian Minority through the Prism of Coptic Monasticism.* Lanham, MD: University Press of America.

Guirguis, Laure. 2016. *Copts and the Security State: Violence, Coercion, and Sectarianism in Contemporary Egypt.* Stanford, CA: Stanford University Press.

Guirguis, Magdi. 2008. *An Armenian Artist in Ottoman Egypt: Yuhanna al-Armani and His Coptic Icons.* Cairo: American University in Cairo Press.

Guirguis, Magdi, and Pieternella van Doorn-Harder. 2011. *The Emergence of the Modern Coptic Papacy.* Cairo: American University in Cairo Press.

Gupta, Akhil, and James Ferguson, eds. 1997. *Culture, Power, Place: Explorations in Critical Anthropology.* Durham, NC: Duke University Press.

Habermas, Jürgen. 1989. *The Structural Transformation of the Public Sphere: An Inquiry into a Category of Bourgeois Society.* Trans. Thomas Burger. Cambridge, MA: MIT Press.

Hacking, Ian. 1990. *The Taming of Chance.* Cambridge: Cambridge University Press.

Haddad, Yvonne, and Joshua Donovan. 2013. "Good Copt, Bad Copt: Competing Narratives on Coptic Identity in Egypt and the United States." *Studies in World Christianity* 19(3): 211.

Haddad, Yvonne, and Jane Smith. 1989. "The Virgin Mary in Islamic Tradition and Commentary." *Muslim World* 79(3–4): 161–87.

Halemba, Agnieszka. 2015. *Negotiating Marian Apparitions: The Politics of Religion in Transcarpathian Ukraine.* Budapest: Central European University Press.

Hamdy, Sherine. 2012. *Our Bodies Belong to God: Organ Transplants, Islam, and the Struggle for Human Dignity in Egypt.* Berkeley: University of California Press.

Handman, Courtney. 2014. *Critical Christianity: Translation and Denominational Conflict in Papua New Guinea.* Berkeley: University of California Press.

Hanks, William F. 2010. *Converting Words: Maya in the Age of the Cross.* Berkeley: University of California Press.

———. 2005. "Explorations in the Deictic Field." *Current Anthropology* 46 (2): 191–220.

————. 1990. *Referential Practice: Language and Lived Space among the Maya.* Chicago: University of Chicago Press.

Hann, Chris, and Hermann Goltz, eds. 2010. *Eastern Christians in Anthropological Perspective.* Berkeley: University of California Press.

Hanna, Michael Wahid. 2013. "With Friends Like These: Coptic Activism in the Diaspora." In *Middle East Report* 267: 28–31.

Hasan, S. S. 2003. *Christians versus Muslims in Modern Egypt: The Century-Long Struggle for Coptic Equality.* Oxford: Oxford University Press.

Haugbølle, Sune, and Daniella Kuzmanovic. 2015. "Introduction: Towards a New Sociology of Icons in the Middle East." *Middle East Journal of Culture and Communication* 8(1): 5–11.

Hefner, Robert W. ed. 1993. *Conversion to Christianity: Historical and Anthropological Perspectives on a Great Transformation.* Berkeley: University of California Press.

Hermkens, A. K., Willy Jansen, and C. Notermans, eds. 2009. *Moved by Mary: The Power of Pilgrimage in the Modern World.* New York: Routledge.

Heo, Angie. 2018. "Imagining Holy Personhood: Anthropological Thresholds of the Icon." In *Praying with the Senses: Transformative Practices in Eastern Orthodoxy,* ed. Sonja Luehrmann, 83–102. Bloomington: Indiana University Press.

————. 2017. "Examining the Role of Media in Coptic Studies." In *Copts in Context: Negotiating Identity, Tradition and Modernity,* ed. Nelly van Doorn-Harder, 52–65. Columbia: University of South Carolina Press.

————. 2015. "Relic Technics and the Extensible Memory of Coptic Orthodoxy." *Material Religion* 11(1): 50–74.

————. 2014a. "Racialized Crossings: Coptic Orthodoxy and Global Christianities." In *Sainthood and Race: Marked Flesh, Holy Flesh,* ed. Vincent Lloyd and Molly Bassett, 150–163. New York: Routledge.

————. 2014b. "The Divine Touchability of Dreams." In *Sensational Religion: Sensory Cultures in Material Practice,* edited by Sally Promey, 435–40. New Haven, CT: Yale University Press.

————. 2014c. "Faces of Authoritarian Mystification." *Material Religion* 10 (4): 523–25.

————. 2013a. "The Virgin Between Christianity and Islam: Sainthood, Media and Modernity in Egypt." *Journal of the American Academy of Religion* 81 (4): 1117–38.

————. 2013b. "Money and Chandeliers: Mass Circuits of Pilgrimage to Coptic Egypt." *Journal of the American Academy of Religion* 81(2): 516–28.

————. 2013c. "The Bodily Threat of Miracles: Security, Sacramentality and the Egyptian Politics of Public Order." *American Ethnologist* 40(1): 149–64.

————. 2013d. "Saints, Media, and Minority Cultures: On Coptic Cults of Egyptian Revolution from Alexandria to Maspero." In *Politics of Worship in the Contemporary Middle East: Sainthood in Fragile States,* ed. Andreas Bandak and Mikkel Bille, 53–71. Leiden: Brill.

————. 2012. "The Virgin Made Visible: Intercessory Images of Church Territory in Egypt." *Comparative Studies in Society and History* 54(2): 361–91.

Herzfeld, Michael. 2009. "The Performance of Secrecy: Domesticity and Privacy In Public Places." *Semiotica* 175: 135–62.

———. 1982. *Ours Once More: Folklore, Ideology, and the Making of Modern Greece.* Austin: University of Texas Press.

Hirschkind, Charles. 2006. *The Ethical Soundscape: Cassette Sermons and Islamic Counterpublics.* New York: Columbia University Press.

Hirschkind, Charles, and Brian Larkin. 2008. "Media and the Political Forms of Religion." *Social Text* 26(3): 1–9.

Ho, Engseng. 2006. *The Graves of Tarim: Genealogy and Mobility across the Indian Ocean.* Berkeley: University of California Press.

Hocart, A. M. 1914. "Mana." *Man* 14: 97–101.

Hofer, Nathan C. 2011. "Sufism, State, and Society in Ayyubid and Early Mamluk Egypt, 1173–1309." Ph.D. diss., Department of Religion, Emory University.

Hoffman, Valerie J. 1997. "The Role of Visions in Contemporary Egyptian Religious Life." *Religion* 27(1): 45–63.

———. 1995. *Sufis, Mystics, and Saints in Modern Egypt.* Columbia: University of South Carolina Press.

Hollywood, Amy. 2012. "Love Speaks Here: Michel de Certeau's *Mystic Fable.*" *Spiritus: A Journal of Christian Spirituality* 12(2): 198–206.

Hourani, Albert Habib. 1947. *Minorities in the Arab World.* Oxford: Oxford University Press.

Howeidy, Amira. February 9, 2010. "The Camilya Conundrum." *Al-Ahram Weekly.*

Howes, David. 1991. *The Varieties of Sensory Experience: A Sourcebook in the Anthropology of the Senses.* Toronto: University of Toronto Press.

Ibrahim, Vivian. 2010. *The Copts of Egypt: The Challenges of Modernisation and Identity.* London: I. B. Tauris.

Immerzeel, Mat, and Jacques van der Vliet. 2004. *Coptic Studies on the Threshold of a New Millennium.* Leuven: Peeters.

Iskander, Elizabeth. 2012. *Sectarian Conflict in Egypt: Coptic Media, Identity, and Representation.* London: Routledge.

Ivanov, Sergey. 2006. *Holy Fools in Byzantium and Beyond.* Oxford: Oxford University Press.

Ivy, Marilyn. 1995. *Discourses of the Vanishing: Modernity, Phantasm, Japan.* Chicago: University of Chicago Press.

Jain, Kajri. 2017. "Gods in the Time of Automobility," *Current Anthropology* 58 (S15): S13-S26.

James, William. 1982 [1902]. *The Varieties of Religious Experience.* New York: Penguin Classics.

Jay, Martin. 1993. *Downcast Eyes: The Denigration of Vision in Twentieth-Century French Thought.* Berkeley: University of California Press.

Johnston, Francis W. 1980. *When Millions Saw Mary: An Account of the Apparitions of the Blessed Virgin Mary at Zeitoun, Cairo, 1968–77.* Devon, England: Augustine Publishing.

Jonsson, Stefan. 2013. *Crowds and Democracy: The Idea and Image of The Masses from Revolution to Fascism.* New York: Columbia University Press.

Kan, Sergei. 1999. *Memory Eternal: Tlingit Culture and Russian Orthodox Christianity through Two Centuries.* Seattle: University of Washington Press.

Kant, Immanuel. 1992 [1766]. "Dreams of a Spirit Seer, Elucidated by Dreams of Metaphysics." In *Immanuel Kant, Theoretical Philosophy, 1755–1770.* trans. David Walford, 301–6. Cambridge: Cambridge University Press.

Kantorowicz, Ernst. 1957. *The King's Two Bodies: A Study in Mediaeval Political Theology.* Princeton, NJ: Princeton University Press.

Kaviraj, Sudipta, ed. 1997. *Politics in India.* Oxford: Oxford University Press.

Keane, Webb. 2014. "Rotting Bodies: The Clash of Stances toward Materiality and Its Ethical Affordances." *Current Anthropology* 55 (S10): S312–S321.

———. 2008. "The Evidence of the Senses and the Materiality of Religion." *Journal of the Royal Anthropological Institute* 14(1): 110–27.

———. 2007. *Christian Moderns: Freedom and Fetish in the Mission Encounter.* Berkeley: University of California Press.

———. 2003. "Semiotics and the Social Analysis of Material Things." *Language and Communication* 23: 409–25.

Keriakos, Sandrine. 2012. "Apparitions of the Virgin in Egypt: Improving Relations between Copts and Muslims?" In *Sharing Sacred Spaces in the Mediterranean: Christians, Muslims, and Jews at Shrines and Sanctuaries,* ed. Dionigi Albera and Maria Couroucli, 174–201. Bloomington: Indiana University Press.

Khalil, Samir. 2003. *Rôle culturel des chrétiens dans le monde arabe, coll. Cahiers de l'Orient Chrétien.* Beyrouth: CEDRAC.

Khalili, Laleh. 2007. *Heroes and Martyrs of Palestine: The Politics of National Commemoration.* Cambridge: Cambridge University Press.

Khan, Naveeda. 2006. "Of Children and Jinn: An Inquiry into an Unexpected Friendship during Uncertain Times." *Cultural Anthropology* 21(2): 234–64.

Khater, Akram Fouad. 2011. *Embracing the Divine: Passion and Politics in the Christian Middle East.* Syracuse, NY: Syracuse University Press.

el-Khawaga, Dina. 1998. "The Political Dynamics of the Copts: Giving the Community an Active Role." In *Christian Communities in the Arab Middle East: The Challenge of the Future,* ed. Andrea Pacini, 172–190. Oxford: Clarendon.

———. 1997. "The Laity at the Heart of the Coptic Clerical Reform." In *Between Desert and City: The Coptic Orthodox Church Today,* ed. Kari Vogt and Nelly van Doorn-Harder, 143–66. Oslo: Novus Forlag.

———. 1993. "Le renouveau copte: La communauté comme acteur politique." Ph.D. diss., Institut d'Etudes Politiques, Paris.

Kittler, Friedrich. 2010. *Optical Media.* Cambridge: Polity Press.

Klein, Holger A. 2006. "Sacred Relics and Imperial Ceremonies at the Great Palace of Constantinople." In *Visualisierungen von Herrschaft,* ed. F. A. Bauer, 79–99. Istanbul: Ege Yayınlar.

Kormina, Jeanne. 2013. "Canonizing Soviet Pasts in Contemporary Russia: The Case of Saint Matrona of Moscow." In *A Companion to the Anthropology of Religion,* ed. Janice Boddy and Michael Lambek, 409–24. Oxford: John Wiley & Sons.

Kormina, Jeanne, and Sergey Shtyrkov. 2011. "St. Xenia as a Patron of Female Social Suffering: An Essay on Anthropological Hagiology." In *Multiple Moralities and Religions in Post-Soviet Russia*, ed. J. Zigon, 168–90. New York: Berghahn.

Krawiec, Rebecca. 2002. *Shenoute and the Women of the White Monastery: Egyptian Monasticism in Late Antiquity*. Oxford: Oxford University Press.

Krueger, Derek. 1996. *Symeon the Holy Fool: Leontius's Life and the Late Antique City*. Berkeley: University of California Press.

Krämer, Gudrun. 1989. *The Jews in Modern Egypt, 1914–1952*. Seattle: University of Washington Press.

Lagnado, Lucette. 2007. *The Man in the White Sharkskin Suit: A Jewish Family's Exodus from Old Cairo to the New World*. New York: HarperCollins.

Lamoreaux, John C. 2002. *The Early Muslim Tradition of Dream Interpretation*. Albany: State University of New York Press.

Landres, J. Shawn, and Michael Berenbaum, eds. 2004. *After the Passion Is Gone: American Religious Consequences*. Lanham, MD: Rowman Altimira.

Lang, Mabel. 1977. *Cure and Cult in Ancient Corinth: A Guide to the Asklepion*. Princeton, NJ: Princeton University Press.

Larkin, Brian. 2013. "Making Equivalence Happen: Commensuration and the Grounds of Circulation." In *Images without Borders*, ed. Patricia Spyer and Mary Steedly. Santa Fe: SAR Press.

———. 2008. *Signal and Noise: Media, Infrastructure, and Urban Culture in Nigeria*. Durham, NC: Duke University Press.

Laurentin, René. 1991. *A Short Treatise on the Virgin Mary*. Washington, NJ: AMI.

Le Bon, Gustave. 2002. *The Crowd: A Study of the Popular Mind*. Mineola, NY: Dover.

Lefort, Claude. 1991. "The Permanence of the Theologico-Political." In *Democracy and Political Theory*, trans. David Macey. New York: Polity Press.

el-Leithy, Tamer. 2006. "Sufis, Copts, and the Politics of Piety: Moral Regulation in 14th-Century Upper Egypt." In *The Development of Sufism in Mamluk Egypt*, ed. Adam Sabra and Richard McGregor, 75–120. Cairo: Institut Français D'archéologie Orientale.

———. 2005. "Coptic Culture and Conversion in Medieval Cairo, 1293–1524 A.D." Ph.D. diss., Department of History, Princeton University.

Lindberg, David. 1976. *Theories of Vision from Al-Kindi to Kepler*. Chicago: University of Chicago Press.

Luehrmann, Sonja, ed. 2018. *Praying with the Senses: Contemporary Eastern Orthodox Spirituality in Practice*. Bloomington: Indiana University Press.

———. 2011. *Secularism Soviet Style: Teaching Atheism and Religion in a Volga Republic*. Bloomington: Indiana University Press.

Lukasik, Candace. 2016. "Conquest of Paradise: Secular Binds and Coptic Political Mobilization." *Middle East Critique* 25(2): 107–25.

Lyster, William, Cornelis Hulsman, and Stephen J. Davis. 2001. *Be Thou There: The Holy Family's Journey in Egypt*. Ed. G. Gabra. Cairo: American University in Cairo Press.

Macalister, Suzanne. 2012. *Dreams and Suicides: The Greek Novel from Antiquity to the Byzantine Empire*. New York: Routledge.

MacCormack, Sabine. 1981. *Art and Ceremony in Late Antiquity*. Berkeley: University of California Press.

MacDougall, David. 2006. *The Corporeal Image: Film, Ethnography, and the Senses*. Princeton, NJ: Princeton University Press.

MacIntyre, Alisdair C. 1984. *After Virtue: A Study in Moral Theory*. Notre Dame, IN: University of Notre Dame Press.

Magdalino Paul, and Maria Mavroudi, eds. 2006. *The Occult Sciences in Byzantium*. Geneva: La Pomme d'Or.

Mahmood, Saba. 2016. *Religious Difference in a Secular Age: A Minority Report*. Princeton, NJ: Princeton University Press.

————. 2005. *Politics of Piety: The Islamic Revival and the Feminist Subject*. Princeton, NJ: Princeton University Press.

Maier, Jean-Louis, ed. 1987. "La Passion des martyrs d'*Abitinae (audience du 12 février 304)*." In *Le Dossier du Donatisme*, Texte und Untersuchungen zur Geshichte der Altchristlichen Literatur, series 134, 57–91.

Makari, Peter E. 2007. *Conflict and Cooperation Christian-Muslim Relations in Contemporary Egypt*. Syracuse, NY: Syracuse University Press.

Makdisi, Ussama. 2008. *Artillery of Heaven: American Missionaries and the Failed Conversion of the Middle East*. Ithaca, NY: Cornell University Press.

————. 2000. *The Culture of Sectarianism: Community, History, and Violence in Nineteenth-Century Ottoman Lebanon*. Berkeley: University of California Press.

Malinowski, Bronislaw. 2002 [1922]. *Argonauts of the Western Pacific*. London: Routledge.

Marks, Laura U. 2000. *The Skin of the Film: Intercultural Cinema, Embodiment, and the Senses*. Durham, NC: Duke University Press.

Margry, Peter Jan, ed. Forthcoming. *Cold War Mary: Ideologies, Politics and Devotional Culture*. New York: Fordham University Press.

————. 2009. "Marian Interventions in the Wars of Ideology: The Elastic Politics of the Roman Catholic Church on Modern Apparitions." *History and Anthropology* 20(3): 243–63.

Martin, Dominic. 2016. "Zealots of Piety: Old Orthodox Religious Revival in a Post-Soviet 'Closed' City (1991–2014)." Ph.D. diss., Department of Anthropology, Cambridge University.

Masco, Joseph. 2010. "Sensitive but Unclassified: Secrecy and the Counter-Terrorist State." *Public Culture* 22(3): 433–63.

Masters, Bruce. 2001. *Christians and Jews in the Ottoman Arab World: The Roots of Sectarianism*. Cambridge: Cambridge University Press.

Mauss, Marcel. 1972 [1902]. *A General Theory of Magic*. Trans. Robert Brain. London: Routledge.

Mavroudi, Maria. 2002. *A Byzantine Book on Dream Interpretation: The Oneirocriticon of Achmet and Its Arabic Sources*. Leiden: Brill.

Mayeur-Jaouen, Catherine. 2012. "What Do Egypt's Copts and Muslims Share? The Issue of Shrines." In *Sharing Sacred Spaces in the Mediterranean:*

Christians, Muslims, and Jews at Shrines and Sanctuaries, ed. Dionigi Albera and Maria Couroucli, 148–73. Bloomington: Indiana University Press.

———. 2010. "Umm Irînî (1936–2006): L'engagement monastique copte au féminin." *Le Mouvement Social* 231(1): 101–21.

———. 2005. *Pèlerinages d'Égypte: Histoire de la piété copte et musulmane (XVe-XXe siècles).* Vol. 107, *Recherches d'histoire et de sciences sociales.* Paris: Éditions de l'Ecole des hautes études en sciences sociales.

———. 1998. "Saints Coptes et Saints Musulmans de l'Egypte du XXe Siècle." *Revue de l'Histoire des Religions* 215(1): 139–86.

Mazower, Mark. 2004. *Salonica, City of Ghosts: Christians, Muslims and Jews, 1430–1950.* New York: HarperCollins.

Mazzarella, William. 2017. *The Mana of Mass Society.* Chicago: University of Chicago Press.

———. 2010. "Branding the Mahatma: The Untimely Provocation of Gandhian Publicity." *Cultural Anthropology* 25(1): 1–39.

———. 2013. *Censorium: Cinema and the Open Edge of Mass Publicity.* Durham, NC: Duke University Press.

McCallum, Fiona. 2012. "Middle Eastern Christian Immigrant Communities as Diasporas." *Border Terrains: World Diasporas in the Twenty-First Century* 23(1) 3–18.

McIntosh, Janet. 2009. *The Edge of Islam: Power, Personhood, and Ethnoreligious Boundaries on the Kenya Coast.* Durham, NC: Duke University Press.

McLuhan, Marshall. 1994 [1964]. *Understanding Media: The Extensions of Man.* Cambridge, MA: MIT Press.

Meinardus, Otto F. A. 2002 [1981]. *Two Thousand Years of Coptic Christianity.* Cairo: American University in Cairo Press.

———. 1996. "The Virgin Mary as Mediatrix between Christians and Muslims in the Middle East." *Marian Studies* 47(10): 88–101.

———. 1970. *Christian Egypt: Faith and Life.* Cairo: American University in Cairo Press.

———. 1962. "The Itinerary of the Holy Family in Egypt." *Collectanea* 2: 5–44.

Meltzer, Françoise, and Jas Elsner, eds. 2011. *Saints: Faith without Borders.* Chicago: University of Chicago Press.

Meri, Josef W. 2002. *The Cult of Saints among Muslims and Jews in Medieval Syria.* Oxford: Oxford University Press.

Messick, Brinkley. 1993. *The Calligraphic State: Textual Domination and History in a Muslim Society.* Berkeley: University of California Press.

———. 1988. "Kissing Hands and Knees: Hegemony and Hierarchy in Shari'a Discourse." *Law and Society Review* 22(4): 637–59.

Meyer, Birgit. 2015. *Sensational Movies: Video, Vision, and Christianity in Ghana.* Berkeley: University of California Press.

———, ed. 2009. *Aesthetic Formations: Media, Religion, and the Senses.* London: Palgrave-Macmillan.

Meyer, Birgit, and Annelies Moors, eds. 2006. *Religion, Media, and the Public Sphere.* Bloomington: Indiana University Press.

Meyer, Marvin, and Richard Smith, eds. 1994. *Ancient Christian Magic: Coptic Texts of Ritual Power.* Princeton, NJ: Princeton University Press.

Meyendorff, John. 1982. *The Byzantine Legacy in the Orthodox Church.* Yonkers, NY: St. Vladimir's Seminary Press.

Mikhail, Maged. 2017. *The Legacy of Demetrius of Alexandria, 189–231 C.E.: The Form and Function of Hagiography in Late Antique and Islamic Egypt.* London: Routledge.

———. 2014. *Byzantine Egypt.* New York: I. B. Tauris.

Miller, Daniel, ed. 2005. *Materiality.* Durham, NC: Duke University Press.

Miller, Patricia Cox. 1994. *Dreams in Late Antiquity: Studies in the Imagination of a Culture.* Princeton, NJ: Princeton University Press.

Mingana, Alphonse, trans. 2012. *Vision of Theophilus: The Book of the Flight of the Holy Family Into Egypt.* Putty, Australia: St. Shenouda Monastery.

Mitchell, Timothy. 1988. *Colonising Egypt.* New York: Cambridge University Press.

Mitchell, W. J. T. 2015. *Image Science: Iconology, Visual Culture, and Media Aesthetics.* Chicago: University of Chicago Press.

———. 2005a. "There Are No Visual Media." *Journal of Visual Culture* 4(2): 257–66.

———. 2005b. *What Do Pictures Want? The Lives and Loves of Images.* Chicago: University of Chicago Press.

———. 1986. *Iconology: Image, Text, Ideology.* Chicago: University of Chicago Press.

Mittermaier, Amira. 2012. "Invisible Armies: Reflections on Egyptian Dreams of War." *Comparative Studies in Society and History* 54(2): 392–417.

———. 2011. *Dreams That Matter: Egyptian Landscapes of the Imagination.* Berkeley: University of California Press.

———. 2008. "(Re)Imagining Space: Dreams and Saint Shrines in Egypt." In *Dimensions of Locality: Muslim Saints, Their Place and Space,* ed. Georg Stauth and Samuli Schielke, 47–66. Bielefeld: Transcript.

Mondzain, Marie-José. 2002. *Image, Icon, Economy: The Byzantine Origins of the Contemporary Imaginary.* Stanford, CA: Stanford University Press.

Morgan, David, ed. 2010. *Religion and Material Culture: The Matter of Belief.* New York: Routledge.

———. 2007. *The Lure of Images: A History of Religion and Visual Media in America.* Berkeley: University of California Press.

———. 1999. *Visual Piety: A History and Theory of Popular Religious Images.* Berkeley: University of California Press.

Morris, Rosalind C. 2000. *In the Place of Origins: Modernity and Its Mediums in Northern Thailand.* Durham, NC: Duke University Press.

Moustafa, Tamir. 2000. "Conflict and Cooperation between the State and Religious Institutions in Contemporary Egypt." *International Journal of Middle East Studies* 32(1): 3–22.

Munn, Nancy D. 1996. "Excluded Spaces: The Figure in the Australian Aboriginal Landscape." *Critical Inquiry* 22(3): 446–65.

———. 1992. *The Fame of Gawa: A Symbolic Study of Value Transformation in a Massim (Papua New Guinea) Society.* Durham, NC: Duke University Press.

Myers, Fred, ed. 2001. *The Empire of Things: Regimes of Value and Material Culture.* Santa Fe: SAR Press.

Naguib, Saphinaz-Amal. 1994. "The Martyr as Witness: Coptic and Copto-Arabic Hagiographies as Mediators of Religious Memory." *Numen* 41(3): 223–54.

Napolitano, Valentina. 2015. *Migrant Hearts and the Atlantic Return: Transnationalism and the Roman Catholic Church.* New York: Fordham University Press.

Napolitano, Valentina, and David Pratten. 2007. "Michel de Certeau: Ethnography and the Challenge of Plurality." *Social Anthropology* 15(1): 1–12.

Nau, François. 1907. "Histoires des Solitaires Egyptiens." *Revue de l'Orient Chrétien* 12: 43–69, 171–89, 393–413.

Naumescu, Vlad. 2008. *Modes of Religiosity in Eastern Christianity: Religious Processes and Social Change in Ukraine.* Münster: Lit Verlag.

Nelson, Cynthia. 1973. "The Virgin of Zaytun." *Worldview* 16(9): 5–11.

Nikolov, Boris. 2008. "Care of the Poor and Ecclesiastical Government: An Ethnography of the Social Services of the Coptic Orthodox Church in Cairo, Egypt." Ph.D. diss., Department of Anthropology, Johns Hopkins University.

Nirenberg, David. 1996. *Communities of Violence: Persecution of Minorities in the Middle Ages.* Princeton, NJ: Princeton University Press.

Norget, Kristin, Valentina Napolitano, and Maya Mayblin, eds. 2017. *Anthropology of Catholicism: A Reader.* Berkeley: University of California Press.

Oraby, Mona. 2015. "Authorizing Religious Conversion in Administrative Courts: Law, Rights, and Secular Indeterminacy." *New Diversities* 17(1): 63–75.

Orsi, Robert A. 1985. *The Madonna of 115th Street: Faith and Community in Italian Harlem.* New Haven, CT: Yale University Press.

Ouspensky, Léonid. 1999. "The Meaning and Language of Icons." In *The Meaning of Icons,* ed. Léonid Ouspensky and Vladimir Lossky, 23–49. Crestwood, NY: St. Vladimir's Seminary Press.

———. 1978. *Theology of the Icon.* Yonkers, NY: St. Vladimir's Seminary Press.

Özyürek, Esra. 2006. *Nostalgia for the Modern: State Secularism and Everyday Politics in Turkey.* Durham, NC: Duke University Press.

Pacini, Andrea. 1998. *Christian Communities in the Arab Middle East: The Challenge of the Future.* Oxford: Oxford University Press.

Palmié, Stephan. 2006. "Thinking with Ngangas: Reflections on Embodiment and the Limits of 'Objectively Necessary Appearances.'" *Comparative Studies in Society and History* 48(4): 852–86.

Pamment, Claire. 2017. *Comic Performance in Pakistan: The Bhand.* London: Palgrave Macmillan.

Pandey, Gyanendra. 1990. *The Construction of Communalism in Colonial North India.* Delhi: Oxford University Press.

Pandolfo, Stefania. 1997. *Impasse of the Angels: Scenes from a Moroccan Space of Memory.* Chicago: University of Chicago Press.

Papaconstantinou, Arietta. 2006. "Historiography, Hagiography, and the Making of the Coptic 'Church of the Martyrs' in Early Egypt." *Dumbarton Oaks Papers* 60: 65–86.

Patton, Kimberley. 2004. "'A Great and Strange Correction': Intentionality, Locality, and Epiphany in the Category of Dream Incubation." *History of Religions* 43(3): 194–223.

Peel, J. D. Y. 2015. *Christianity, Islam, and Orisa-Religion.* Berkeley: University of California Press.

Peirce, Charles Sanders. 1955. *Philosophical Writings of Peirce.* Ed. Justus Buchler. New York: Dover.

———. 1902. "Virtual." In *Dictionary of Philosophy and Psychology,* vol. 2, ed. James Mark Baldwin, 763. New York: Macmillan.

Pelikan, Jaroslav. 1996. *Mary through the Centuries: Her Place in the History of Culture.* New Haven, CT: Yale University Press.

———. 1990. *Imago Dei: The Byzantine Apologia for Icons.* Princeton, NJ: Princeton University Press.

———. 1977. *The Christian Tradition.* Vol. 2. Chicago: University of Chicago Press.

Pennington, J. D. 1982. "The Copts in Modern Egypt." *Middle Eastern Studies* 18(2): 158–79.

Pfeiffer, K. Ludwig. 1994. "The Materiality of Communication." In *Materialities of Communication,* eds. Hans Ulrich Gumbrecht and K. Ludwig Pfeiffer, trans. William Whobrey, 1–14. Stanford, CA: Stanford University Press.

Pietz, William. 1987. "The Problem of the Fetish II: The Origin of the Fetish." *RES: Anthropology and Aesthetics* 13: 23–45.

———. 1985. "The Problem of the Fetish." *RES: Anthropology and Aesthetics* 9: 5–17.

Pinney, Christopher. 2003. *Photos of the Gods: The Printed Image and Political Struggle in India.* London: Reaktion.

Plate, Brent S., ed. 2004. *Re-Viewing the Passion: Mel Gibson's Film and Its Critics.* New York: St. Martin's Griffin.

Pop, Simion. 2017. "'I've tempted the saint with my prayer!' Prayer, Charisma and Ethics in Romanian Eastern Orthodox Christianity." *Religion* 47(1): 73–91.

Pope Paul VI. 1973. "A Summo Pontifice Paulo Pp. VI et a S.S. Shenouda III, Patriarcha Sedis Sancti Marci Alexandriae." *Acta Apostolicae Sedis* 65: 299–301.

Pope Shenouda III. 1991. "Anchorites." In *The Coptic Encyclopedia,* vol. 1, ed. Aziz S. Atiya. New York: Macmillan.

———. 1975. *The Beholder of God: St. Mark the Evangelist and Martyr.* Cairo: al-Kuliyah al-Iklirikiyah bi-l-Abbasiya.

Promey, Sally M., ed. 2014. *Sensational Religion: Sensory Cultures in Material Practice.* New Haven, CT: Yale University Press.

al-Qattan, Najwa. 2007. "Inside the Ottoman Courthouse: Territorial Law at the Intersection of State and Religion." In *The Early Modern Ottomans: Remapping the Empire,* ed. Virginia H. Aksan and Daniel Goffman, 201–12. New York: Cambridge University Press.

Rafael, Vincente L. 2003. "The Cell Phone and the Crowd: Messianic Politics in the Contemporary Philippines." *Public Culture* 15(3): 399–425.

Rajagopal, Arvind. 2001. *Politics after Television: Hindu Nationalism and the Reshaping of the Public in India.* Cambridge: Cambridge University Press.

Ramzy, Carolyn M. 2014. "To Die is Gain: Singing a Heavenly Citizenship among Egypt's Coptic Christians." *Ethnos* 80(5): 1–22.

Raymond, André. 2000. *Cairo.* Trans. Willard Wood. Cambridge, MA: Harvard University Press.

Reinhardt, Bruno. 2015. "Flowing and Framing: Language Ideology, Circulation, and Authority in a Pentecostal Bible School." *Pragmatics and Society* 6 (2): 261–87.

René, Monica. 2014. "Contemporary Coptic Art." In *Coptic Civilization: Two Thousand Years of Christianity in Egypt,* ed. Gawdat Gabra, 273–84. Cairo: American University in Cairo Press.

Rév, István. 2005. *Retroactive Justice: Prehistory of Post-Communism.* Stanford, CA: Stanford University Press.

Riesebrodt, Martin. 1998. *Pious Passion: The Emergence of Modern Fundamentalism in the United States and Iran.* Berkeley: University of California Press.

Robbins, Joel. 2004a. *Becoming Sinners: Christianity and Moral Torment in a Papua New Guinea Society.* Berkeley: University of California Press.

———. 2004b. "The Globalization of Pentecostal and Charismatic Christianity." *Annual Review of Anthropology* 33: 117–43.

———, ed. 2003. *The Anthropology of Christianity.* Special issue of *Religion* 33(3).

Robbins, Joel, and Matthew Engelke. 2010. "Introduction to Special Issue: Global Christianity, Global Critique." *South Atlantic Quarterly* 109: 623–31.

Robbins, Joel, and Naomi Haynes, eds. 2014. *The Anthropology of Christianity: Unity, Diversity, New Directions.* Special Issue of *Current Anthropology* 55 (S10).

Rogers, Douglas. 2009. *The Old Faith and the Russian Land: A Historical Ethnography of Ethics in the Urals.* Ithaca, NY: Cornell University Press.

Rowe, Paul S. 2007. "Neo-millet Systems and Transnational Religious Movements: The Humayun Decrees and Church Construction in Egypt." *Journal of Church and State* 49(2): 329–50.

Rowe, Paul S., John H.A. Dyck, and Jens Zimmerman, eds. 2014. *Christians and the Middle East Conflict.* New York: Routledge.

Rydén, Lennart. 1983. "The Holy Fool." In *The Byzantine Saint,* ed. Sergei Hackel, 106–13. San Bernardino, CA: Borgo.

Safi, Omid. 2000. "Bargaining with Baraka: Persian Sufism, 'Mysticism,' and Pre-Modern Politics." *Muslim World* 90 (3–4): 259–88.

Sahlins, Marshall. 1976. *Culture and Practical Reason.* Chicago: University of Chicago Press.

Salomon, Noah. 2016. *For Love of the Prophet: An Ethnography of Sudan's Islamic State.* Princeton, NJ: Princeton University Press.

Samir, Samir Khalil. 1997. *The Significance of Early Arab-Christian Thought for Muslim-Christian Understanding.* Washington, DC: Center for Muslim-Christian Understanding.

Sánchez, Rafael. 2016. *Dancing Jacobins: A Venezuelan Genealogy of Latin American Populism.* New York: Fordham University Press.

Sanders, Paula. 1994. *Ritual, Politics, and the City in Fatimid Cairo.* Albany: State University of New York Press.

Saward, John. 1980. *Perfect Fools: Folly for Christ's Sake in Catholic and Orthodox Spirituality*. Oxford: Oxford University Press.

Scheer, Monique. 2013. "What She Looks Like: On the Recognition and Iconization of the Virgin Mary at Apparition Sites in the Twentieth Century." *Material Religion* 9(4): 442–67.

———. 2012. "Catholic Piety in the Early Cold War Years; or, How the Virgin Mary Protected the West from Communism." In *Cold War Cultures: Perspectives on Eastern and Western European Societies*, ed. Annette Vowinckel, Marcus M. Payk, and Thomas Lindenberger, 129–151. New York: Berghan.

Schielke, Samuli. 2012. *The Perils of Joy: Contesting Mulid Festivals in Contemporary Egypt*. Syracuse, NY: Syracuse University Press.

———. 2008. "Policing Ambiguity: Muslim Saints-Day Festivals and the Moral Geography of Public Space in Egypt." *American Ethnologist* 35(4): 539–52.

Schleifer, Aliah. 1998. *Mary the Blessed Virgin of Islam*. Louisville, KY: Fons Vitae.

Schmidt, Jalane D. 2015. *Cachita's Streets: The Virgin of Charity, Race, and Revolution in Cuba*. Durham, NC: Duke University Press.

Schmitt, Carl. 1985. *Political Theology: Four Chapters on the Concept of Sovereignty*. Chicago: University of Chicago Press.

Schroeder, Caroline. 2007. *Monastic Bodies: Discipline and Salvation in Shenoute of Atripe*. Philadelphia: University of Pennsylvania Press.

Scott, Rachel M. 2010. *The Challenge of Political Islam: Non-Muslims and the Egyptian State*. Stanford, CA: Stanford University Press.

Sedra, Paul. 2014. "Copts and the Millet Partnership: The Intra-Communal Dynamics behind Egyptian Sectarianism." *Journal of Law and Religion* 29 (3): 491–509.

———. 2012. "Activism in the Coptic Diaspora: A Brief Introduction." *Jadaliyya* 13, www.jadaliyya.com/Details/27046/Activism-in-the-Coptic-Diaspora-A-Brief-Introduction (accessed May 28, 2018)

———. 2011. *From Mission to Modernity: Evangelicals, Reformers and Education in Nineteenth Century Egypt*. New York: I.B. Tauris.

———. 1999. "Class Cleavages and Ethnic Conflict: Coptic Christian Communities in Modern Egyptian Politics." *Islam and Christian-Muslim Relations* 10(2): 219–35.

Seikaly, Samir. 1970. "Coptic Communal Reform, 1860–1914." *Middle Eastern Studies* 6(3): 247–75.

Seremetakis, C. Nadia. 2009. "Divination, Media, and the Networked Body of Modernity." *American Ethnologist* 36(2): 337–50.

———, ed. 1994. *The Senses Still: Memory and Perception as Material Culture in Modernity*. Boulder, CO: Westview.

———. 1991. *The Last Word: Women, Death, and Divination in Inner Mani*. Chicago: University of Chicago Press.

Sha'lan, Husayn. 1986. "Jerusalem and the Copts." *Journal of Palestine Studies* 15(4): 178–80.

el-Shamy, Hasan. 1980. *Folktales of Egypt*. Chicago: University of Chicago Press.

Sharkey, Heather J. 2017. *A History of Muslims, Christians, and Jews in the Middle East*. Cambridge: Cambridge University Press.

———. 2008. *American Evangelicals in Egypt: Missionary Encounters in an Age of Empire*. Princeton, NJ: Princeton University Press.

Sharp, Lesley A. 2000. "The Commodification of the Body and Its Parts." *Annual Review of Anthropology* 29: 287–328.

Shatzmiller, Maya ed. 2005. *Nationalism and Minority Identities in Islamic Societies*. Montreal: McGill-Queen's University Press.

Shenoda, Anthony. 2012. "The Politics of Faith: On Faith, Skepticism, and Miracles among Coptic Christians in Egypt." *Journal of Anthropology* 77 (4): 477–95.

———. 2010. "Cultivating Mystery: Miracles and a Coptic Moral Imaginary." Ph.D. diss., Department of Anthropology, Harvard University.

Shenoda, Maryann M. 2007. "Displacing Dhimmi, Maintaining Hope: Unthinkable Coptic Representations of Fatimid Egypt." *International Journal of Middle East Studies* 39: 587–606.

Shulman, David, and Guy G. Stroumsa , eds. 1999. *Dream Cultures: Explorations in the Comparative History of Dreaming*. Oxford: Oxford University Press.

Simmel, Georg. 1950 [1908]. "The Stranger." In *The Sociology of Georg Simmel*, trans. Kurt Wolff, 402–8. New York: Free Press.

Skalova, Zuzana, and Gawdat Gabra. 2001. *Icons of the Nile Valley*. Cairo: Egyptian International Press.

Sloterdijk, Peter. 1988. *Critique of Cynical Reason*. Trans. Michael Eldred. Minneapolis: University of Minnesota Press.

Snoek, Godefridus J. C. 1995. *Medieval Piety from Relics to the Eucharist: A Process of Mutual Interaction*. Leiden: Brill.

Sobchack, Vivian. 2008. "Embodying Transcendence: On the Literal, the Material, and the Cinematic Sublime." *Material Religion* 4(2): 194–203.

Spadola, Emilio. 2009. "Writing Cures: Religious and Communicative Authority in Late Modern Morocco." *Journal of North African Studies* 14(2): 155–68.

Spyer, Patricia. 2008. "Blind Faith: Painting Christianity in Postconflict Ambon." *Social Text* 96(3): 11–37.

Spyer, Patricia, and Mary Margaret Steedly, eds. 2013. *Images That Move*. Santa Fe, NM: SAR Press.

Starrett, Gregory. 1998. *Putting Islam to Work: Education, Politics, and Religious Transformation in Egypt*. Berkeley: University of California Press.

Stewart, Charles. 2012. *Dreaming and Historical Consciousness in Island Greece*. Cambridge, MA: Harvard University Press.

———. 1991. *Demons and the Devil: Moral Imagination in Modern Greek Culture*. Princeton, NJ: Princeton University Press.

Strathern, Marilyn. 1988. *The Gender of the Gift: Problems with Women and Problems with Society in Melanesia*. Berkeley: University of California Press.

Stolow, Jeremy, ed. 2012. *Deus in Machina: Religion, Technology, and the Things in Between*. New York: Fordham University Press.

———. 2005. "Religion and/as Media." *Theory, Culture, and Society* 22(4): 119–45.

Sullivan, Winnifred Fallers, et al., eds. 2015. *Politics of Religious Freedom.* Chicago: University of Chicago Press.

Swanson, Mark N. 2015. "The Martyrdom of Jirjis (Muzahim): Hagiography and Coptic Orthodox Imagination in Early Fatimid Egypt." *Medieval Encounters* 21: 431–51.

———. 2010. *The Coptic Papacy in Islamic Egypt (641–1517).* Cairo: American University in Cairo Press.

Tadros, Mariz. 2013. *Copts at the Crossroads: The Challenges of Building Inclusive Democracy in Egypt.* Cairo: American University in Cairo Press.

———. 2011. "Sectarianism and Its Discontents in Post-Mubarak Egypt." *Middle East Report* 259: 26–31.

———. 2009. "Vicissitudes in the Coptic Church-State Entente in Egypt." *International Journal of Middle East Studies* 41(2): 269–87.

Tambar, Kabir. 2014. *The Reckoning of Pluralism: Political Belonging and the Demands of History in Turkey.* Stanford, CA: Stanford University Press.

———. 2009. "Secular Populism and the Semiotics of the Crowd in Turkey." *Public Culture* 21(3): 517–37.

Tarde, Gabriel. 1989. *L'opinion et la foule.* Paris: Presses Universitaires de France.

Taussig, Michael. 1993. *Mimesis and Alterity: A Particular History of the Senses.* New York: Routledge.

———. 1991. "Tactility and Distraction." *Cultural Anthropology* 6 (2): 147–53.

Taylor, Charles 2004. *Modern Social Imaginaries.* Durham, NC: Duke University Press.

Taylor, Christopher. 1999. *In the Vicinity of the Righteous: Ziyara and the Veneration of Muslim Saints in Late Medieval Egypt.* Leiden: Brill.

Timbie, Janet A. 2010. "Coptic Christianity." In *The Blackwell Companion to Eastern Christianity,* ed. Ken Parry, 94–116. New York: Wiley.

Trainor, Kevin. 2010. "Pars pro toto: On Comparing Relic Practices." *Numen* 57(3): 267–83.

Trossen, Jean-Pierre. 1948. *Les relations du Patriarche Copte Jean XVI avec Rome (1676–1718).* Luxembourg: Imprimerie Hermann.

Tomlinson, Matt. 2014. *Ritual Textuality: Pattern and Motion in Performance.* Oxford: Oxford University Press.

Torallas Tovar, Sofía. 2017. "The Reverse Case: Egyptian Borrowing in Greek." In *Greek Influence on Egyptian Coptic: Contact Induced Change in an Ancient African Language,* ed. Peter Dils et al., 97–113. Hamburg: Lingua Aegyptia 17.

Turner, Victor, and Edith Turner. 1978. *Image and Pilgrimage in Christian Culture.* New York: Columbia University Press.

Valtchinova, Galia. 2010. *Religion and Boundaries: Studies from the Balkans, Eastern Europe, and Turkey.* Istanbul: Isis Press.

van der Veer, Peter. 1994. *Religious Nationalism.* Princeton, NJ: Princeton University Press.

van der Veer, Peter, and Hartmut Lehmann, eds. 1999. *Nation and Religion: Perspectives on Europe and Asia.* Princeton, NJ: Princeton University Press.

van der Vliet, Jacques. 2014. "Magic in Late Antiquity and Early Medieval Egypt." In *Coptic Civilization: Two Thousand Years of Christianity in Egypt,* ed. Gawdat Gabra, 145–52. Cairo: American University in Cairo Press.

———. 2009. "The Copts: 'Modern Sons of the Pharaohs'?" *Church History and Religious Culture* 89(1–3): 279–90.

van Doorn-Harder, Pieternella. 2017. *Copts in Context: Negotiating Identity, Tradition, and Modernity.* Columbia: University of South Carolina Press.

———. 1995. *Contemporary Coptic Nuns.* Columbia: University of South Carolina Press.

Verdery, Katherine. 1999. *The Political Lives of Dead Bodies: Reburial and Postsocialist Change.* New York: Columbia University Press.

Vinea, Ana Maria. 2015. "'May God Cure You': Contemporary Egyptian Therapeutic Landscapes between Qur'anic Healing and Psychiatry." Ph.D. diss., Department of Anthropology, City University of New York.

Virilio, Paul. 2006. *Speed and Politics.* Trans. Mark Polizzotti. Cambridge, MA: MIT Press.

Viswanathan, Gauri. 1998. *Outside the Fold: Conversion, Modernity, and Belief.* Princeton, NJ: Princeton University Press.

Voile, Brigitte. 2004. *Les Coptes d'Egypte sous Nasser: Sainteté, miracles, apparitions.* Paris: Centre National de la Recherche Scientifique.

Volk, Lucia. 2010. *Memorials and Martyrs in Modern Lebanon.* Bloomington: Indiana University Press.

Warner, Michael. 2002. *Publics and Counterpublics.* New York: Zone.

Waterbury, John. 2014. *The Egypt of Nasser and Sadat: The Political Economy of Two Regimes.* Princeton, NJ: Princeton University Press.

Watson, John. 2002. *Among the Copts: Beliefs and Practices.* Eastbourne, UK: Sussex Academic Press.

Weber, Max. 2013 [1922]. *Economy and Society.* Vol. 1. Ed. Guenther Roth and Claus Wittich. Berkeley: University of California Press.

Weber, Samuel. 1996. *Mass Mediauras: Form, Technics, Media.* Stanford, CA: Stanford University Press.

Wedeen, Lisa. 1999. *Ambiguities of Domination: Politics, Rhetorics, and Symbols in Contemporary Syria.* Chicago: University of Chicago Press.

Weiss, Max. 2010. *In the Shadow of Sectarianism: Law, Shi'ism, and the Making of Modern Lebanon.* Cambridge, MA: Harvard University Press.

Weitzmann, Kurt, ed. 1980. *The Age of Spirituality: Late Antique and Early Christian Art, Third to Seventh Century.* New York: Metropolitan Museum of Art.

Wessel, Klaus. 1965. *Coptic Art in Early Christian Egypt.* New York: McGraw-Hill.

Westermarck, Edward. 1968 [1926]. *Ritual and Belief in Morocco.* Vol. 1. New York: Routledge.

———. 1916. *The Moorish Conception of Holiness (Baraka).* Helsinki: Akademiska Bokhandeln.

Wheeler, Brannon. 2006. *Mecca and Eden: Ritual, Relics, and Territory in Islam.* Chicago: University of Chicago Press.

Wickham, Carrie Rosefsky. 2013. *The Muslim Brotherhood: Evolution of an Islamist Movement.* Princeton, NJ: Princeton University Press.

Winegar, Jessica. 2006. *Creative Reckonings: The Politics of Art and Culture in Contemporary Egypt*. Stanford, CA: Stanford University Press.

Wolf, Eric R. 1958. "The Virgin of Guadalupe: A Mexican National Symbol." *Journal of American Folklore* 71(279): 34–39.

Woodward, Kenneth L. 1996. *Making Saints: How the Catholic Church Determines Who Becomes a Saint, Who Doesn't, and Why*. New York: Simon and Schuster.

Ye'or, Bat. 1985. *The Dhimmi: Jews and Christians under Islam*. Trans. David Maisel. Madison, NJ: Fairleigh Dickinson University Press.

Yurchak, Alexei. 2015. "Bodies of Lenin: The Hidden Science of Communist Sovereignty." *Representations* 129(1): 116–57.

———. 2006. *Everything Was Forever, Until It Was No More: The Last Soviet Generation*. Princeton, NJ: Princeton University Press.

Zaki, Pearl. 1977. *Our Lord's Mother Visits Egypt in 1968 and 1969*. Cairo: Dar El Alam El Arabi.

Zeghal, Malika. 2009. "On the Politics of Sainthood: Resistance and Mimicry in Postcolonial Morocco." *Critical Inquiry* 35(3): 587–610.

———. 1999. "Religion and Politics in Egypt: The Ulema of al-Azhar, Radical Islam, and the State (1952–1994)." *International Journal of Middle East Studies* 31(3): 401–27.

Zeidan, David. 1999. "The Copts—Equal, Protected or Persecuted? The Impact of Islamization on Muslim-Christian Relations in Modern Egypt." *Islam and Muslim-Christian Relations* 10(1): 53–67.

Ziedan, Youssef. 2012. *Azazeel*. Trans. Jonathan Wright. Chicago: Atlantic.

Zigon, Jarrett. 2010. *"HIV is God's Blessing": Rehabilitating Morality in Neoliberal Russia*. Berkeley: University of California Press.

Index